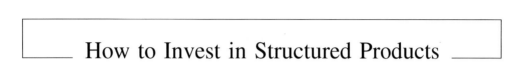

# How to Invest in Structured Products

# How to Invest in
# Structured
# Products

*About the author*

ANDREAS BLÜMKE is Head of Structured Products at VP Bank. He obtained a degree in economics, option business management, from the HEC University of Lausanne in 1992. He became a Certified International Investment Analyst (CIIA) in 2000. Before starting a banking career, he was a commodity trader from 1992 to 1995, working for Continental France in Toulouse as a soft-seed trader, and later at Deutsche Conti in Hamburg as edible oil trader. He began his banking activities at UBS AG in 1996 in Zürich, where he briefly traded bonds and bond futures, before he joined Cantrade Privatbank AG in 1997 to trade OTC options. Shortly after, he created and built the structured products desk. As the structured products business expanded successfully, he managed a team of up to 6 people, including an Advisory desk. Cantrade subsequently became Ehinger & Armand von Ernst AG, and was acquired by Julius Baer AG in 2006.

He is married with two children, and fluent in French, German and English. Structured products have been his passion for the last 12 years.

# How to Invest in Structured Products

A Guide for Investors and Investment Advisors

**Andreas Blümke**

A John Wiley and Sons, Ltd., Publication

*Registered office:*

John Wiley & Sons Ltd, The Atrium, Southern Gate, Chichester, West Sussex, PO19 8SQ, United Kingdom

For details of our global editorial offices, for customer services and for information about how to apply for permission to reuse the copyright material in this book please see our website at www.wiley.com.

*Library of Congress Cataloguing-in-Publication Data*

Blümke, Andreas.
  How to invest in structured products : a guide for investors and asset
managers/Andreas Blümke.
      p. cm.
  Includes bibliographical references and index.
  ISBN 978-0-470-74679-0 (cloth)
  1.  Investments.  2.  Asset management accounts.  I.  Title.
  HG4521.B562 2009
  332.63'2 – dc22

                                                    2009015952

A catalogue record for this book is available from the British Library.

ISBN 978-0-470-74679-0

Typeset in 10/12pt Times-Roman by Laserwords Private Ltd, Chennai, India

This book is dedicated to my wife and children

# Contents

# Disclaimer

This book has been written for the purpose of information and discussion only. All information is indicative only, and should not be considered as advice in any way whatsoever including, but not limited to, legal, tax or other advice. This book shall not be construed as, and does not form part of, an offer, nor invitation to offer, nor a solicitation or recommendation to enter into any transaction. Some calculations are expressed in their simplest form and may differ from those used by practitioners. Some definitions are related purely to the contents of this book and may not fit in other circumstances. Although all material has been prepared with care, no representation, warranty or assurance of any kind, express or implied, is made as to the accuracy or completeness of the information contained herein. No act or omission of the author or the publisher in relation to the information contained herein shall constitute or be deemed to constitute, a representation, warranty or other undertaking of the author or the publisher. No representation is made as to the reasonableness of the assumptions made within or the accuracy or completeness of any back-testing. Any data on past performance or back-testing contained herein is no indication as to future performance. Neither the author nor the publisher can be held accountable for any direct, indirect, incidental or consequential losses arising from the use of this book or reliance on parts of its contents, or other information contained herein. The author is not sponsored, funded or otherwise financially supported by any corporation or firm cited herein. All rights reserved.

# Foreword

In general, investment product clients include pension funds, foundations, endowments, insurance companies, banks, investment intermediaries and retail investors. Each group faces a unique set of investment objectives and constraints that must be addressed in order to effectively manage their investment portfolios. Reality shows that these considerations are, unfortunately, rarely confronted in a systematic way, which leads to avoidable misallocations of investments. This book is one of the first contributions on the topic that includes a comprehensive list of factors an investor needs to take into consideration before investing. This makes it a great help to any buyer of structured products. It also gives guidance on how to construct a portfolio of structured products. Given the large number of products typically present in portfolios nowadays, this is a significant addition to the existing literature.

It is essential to identify the needs, targets, and risk tolerance of the investor, as well as the constraints under which the investment portfolio must act, and to formulate an investment strategy that consolidates these potentially conflicting requirements.

The next step, after identifying the client's objectives and constraints, is to determine the investor's expectations regarding the development of the capital markets, by separately identifying his views about different asset classes and sectors. These forecasts of risk and return characteristics form the basis for constructing portfolios that maximize the expected return for a given level of risk.

Once this is done, the strategic asset allocation for the investor can be determined. Here one combines the above gathered information regarding expectations, risks, needs and constraints to determine target asset class weights. The definition of maximum and minimum asset class weights is an optimal way to build up a simple risk-control mechanism. The investor may seek both single-period and multi-period horizons in the return and risk characteristics of asset allocations. A single-period horizon has the advantage of being straightforward but a multi-period horizon better addresses the liquidity and tax considerations that arise from rebalancing portfolios over time.

Many institutional and retail investors make portfolio allocations to alternative investments, such as structured products and hedge funds, that are comparable in size to those they make to traditional asset classes, like equity and bonds. In doing so, such investors may either seek risk diversification and/or yield enhancement. Investors who take advantage of the opportunities presented by alternative investments may have a substantial advantage over those who do not, as long as they fully understand the risk and return potentials of these investments. Therefore, performance evaluation and attribution provide an essential measurement service to investment managers and investors themselves.

Although there are many books describing the functionalities of structured products, the above-mentioned issues, especially the use of structured products in a portfolio context, remain mostly untouched. The main contribution of this book lies in focusing on the above issues and finding solutions that are suited to the daily use for investment advisors and portfolio managers. The contributions can be divided into four parts.

First, the distribution of returns cube is a development of the risk and return decision of an investor, since it widens the definition of risk by allowing the skew and kurtosis to enter in addition to the standard deviation. While a low standard deviation is always preferable for a risk averse investor in a non-portfolio context, the choice of the correct skew and kurtosis also depends on other preferences.

Second, to determine these preferences, the book provides a comprehensive questionnaire. By applying the latest results from the field of behavioral finance, it seeks to prevent investment advisors and investors from applying less than ideal decisions.

Third, it offers an analysis of the return distributions of common structured products, which not only provides useful results but also offers valuable advice on how to analyze future investment options. This is done by approximating not only the mean and standard deviation, but also the skew and the kurtosis of the distribution, which must not be neglected in investment decisions.

Finally, the book's contribution lies in combining all the above-mentioned results to show how to ideally construct portfolios and how to implement structured products to reach the most value added.

Jan Schoch
**EFG Financial Products AG**
Partner
Manager Financial Engineering & Distribution

# Acknowledgements

It is a particular concern of mine to thank those who helped me to write this book.

My first thanks go to my team colleague, Dr Christian Bührer, whose input I always appreciated; to Daniel Huber for reading the first draft of the book and providing feedback before anybody else; to Jan Schoch, Christoph Baumann and Christian Sperschneider for their early support of the project and back-test spreadsheet programming; to Florence Tato for her insights on customized indices.

I am deeply indebted to John Marion, as well as to Matthew Cornes, Janis Nitsios and Edward Ennis, for their helpful grammatical revision and constructive content suggestions for various parts of the book.

A warm thanks go to the Wealth Engineering crew: Christoph Boner for guiding my thoughts in the search for a model integrating structured products in a portfolio context; Dr Ana-Maria Matache and Dr Ilya Karmilov for teaching and assisting me with the kurtosis and skew of return distributions; Dr Thomas Stadler for the tool to calculate a product's behavior during its lifetime; Jürg Sturzenegger and Ernst Näf for their encouragement and support to finish the project.

I also wish to thank Peter Pilavachi, Alain Krüger, Alain Alev, Jad Nahoul, Christoph Roos, Markus Engeler, Konstantin Gapp, Lorenz Roder, Jacques Sebban, Markus Jetzer, Richard Baker, François Péningault, Marcel Köbeli, Guillaume Subias, Karim Shakarchi, Robert Zimmermann, Sascha Ziltener, Patrick Stettler, Michela Borgia, Miguel Haupt, Thilo Wolf, Urs Kunz, Christina Halin, Christoph Roos, Mario Koglin, Jan Auspurg, Thomas Frauenlob, Pierre Bès, and the many other product specialists not listed here, for sharing their knowledge of structured products and providing numerous examples, as well as for the discussions on market views and appreciated comments about the structured product industry.

Thank you to all the client advisors I have had the pleasure to work with; you are too numerous to be mentioned here, but you are remembered.

I really enjoyed every step of the publication process with Pete Baker and Aimee Dibbens at Wiley Finance, whom I thank for their support, encouragement and guidance for a first-time writer.

I thank my parents, especially for granting and supporting my education. Without you, I would not be where I am today.

Last but not least, a very big thank you to my family, for the long hours of solitude they endured while I wrote chapter after chapter of this book. The door will stay open from now on.

# Goal of this Book

The intention of this book is to familiarize financial practitioners with structured products commonly used in Europe. It is specifically designed for investors already using or considering the use of structured products in their portfolios, and for investment advisors[1] working in private banking who may recommend products to their clients. Professional money managers such as asset and portfolio managers will also find valuable processes and criteria for use in evaluating structured products as potential investments in their portfolios. The products are not only considered as stand-alone financial constructs, but also in the context of the portfolio into which they would fit. Further consideration is given to the market conditions at the time of investment, and which type of products qualify for the given conditions. In addition, an original approach of establishing an investor's risk-return profile is developed and a method to build a preferred portfolio including, but not limited to, structured products is presented.

After reading this book, investors will be able to differentiate and classify the products they see in the market, on the different issuers' websites or in newspaper advertisements, and know which ones would roughly fit into their portfolio. Structured products end-users will understand the fine points of the products and learn how their secondary valuations evolve during their lifetimes.

Investment advisors will be able to better comprehend the use of structured products in everyday banking. Quickly analyzing a product, assessing which of their clients it fits, and recognizing its major pitfalls will become common practice with the help of the methods included in this book. Advisors will be able to see the added value versus the cost of a product and whether the payoff is compatible with their market expectations. Elements of behavioral finance theory help the advisor understand the choices of his[2] clients and advise them correctly on structured products investments.

In addition to the above, the book proposes a practical process for selecting between basic assets (like bonds or stocks) and structured products having those basic assets as underlying. Portfolio and asset managers can take advantage of this method to structure their portfolios

---

[1] For the sake of simplicity, the name *investment advisor* will be used throughout this book. It refers also to titles such as CROs (customer relationship officers), relationship managers, client advisors, etc.

[2] Unless specifically noted to the contrary, any reference to a gender shall automatically refer to the opposite sex also.

efficiently with different types of return distributions. Timing, structure and characteristics of products in relation to those of their underlying assets are discussed. Classical theories like Modern Portfolio Theory are analyzed from a structured products perspective. An innovative approach to asset allocation and asset classification opens new horizons compared to the classical risk-return methodology. Portfolio and asset managers will be able to integrate fully structured products into their investment processes.

Abundant studies about the effect of options of any sort on portfolios have been published in the specialized press such as *The Journal of Finance* or *The Journal of Portfolio Management*. However, these articles are written in a high-level technical way and are intended for a professional audience. An end-investor, and probably even some of the professional money managers, would be hard-pressed to find the advice or knowledge they were looking for in these publications. In this book, care has been taken to keep the text flowing easily, with the help of diagrams and tables. The products and the concepts are described simply, but encompassing enough detail that the reader can make a complete image of them.

# Who Should be Interested

In this book, the whole value chain of structured products is considered using an impartial, unbiased approach. From the conception of the product to the end-user, who is the final investor in the product, every aspect is analyzed. Hence, the book addresses the following large audience:

- private individuals investing in financial markets;
- high net worth individuals;
- investment advisors of banks (otherwise known as relationship managers, customer relationship officers, client advisors);
- independent investment advisors;
- investment consultants;
- asset managers;
- portfolio managers;
- mutual fund managers;
- pension fund managers;
- structurers (buy-side and sell-side);
- family offices;
- education officers.

The book focuses on products typically used in private banking. Institutional investors will also find many useful explanations and descriptions of products, but CDOs, structured finance (like for the municipal market), and mortgage- or asset-backed types of products are not treated herein.

The book does *not* include many mathematical formulas. Many concepts are explained in words, graphics and examples rather than in formulas or complex diagrams, as it is not the goal of the book to prove known mathematical concepts, nor is the target audience interested in crunching numbers.

However, some prerequisite knowledge is required. It is assumed that the basic option theory (calls and puts) as well as the definitions of yield, interest rate and the time value of money are understood. In short, having a rough idea how financial markets generally work makes the reading easier.

# Content Summary

This book is divided into two parts. The first deals with structured products as individual, stand-alone investments. The second examines structured products in the portfolio context.

The first part can be read in chronological order for readers who have little or no experience in structured products. The first chapters are used to introduce basic concepts in an easy and understandable way. People familiar with the concept might want to skip some chapters, like "Reading a payoff diagram". After the reader has familiarized himself with the terminology and basic characteristics, the approach and analyses become more complex. In the later chapters, the reader will discover how a product behaves during its lifetime, why it does so, and how to avoid common and less common pitfalls. Products across all asset classes are considered.

The second part addresses the implementation of structured products in portfolios considering investment preferences. Not only private investors, but also portfolio and asset managers, will find helpful concepts for integrating structured products in their decision processes and ultimately their managed portfolios. Classical modern portfolio theory is revised to adapt to the asymmetrical return distributions of structured products, and the investor's classic investment preferences of risk and return (sometimes in the light of behavioral finance aspects) are enhanced with skewness and kurtosis of returns, both concepts being duly described. A questionnaire will help to define the investment preferences, and extensive back-testing of products yields the typical distribution of returns for major product types. Ultimately, examples of portfolios combining the investment preferences with the analyzed products are built.

At the end of the book, a glossary of technical terms will help the reader understand the jargon used in connection with structured products. An intuitive description of return distribution shapes and a list of websites referring to issuers of structured products and related topics are also provided.

# Part I
## Individual Structured Products

# 1
## Introduction

Structured products have been on the rise since the late 1990s but then lost the trust of the investors in the credit crisis of 2008. Global statistics are difficult to gather, but an estimated EUR 1000 billion of structured products investments were held in portfolios worldwide as of 2007. According to the Swiss Association of Structured Products SVSP[1], assets of over EUR 220 billion were invested in structured products held at Swiss banks in 2007, which amounted to roughly 6.5% of total assets under management in Switzerland. In Germany, the second-biggest market, about EUR 134 billion were held in portfolios. Since then, the amounts have sharply decreased. Nevertheless, individual as well as institutional investors have recognized the benefits structured products generate with their specific risk-return profile that cannot be replicated by the usual investment vehicles such as equities or bonds.

In fact, the structured product market grew so fast and became so diverse with thousands of payoff profiles in all asset classes, that many stakeholders, be they banks, financial regulators or private or institutional investors, were caught unaware and had no systems, rules, laws or processes to cope with the sheer amount of innovation that appeared in so little time. However, professionals in their respective fields reacted quickly and allocated enough resources to handle structured products: systems were programmed, rules and laws came into effect, and processes were implemented. The two stakeholders that were partially left out in the resource allocation were those furthest out in the value chain: the investment advisor and the end-user. Structured products knowledge was slow to come to private banking investment advisors, and hence to investors being advised by them.

The success of the financial industry as a whole, as well as that of individual products, is measured by the revenues they generate. Consequently, the industry's best interests are served by satisfying the needs of the investors. Whatever type of product sold most must therefore inevitably be the one preferred by investors. But does the end-user really know what he is buying, even though the terms are written on the final term-sheet? Have his preferences correctly been assessed, or have they possibly been framed in such a way that the investor only *believes* that one or the other product corresponds to his preference? The author supposes that a majority of private and institutional investors do not have a deep enough understanding about the products' functioning and the associated risks. How could they? Even the professionals do not always agree and sometimes are not aware or don't consider all the risks embedded in the products.

The volume-driven incentive structure of the industry and the relatively poor end-user knowledge has led to markets becoming overwhelmingly concentrated in a certain type of product, based on investors' uninformed preferences and decisions. In one of the largest structured product markets, Switzerland, the private banking clientele's appetite for one particular type of product from 2004 onwards outshone any other product category offering, despite the fact that more attractive and financially superior (on an after-tax basis), products could be invested in. This ravenous consumer appetite caused issuers to push the

---
[1] Schweizerische Verband für Strukturierte Produkte, www.svsp-verband.ch

cost-minimizing and volume-maximizing structure known by the name of "worst-of barrier reverse convertible"! It first brought about the assignment to investors of financial stocks in the subprime crisis of 2007/08 and distorted many portfolios' risk structure in addition to producing heavy losses. As the crisis deepened and stocks plunged on a broad basis, all kind of stocks were assigned. In another large market, Germany, it was the "discount certificate" that took the lion's share of the investor's attention. A similar tendency happened on the other side of the globe, where clients in Hong Kong, Singapore and other Asian countries rushed to the "leveraged stock accumulator". In Korea, the attention was focused on the "autocallable reverse convertible". All the above-mentioned products were based on similar construction techniques and met with the same fate: a large number of their barriers were broken through, thus knocking the embedded short options in, much to the chagrin of the investors.

Structured products, which have never enjoyed a particularly good image, have become disreputable, particularly after the subprime/credit crisis. Especially since the demise of Lehman Brothers, structured products have come under heavy criticism. Aren't CDOs[2] structured products? Aren't bad mortgages repackaged by financial institutions and sold as CDOs? Isn't the source of the subprime crisis bad mortgages? Didn't the subprime crisis develop into the worst financial crisis since the 1930s and make everyone the poorer? Yes, yes, yes and again, yes. Yet it's not the investment vehicle that is to blame; rather it is the people participating in the game, and that includes everyone from the structurer to the final investor.

If anyone opens a European financial newspaper, journal or review and takes a look at the advertisements, he will notice that many of them are about structured products. Those ads are not about complex structures like CDOs, which are products used by institutional investors such as insurance companies or pension funds. Instead, most ads are promoting what seem to be simple investment strategies based on popular themes or commonly-known stocks or indices. Their content usually consists of great sounding but meaningless slogans, double-digit coupons or bonuses, nice pictures, fancy product names not found in any dictionary and colorful graphics as well as a lot of small print. In fact, structured product promotions don't differ that much from car or holiday ads. The only difference is that product names like "Reverse Convertible", "Bonus Certificate" or "Capital Guaranteed Product", commonly-found word combinations in structured products, are not as explicit as "The new Toyota Avensis" or "Sunny Holidays in Ibiza". However well conceived or badly presented, structured product advertisements are still only just that: advertisements. They simply represent a means for a product issuer to tell its potential clients that there is a new product on the market, and to encourage investment in it. Beyond that, the advertisement isn't helpful to the private investor. A sensible person doesn't buy a car or book a trip based only on the information included in the advertisement. The car is a complex machine, which needs to be examined closely, test-driven, have its options tried out ... The holiday needs to be analyzed, flights checked, hotel rooms and locations scrutinized ... The same goes for a potential investment in a structured product which – if anything – is a complex form of investment. Not only must the structure fit in the investor's portfolio, but also its maturity must match – or at least not exceed – his estimated holding period; the worst-case scenario should be considered and the potential effect such a scenario would have on the portfolio measured, etc. Falling into a habit of investing in the same structure repeatedly just because

---

[2] Collaterized Debt Obligations, a specific product type primarily used by institutional investors.

it seems to work well is one of the worst mistakes that investors can make. Unfortunately, besides the four universally acknowledged fundamental forces of nature (strong, weak, electromagnetic and gravitational), in the author's view, there is a fifth, obviously stronger than all the others: the force of habit. In the years from 2003 to 2007, numerous private investors found structured products attractive, cashed in high coupons or bonuses and were happy. Many repeated, multiplied and even leveraged investments as if they were a bonanza, until a bear market and the bankruptcy of Lehman Brothers came along. Suddenly everybody was finger-pointing structured products as being responsible for the whole disaster. Many structured product investments turned out to be unsuitable for some portfolios, and at least some investors found out that the worst-case scenario could not be borne. Many complained about having received bad advice. Despite the products' poor performance in the recession that followed the bull markets, the products themselves should not be seen as the cause of the investor's ire. As in a car crash, it's not the car that is responsible for the harm done, it's the driver behind the wheel. If the car had an unknown technical flaw, one can blame the constructor. If it had a known flaw, blame the seller or reseller. Finally, if the car was not fit to be driven on the road, one could even blame the authority that gave it permission to be driven in the first place. In any case, the car is not responsible. The same goes for structured products. The structurer constructing it, the seller marketing it, the client accepting it, the regulator watching it, the management cashing it, all bear a partial responsibility, but the product itself is innocent. Whatever may have been, it's useless to play the finger-pointing blame-game or dwell on the things of the past. So why not take a fresh start and reconsider structured products as just what they are: an investment vehicle or tool that can be useful when searching for investments that match one's risk-return profile.

This book casts a critical eye on the world of structured products and the factors that influence it. It helps end-investors to consider structured products from different angles and take rational, considered investment decisions. Have a look at the advertisements in the newspapers again after reading this book; they will surely appear different.

# 2
# Generalities About Structured Products

## 2.1  A DEFINITION BY ANALOGY

A strict definition of structured products would state that:

Structured products are financial assets, which consist of various elemental components, combined to generate a specific risk-return profile adapted to an investor's needs.

So far, so good; but which components are combined together, what's a specific risk-return profile and how does an investor know that it's adapted to his needs? For one, there is no limit to the possible permutations; think of Lego bricks – dozens of different objects can be built with the same bricks. Given enough bricks, the possibilities become quasi-infinite. Likewise, structured products are formed by combining options with bonds or options with other options, and there are millions of options and bonds. The options themselves must be based on something: a stock, an index, a yield curve or a commodity – options exist on practically everything. When an option allows (or forces) an investor to buy or sell a certain asset, it creates a certain return profile linked to a particular risk. So the combination of options on certain assets with or without a bond component creates a specific risk-return profile. Options are often considered as risky instruments best left to the speculators but, in certain arrangements, they rather reduce the risk of an investment when comparing it to the underlying asset. Whether any particular arrangement of options is suitable for an investor remains for him to decide. The second part of this book helps the investor to determine which kind of risk (and return) is likely to be suitable for his needs.

The product's mathematical payoff formula[1] could be of help. The "specific risk-return profile" of each product is after all fully defined in it. Indeed, the final value of a product can be directly calculated by its payoff formula. However, few people really have the time to replace symbols with numbers in complex, often unintuitive, equations written on the term-sheets. Even if that exercise is performed, it tells the investor less than it should because the probability of actually getting any specific result is not included in the calculation. In fact, it is not even necessary to understand the full mathematics behind every term-sheet. Think of it like a toaster or coffee machine: it's pointless knowing what amount of electricity is needed to toast the bread or heat the water, only the purpose and the operation of the machines must be known. As with everyday household objects, investors only need to know how and when to use the products, and not necessarily how they are constructed. It is nevertheless important to know the general purpose as well as the most important key points of a structured product. For most people, understanding the purpose of a product in words or through a graphic is much easier than studying the math behind it and then drawing the conclusions from them.

To begin with, let's first examine the purpose of structured products through an example that everyone, even somebody altogether without financial experience, can understand.

---

[1] See Section 2.4, Reading a Payoff Formula, page 16.

Let's imagine a person, Dominique, who wants to drive from Paris to Milan. To do so, he would buy a car. Now, imagine that Dominique wants to invest in equities: he would buy a stock. Reverting to his trip from Paris to Milan, he might think: "Hmm, the road could be long and dangerous; maybe I should buy a car with an airbag and an anti-lock braking (ABS) system, to increase safety." The stock market equivalent of buying an airbag and ABS system would be buying a capital guarantee on top of his stock investment. This simple action, combining stock exposure with a capital guarantee, would already form a structured product.

Dominique further reflects that he wouldn't know how to get from Paris to Milan and that a global positioning system (GPS) in the car would be helpful. He doesn't know either if this is the right moment to enter the stock market. Similarly, Dominique could add a look-back option to his stock investment together with the capital guarantee. This would add another optional feature to his structured product. Table 2.1 summarizes the situation.

**Table 2.1**  Structured products and car analogy

| Building a car | | Building structured products | |
| --- | --- | --- | --- |
| Dominique wants to drive from Paris to Milan | He buys a car | Dominique wants to invest in equities | He buys a stock |
| The road is long and could be dangerous | He adds an airbag and an ABS system | Equities could fall and hurt the performance of his portfolio | He adds a capital guarantee |
| Dominique doesn't know exactly how to get from Paris to Milan | He adds a GPS system | Dominique doesn't know if this is the right moment to buy | He adds a look-back option |

It is thus possible to compare the construction of structured products to the construction of a car and its various options. As mentioned, structured products often consist of a financial underlying asset and an option pasted together. The financial asset can be a stock, an index, a commodity, a fund, etc. The option can be a call or a put; it can be plain vanilla or exotic. Several options can be added to the underlying. Also, a single structured product may be linked to several underlying assets. So a product may quickly become complex, and with all the different option strategies and the different underlying assets to choose from, the number of possibilities rapidly becomes tremendously large. Add to that the fact that several underlying assets can be combined with several options and the number of possibilities approaches infinity. Add the time dimension (the same product issued one day later will not have the same parameters due to market movements) and the possibilities are indeed infinite.

Adding options does cost money and leaves investors like Dominique with less to begin with. Does it pay off? How does one know? As with the car, it might be a good idea to include some features that are or may become useful, even though no one would ever *hope* to use some of them. Including an airbag with the car is a sensible thought to protect the driver, but he would actually do his utmost to prevent its use. The ABS also comes in handy, but it also comes into play only as a last resort. These options are not free, they each have a specific cost and they can be thought of as *insurance*. They prevent or lessen the impact of the worst-case scenario, a crash. A structured product with a capital guarantee relates to this category. No matter what the underlying does, the investor will not lose his capital, since it is protected. Does an investor want a capital guarantee to be triggered when his product matures? Certainly not, since if that scenario were to occur, it would mean that the underlying did not behave as expected and the return on capital would likely be zero percent. Yet a logical reason to spend money on a capital guarantee would be the uncertainty about the future performance of an underlying asset. Since it is seldom possible to know beforehand how an asset price will evolve in the future, investors with low risk appetite will be better off with the option than without.

What about the GPS in the car? This feature can be considered as a *performance enhancement*. It allows a driver to reach a destination faster without losing his way. In structured products, it can be compared to the look-back feature. A look-back allows the buyer to set the level of strike of an option some time *after* it was bought. The buyer will always select the best point for himself: if he bought a look-back call, he will choose the lowest point the market reached within the look-back period; if it was a put, the highest point will be selected. Hence the name of the option, look-back: the buyer looks back at what the market did and chooses the best strike for himself, improving his performance. Obviously, this feature can be quite expensive.

The two paragraphs above discuss the investor's possibilities and needs. Assessing them correctly is a tricky exercise, which is often neglected or assessed too quickly and without proper consideration. Yet, that need assessment is the most important step in the value chain of investing in structured products.

Extending the above reasoning to encompass all possibilities on all assets, structured products can be defined as a *toolbox of options*, with which investors build their preferred risk-return profile by specifying their desired options, as they would build the car of their dreams *according to budget*. The cost of too many options may become prohibitive and needlessly increase the complexity of a product; is it useful to have a mini-bar and two large LCD TV screens in the car? It may be nice to have, yes, but superfluous to fulfill the car's primary mission, which is to transport someone from A to B. When constructing or choosing a structured product, best avoid features that are not necessary, but stick to those features deemed essential.

Structured products are not an asset class by themselves, even though some practitioners like to think so. Rather they are means to either enhance the performance or reduce the risk of an asset or a portfolio, independent of the asset class on which they are based. Structured products are no freebies, and there's no such thing as a "Harry Potter" product summoned with a magic wand. A product always has a cost associated, even if it is only an opportunity cost. Whether a particular product is of use to any particular person is an analysis that only this person can make, because only he knows his own risk-reward profile.

## 2.2 BUYERS, SELLERS AND REASONS FOR INVESTING IN STRUCTURED PRODUCTS

### 2.2.1 Institutional buyers

Institutional investors around the world buy, hold and trade structured products. They include pension funds, insurances, banks, municipalities, non-profit institutions, asset managers, hedge fund and mutual fund managers. An institutional investor will select structured prod-ucts as an investment vehicle when other, classical, vehicles are not available or do not fit his investment needs. Suppose, for instance, that a pension fund has a future liability stream whose payoff depends on the level of the interest level of the EUR 3-month Libor (EURIBOR) interest rate and the yearly stock performance starting in five years and for the next 10 years after that date. Such a liability can seldom be matched by classical assets like single bonds. It requires a structured product. The product could have a payoff that pays a low fixed coupon for the first five years and then switches to a floating coupon linked to the 3-month EURIBOR. In addition, the floating coupon increases by 3% if the yearly stock performance is positive. This product will match the liability stream more closely than other investments, which is (or should be) the primary reason for an institutional entity to invest in a structured product. Another frequent reason for institutional investors to choose structured products as an investment vehicle is the replication of strategies that would not be possible or be too onerous by means of classical instruments.

### 2.2.2 Private buyers

Private investors usually have simpler needs and targets. Their reasons for holding structured products are the prospect of gaining more than a riskless interest rate would otherwise yield, optimizing returns, or participating in the performance of an underlying asset while protecting their notional conditionally or unconditionally.

Take the case of our fictional character Dominique, who would like to invest EUR 8 million but who needs those funds in three years' time for a project he has pledged to support. While he could purchase bonds maturing in three years, he is not satisfied with the yield of the risk-free rate. In other words, he would like an investment with upside potential without putting his capital at risk. Dominique does not rely on a steady coupon stream for the next three years (suppose he has other sources of income) and would consider risking the interest he would otherwise have gained with bonds to purchase calls on various underlying assets. Such an investment strategy can be achieved by means of a capital guaranteed product portfolio. After consulting with his advisor on the current market opportunities, forecasts and structuring factors, he decides to allocate his capital as shown in Table 2.2.

**Table 2.2** Sample structured product portfolio[2]

| Product | Maturity | Weight | Payoff |
|---|---|---|---|
| Capital guaranteed note on Eurostoxx50 | 3 years | 33% | 100% participation up to a cap of +40% |
| Emerging market currency note | 1.5 years | 33% | 200% participation on a basket composed of the Turkish Lira, Brazilian Real and Russian Ruble |
| Callable daily range accrual | 3 years (max) | 34% | Coupon of 6% as long as the short-term interest rate level stays below 7% (currently 2.5%) |

---

[2] The weighting has been equally set for all three products for illustration purposes.

The products need not be described or understood down to the last detail at this point. Suffice to know that all of them are 100% capital guaranteed in EUR at maturity and all have the *potential* to generate a return that is higher than the risk-free rate. Thus, they correspond to his prerequisites as mentioned above.

It is, however, worthwhile to elaborate on the reasoning of the portfolio construction. Dominique's target is an above risk-free return. Suppose that for a three-year maturity, the EUR risk-free rate was 3.5%. The total return over that period for a risk-free bond portfolio would thus be:

$$(1 + 3.5\%)^3 - 1 = 10.87\%$$

Let's look at the products' potential performance. The first one can appreciate up to 40% (the level of the cap) and performs if the European equity market rises. The second, betting on the appreciation of a basket of emerging currencies against Dominique's reference currency (the EUR), has unlimited upside potential. Finally, the third product generates an interest nearly double that of the risk-free rate as long as the short-term interest rates stay below a certain threshold, which is far away from the present level (the threshold is 7%, and the current level is 2.5%[3]). The large upside potential of the first two products means that if only one of them performs well, it is likely that the performance of the whole portfolio will be higher than the risk-free rate.

On the portfolio construction side, it is interesting to note that the third product, linked to the level of the short-term interest rate, is somewhat uncorrelated or even negatively correlated with the first two.[4] Consequently, if the equity and the emerging market currency notes do not perform, then it is likely that at least the interest rate note will generate a positive performance.

Another important point in the portfolio's construction is the shorter maturity of the emerging market currency note than Dominique's investment horizon. The currency note expires after 1.5 years, either on the capital guarantee if the currencies did not appreciate against the EUR (case a) or above it if they did (case b). In both cases, a reinvestment is necessary. In case a), he gets a second chance to "re-strike" a new product: if the emerging market currencies did not appreciate, then it is likely that they depreciated, (they seldom stay at the same level) and the product would have poor chances to perform going forward anyway. Constructing a new product with a new at-the-money strike will raise the chances for a positive performance for the remaining 1.5 years. In case b), the positive performance of the first product can be "locked-in" by constructing a new capital guaranteed product that would include the original notional plus the performance to date. That performance, being now capital guaranteed, cannot be lost again. Note that the new product need not be based on the same underlying currencies than the previous one. It need not even be a product on emerging market currencies. After the product's expiry, a new assessment of the macro-economic and micro-economic situation should be undertaken. Subsequently, the structuring factors should be assessed in order to determine the final structure of the new

---

[3] Note that the short-term rate of 2.5% is lower than the yield of longer-dated bonds (3.5% for a 3-year maturity), implying a rising yield curve. Yield curves and fixed-income products are explained on page 169.

[4] Historically, weak stock markets in the developed countries have led to depreciations of emerging market currencies. Such a market development is negative for the first two products, but usually led central banks to lower the interest rates (i.e. reduce the cost of borrowing) to stimulate the economy, which is in turn positive for the last product.

product for the remaining 1.5 years. This procedure shows that products with a shorter maturity than the investor's investment horizon can be implemented in a portfolio without difficulty. The third product's maturity is mentioned to be 3 years (max); in fact, the issuer of the product can redeem it prior to maturity in certain circumstances.[5] Suffice to say that, at this point, Dominique isn't certain as to when the product will be redeemed, only that it cannot be after 3 years. Hence, a similar approach as for the second product will be used if an early redemption occurs.

Would there be an alternative investment strategy for Dominique to reach his goal? Several can be envisioned; for instance, convertible bonds would match the request. They have the same payoff structure as capital guaranteed products; they even pay a minimum coupon. However, they are principally linked to the equity market. Investing the whole portfolio in convertible bonds would link the portfolio's risk too much to the equity market. In bearish times, convertible bonds fare poorly, usually yielding less than the risk-free rate. Another possibility would be an investment in high yield or emerging market bonds. The yield on those instruments is usually far above the risk-free rate, which also fits the request. Yet that would mean taking an additional credit risk, because the high yield principally reflects the issuer's default probability. Note that Dominique also bears the issuer risk when investing in structured products. However, this risk can be lowered substantially by selecting product issuers that boast a high credit rating. Such a strategy maintains the upside potential of the portfolio and minimizes the downside risk, which is not feasible with a high yield or emerging market bond portfolio.

This sample case illustrates the usefulness of structured products in reaching an investment target. Buyers should always keep their targets/constraints in mind when investing. Structured products can be of help to reach or to optimize those targets.

### 2.2.3 Sellers (issuers) of structured products

Structured product sellers mushroomed until the subprime and credit crises of 2008. Nearly every major and middle-sized financial participant in the banking sector built a structured product offering for its internal or external clients. Investment banks, wholesale banks, retail and private banks, state-owned banks, brokers and finance boutiques – all were entering and subsequently expanding their structured product business. The main reason for financial actors to enter the structured product business was profit. As with every business in this world (from pizza restaurants to computer chip manufacturers), structured products supposedly generate a profit for the manufacturers and sellers. Or at least everyone thinks they do. Unlike a pizza that earns EUR 1.00 for the restaurant the minute it changes hands if it is sold for EUR 6.00 and cost EUR 5.00 to manufacture, a structured product's profit can only be measured at its expiry. When the product is sold (which would be the moment the investor buys it), its manufacturing costs are not known. A mathematical model determines a "fair value" for the product at the issue date, which the issuer raises by a spread; the total amounts to the issue price. The spread is supposed to be the issuer's profit, but it also serves to pay for the service the issuer has to deliver for the lifetime of the product: secondary market prices, listing costs, term-sheet production, adjustments for corporate actions, settlement, etc., and last but not least, hedging. All these factors apart from hedging can be more-or-less determined at the issue date. Hedging, simply put, are the

---

[5] It will be shown later how "callable" products function.

trading activities the issuer must undertake during the lifetime of the product to transform the mathematical model's "fair value" plus the spread into a real profit. For example, the mathematical model will tell the trader every day of the product's life: "buy 100 shares of company XYZ", or "sell 20 shares of company XYZ". Several times a day, the trader will have to make one or more deals to hedge the risks embedded in the product. Depending on how well the mathematical model has been programmed and how efficiently the issuer's trader can execute the orders will determine the issuer's ultimate profit. Product issuers usually hedge every risk they can. They try to live on the spread they take at the issue date of the product, or on the bid-ask spread in the secondary market. However, even the most advanced trading models cannot hedge every single risk of some structured products. The issuer's profit, if any, can therefore only be determined at maturity. Of course, in normal market situations, the spread the issuer takes is more than enough to cover the hedging risks, but in market turmoil, hedging may become difficult or outright impossible. If the situation is severe, like in the financial crisis that began in 2008, hedging costs can wipe out several years of an issuer's past profits.

To offset some of the risks, an issuer's interest is to have a large trading book, with as many positions (or products) as possible. The reason is cross-hedging: some of the products cancel each other out, in terms of risk. A simple example: a bank simultaneously issues a call warrant and a discount certificate on the stock of Assicurazioni Generali SpA (an Italian insurer). Taken from the issuer's perspective, if both have the same maturity and strike, the risks are reduced, because the short volatility position of the warrant is offset by the long volatility position of the discount certificate.[6] The issuer can lock-in the bid-ask spread of the volatility with little risk. Having many such positions associated with a large client base creates economies of scale in terms of hedging. The more clients that buy and sell the bank's products, the higher the chance that hedges offset themselves, creating low-risk benefits. The concept is similar to that of the FX market: if on the same day, an investor buys EUR 1 million against USD while another does the reverse trade, the bank locks in the margin between the two trades, taking no risk, and books a profit. A large trading book with many underlying assets also allows an issuer to become more competitive against smaller rivals. Prices for product buyers will be more attractive, as the spread the issuer takes diminishes.

This all sounds very complex, doesn't it? It really is; structured products *are* ruled by mathematics. But then, so is the GPS in the car and even more so a computer or a portable telephone. Nearly every household object is controlled by mathematical formulas and functions, even the fridge and the coffee machine. But the end-user doesn't necessarily need to understand the program code in his cell phone that enables him to call a friend, just how to use the object efficiently; the same is true for structured products. If some of the above reasoning seems unclear or difficult to understand, take heart! The next chapters will clarify all there is to know, step by step.

Just one more comment before going into detailed matters on the products: issuers are also interested in the marketing potential that structured products offer. New products are a way to access the wealthy individuals and institutional asset managers. It gives the issuer the opportunity to contact its clients with a new story. A bank issuing a new product would typically advertise it in newspapers, on websites or per email, its sales force ordered to call its internal or external clients boasting of the product's advantages. The bank's brand

---

[6] Indeed, the issuer sells the call embedded in the warrant and is short volatility. The discount certificate has a payoff profile of a short put, which is the reverse in terms of volatility for the issuer.

gains in awareness; its name is recognized by an increasing part of the investor population. A larger audience raises the amount of potential business. There is a saying in investment banking that "volume attracts volume". Hence, some banks' strategy is to issue dozens or even hundreds of products simultaneously in order to show presence in the market. It doesn't matter if the products attract no volume at the issue date. Some stock exchanges, like Frankfurt or Stuttgart (Euwax) in Germany have lowered listing costs so much that listing a product there costs virtually nothing. But in terms of product statistics compiled by the exchanges, the issuers with most products rank in the first quartile, and are perceived as strong players in the market. Private clients are attracted to the issuers with the largest product palette and often tend to be more sceptical towards smaller players.

## 2.3   READING A PAYOFF DIAGRAM

The most intuitive way to understand structured products is in graphical form. This section focuses on the so-called payoff diagrams, which are graphical representations of the mathematical formulas that characterize each product. It is important for the reader with little experience in structured products to fully understand how a payoff diagram is read, as it is the basis for many product illustrations not only in this book, but also in every other publication, newspaper advertisement or industry-specific website.

Figure 2.1 is an example of a payoff diagram showing a capital guaranteed product on an asset (for example the Eurostoxx50) with 100% capital guarantee, 100% participation to the positive performance up to a cap of 120% of spot price.

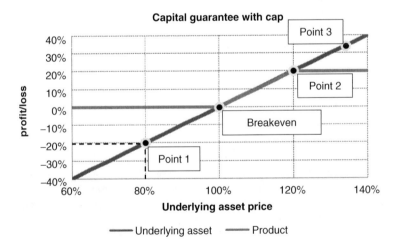

**Figure 2.1**   Capital guarantee with cap
*Source:* Bloomberg, own calculations

Formally, the payoff diagram illustrates the profit and loss of a product as a function of the underlying asset's price. It consists of two axes and one or more payoff lines. In our example, two payoff lines are drawn.

*The horizontal (x) axis* represents the market price of the underlying asset. It may be scaled in percent as in the example or in absolute values. Its value increases from left to right. The price level of the underlying asset at which the product was issued is usually normalized at 100% and placed around the middle of this axis, as shown in the example.

*The vertical (y) axis* represents the gain (if above zero percent) or the loss (if below zero percent) the investor realizes at maturity. The point at which the vertical axis has a value of 0% is called the *breakeven* point. This is the point at which the investor neither gains nor loses money (in nominal terms). On the payoff graphs of some issuers and publications that point has a value of 100%, which then denotes the value of the product at inception. In that case, the reference of the axis is not the profit and loss the investor makes when the product expires, but the redemption price of the product at maturity in percent of its issue price. To calculate his profit or loss, the investor must deduct the sum initially invested from the result shown by the payoff line.

*The market payoff line* shows the underlying asset's profit or loss as a function of its market price. It is usually represented by a 45° straight line. Of course, depending on the scale of the axes, it may appear to be steeper or flatter. In Figure 2.1, the slope is flatter because the graphic is slightly elongated. As long as the scales are correctly labeled, it is of no consequence. *Point 1* correctly shows that a drop in the price of the underlying asset by 20% results in a corresponding loss of 20% for an investor who would have bought the underlying asset (not the product) at 100%.

*The product payoff line* symbolizes the product's profit and loss as a function of the market price of the underlying asset. One can observe that the loss is limited to 0% and the gain to 20% in the case of the example above. The breakeven point is located where the product payoff line crosses the vertical axis from negative to positive profit and loss. Since this product is capital guaranteed to 100%, the line runs parallel to the 0% level when the underlying asset drops below 100%. In this example, *Point 2* shows the maximum return an investor can achieve with the product. Note that *Point 1* cannot be reached with the product, and neither can *Point 3*, which depicts an increase of 30% of the underlying asset. Both *Point 2* and the breakeven are called inflection points. Each inflection point is linked to a special level of a structured product, such as the strike or the barrier of an embedded option. In some special cases, a payoff in graphical form is not possible or practical.[7] In those cases, the product can only be described in words, flowchart diagrams[8] or tables. The shape of the product's payoff gives the investor a rough indication about whether that product appeals to him or not.

In its classical form, the payoff diagram only shows what the investor can gain or lose *at maturity*. Nothing is said about how the product behaves during its lifetime and, furthermore, no indication is given about the chances or risks of realizing the indicated product outcome. In other words, the graphic tells nothing about the chances of ending on any specific point of the product line. This is annoying for the end investor, as some payoffs may demonstrate incredibly attractive payoffs, but the best case might actually have very little chance of being achieved. Thankfully, at least some of the issuers (e.g. EFG Financial Products) are moving in the right direction and now discloses some of the risk figures either directly on their term-sheets and/or on their website. The difficulty for the end-user then lies in the interpretation of the numbers, but at least when they are available they can be analyzed.

With their Derivative Map, the SVSP has been trying to create a standard for representing structured products in a graphical form. Unfortunately, the standard that the SVSP wants

---

[7] Especially for callable products.
[8] The Express Certificate's payoff is often depicted with such a method.

to generalize has not been adopted by all market participants, so similar payoffs are often represented differently, depending on the issuers' marketing departments. As the issuers strive to improve their marketing material, they may change the design of their diagrams, which sometimes makes it difficult for the occasional user of structured products to find the diagram they are accustomed to. To illustrate this point, Figure 2.2 shows two diagrams of the same payoff type: a worst-of barrier reverse convertible on three stocks.[9] These diagrams were extracted from term-sheets of well-known product issuers in Switzerland: Julius Baer and EFG Financial Products.

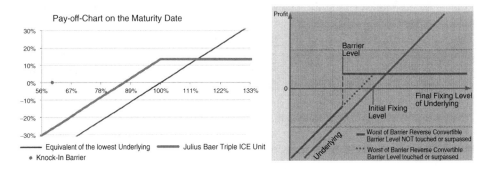

**Figure 2.2**   Different representations for similar products
*Source:* Julius Baer, EFG FP

A closer look at the Julius Baer graph will reveal that the barrier is shown as a dot on the horizontal axis. Both payoffs are in fact identical, only the chosen representation is different. Note that while the Julius Baer representation illustrates the effective payoff for a specific product with the correct scales, EFG FP uses a template without scales that fits all products of this category, in this case barrier reverse convertibles. At least the two mentioned issuers do provide payoff diagrams on their term-sheets. Sadly, the majority of other issuers do not even include one in their sales documents.

## 2.4   READING A PAYOFF FORMULA

The payoff formula, which is an exact mathematical expression or a decision tree, describes how to calculate the precise amount of money an investor gets back at maturity when the product expires. It is useful to know how to read a payoff formula, as only few issuers provide payoff diagrams on their term-sheets. Moreover, some payoffs cannot be displayed efficiently in graphical form. For example, in a decision tree, if there are too many "if – then – else" clauses, the payoff diagram becomes impossible to draw.

The diversity of formulas is large as there are many product variations. Here is a simple payoff formula example of a capital protected note on an index:

$$\text{Payoff} = \text{Nominal}^* \left\{ 95\% + 90\% * \text{Max} \left[ 0; \frac{\text{Index}_{\text{Final}} - \text{Index}_{\text{Initial}}}{\text{Index}_{\text{Initial}}} \right] \right\}$$

[9] The characteristics of this product type will be explained in more detail on page 45 and following.

One of the easiest ways of reading it is to take the formula apart, starting from inside out and from right to left. Take the last term first:

$$\text{Max}\left[0; \frac{\text{Index}_{\text{Final}} - \text{Index}_{\text{Initial}}}{\text{Index}_{\text{Initial}}}\right]$$

Inside the square brackets, there are two terms, a zero, and a quotient. Let us disassemble the quotient. It is in fact a simple performance calculation: first, the difference between the level of the index at maturity ($\text{Index}_{\text{Final}}$) and that of the index level at the issue date ($\text{Index}_{\text{Initial}}$) is taken. The result can be either a positive or a negative number. This is then divided by $\text{Index}_{\text{Initial}}$, which is the basis; the result of the operation is the index performance expressed as a percentage. If the index has risen since the product was initially launched, the percentage will be a positive number, and if it has fallen, it will be negative. Therefore, inside the square brackets, the first term is equal to 0 and the other can be either positive or negative. Looking just outside the brackets, there is the word "Max". This is a mathematical function for selecting the *maximum* (higher) result from the two terms inside the brackets. So if the result of the division is positive, that term will be selected; if negative, then the term 0 will be selected. This part of the formula forms in fact the capital guarantee; negative performances are not taken into account.

The whole term is then multiplied by 90%. This calculates the level by which the product participates to the upside performance of the underlying asset, as this number multiplies the positive performance of the index.

Finally, the first number inside the outer parenthesis is taken: 95%. This designates the level of the capital guarantee, because it is a constant. Here the capital is not fully guaranteed, and the investor may incur a maximum loss of 5%.

The whole of the previous calculations is then multiplied by the "Nominal", which stands outside the curly brackets. The Nominal designates the amount of money that was necessary to buy one note (i.e. 1000) or just the amount of money used by the investor when the product was purchased. The Nominal is also multiplied by 90% of the positive performance. Thus, by adding 95% of the initial Nominal and 90% of the positive performance, one obtains the final sum that the issuer repays when the product reaches its maturity. Two numerical examples follow:

1. An investor invested EUR 250 000 in the above-mentioned capital guaranteed note. The note's maturity was 4 years, and the purchase price was 100%. The spot price of the index at issue date was 3600 ($\text{Index}_{\text{Initial}}$) and at maturity the index had risen to 5400 ($\text{Index}_{\text{Final}}$). We have:

$$\text{Payoff} = \text{EUR } 250\,000^* \left\{ 95\% + 90\% * \text{Max}\left[0; \frac{5\,400 - 3\,600}{3\,600}\right] \right\}$$

which equals:

$$\text{Payoff} = \text{EUR } 250\,000^* \{95\% + 90\% * \text{Max }[0; 0.5]\}$$

Determining Max:

$$\text{Payoff} = \text{EUR } 250\,000^* \{95\% + 90\% * 0.5\}$$

Distributing the nominal of EUR 250 000 invested:

$$\text{Payoff} = \text{EUR } 237\,500 + \text{EUR } 112\,500 = \text{EUR } 350\,000$$

Note that in this example, as the capital is only guaranteed to a level of 95%, the first ~5% of the index performance is lost to the investor. More precisely, as the participation amounts only to 90% and not 100%, the first 5%/90% = 5.55% positive performance is lost. In other words, the index needs to rise 5.55% for the investor to recoup his initial investment.

2. An investor places USD 150 000 in the following capital guaranteed note:

$$\text{Payoff} = \text{Nominal}^* \left\{ 102\% + 85\% * \text{Max}\left[0; \frac{\text{Index}_{\text{Final}} - \text{Index}_{\text{Initial}}}{\text{Index}_{\text{Initial}}}\right] \right\}$$

The initial price was again 100%, and the index spot fixing was 1250. After 4 years, the note redeems with the index at 980. We have:

$$\text{Payoff} = \text{USD } 150\,000^* \left\{ 102\% + 85\% * \text{Max}\left[0; \frac{980 - 1\,250}{1\,250}\right] \right\}$$

which equals:

$$\text{Payoff} = \text{USD } 150\,000^*\{102\% + 85\% * \text{Max}\,[0; -0.2160]\}$$

Determining Max:

$$\text{Payoff} = \text{USD } 150\,000^*\{102\% + 85\% * 0\}$$

which results in:

$$\text{Payoff} = \text{USD } 150\,000^*\{102\%\} = \text{USD } 153\,000$$

In this example, the index fell by 21.60% but the loss was avoided by the capital guarantee. The note paid a minimal return of 2% over 4 years as the capital was guaranteed to a level of 102%, which amounts to approximately 0.5% per annum.

This was the worst section in terms of math! With the exception of a few numerical examples, the mathematical calculations will be few and far between in the rest of this book.

## 2.5   READING A TERM-SHEET

When an investor, a representative or an investment advisor is confronted with a structured product, the most important document is its term-sheet, sometimes referred to as the sales-sheet. In this two-pager (which tends to become a four-pager due solely to the lengthy small-print disclaimers), the main terms of the product are defined.

The final investor should always carefully study the terms and conditions stated in the term-sheet, as it forms the basis for the product and all key factors are stated therein. This is easier said than done; if the investment advisor deems that his client does not have the knowledge necessary to evaluate a product, the advisor should thoroughly go through the document himself and highlight the opportunities as well as the risks to his client in a way that can be easily understood. The description can be made by analogy or by example, but as long as the end-investor is not a discretionary managed client and has to take a decision himself, his advisor has the duty to inform and advise him about the characteristics of the product.

There also exists another much longer document, called the prospectus (in some cases called the pricing supplement), which is usually about 40–60 pages long. It is a document that regulates and describes every aspect of the product, including conventions (i.e. business days, yield calculation conventions, etc.), the full description of the issuer, regulators, etc. It is rarely seen by anybody but the legal unit of the issuer, but can be requested on demand. Although this document does constitute the legally binding document between the investor and the issuer, it will not be further mentioned in this book, the term-sheet being an adequate basis.

A sample term-sheet of medium complexity is shown below. It is followed by comments illustrating the most important points an investor should be aware of. Persons with little knowledge of structured products should switch from the comments back to the term-sheet with the corresponding numbers of the headings in the first column.

### 2.5.1   The name and the final conditions (1)

The name is the most confusing part of a product. It's often difficult to interpret because it's been chosen to "sound" good or to have an easy to remember abbreviation, but doesn't necessarily tell anything about the payoff, the opportunity or the risk. What's more, the same payoff has been attributed different names by each issuer purposely for marketing reasons. Fortunately, the SVSP association has defined a table with generic product names whose usage is spreading across the industry. Nevertheless, even some generic names tend to be unclear. For instance, the name "Express Certificate", being one of the standard 25 products defined by the SVSP, doesn't tell the investor that it's really an autocallable barrier coupon accumulator.[10] Obviously these four words have little meaning for a non-professional as well, but once a few concepts are known, the investor would at least have a hint about some of the components embedded in the product, giving him a rough indication about the structure of the product. The name of the sample term-sheet sounds complex and foggy as

---

[10] Products of this type will be explained in Chapter 5, Section 5.3 on Autocall and callable options on page 128. Express certificates are explained in section 5.3, page 124.

| 1 | Final Terms and Conditions<br><br>**_Early Redemption Shark note[11] on ABC 30 Index (in EUR)_** | |
|---|---|---|
| 2 | **Instrument Type** | Index Linked Redemption Instrument (EMTN) |
| 3 | **Issuer** | Issuer Ltd. |
|   | **Guarantor** | G Bank |
|   | **Rating of Guarantor** | AA / Aa1 |
|   | **Lead Manager** | LM Ltd. |
|   | **Documentation** | Issuer Ltd. MTN Programme |
|   | **Calculation Agent** | CA Bank |
|   | **Principal Paying Agent** | PPA Bank |
| 4 | **Underlying Index<br>(Reference Asset)** | ABC 30 Index (ABC 30)<br>_Bloomberg: ABC30; Reuters: .30ABC_ |
| 5 | **Trade and Pricing Date<br>(Initial Valuation Date)** | 10 January 2008 |
|   | **Issue & Payment Date** | 21 January 2008 |
|   | **Expiration Date<br>(Valuation Date)** | 10 July 2009 |
|   | **Redemption Date** | 15 July 2009 |
| 6 | **Denominated Currency** | Euro ("EUR") |
| 7 | **Denomination (DN)** | EUR 1,000 per Instrument |
|   | **Notional Amount** | EUR 20,000,000 |
|   | **Number of Instruments** | 20,000 |
|   | **Issue Price** | 100% (of Denomination) |
| 8 | **Knock-Out Event** | A Knock-Out Event shall be deemed to occur if, on any exchange business day during the period from and including the Pricing Date to and including the Expiration Date, the level of the Underlying Index trades at or above the Knock-Out Barrier. |
|   | **Knock-Out Barrier** | 132% (Index level: 4647.06) |
|   | **Capital Protection** | 100% in the case of Early Redemption or Redemption, as defined below |
|   | **Participation Factor (PF)** | 100% |
|   | **Rebate** | $7.50\% \times (n/N)$ |
|   | **where** | n is the number of exchange business days from and excluding the Initial Valuation Date to and including the date on which the Knock-out Event has occurred.<br>N is the number of exchange business days from and excluding the Initial Valuation Date to and including the Expiration Date. |
|   | **Early Redemption** | **If a Knock-Out Event has occurred** before or on the Expiration Date, each Instrument will be redeemed ten business days after the date on which this Knock-Out Event occurred, and the investor will receive a cash amount in EUR calculated according to the following formula:<br>$DN * (100\% + \text{Rebate})$ |

**Figure 2.3**   Mock term-sheet

| | Redemption | If a **Knock-Out Event has not occurred** before or on the Expiration Date, each Instrument will be redeemed on the Redemption Date and the investor will receive a cash amount in EUR calculated according to the following formula: |
| | | $$DN * \left[100\% + PF * Max\left(0\%; \frac{ABC30_F}{ABC30_I} - 1\right)\right]$$ |
| | **where** | $ABC30_F$ is the official closing level of the Underlying Index on Expiration Date |
| | | $ABC30_I$ is the official closing level of the Underlying Index on Pricing Date (3520.50) |
| | **Settlement of the Instruments** | Cash settlement |
| | **Listing** | Application will be made to list on the X Stock Exchange |
| | **Minimum Trading Size** | 1 Instrument and multiple of 1 thereafter |
| | **Governing Law/Place of Jurisdiction** | As per the Issuer's programme |
| 9 | **Selling Restrictions** | US, US Persons, UK, Singapore |
| 10 | **Secondary Market** | Under normal market conditions, indicative clean prices will be provided on Y with a bid offer spread of 1.00% |
| | **ISIN Code** | CH0022334455 |
| | **Valoren Number** | 2233445 |
| 11 | **Ric Code** | CH002233445=IL |
| | **Clearing System** | Z Clearing System |
| 12 | **Taxation** | [not represented] |
| 13 | **Disclaimers** | [not represented] |

**Figure 2.3** *(continued)*

well: "Early Redemption Shark note on ABC Index in EUR". Splitting the name into its individual parts provides some information:

- *Early Redemption:* these two words imply that the product may be redeemed prior to the final maturity date.
- *Shark:* apart from being a carnivorous fish, the word "Shark" is not offering any information. One has to know that the final payoff of the product resembles a Shark's fin to understand the analogy.[12]
- *Note:* a note invokes a bond of some sort. Investors may be familiar with T-Notes or medium-term notes. A bond component is probably embedded in the product.
- *On ABC Index:* this obviously refers to the underlying asset on which the product is based.
- *In EUR:* means that the product is denominated in EUR. The underlying asset may not be referenced in EUR but in another currency instead, hence the specification. But in this case, the assumption is that the reference currency of the ABC30 index is the EUR.

---

[11] To see the payoff diagram of this hypothetical product, flip to page.
[12] See Figure 2.4 page 26 for a graphical representation.

Structured products' names and descriptions are as abundant as grains of sand on a beach: every issuer labels his products differently, despite their equality. The plain fact is that a product's components stay the same, and a different name will not differentiate it from a performance point of view, which was often all that mattered to the investor in the past. Branding a commodity has never been an easy undertaking. Efforts have been made by several market participants to standardize them, but few issuers actually name their products according to the standard. At best, a mention somewhere in the term-sheet is made that their fancy name product corresponds to a certain name or category of the standard. The branding efforts by the issuers for their own products are unabated as each one tries to differentiate its offering from the others. Similar products are actually differentiated by a few factors like, for instance, secondary market-making, after-sales support, issuer credit rating and the quality of the issuer's website. These factors have drawn more attention of late, at least since the bankruptcy of Lehman Brothers.

The document shown here is the *final* term-sheet. More often than not, the marketing for new structured products is done via a document with *indicative* terms and conditions. The product, calculated with market conditions at the time the product goes into subscription, will be fixed only after a subscription period of several days. For instance, an indicative term-sheet labeled "13% reverse convertible on. . ." may become "13.5% reverse convertible on. . ." when the product is finalized. It is standard procedure to present clients with indicative documents, where all but a few (but essential) parameters are already fixed. The product is only issued if enough money can be raised; otherwise it is canceled, as the issuer may need a certain volume for the product to cover the issuing costs in order that it is profitable for him. After the subscription period is over, the final conditions of the product will likely be slightly different to the ones calculated previously, because the market will have moved not only in terms of spot price, but also in terms of volatility, interest rate, etc. The differences between the final terms will often be a slight difference in a barrier, a participation rate or a strike. Once the product is fixed, in order for the end-investor to track and manage any product in his portfolio, the final terms must be known.

### 2.5.2 The investment type (2)

The investment type[13] determines the legal form through which the investor will have access to the product. In its most common form, the product will be structured as a Medium Term Note (MTN). If denominated in Euro-currency, they are referred to as Euro MTNs. Each MTN is linked to a funding program used by issuers to issue bond debt on a regular and continuous basis. The advantage to issuers is simplicity: they are not required to produce a full suite of legal documents each time a new note (linked to a structured product) is issued. Instead, the existing template documents are amended with each new issue by means of a pricing supplement, which sets out the terms of each specific issue of notes. The access to debt funding is easier, takes little time and above all is cheaper. The drawback to the investor is that it does not eliminate the counterparty risk, which he bears.

Apart from MTNs, of all the other possible investment vehicles, only certificates will be of interest herein. Certificates are of interest in this book because they are most often the form used by issuers when no funding (i.e. bond component) is needed for the structure of the product. Certificates have been particularly prolific in Germany, Italy and the Benelux

---

[13] Named "Instrument Type" in this example.

states. Certain types of investment vehicles sometimes referred to as structured products may be constructed via funds or special purpose vehicles (SPVs). These legal forms are seldom used in the private banking business and will not be described further.

### 2.5.3 The counterparties involved (3)

Each structured product is issued by a legal entity, often domiciled in a foreign country. Common issuers are seated in Guernsey, Jersey, the Cayman Islands, Luxemburg, etc. The reason for issuing from abroad is solely for corporate tax optimization. Products issued from jurisdictions like those named above are not subject to tax at source. On the other hand, if a product is not taxed at source because of local regulation, then it might well be issued by an issuer in the residence country. This is the case for Germany, which does not tax certificates.[14] The issuer in most cases is also the guarantor of the product, but sometimes they are different legal entities. The guarantor is of great importance to the investor, as this legal entity determines the credit risk (commonly called counterparty risk) the holder of the product bears. The calculation agent is the entity who determines the price of the product at inception and during the whole life of the product. The calculation agent is not always mentioned on the term-sheet.

The issuer, guarantor and calculation agent can be one and the same. However, in some cases, it is advantageous to have a guarantor different from the calculation agent. Since the calculation agent is often an investment bank with a relatively low rating in terms of financial strength by the international rating agencies (such as Moody's or S&P), investors are seldom willing to take that counterparty risk for products with long maturities. Hence, the low rated (investment) banks swap their rating for one of a higher rated financial institution who is willing, for a small fee, to finance the product, thus lowering the default (bankruptcy) risk for the product holders. What happens when an investment bank acting as a calculation agent defaults? In that case, the issuer must find a new calculation agent who will take over the price calculation of the product. In theory, that may sound perfectly reasonable; in practice, it is likely that the product will remain illiquid until its maturity.[15]

Additionally a lead manager and a co-lead manager can sometimes be found. These names designate the parties in charge of the distribution of the product. They are not always mentioned.

For the sake of simplicity, the generic appellation of "issuer" will be used throughout this book for a reference to the products, even if it would be technically correct to use "calculation agent", "lead manager" or "guarantor" in some instances.

### 2.5.4 The underlying asset(s) (4)

This part of the term-sheet describes the underlying assets and their identification numbers for the specific product. Any fixing levels, barriers, caps, guarantee and other payoff relevant levels should be clearly mentioned here, unless they are grouped later in the payoff section. In products with multiple assets, the table of underlying assets can grow quite large. In

---

[14] Status 2008. In 2009, the new "Abgeltungssteuer" (Flat Tax Rate) will be introduced as part of the "Corporate Tax Reform", with the effect that all forms of income or capital gain will be taxable.

[15] See also "Funding rates and counterparty/credit risk", page 145

this example, the fixing levels are spread out somewhere in the payoff formula. Note that corporate actions[16] on assets during the lifetime of the product are not always kept up-to-date on the term-sheet by all issuers. For instance, if a product included five Nestlé shares before it split 10:1 on 30 June 2008, some issuers will produce a new term-sheet correctly indicating 50 shares after that date, while others will not, thus saving them the effort of adjusting the document to the new conditions. However, the trading books of the issuer take corporate actions into account, and hence the price of the product should be fair at all times.[17]

Again, there is no standard practice, which is regrettable. The main reason that some of the issuers do not systematically adjust their term-sheets is the cost: initially, when the pricing of the product is done, the buyer pays little or no attention to whether the issuer will amend the term-sheet for corporate actions on the assets included in the product or not. The initial conditions of the product are those that matter, as the trade often goes to the most aggressive offer. The issuer may price aggressively if he saves himself the cost of a team dedicated to the after-service of their products. Nevertheless, as some issuers cut corners, an investor or an investment advisor may be well advised to ask for a new term-sheet or at least confirmation of the pricing in case of changes in the underlying assets of their products.

### 2.5.5 The product calendar (5)

Four main dates determine the product's lifetime: the pricing, issue, final valuation and redemption dates.

*The pricing date*, also referred to as the trade or strike date, designates the date at which the product was traded for the first time. It is usually from this point onwards that any embedded option is active and running. It is also the date at which the product is valued initially and from which any performance calculations start (with the reference level set at 100%). In short, this date sets the beginning of the product's life.

*The issue date*, also referred to as the value or payment date, designates the date at which the money flows take place initially. The investor's bank account is debited of the necessary cash and the product is booked into his deposit account. Any coupon accruals start from this date. The issue date is normally set between one and two weeks after the pricing date to allow the issuer to set up the product in a formal way (setting up the funding, requesting security numbers, writing the final term-sheet and prospectus, etc.). The time between the pricing and the issue date is commonly referred to as the *grey market*. From the issue date onwards until the final valuation date, the product is said to be trading in the *secondary market*.

*The final valuation date*, also referred to as the final observation or expiration date, designates the day on which the product's performance is measured for the last time. Any embedded option expires on this date. The product cannot be traded after the final valuation date.

*The redemption date*, also referred to as the settlement or maturity date, designates the date at which the inverse money flows take place. The notional plus or minus of any performance or coupon is credited to the investor, and the product is removed from his deposit account. The redemption usually takes place between three days and two weeks after

---

[16] For example stock splits, acquisitions, divestments or mergers of companies.

[17] If that were not the case, the trader who manages the product for the bank may incur huge losses on his trading book.

the final valuation date, the time necessary for the issuer to calculate the final value, deliver stocks or cash and settle the product in general. The product ceases to exist after that date.

The above definitions are sometimes mixed by the issuers as there is no standard practice in the industry. Other intermediary dates are sometimes mentioned.

*Observation dates:* when the product has a path-dependent option embedded, intermediary fixings of relevance to the product's final payoff are performed. This is, for example, the case for average (or Asian) options and for products with an (auto)callable[18] feature.

*Early redemption dates:* mostly used with (auto)callable products, these designate the dates prior to the final maturity at which the issuer must or can redeem the product, as a result of the observation of the underlying asset(s). The mock term-sheet includes an early redemption as specified in the name, but the topic appears only later within the payoff formula (see point 8 of the Mock term-sheet).

Unless otherwise stated, all the fixings are taken at the closing times of the relevant exchanges. Sometimes, especially when the volume is large in relation to the underlying asset's liquidity, the initial and the final fixings can be spread over a time span from several hours to several days. It can also happen that the issuer deems it necessary to avoid redeeming a particular product based on the underlying asset's closing price, because of poor liquidity or to discourage arbitrage attempts by third parties. In those instances, the issuer may defer redemption or prolong the time necessary to unwind a product, in an attempt to consider the product holders' best interests. This can be tricky for the issuer, since his actions may have a positive or a negative effect on the product. Not all issuers attempt this course of action, and rather hold themselves strictly to the product's calendar.

### 2.5.6 The currency (6)

The product can be either denominated in the same reference currency as the underlying asset or in a different one. In the latter case, the product can be either composite or quanto.[19] Composite products are subject to variations in the currency exchange rate between the asset's and the product's currency. Quanto products eliminate currency exchange risks.

### 2.5.7 The value parameters (7)

These numbers define the minimum trading and maximum outstanding amounts.

*The denomination* is sometimes referred to as the reference amount. This represents the smallest tradable unit, which is nondivisible. It is the lowest amount one investor can hold, usually ranging from 100 to 1000. Some products have a high initial denomination, like 50 000 and multiples of 1000 above. These products target more informed investors, called "qualified" investors in some jurisdictions.

*Number of units* means the amount of units issued. At inception, the whole size is seldom traded. The issuer normally sets the number of units higher than the original subscription amount, in order to give other investors the possibility of buying the product in the secondary market.

---

[18] See Section 5.3 for more information.
[19] See Section 5.1 for more information.

*The notional amount* is the result of the number of units multiplied by the denomination. This figure determines the maximum volume outstanding – in other words, the maximum size in its denomination currency the product can reach if all the units are held by investors. Note that, as a general rule, the issuer may decide to increase that amount at any time if he chooses. In contrast to stocks, where a bigger market capitalization is often a sign for better liquidity and smaller spreads, structured products with higher open interest do not enjoy greater liquidity than smaller issues.

### 2.5.8   The payoff formula (8)

In this sample product, the payoff formula is spread over several lines.[20] Unlike hedge funds, where a secret and totally discretionary strategy known only to the fund's manager – often referred to as a "black box" – determines the profitability, each structured product has a mathematic payoff formula that calculates the amount to be redeemed at maturity.[21] Normally, the formula can be replicated on a computer spreadsheet in order to simulate the returns according to several scenarios.[22] Plotting the results of the formula with all the possible levels the underlying asset can take at maturity results in the payoff diagram. Since the mock term-sheet does not include a graphic, it has been represented in Figure 2.4 for illustration purposes, using its formula.

To read and understand the "if-this-then-that-and-if-not-then-else" decision tree of the text appears to be a daunting undertaking. For an investor, unless he is a mathematician, Figure 2.4 describes the payoff of the product far better than any formula could. The dotted black line represents the (fictitious)ABC30 index. The solid line determines the payoff of the product as long as no knock-out occurred, and the dashed line replaces the solid line

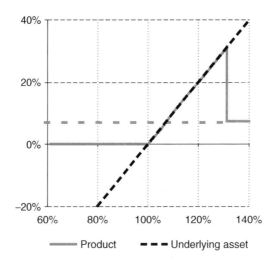

**Figure 2.4**   Payoff 2: sample Shark note

---

[20] All those within the range marked "8", including the cells "Knock-out Event" to "Redemption".

[21] Unless it is actively managed. See Section 8.2.

[22] See the second part of this book, from page 259 onwards, where the back-tested performance of a multitude of products has been plotted in the form of payoff diagrams.

once a knock-out has occurred. Standard practice in the structured products industry is to draw full lines for initial payoffs and dashed lines if a particular event occurs. In this Shark note, an investor participates with 100% to the positive performance and with 0% to the negative performance of the ABC30 Index up to a barrier (this part is represented by the solid line). If this barrier is touched any time during the life of the product, the positive participation is lost and the product is redeemed early at 100% plus a rebate (represented by the dashed line).

### 2.5.9   Sales restrictions (9)

The regulators of most countries make the sales and marketing efforts of structured products distributors difficult. Each country has its local rules and regulations, intended to prevent abuses relating to the offering and sale of securities. For instance, since most products issued are not registered with the SEC[23] in the USA, it is forbidden to market these to US persons or residents. In the UK, the law states that in order to be used for marketing financial products to retail clients, the sales documents must be "clear, fair and not mis-leading";[24] an ambiguous statement for any corporate lawyer, to say the least. In the EU, rules governing the distribution of financial products are given by the Prospectus Directive, which came into effect on 1 July 2005. In Switzerland, the Simplified Prospectus Directive outlines what an issuer must write on a term-sheet for a product to be offered to the public.[25] There is no doubt that all these regulations are necessary ensure smooth market development, but they are of little relevance to the end-investor who is seldom accustomed to reading the small print in legal language and cares more about a clear explanation of how his product actually works. In fact, the term-sheets have been written from the seller's point of view and not from the buyer's, which is one of the reasons why structured products are mistrusted and deemed non-transparent by the general public. Friendlier end-user documentation with graphics and tables would help investors to understand a product far better than dozens of legal points that ultimately have nothing to do with the product's payoff or performance.

Apart from protecting the investor from financial abuse, it is the author's view that these local laws are intended to function as entry barriers for foreign issuers and tend to confuse the end-user more than they help him. To understand the peculiarities of each country's banking laws requires much local knowledge, and accessing the market requires *local* banking or distribution licenses, making the cost of entering a foreign market daunting for a medium-sized institution. This can become very confusing for investors. An illustration of this is the website of ABN AMRO, www.abnamromarkets.com, which is one of the best websites in the world for structured[26] products. Due to the different local country laws, the bank has split its product offering by country. If a *private* investor wishes to enter the site, he has first to declare the country he lives in. Then he must click on a disclaimer (which no one bothers to read anyway). Finally, he can access the products that were cleared for

---

[23] Securities and Exchange Commission, the regulating body enforcing the federal securities laws in the United States.
[24] Much simplified.
[25] Note that if a product is listed on the SIX by its issuer, the latter does not need to provide a Simplified Prospectus.
[26] Now RBS, markets.rbs.com.

his country by ABN's legal department. The following table summarizes the offering by
country:

**Table 2.3** ABN AMRO (now RBS) website products by country

| Selected country | Number of products[27] |
| --- | --- |
| **France** | Less than 200 |
| **Italy** | 959 |
| **USA** | Less than 1000 |
| **Switzerland** | 1938 |
| **Germany** | 18 355 |

Source: www.abnamromarkets.com and country-specific sites

What is even more astonishing is that similar payoffs can be found for each country, but
that the number of offered products is different. A simple check for specific products shows
that there are 427 products of the "mini future" type on ABN's Swiss website[28] and 4070 on
the German one. Effectively, the Swiss private investor is given less choice than is globally
available. Though from an investment point of view there is no difference between the
products, ABN must provide one website per country because of their different legal rules.
Since the legal setup doesn't differentiate the payoffs of the products but only decreases
their numbers, it can be considered as inefficient protectionism.

Of course, ABN also provides an option to institutional investors, showing all 23 866
products. Indeed, any private investor can click on "*I am an institutional investor*" and
accept the disclaimer. He then gains access to all ABN's products. Of course, if the investor
then buys a product not designed for his country, he may lose the protection of his local
law, whatever that protection may be worth.

### 2.5.10 Secondary market (10)

The secondary market plays an important role in portfolio management for an investor. It
allows him to increase or decrease existing positions, close certain investments, or switch
from one investment to another. To the investor, several factors determine the efficiency of
an asset's secondary market:

- the liquidity (intraday, daily, monthly…);
- the depth (ability to trade large sizes without moving the market);
- the bid–ask spread width;
- the settlement efficiency.

Popular belief has it that structured products are illiquid, non-transparent and that one must
hold them to maturity without any possibility of selling them in the meantime. While it is

---

[27] As of 23 May 2008.
[28] Accessed by stating that the visitor is Swiss.

true that the price availability for some products may be weak (for a private investor, the only price source for a product is sometimes the issuer's internet page), a structured product will always have a secondary market price, and its bid–ask spread will seldom exceed 1%. It can even go as low as 0.1% for small sizes, for instance in Germany. In any case, products can be traded on an intraday basis as long as their underlying asset also does. This characteristic increases the liquidity of structured products beyond that of emerging market or corporate bonds (which are often trading at over 1% bid–ask spread) and, depending on the view from which liquidity is considered, even mutual funds (which cannot be traded intraday, but are booked on an end-of-day valuation basis). Not to mention hedge funds, in which liquidity is provided on a quarterly basis, often associated with a monthly or quarterly notice period. More and more issuers are making it possible to place buy or sell limits on their products. The listing of many products on a regular exchange[29] improved the liquidity of those products in the secondary market. Their price quotes can be followed more easily over the internet by investors.

On the term-sheet, the secondary market spread will always be indicated with a provision "under normal market conditions". The definition of "normal" markets for structured products includes not only the liquidity of the underlying asset, but also its option's market liquidity. In fast markets, where market-makers withdraw their quotes from the option markets, structured products may be quoted with much larger spreads or not at all simply because the issuer has difficulties in hedging[30] himself properly on the option part. However, when the market returns to normal, the product will be quoted as before. Of course, the liquidity of some asset classes is lower or more volatile and spreads can widen, as the commodity, private equity or hedge fund markets show.

### 2.5.11   Listing, settlement details and security number (11)

Structured products are securitized financial instruments like any stock or bond. They have a seven-digit Swiss security number ("Valoren"), an ISIN code beginning with the country code (CH, DE, NL...) plus 11 digits and specific country codes like WKN ("Wertpapierkennnummer") for Germany, etc. Hence, they are settled through clearing houses. In the EU and Switzerland, the main houses are Clearstream, Cedel and SIS Intersettle. As a consequence, they are transferrable and an investor does not need to sell his structured products holdings if he decides to move his deposit account from one bank to another.

Nowadays, most products also have either a Bloomberg or a Reuters (RIC) code to let private banks easily follow the products they bought for their clients on spreadsheets or outright from their back-office systems. In the example, the Reuters code is the ISIN followed by "=IL", meaning that the product will also be quoted live on Reuters. On Bloomberg, the majority of the products can be found via the ISIN code plus the function key "Corp".

---

[29] Scoach in Switzerland, Euwax in Germany.

[30] A hedge is a specific investment that reduces the risk of another investment. In structured products, the issuer seldom wants to be exposed to the price variation of the underlying asset, preferring instead to be exposed solely on the volatility of that asset. Hence, the issuer's trader hedges the so-called "bullet risk" by buying or selling a certain amount of the underlying asset. In order to know how much, he must know where the volatility trades.

The end-of-day valuation is published by the issuer, who feeds the price to a clearing-house, which then feeds the bank's internal systems to be reflected in the clients' accounts. If the client's account statement does not show the correct mark-to-market price of a structured product, it is likely that some element in the end-of-day valuation chain may be broken, stale or missing.

### 2.5.12   Taxation (12)

In the example, the tax treatment is not represented because it differs widely from one country to another. This book does not intend to give tax advice on the different products for different jurisdictions. The main reason for not delving into tax matters is the changing legal environment that makes it difficult to keep up with changes and the special tax situations of the different investors. A pension fund investing in a product is likely to be treated differently by its local tax authorities than a private person, a trust or a corporate investing in the same product. Hence, it is advisable for an investor to consult with a tax advisor. Private individuals should at least ask their investment advisor about the taxation of the products they hold in their portfolio. If the advisor himself cannot help, he can recommend somebody who can. It will be shown later that the after-tax performance of two similar products can differ by varying their construction. However, an investor should know a few general guidelines.

The tax treatment of structured products is determined by the local tax authorities. In Switzerland, taxation is ruled by the Swiss Tax Authorities;[31] in Germany, it's the BaFin.[32] For products distributed in Switzerland, the information about two tax treatments should be mentioned on the term-sheet:

1. the Swiss tax treatment;
2. the EU savings tax treatment.

If these two elements are missing, the product may be classified as non-transparent by the tax authorities, and the taxation may be disadvantageous for the investor. In Germany, a new law, the "Abgeltungssteuer", which is a flat tax rate affecting all financial products, has been introduced at the beginning of 2009.

### 2.5.13   Disclaimer (13)

It is unclear if disclaimers are a blessing or a curse for investors. It's certainly paper-consuming: a single term-sheet has often more disclaimer pages than product details. The author declines to reproduce the disclaimer from the sample term-sheet, which is three to four pages long, written in small print. The disclaimer for Swiss products includes information related to the previously-mentioned Prospectus Directive, conflicts of interest that the issuer may have, index copyright disclaimers, etc. The purpose of the disclaimer is to protect the issuers from lawsuits. However, it doesn't protect third party distributors. If an investor feels he has been wrongly advised by his investment advisor on a complex

---

[31] Eidgenössische Steuerverwaltung, ESTV.
[32] Bundesanstalt für Finanzdienstleistungsaufsicht.

product, he can try to sue the company who the investment advisor represents. Needless to say, a disclaimer is only worth the paper it is written on, and investors (particularly institutional investors) can also sue the issuer directly if they feel that bad advice or a poorly structured product has been recommended to them. Of late, legal cases have been surging against investment banks because of some products based on mortgage-backed securities which have lost their entire value in the subprime crisis.[33] The outcome of most cases is still pending. It is common practice for banks to settle cases out of court in order to avoid bad publicity.

---

[33] In particular the Collaterized Debt Obligations, CDOs.

# 3
# The Categories of Structured Products

In April 2006, one of the goals of the SVSP was to map the structured products world in a few global but comprehensive groups. The association created four categories, of which three are "real" structured products: Capital Guarantee, Yield Enhancement and Participation. The fourth is called Leverage, but it consists only of warrants, which are securitized options. As warrants cannot really be considered structured products, there are only a few references to them in this book. The categories are differentiated by their risk-return profile (Figure 3.1), comparing the generic risks of structured products with familiar asset classes.

Figure 3.1 (without the chevrons at the bottom which show standard asset classes) is the standard illustration used by the structured products industry to represent the four product classes graphically. The horizontal scale goes from low risk on the left-hand side to high risk on the right-hand side. The leftmost product category is Capital Guaranteed products, which are fairly low-risk instruments that have a similar risk/return profile to cash and bonds. Yield Enhancement and Participation products have an average-to-high risk, and compare to stocks. The more aggressive Participation products fit alongside riskier stocks and commodities. On the upper and rightmost side are warrants, which carry the same risk as options and futures. These are high-risk instruments, as they include leverage as one of their key features. The vertical scale suggests that the higher the risk taken, the higher the expected return should be. Since volatility is often taken as a proxy for risk, Figure 3.1 seems to be accurate at first glance, making the reader think of the Efficient Frontier of Markowitz.[1] Most investors will be familiar with the hypothesis that cash is usually safer than bonds but yields less, while bonds are safer than stocks but also have a lower expected return, etc. The flaw with this reasoning when applied to structured products is that they have asymmetric return distributions. Indeed, it is perfectly reasonable to imagine that a capital guaranteed product which participates to the upside performance of a risky asset (e.g. a stock index) can have a higher expected return than a yield enhancement product with a capped upside potential.[2] It is possible to structure a capital guaranteed product on a "risky" commodity or to construct a participation product on a bond index. As there are almost limitless possibilities for structuring any product type, the risk of each product will vary with its construction parameters. This fact blurs the simplicity of the classical product categorization as shown in Figure 3.1, which should consider parameters other than risk and return to be accurate. It will be improved in the second part of this book. For now, the three main product categories, excluding warrants, are detailed in the next section.

---

[1] The Efficient Frontier is discussed in Section 10.2.
[2] Some terms or reasoning may sound unfamiliar to the reader with little investing experience; however all will be made clear in the respective chapters.

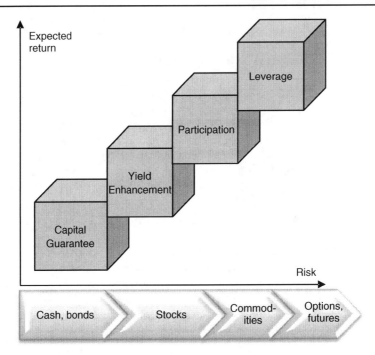

**Figure 3.1**    Classical structured products representation

## 3.1    CAPITAL GUARANTEED PRODUCTS

The payoff and the formula for the capital guaranteed product have already been described previously. Let's continue by giving a definition:

Capital guaranteed products guarantee the redemption of the invested capital at maturity in addition to participating to a certain degree in the performance of an underlying risky asset.

Hence, capital guaranteed products are characterized by three factors:

- loss potential limited to the level of the capital guarantee[3] (on a nominal basis);
- participation of some sort in an underlying asset; and
- no (or small) guaranteed income.

Therefore, the goal of a capital guaranteed product could be to invest in an average-to-high risk asset like stocks, commodities or FX, but limiting the downside risk. In this case, the product needs to be compared ("benchmarked") to the underlying asset(s). Alternatively, it can be structured with the goal of outperforming a yield, say the 5-year swap rate or the 3-year government bond yield. In this case, the product must be compared to the yield that would have been earned by investing in this swap or bond.

---

[3] Not considering the credit risk of the issuer.

It is important to know in advance what the goal of a capital guaranteed product is because that is the only way of determining the *opportunity costs*. For instance, if the goal of the product is the participation in a risky asset's performance, for example the Eurostoxx50 Index (a stock index comprised of the 50 largest European companies), then the opportunity costs are the foregone dividends of those stocks (as well as voting rights, but that is usually a minor issue) for the lifetime of the product. On the other hand, if the product's goal is to beat the 5-year EUR swap rate, then the opportunity costs would be the riskless swap rate that could have been earned by investing in a swap (or a government bond) for five years.

Another reason to keep an investment's goal (target return and risk) in mind prior to choosing a product is that the structure will have different parameters for different investment goals. Suppose, for example, that an investor has a positive view on a risky asset. A capital guaranteed product should not be capped if the aim is to participate in the performance of that risky asset without the risk of incurring losses. But if the target return is slightly above the risk-free rate, a cap of some sort, limiting the upside but reducing the time to maturity, will heighten the chances to achieve that target. Another important factor is the psychology of the investor, especially in private banking. For most private investors, the capital guaranteed product looks quite attractive when issued: either "riskless" participation in a risky asset (goal = participation) or the outlook of a high yield (goal = yield outperformance). What could go wrong? Of course, the investor has his own view on the underlying asset(s) or an investment advisor sold him the idea. But at maturity, things look quite different: either the expectations materialized, or they didn't. In the former case, the investor would have been better off investing directly in the underlying asset (he didn't need the capital guarantee). In the latter case, the investor would have been better off not investing at all! Thus, the potential for disappointment is big: capital guaranteed products could be compared to half-full glasses when issued, and half-empty glasses when redeemed at maturity. But it is easy to look back in hindsight, knowing what should have been done. Yet this doesn't help the investor decide today what will be best in the future. So a capital guaranteed product can be a good compromise for an investor who doesn't want to stay in cash, but doesn't have a strong conviction as to the future either. If the investor bears in mind the product's goal *and the minimized or avoided risks* compared to a straight investment in a risky asset, it will help him comprehend the product's raison d'être.

For the occasional structured product investor, a source of confusion often exists between capital guaranteed and (conditionally) capital protected products. To make matters clear, capital guarantee is unconditional, whereas capital protection is often linked to the underlying asset not falling below (or in rare circumstances, not rising above) a certain threshold. If the threshold is reached, the capital protection disappears and the investor is likely to incur a loss at the redemption of the product. Barring the bankruptcy of an issuer, a capital guaranteed product is always redeemed at least at the guarantee level (i.e. at 100% if the level was set at 100%, 95% if the level was set at 95%, etc.). Note that not all issuers hold themselves to this definition, hence the need for the investor to be very careful when reading a term-sheet.

From an academic point of view, capital guaranteed products create convex payoffs. As will be shown in the second part of this book, an investor holding capital guaranteed products buys the positive skewness,[4] or insurance, of returns, which is positively valued by the market. In theory at least, the expected return of capital guaranteed products should be

---

[4] Skewness is a measure of the symmetry of an expected return distribution (actually it measures the *lack* of symmetry) and is discussed extensively in the second part of the book.

lower than the expected returns of their underlying asset(s). It will be shown in the second part of the book that this is far from being always the rule.

The variety of participation forms is quasi-infinite. The most common forms are unlimited or limited upside (with the use of caps or knock-outs), but may also be conditional coupon payments, downside or absolute participation, ranges, etc.

### 3.1.1 Classical capital guaranteed products

Let's now look at how classical capital guaranteed products are constructed. In its basic form, the product consists of two elements. First, a zero-coupon bond is issued for the maturity concurrent with that of the product. Then a call option on the underlying risky asset is bought. Adding the two lines on the payoff diagrams (Figure 3.2) results in the finished product, a capital guaranteed note.

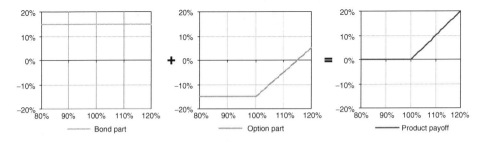

**Figure 3.2**   Payoff 3: capital guaranteed product construction

A zero-coupon bond is simply a bond without a coupon (hence its name), which is issued at a discount. It redeems at par at maturity. The yield at the time of the issue determines the level of discount at which the bond is issued.

For example: current interest rate is 4%; maturity 5 years:[5]

$$\text{Zero-bond Price} = \frac{100\%}{(1 + 4\%)^5} = 82.19\%$$

The issue price of the zero-coupon bond is thus 82.19%. The discount to par then amounts to 17.81%.

The discount represents the amount of money available to buy call options on the underlying risky asset (i.e. an equity index) for a 100% capital guaranteed product. If a 5-year call option on the risky underlying asset costs exactly 17.81% of that asset's spot price, then the participation amounts to exactly 100%. If the option costs more or less, then the participation either dwindles below or rises above 100%.

For example, discount = 20%, option cost = 25%:

$$\text{Participation} = \frac{20\%}{25\%} = 80\%$$

Represented in graphical form, the evolution of the individual component values of a capital guaranteed product as in the example above are best illustrated as in Figure 3.3.

---

[5] Calculation assumes annual basis. In practice, semi-annual basis or compounded calculations may be used.

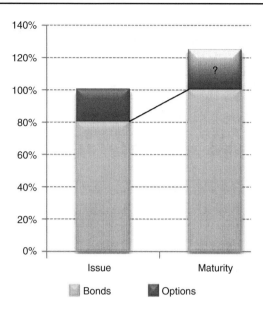

**Figure 3.3** Capital guarantee components value at issue and maturity date

At the issue date, the product is composed of 80% bonds and 20% call options. At maturity, the bond component will increase up to the level of the capital guarantee (in this case from 80% to 100%), and the value of the option component will depend on the performance of the underlying asset.

In some situations, the discount is simply not high enough to generate a participation rate on the risky underlying asset that looks attractive. This is often the case when the product has to be denominated in a currency with low interest rates (i.e. JPY or CHF), or when the volatility of the underlying risky asset is simply too high and the call option becomes too expensive. In these cases, there are many alternatives to increase it, such as reducing the capital guarantee to a level below 100%, or making the option cheaper by placing a cap or a knock-out barrier or other "exotic" feature that will be described in later chapters.

There exists one other alternative to "classical" zero-bond + call capital guaranteed products: CPPI structures. CPPI stands for Constant Proportion Portfolio Insurance. These products are usually long-term investments (5–15 years), mostly used for products on mutual funds or hedge funds where either the liquidity is thin or the volatility can only be determined with difficulty. These instruments are outside the scope of this book, and no further mention of them will be made.

As mentioned above, two factors are most important when structuring a capital guaranteed product: the *interest rate level* and the *volatility* of the underlying risky asset. The interest rate must be as high as possible and the volatility as low as possible.

- A higher interest rate will lower the value of the zero-bond at the issue date, thus freeing more capital to purchase call options.
- A lower volatility decreases the value of the call option; thus more options can be bought with the same amount of money.

When all goes well and the risky assets' performance rises day by day (like the bull run in stocks worldwide from mid 2003 to mid 2007), there is little demand for capital guaranteed products. But when a bear market emerges, the volatility has often already risen and it is too late to structure an appealing product. When the market enters full bear mode, then it's usually too late to even attempt to structure a capital guaranteed note. Not only does volatility spike but, as central banks tend to lower interest rates in such situations, the two main factors for the construction of the product, volatility and yield, are precisely the opposite of what they need to be. Any product with capital guarantee will have unattractive conditions and is likely to perform poorly.

### 3.1.2   Capital guaranteed products with knock-out (Shark notes)

One of the biggest problems with traditional capital-protected products is that they have relatively long terms until maturity. If the underlying asset falls, investors can suffer substantial mark-to-market losses prior to expiry. Rising interest rates and declining volatility also have a negative impact on the price of long-term capital-protected products, as will be demonstrated later. Shortening the tenor can mitigate these unforeseeable effects. So-called shark notes combine full capital protection with a short- to medium-term investment horizon.

*Construction and description*

Shark notes are comprised of two components: a zero-coupon bond (for the capital guarantee) and an up-and-out call option (for the participation). This combination creates the payoff profile that gives the product its name, resembling a shark's fin (Figure 3.4).

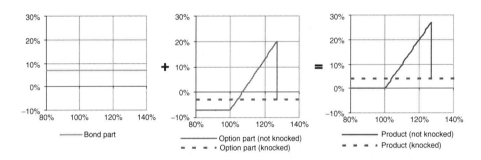

**Figure 3.4**   Payoff 4: Shark note construction

In Figure 3.4, the discount of the zero-coupon bond is 7%. The up-and-out call on a risky underlying asset for the same maturity equally costs 7%. Adding the lines of the first two graphics results in the line in the third, that shows the final payoff of the product. The up-and-out call option features a barrier[6] ("knock-out") that is set well above the spot price of the underlying at issue. What effect does this barrier have? Upon reaching the barrier, the option "dies", i.e. its value falls to zero and the upside participation is lost to the holder

---

[6] See Section 5.2, Barrier Options.

of the product. While this may seem a rather disadvantageous feature to the investor, it may be useful in some situations, as will be seen shortly.

Sometimes the option includes a *rebate*, which is a compensation of sort that is paid back to the buyer of a barrier option if a barrier event occurs during its life. In that case, the value falls not to zero, but to the level of the rebate, which is determined at issue and remains constant. In the above example, the rebate is set at 4%. Once knocked out, regardless of how the underlying performs thereafter, the value of the option at expiry equals the rebate (dotted lines in the graphics). If a rebate has been included in the construction of the product, its amount often corresponds to the level of a coupon of a bond with comparable maturity, as with the Shark note in the example. It can already be guessed that a Shark note featuring a high rebate is better suited to outperform a given bond yield than to participate in the performance of the product's underlying risky asset.

In order to determine how many scenarios are possible at expiry for the Shark note, the number of kinks in the payoff diagram can be counted and one added.[7] In Figure 3.4 above, there are two kinks: one at the strike of the up-and-out call, and one at the level of the barrier. There are thus three possible scenarios at expiry (Table 3.1).

**Table 3.1**  Shark note redemption scenarios

| Market | Redemption |
|---|---|
| Underlying < 100% | 100% (capital guarantee level) |
| Underlying > 100% (barrier never touched) | 100% + participation |
| Barrier touched | 100% + rebate |

*Example*

An example will illustrate the benefits of the shark note as compared to a classical capital guaranteed product without an up-and-out barrier. Let's assume that an investor buys a capital-protected product in EUR on the Eurostoxx50 index with a term of five years, a 100% capital guarantee and 100% participation. Suppose furthermore that after 18 months, three market scenarios are possible: an increase of 20%, a decrease of 20% and a flat market. Table 3.2 summarizes the three scenarios and shows the calculated mark-to-market value of the product:

**Table 3.2**  Secondary market values of a capital guaranteed product[8]

| Market | Value of product | Performance |
|---|---|---|
| +20% | 113.3% | +13.3% |
| Flat | 101.2% | +1.2% |
| −20% | 92.3% | −7.7% |

---

[7] This method can be applied for most payoff diagrams.
[8] More on a product's value during its lifetime on page 71 and following. For an explanation of the mark-to-market value of a capital guaranteed product, please refer to Section 4.2 on page 78.

If the investor now changes his mind and wishes to exit the product, the capital guarantee has served no purpose in two out of three cases (positive and flat market scenarios) as the market is above or at the capital guarantee level. In the third case – in which the capital guarantee is really needed – the investor still suffers a loss of nearly 8%. The longer the maturity of the product, the bigger this number becomes.

The Shark note's up-and-out call option is much cheaper than a normal call option with the same term to expiry. Compare an 18-month plain-vanilla call option on the Eurostoxx50 index with an up-and-out call (Table 3.3).

**Table 3.3** Plain vanilla call versus up-and-out call costs

| Option type | Price in % of underlying |
| --- | --- |
| Normal call | 11.5% |
| Up-and-out call | 6.2% (barrier at 135%, rebate 0%) |

With yields in Euro around 4.5% p.a., it is therefore possible to create a 100% capital-protected product with 100% participation and an 18-month term if a barrier is set at 135% and the rebate fixed at zero (Table 3.4). The term is 70% shorter than in the 5-year previous example, the disadvantage being that the participation rate falls to zero if the Eurostoxx50 advances by more than 35%. Without the barrier, the participation in an 18-month product would amount to no more than around 45% with this short term.

**Table 3.4** Shark note versus classical capital guarantee

| Product | Characteristics |
| --- | --- |
| Classical capital guarantee | 100% participation, 5 years maturity |
| Shark note | 100% participation, barrier at 135%, rebate 0%, 18 months maturity |

Investors should therefore form an opinion regarding the market's upside potential. If the belief is that a gain of more than 35% in the Eurostoxx50 is possible or even probable over the next 18 months, the Shark note is the wrong structure to opt for. If, on the other hand, a 35% gain is considered unlikely, the product could be a good alternative to a direct investment in the index for investors who are risk averse. Table 3.5 gives the values of the Shark note after 18 months (which corresponds to its maturity) with the same market scenarios as in Table 3.2.

**Table 3.5** Value of the Shark note after 18 months

| Market | Value of the product | Performance |
| --- | --- | --- |
| +20% | 120% | 20% |
| Flat | 100% | 0% |
| −20% | 100% | 0% |

Source: own calculations

Compared to Table 3.2, the worst-case scenario has been increased to 0% from −8%, and the best-case scenario has increased to +20% from +13.3%.[9] This example shows that shortening the maturity through an up-and-out barrier can indeed be worthwhile. However, investors must keep in mind that a knock-out event will cause the product to be redeemed at par at maturity no matter what the market does after the knock-out occurred.

*Defining the objective: equities or bonds?*

As mentioned above, with capital guaranteed products investors should be sure about which objective they want to achieve, whether it is to participate in equity upside with limited downside risk, or to achieve a return slightly higher than that of a bond. Both can be accomplished with shark notes, but the structure has to be adapted according to the objective.

For investors who want to profit from *stock price gains*, the barrier should be set as high as possible in order to minimize the probability of a knock-out event and the rebate should be fixed at zero. In contrast, if an above-average *bond-like return* is the goal, the rebate should be fixed as high as possible. The rebate will be paid out if a knock-out (barrier) event occurs.

The following example shows how a Shark note can be structured to fit either objective: with or without rebate (Table 3.6). The zero-rebate example where the objective is the stock price appreciation (SN1) is taken from Table 3.4: shark note on Eurostoxx50 Index with 18-month term.

**Table 3.6**   Objective selection with Shark notes

| Name | Objective | Barrier | Rebate | Value |
|---|---|---|---|---|
| **Shark note 1 (SN1)** | **Stock-price appreciation** | 135% | 0% | 100% |
| **Shark note 2 (SN2)** | **Bond return +** | 125% | 8.5% | 100% |

Source: Bloomberg, own calculations

SN2 has the same maturity and costs the same as SN1. SN2's barrier has been lowered to allow the payout of an 8.5% rebate in case of knock-out. It is interesting to note that, when an above-average bond return is the target, a breakout above the barrier is actually desirable. If the barrier is reached, the product returns 5.6%[10] per annum (compared with an interest-rate level of 4.3% of p.a.), thereby outperforming the return on a comparable bond by an impressive 32%.

*Fine-tuning through autocall[11]*

There is one important element to take into consideration, particularly if the aim is to participate in equity performance without risk. Consider the following for a shark note without rebate: if, contrary to the investor's expectations, the barrier is breached during the lifetime of the product, it is unlikely to happen precisely at the stock market's peak. On the contrary, it is reasonable to assume that the market will rise further. However, a barrier breach means that the shark note is converted to a zero-coupon bond, and the investor misses

---

[9] Assuming that the barrier of 135% has not been hit.

[10] $\frac{8.5\%}{1.5\% \text{ years}}$

[11] See also Section 5.3 Autocall and callable options.

out on a part of the market upswing while waiting for the product to expire. A possible solution to this situation would be to enhance the Shark note with an *autocall on a barrier event* feature. The autocall causes the immediate redemption of the product at 100% of nominal value as soon as the barrier is breached. The investor therefore does not have to wait until the product expires and can immediately invest in a new shark note in order to participate in any further upside, provided that such an investment still fits his portfolio. The cost of an autocall feature on a shark note without a rebate is low, amounting to −2.5 percentage points on the barrier in the example of Table 3.6 above (i.e. reducing the barrier to 132.50%).

However, an autocall can become very expensive if a rebate that roughly amounts to or exceeds the level of the actual yield is included in the up-and-out call. In fact, the author does *not* recommend including an autocall feature in a shark note whose purpose is to outperform bonds and includes a high rebate. This is because the goal of the product is reached when the barrier in the up-and-out option is triggered: the rebate kicks in and will be paid out at expiry, no matter what the underlying asset does from that point on. The investor only has to wait until the product, now transformed into a high coupon-bearing bond, expires. For investors who would still like to include an autocall provision in a shark note paying a high rebate because they wish to reinvest in a new product once a knock-out occurs, a solution can be found whereby the rebate is paid out pro rata temporis. In the example with a 125% barrier and an 8.5% rebate, the product would be redeemed at 104.25 if the barrier was breached after nine months. The cost of such an autocall is low, reducing the rebate by a mere 0.25 percentage points.

*Shark note conclusion*

It can be observed through the above example, which started with a simple capital guaranteed product and ended in an autocallable Shark note with rebate featuring multiple exotic options, how quickly a product can become complex. In itself, complexity in a product isn't a bad thing; it is admissible as long as it serves a purpose to the investor. In practice, however, the complexity of some products often only serves the issuer, who confuses the investor with dazzling payoffs that often have only a small chance to perform in a way satisfying to the investor. By way of an example, a lot of capital guaranteed products featuring baskets of 20 stocks or more and a complex payoff structure are often "optimized" to have an attractive look, but have actually very few chances to end above the capital guarantee level.

### 3.1.3  Dos and don'ts

Throughout the book, the author wishes to share his personal views on some features and pitfalls of structured products under the sections named "Dos and Don'ts". While these views cannot be systematically applied to all products, they are designed to encourage the reader to open his eyes when he sees a product fitting one of the descriptions given. It may be that the product is perfectly sound and appropriate, but a closer look is recommended to fully appreciate all the features.

- Try to find a product that roughly fits the investor's investment horizon. For example, do not engage in a capital guaranteed note with a maturity of 6 years, when the horizon is at most 3 years.

- Be aware that the capital guarantee is only valid at maturity. During the lifetime of the product, the mark-to-market price can decline substantially under par, the more so if the maturity of the product is long.
- Avoid buying products where the capital protection is more than 10% lower than the strike price of the option, because the difference between the two determines the amount of performance that is lost. For example, in a capital guaranteed product with 85% capital guarantee level and 100% participation, if the strike of the call is set at 100% of the spot, then the 15% initial performance is lost to the investor. This means that the underlying asset must perform by more than 15% to break even, not considering any opportunity cost.
- Don't invest in a product where the participation is too low when the portfolio is compared to a benchmark that tracks the underlying asset(s). For instance, imagine that the client's goal is to track the S&P500 and the product's characteristics are 2 years maturity, 100% capital guarantee and 50% participation. Suppose that the riskless interest rate (for example the 2-year treasury) is at 4.5%. The S&P500 must perform 9% per annum over two years just to break even with the yield. If the product only delivers 50% participation, then the index has to rise by 18% to break even. As a general rule, an acceptable level of participation starts at 80% or so.
- Pay attention to the rating of the issuer of the product. Especially for long maturity products, the rating is important, as the holder of the product bears the counterparty risk, as with fiduciary placements. Don't invest in products with capital guarantee where the issuer is rated lower than A-, otherwise the capital guarantee may well become meaningless if the issuer goes belly up. For medium or longer maturities (two years or more), select issuers with AA ratings and above.
- For Shark notes, clearly define the objective to be achieved (participation or yield outperformance).
- Avoid shark notes with more than two to three years maturity, especially those without rebate. The added value of the last year is small in terms of the level of the barrier.

## 3.2 YIELD ENHANCEMENT

This category covers the largest number of structured products both in the variety of commonly-known structures and the volume invested throughout Europe. Let's start by giving a definition for this group of products:

Yield enhancement products are financial constructs with capped upside potential and without capital guarantee that aim to generate a high return relative to bond yields; the risk may become comparable to their underlying asset(s) in case of adverse market conditions.

Despite their bond-like look, yield enhancement products should never be implemented as a replacement for bonds, as their risk profile is fundamentally different from classical fixed-income instruments. Typically, yield enhancement products pay a relatively high coupon, are issued at par (100%), and trade in percent of nominal in the secondary market. Alternatively, they are issued at a relatively high discount compared to the spot prices of the underlying asset(s) they are based upon and trade in units. Historically, all yield enhancement products had a capped upside performance, represented either by the level of the coupon or the height of the discount. Nowadays, the border between participation[12] and yield enhancement products has become permeable, as some products feature both unlimited upside potential and coupons or discounts. However, keep in mind that more features doesn't necessary mean better chances of high performances.

Yield enhancement products have concave payoff functions. In essence, these payoffs are done by selling puts. Investors holding these instruments have sold positive skewness,[13] or insurance, of returns and received a premium as compensation. In Europe, the most widely-held products are the reverse convertible and the discount certificate. These have the exact same payout profile but their construction is different.

### 3.2.1 The reverse convertible

Figure 3.5 shows the construction elements that are used to build a reverse convertible.

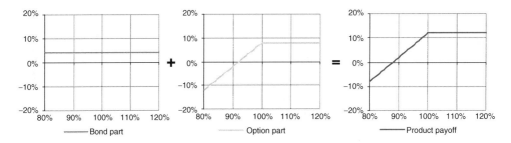

**Figure 3.5** Payoff 5: reverse convertible construction

First, a zero-coupon bond is purchased for the lifetime of the product. Then a plain vanilla[14] put is sold short on the underlying risky asset. The combination of these two financial assets forms the reverse convertible. In the example shown in Figure 3.5, with a maturity of one year (which is the typical maturity for reverse convertibles), the zero-coupon yields 4%, and the short put garners a premium of 8%. The addition of those two numbers results in a coupon of 12%. Thus, the risky asset can fall by 12% before the investor incurs a loss. The opportunity costs should always be measured against the underlying risky asset, i.e. the performance of a stock, and *not* on any bond yield that the investor might get by means of investing in an equivalent bond. Even though the word "coupon" always evokes a bond in the mind of the investors (as also mentioned in the definition above), the risk is always based on that of the underlying risky asset(s). There is no capital guarantee comparable to bonds in yield enhancement products.

The payoff of the reverse convertible is capped to the upside: the investor cannot gain more than the coupon (which is guaranteed). However, he can lose much of his entire

---

[12] Participation products will be treated extensively in Section 3.3.

[13] Positive skewness denotes return distributions where the tail to the right is more pronounced than the tail to the left.

[14] A plain vanilla option designates an option without exotic features, like barriers or asian tails. It is the most basic form of an option. Calls and puts are the two plain vanilla options. In contrast, a knock-in put is an exotic option.

investment if the underlying risky asset declines strongly. In the extreme case, where the underlying loses all value (i.e. bankruptcy for a stock) the investor might lose the whole of his investment, leaving him with only the coupon. It is of utmost importance to consider a reverse convertible type of structure like an equity investment if the underlying asset(s) is/are equity(ies). The same argument is valid for commodities, FX or any other risky underlying asset. Just because the product pays a coupon doesn't mean it's comparable to a bond. This can't be said often and loud enough.

### 3.2.2   The worst-of barrier reverse convertible

The reverse convertible, which is the predominant product type especially in Switzerland, has evolved into many sub-categories. Some of them will be briefly explained in later chapters, but one is of particular interest due to its wide acceptance by investors, from grandmothers to pension funds: it is worst-of knock-in reverse convertible, more commonly known as the worst-of barrier reverse convertible.

The structure is that of a classical reverse convertible with some additional elements: the product is based on *several underlying risky assets* and incorporates a *knock-in barrier*. The final payoff is based on the worst performing of the risky assets.

The common representation of the worst-of knock-in reverse convertible payoff (Figure 3.6) does not differ from that of the knock-in reverse convertible on a single underlying asset, because it is not practical to represent multiple assets in the same graphic. One would have to make a three dimensional graphic to show the single barriers on each asset, but that would probably be more confusing than helpful to the end investor. The investor has to keep in mind that the payoff line always represents the *worst performing asset* of those included in the structure.

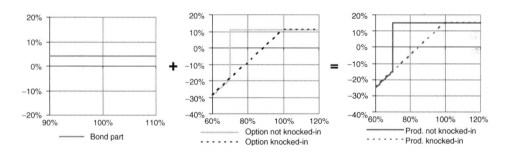

**Figure 3.6**   Payoff 6: (worst-of) barrier reverse convertible construction

Note that the payoff for a barrier reverse convertible which has been knocked-in is identical to that of a reverse convertible without a knock-in feature (in case a knock-in occurs, the solid line disappears and the payoff assumes the shape of the dotted line).

Let's define the knock-in barrier first. A down-and-in barrier[15] has been added to the short plain vanilla put option of the classical reverse convertible, thus making it an exotic

---

[15] More on exotic barrier options in Section 5.2.

option. The "down" means that the underlying asset has to go down for something to happen with the option. The "in" means that once the underlying asset has fallen by more than a predefined amount, the option knocks-in; in and becomes "alive";[16] in other words, the option begins to exist and transforms itself into a short plain vanilla put once the barrier has been touched. Effectively, the option was "dead" (as if it didn't exist) prior to the underlying asset breaking through the barrier. This implies two things: first, the product is *conditionally* capital protected; i.e. unless the underlying asset breaks through the barrier, the investor will not lose any invested capital. Second, the product's payoff diagram has now an asymptote (a vertical inflexion point) at the level of the barrier. So, if the down-and-in level of the barrier is set at 70% of the underlying asset's spot price at issue, the product could be worth either 100% or 70% from one second to the next.

Now let's define the worst-of feature. This feature causes the short put to knock-in when the worst performing of the underlying assets reaches its respective barrier level. For the sake of simplicity, the description will be made through a practical example. Table 3.7 summarizes the product's characteristics.

**Table 3.7**  Worst-of barrier reverse convertible example

| Type | Worst-of barrier reverse convertible |
|---|---|
| Underlying stocks | Nestlé, UBS, Roche |
| **Currency** | CHF |
| **Strike** | 100% of spot |
| **Knock-in barrier** | 70% of spot |
| **Maturity** | 1 year |
| **Coupon** | 15% |

Source: Bloomberg, own calculations

The payoff can be described in the following two steps:

1. As long as none of the three stocks has ever declined by more than 30% anytime during the lifetime of the product *or* all the stocks close above their initial values, the product is redeemed in cash at 100% + 15% coupon on the invested nominal.
2. If at least one of the three stocks has declined by more than 30% during the lifetime of the product *and* at least one of the stocks is still below its spot at issue date, the product is redeemed in shares[17] of the worst performing stock plus the 15% coupon.

There are two main points to remember from a risk point of view: first, if scenario 2 is validated, the investor receives the worst performing stock of the three. That means that the whole invested notional is dependent on the worst performing stock, not only one third of it. There is therefore a *concentration of risk*, not a diversification. Second, the number of shares received in scenario 2 is fixed and linked to the spot of the three underlying stocks

---

[16] This is the exact opposite of the up-and-out from the Shark note described earlier.
[17] There are in fact two variants for the redemption for scenario 2: some issuers will physically deliver the stocks as in the example, whereas others will redeem in cash. The actual variant is always indicated on the term-sheet.

*at the issue date*. Table 3.8 is a practical example taken from Table 3.7, based on a nominal per note of CHF 1000.-:

**Table 3.8** Reverse convertible share delivery calculation

| Stocks | Spot at issue date | Amount of shares in case of physical delivery |
|--------|--------------------|-----------------------------------------------|
| **Nestlé** | CHF 450.- | 2.22 |
| **UBS** | CHF 70.- | 14.29 |
| **Roche** | CHF 200.- | 5 |

Source: own calculations.

Suppose that at maturity, UBS has fallen to CHF 30, Nestlé, Roche stayed flat, and the worst-of knock-in reverse convertible is redeemed. UBS has clearly broken through the barrier (loss of 100% − 30/70 = 57%, which is more than the 30% protection planned at the inception of the product) and the product is redeemed in UBS shares. At redemption, per CHF 1000 nominal, the investor gets 14 shares worth 14 * 30 = CHF 420 plus a small amount of cash (0.29 * 30 = CHF 8.70) totaling CHF 428.70, which amounts to a loss of 57%. Added to that, the 15% guaranteed coupon reduces the loss to 42%.

Note that the investor will not necessarily receive the stock that broke through the barrier in the first place. In the above example, if after dropping to CHF 30 UBS recovers to CHF 60 (loss of 1 − 60/70 = 14.3%) and Roche declines to 150 (loss of 1 − 150/200 = 25%), the product will be redeemed in Roche shares, even though UBS broke through the barrier and Roche didn't.

### 3.2.3 The discount certificate

The discount certificate has an identical payoff profile to that of the reverse convertible, only its construction elements differ (Figure 3.7).

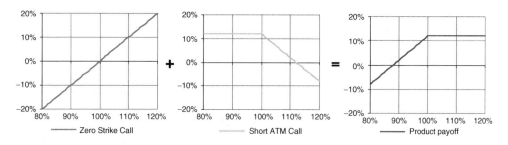

**Figure 3.7** Payoff 7: discount certificate construction

The right-hand side of Figure 3.7 shows that there is no difference when comparing the payoff diagram of the discount certificate to that of the reverse convertible. The discount certificate is just constructed differently: a long zero-strike call, sometimes referred to as LEPO,[18] is combined with a short call option with a strike at- or out-of-the-money.

As a matter of fact, most structured products can be constructed in two ways. This is a consequence of the call-put parity: a long call can be replicated by going long a LEPO on the underlying asset in addition to a long put with the same strike minus the cost of financing the underlying asset at money-market rates. By rearranging that equation, it can be adapted to the case of the reverse convertible and discount certificate (Table 3.9).

**Table 3.9**  Economically equal discount certificate and reverse convertible

| Money market + short put | = | LEPO + short call |
|---|---|---|
| **Reverse convertible** | = | **Discount certificate** |

The discount certificate construction implies that the investor will pay less than the spot price at the issue date of the product, since the premium received on the short call reduces the purchase price of the zero-strike call. So instead of receiving a coupon at maturity as with the reverse convertible, the investor simply pays less at the issue date.

*A word about taxes*

The reverse convertible/discount certificate equality gives an opportunity to discuss briefly a subject that concerns all investors: taxes on structured products. Because taxes vary from one country to another, are dependent on each individual's situation and on top of that vary over time, only a simple example will be represented here. The example focuses on an investor taxable in Switzerland.

A misconception held by many Swiss investors is that receiving a coupon at maturity is somehow better than paying less on the issue date, while the reverse is true. For Swiss investors there is indeed an appreciable difference between the reverse convertible and the discount certificate in favor of the latter when considering taxes.

Because the Swiss Tax Authorities tax income but not capital gains, the coupon of a reverse convertible is usually split for tax purposes on the term-sheet. If that were not the case, the product would risk being classified as "non transparent" and the whole coupon could be taxed by the authorities. The split is made according to the current interest rate level: on issue date, the 10% coupon of a one-year maturity product when the interest rate is 3% will be split into 3% taxable income and 7% tax-free capital gain. The maturity of the reverse convertible does not matter. Whether it is greater or less than one year, the interest-linked part of the product's return will still be taxed.

The matter is different for discount certificates and depends on the maturity. If the maturity is greater than one year, the part of the discount that is attributable to interest will also be taxed, as with the reverse convertible. However, as long as the maturity is less than one year, the discount is free of tax!

Therefore, if a private individual who is taxable in Switzerland invests in a Reverse Convertible with a one-year maturity, he is actually choosing to give the state taxes of his

---

[18] Low Exercise Price Option. To simplify, it is assumed that no dividends are paid,

own free will. His net revenue drops by the amount of the taxes. Let's see this through the examples given in Tables 3.10 and 3.11.

**Table 3.10** Swiss tax treatment example 1

| Example in % | Reverse convertible | Discount certificate |
| --- | --- | --- |
| **Underlying** | SMI | SMI |
| **Maturity** | 1 year | 1 year − 1 day |
| **Coupon** | 10% | Discount: 10% |
| **Interest rate** | 3% | 3% |
| **Tax (35%)** | 1.05% | 0% |
| **Net revenue** | **8.95%** | **10%** |

**Table 3.11** Swiss tax treatment example 2

| Example in numbers | Reverse convertible | Discount certificate |
| --- | --- | --- |
| **Initial cost** | 100% | 90% (10% discount) |
| **Initial investment** | CHF 100 000 | CHF 90 000 |
| **Payoff at maturity** | 110 000 | 100 000 |
| **Pre-tax revenue** | 10 000 | 10 000 |
| **Tax (35%)** | 1 050 | 0.00 |
| **Net revenue** | **CHF 8 950** | **CHF 10 000** |

The case demonstrates the absolute superiority of the discount certificate as compared to the reverse convertible for Swiss taxpayers. Note that this also holds for barrier reverse convertibles versus barrier discount certificates, worst-of barrier reverse convertibles versus worst-of barrier discount certificates and so on.

So why is it that the Swiss invest in so many reverse convertibles? There could be several reasons.

*The coupon.* Reverse convertibles pay a coupon while discount certificates do not. This makes the reverse convertible *look* more like a bond than the discount certificate; especially the Italian-speaking customers of banks, who were used to high Lira denominated coupons (10% or more) were disappointed when these disappeared to be replaced by the Euro denominated bonds, which had coupons of around 3%. The high coupon also seduced other customers, especially when it was linked to blue chip equity like Roche or UBS. Unlike the discount certificate, the customer sees a money flow in form of a coupon at the maturity of the reverse convertible.

*Lack of knowledge.* Structured products are relatively new instruments in the financial world. They didn't exist until the late 1980s, and really boomed only from the late 1990s onwards. Few people know how they are constructed, and fewer still know their subtleties. Even some investment advisors have limited knowledge. In the early years of the reverse convertible, the coupon was of more importance to the majority of the investors, and the advisors sold their clients what they wanted. It may be that few investors understand the tax differences between the two instruments.

*Habit and customer psychology*. As already mentioned in the introduction, the *force of habit*, a very strong and difficult human behavior to break once rooted may apply here. After an investor has had a good experience with a new instrument like a reverse convertible, he tends to stick to that instrument, regardless of the market conditions or expectations. The investment advisor, even if he knows the tax advantage of the discount certificate and is willing to make the effort, will have difficulty making the client switch instruments once a habit has been formed.

*Market size*. The tax advantage of below one-year maturity discount certificates versus reverse convertibles is only valid for investors taxed in Switzerland. A large part of the invested volume remains with foreigners taxed in other countries, where practices differ.

*Lack of offer*. A client is seldom offered the choice between a reverse convertible and a discount certificate on the same underlying. There are many more issues of reverse convertibles than there are of discount certificates, and they are much more advertised. Indeed, the worst-of barrier reverse convertibles are so popular nowadays, that few issuers bother to issue worst-of barrier discount certificates.

None of these reasons is grounded in economics. They are all related to the psychology of the market participants, from the issuer of the product to the final investor. Note that in Germany, where until 2009 the reverse convertible was also at a tax disadvantage,[19] the discount certificates boomed. Hence, the Germans seem to have a more acute feeling toward taxes than the Swiss.

### 3.2.4 Yield enhancement variations

Many more yield enhancement products exist, but they are less well known and are usually variations of the reverse convertible or the discount certificate. As the possibilities are virtually limitless, it would be fruitless to enumerate them all. Instead, a list of additional features to a standard reverse convertible (or discount certificate) and its effect on the payoff is shown below, followed by a table of selected variations (Table 3.12).

- Putting the coupon of the reverse convertible at risk: linking the coupon to a breakthrough of the barrier.
  *Effect:* increases the coupon quite significantly. Best used in situations where the expected market scenario is unlikely to hit the barrier and the investor seeks higher coupons.
- Same as above, but adding a second barrier to the upside of the product (coupon is lost if either barrier is touched).
  *Effect:* increases the coupon even more. Best used for situations where the market scenario is volatile, but with a range bound outlook and volatility is expected to decrease.
- Instead of having a fixed barrier, the barrier can be relative to another underlying asset like an index.
  *Effect:* makes the product independent of market movement. Regardless of the market direction, it is then essential that the underlying asset(s) of the product move in parallel with the underlying asset they are measured against. Can be used when the correlation

---

[19] The introduction of the Flat Tax Rate ("Abgeltungssteuer") will level that disadvantage from a tax point of view in the future.

between the product's underlying asset(s) and the reference asset is historically low and expected to rise.

• In a worst-of barrier reverse convertible, instead of putting all the barriers at the same level, use individual levels for each underlying

  *Effect:* allows for volatility adjustments. If a worst-of barrier reverse convertible is structured with two underlying assets, one with a high volatility and the other with a low one, use a deep barrier for the volatile asset and a shallow barrier for the less volatile asset. Thus, both assets add equally to the risk (and thus the coupon) of the product.

• In a worst-of barrier reverse convertible, use European style[20] barriers instead of American style.

  *Effect:* lowers the coupon, but a knock-in can only take place at maturity, not during the lifetime of the product.

Table 3.12 overleaf shows an enhanced (without pretending to be complete) list of reverse convertible variations.

In this jungle of possibilities, it is not easy to find the right product. The best way to select a fitting variant is to begin by assessing the market conditions and selecting an underlying asset (stock, index, commodity...), followed by a clear target return objective, and finally to define the maximum acceptable risk. Make sure that the product fits in the portfolio from a risk and diversification point of view. If unsure, keep it simple; a host of features, as dazzling as they seem, often tends to dilute the performance of the product.

*Dos and don'ts*

• Invest in a yield enhancement product only when the worst-case scenario risk can be borne. Remember, there is no capital guarantee, even if the barrier is optically set very low.

• As a representative, always explain the risks when recommending yield enhancement products. Never suggest that a yield enhancement product could be a bond replacement, only with "enhanced yield". Again, just because a coupon is paid at maturity doesn't qualify the product for a bond type of risk.

• As an investor, consider the level of the coupon (or the discount in case of a discount certificate) to gauge the risk of the structure: suppose that the coupon of a one-year product is 15% and the riskless money-market rate is 3%. Regardless of the level of the barrier and other features if any, this is a relatively high risk product. Be prepared to take full underlying asset risk.

• In products featuring worst-of options, be aware of concentration risk in the underlying assets on a portfolio basis. For example, consider the portfolio shown in Table 3.13 (see p.53) with three worst-of reverse convertibles (with or without barrier) including the following Swiss stocks.

  The portfolio's risk is concentrated on a single stock! If for example Credit Suisse dropped significantly, the value of the portfolio would be 100% linked to Credit Suisse and might even become worthless if the company goes broke. It may seem surprising, but the author has effectively seen similar portfolios on several occasions.

---

[20] See American and European barriers, page 123.

**Table 3.12**  Reverse convertible (RC) variations

| Generic name | Features | Best market conditions | Optimal market scenario |
|---|---|---|---|
| **RC** | Plain vanilla option | High volatility | Lower volatility, sideways market expected |
| **Barrier RC** | Barrier protecting the capital | High skew | Sideways, lower trending, market expected |
| **Barrier worst-of RC** | Barrier can be breached by worst performing stock | High skew, low correlation | Rising correlation, sideways, lower trending market expected |
| **Barrier best-of RC** | All stocks must breach the barrier for the capital guarantee to disappear | High skew, high correlation | Correlation drops, sideways market expected |
| **Callable RC** | Product can be called by the issuer at certain dates | High interest rates, high volatility | Falling volatility, slightly rising market scenario |
| **Trigger worst-of barrier RC** | Barrier + early redemption with full coupon if all stocks above trigger level | Low correlation, expected to rise in the short term | Broad, parallel market movement expected |
| **Barrier worst-of RC with participation on the worst-of** | Barrier + participation on the worst performer if positive | Low correlation | Correlation expected to rise, chances of rising market |
| **Callable yield note** | Barrier + long term (2–3 years), worst-of, usually indices. Called by the issuer if market rises | High interest rates, high volatility | Falling volatility, slightly rising market scenario, long-term horizon |
| **Relative worst-of barrier RC** | Barrier is set relative to a benchmark, usually an index | Low correlation, high volatility, | Rising correlation expected. Asset performance equal to index performance |
| **Individual barrier worst-of RC** | Barriers are set at different levels for each stock | Different asset volatilities | Individual stock worst-case scenario expected |
| **Multichance RC** | 3 out of 5 stocks must hit the barrier before the capital guarantee disappears | High correlation, high volatility | Lower correlation expected |
| **Lookback RC** | The strike is set a few weeks after the product has been launched | Low volatility, low skew | Market declines further then bottoms out or rebounds |
| **Window barrier RC** | The barrier is only observed during a certain time window (at the end) | Strong rising volatility term structure | Volatility terms structure flattens |

**Table 3.13**  Example of suboptimal barrier
worst-of reverse convertible portfolio

| | |
|---|---|
| **Product 1** | ABB/Nestlé/Crédit Suisse |
| **Product 2** | Roche/Crédit Suisse/Swiss Re |
| **Product 3** | Novartis/Zürich/Crédit Suisse |

- In products featuring a worst-of option, never invest in products based on too many underlying assets. In fact, keep the amount as low as possible, preferably two. Avoid products featuring "worst-of four", "worst-of five" or more assets. The added value of the fourth, fifth or $n^{th}$ asset is most of the time very low, in the range of 0% to 2% additional coupon or discount at best. Dramatically increasing the unsystematic risk with the addition of another asset for a very small increase in the potential yield generally doesn't pay off.
- In the case of barrier reverse convertibles, invest in products where the conviction is pretty high that the barrier will hold. Nothing is worse than a barrier reverse convertible "knocking-in", therefore, it is better to take 5% more protection on the barrier than necessary and accept a slightly lower coupon. Also consider lowering the strike of the option instead of placing a barrier.
- Think about investing in "best-of" options when the correlation is high and expected to fall.
- Use a European barrier when uncertain about the market's medium term evolution and the volatility is high. It often happens that a stock's price falls more than anticipated but rebounds within the lifetime of the product.

## 3.3  PARTICIPATION

Participation products are the group of products that have upside potential and no, or only conditional, capital protection.[21] Let's formally define participation products:

Participation products are financial constructs closely linked to the performance of their underlying asset(s), which sometimes feature a conditional downside protection or a leveraged upside.

Of the three product categories (four including warrants), participation products are the riskiest. They have no certain capital guarantee, they neither pay a guaranteed coupon nor are they issued at any significant discount. Nevertheless, they offer partial, full or even leveraged participation on the underlying risky asset. The most known products are:

- tracker certificate (basket);
- bonus certificate;
- twin-win certificate;
- airbag certificate;
- turbo certificate (also called capped outperformance certificate);
- outperformance certificate.

These products are frequently equity based, but can be based on any underlying asset.

---

[21] Not to be mistaken for capital guarantee, which is unconditional.

### 3.3.1 Tracker certificate

Tracker certificates are structures that simply track an underlying asset or multiple underlying assets. There is no cap or protection. They are structured with a zero-strike call (LEPO), in which the strike has been set to a level of zero. Since a zero-strike call always has an intrinsic value of 100% and no time value, its value always equals the spot price of the underlying minus any discounted dividends or present value yields. The payoff diagram of a tracker looks like the payoff diagram of the underlying asset (Figure 3.8).

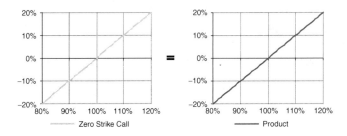

**Figure 3.8**   Payoff 8: tracker certificate payoff

A tracker can be structured either with total return or with excess return underlying assets. A total return tracker includes any dividends or yield. An excess return index includes neither of the two mentioned attributes, and always underperforms a total return index on the same underlying asset. Unless the tracker is issued or trading at a discount, the costs for the investor when investing in an excess return based tracker are the foregone dividends or yield. In practice, trackers are usually constructed with excess return assets, like a basket of stocks, or an index like the S&P500, the Eurostoxx50 or the SMI. Total return assets like the DAX index are very seldom used in structured products, because they have to be issued above par due to structuring costs, and they seldom look attractive.

The cost of a tracker on an ex-dividend asset is symbolically represented in the graphic of Figure 3.9. Imagine a stock index like the Eurostoxx50 or the S&P500 with a dividend

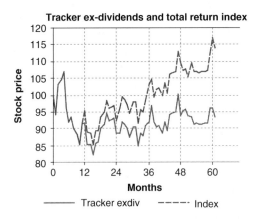

**Figure 3.9**   Ex-dividend and total return index
*Source:* Bloomberg, own representation

of 4% per annum. For illustrative purposes, assume that the dividend is paid once every 12 months. Now suppose that Bank XY has issued a certificate tracking that excess return index with a maturity of 5 years. Excluding the effect of taxes on dividends, the total return asset outperforms the tracker by the cumulated dividends, assumed to be reinvested. On a one-year scale, that doesn't amount to much, but on a five-year scale the outperformance of the index including dividends, as compared to the tracker without dividends, is significant.

Nowadays, trackers on excess return underlying assets, as for example the one on the Eurostoxx50 mentioned above, are often very liquid and efficient investment vehicles to use for investing in a certain sector, market, theme or region. Among other reasons, this is because of the competition coming from exchange-traded funds (ETFs). In principle, it should trade (on the offer side) approximately at the spot price minus discounted dividends to maturity plus structuring costs and any bid-ask spread. If it trades above, then it's too expensive, and below would be too cheap. This implies that the investor must know the implied dividends to maturity in order to determine whether the price of a tracker is fair or not, which is not an easy feat. For instance, investment banks keep their forecasts on expected dividends secret, because their level influences the price of a broad range of products. One free source for an investor to estimate dividends is the internet, where information can be found on various financial websites.[22] The investor could also ask his investment advisor to provide the information.

Trackers that are issued on total return assets, like the MSCI Total Return index or a total return commodity index, will often be issued above the spot price, due to structuring costs. Otherwise, they include periodic management fees to pay for the hedging and market-making costs. In the secondary market, they should trade fairly tight around the spot price of the underlying asset.

A tracker, basket of shares or index certificate competes on the market with long-only funds or exchange-traded funds. Historically, tracker certificates were constructed with static underlying assets. Once the certificate's underlying assets were fixed at the issue date, they were not changed until maturity (barring corporate actions and the like). In the late 1990s tracker certificates were developed with changing underlying assets. However, these were rule based, with objective criteria deciding which asset was part of the tracker and which not. For instance, every quarter the basket would be rebalanced to contain the 10 stocks with the highest dividend yield growth, or those with the lowest P/E, etc. Although many such mathematically determined strategies have been invented and promoted in the last 10 years, few have constantly outperformed their respective benchmarks to the knowledge of the author.

Since 2007, a new kind of tracker certificate has been made possible in Switzerland as a result of changes in the regulation: the *actively managed certificate* (AMC). It is a fully discretionary managed investment vehicle. AMCs are so flexible that they allow an investment advisor to manage the underlying portfolio of the AMC like a fund but without the regulatory burden required by mutual funds. The AMC can even be structured in the form of a hedge fund, allowing leverage, short positions, and investments in complex instruments

---

[22] For instance Yahoo Finance, but also UBS quotes, Zacks.com and other financial service websites provide this information for free, though the source of the estimate may not always be reliable or accurate. On the Bloomberg.com website, expected dividend yields are also provided, based on financial analysts forecasts. This is often the most accurate source one can find for free.

like exotic OTC options, swaps of all kinds as well as structured products. AMCs will be discussed in depth in Section 8.2.

Tracker certificates are most useful to investors when they track underlying assets that are difficult or downright impossible to invest in with classical instruments, for example:

- commodities;
- private equity;
- real estate;
- some hedge funds or fund-of-funds;[23] and
- insurance-linked products.

At another level, trackers are often used to invest in a specific market segment, for example:

- European pharmaceutical;
- high dividend stocks of the S&P500; and
- China Water exposed companies.

One of the advantages of tracker certificates is that they allow an investor to get exposure to a theme or industry segment while staying diversified and keeping the costs low. Investors should keep in mind the many possibilities offered by these apparently simple instruments. Are they denominated in the same currency as the underlying asset, or in a different one? Are the expected dividends correctly reflected in the tracker's price? Is the strategy sound? A tracker's name does not necessarily reflect its underlying asset's full business exposure. For instance, the China Water exposed companies tracker mentioned above might include mainly European and US stocks like Veolia Environment and Valmont Industries instead of Chinese companies. Even if these stocks have some exposure to the China Water theme, their main exposure remains in Europe and the US respectively, and the price of these stocks will be primarily influenced by other factors than China Water investments.

If the underlying assets are dividend-paying stocks, the investor does not incur the dividend risk any more. It is borne by the issuer. Therefore, if an investor expects falling dividends but wants (or has) to remain invested in stocks, one way of getting rid of the dividend risk is to switch the stocks for a tracker certificate on the stocks. But there are other ways, such as transforming the dividend into protection as with the bonus certificate.[24] Yet another potential advantage is that a tracker certificate may be taxed less than its underlying constituents in certain jurisdictions.

The main disadvantage with a static tracker is that it is just that – static. Once set up, there is no way of modifying its constituents. This can become bothersome; imagine a certificate that tracks 20 stocks in the high-tech sector. The scenario is that these 20 stocks should outperform the sector as a whole. The product is issued but, 10 days later, a competitor not included in the basket announces a technological breakthrough making the business model of three stocks within the basket obsolete. These three stocks immediately lose 15%, but the investor thinks they could well fall by another 20% or even go out of business. The investor has no other choice but to sell the whole tracker, including the 17 stocks that he might want to keep.

---

[23] An investor would be well advised to pay attention to the total expense ratio (TER) of such instruments, as multiple fee layers can reduce the performance dramatically.

[24] See Section 3.3.2 below for more information.

### 3.3.2 Bonus certificates

Bonus certificates are tracker certificates with conditional downside protection. They are popular among investors who are bullish on the underlying asset but wouldn't like to lose money if the asset declines in value. A bonus certificate on a stock (or stock index) participates fully in its upside performance, pays a positive amount (the "bonus") if the underlying asset doesn't perform better than the predefined bonus level or worse than a predefined barrier, but loses the bonus and protection if the barrier is touched. Like the barrier reverse convertible, the bonus certificate is said to be "conditionally capital protected". Conditional, because the capital protection disappears if the underlying asset falls too much and breaches the barrier. A typical bonus certificate, like the one shown below in Figure 3.10 has the features described in Table 3.14.

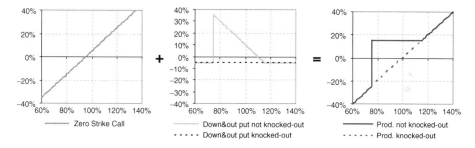

**Figure 3.10** Payoff 9: bonus certificate construction[25]

**Table 3.14** Example of bonus certificate

| | |
| --- | --- |
| Upside participation to the risky asset | 100% |
| Bonus level | 15% |
| Barrier in % of spot | 75% |
| Maturity | 2 years |

In this example, if the asset doesn't rise by more than 15% by maturity, the return on the invested capital will be at least 15%, provided that it hasn't touched the barrier, i.e. 75% of spot. Should the latter have occurred, the bonus certificate is transformed into a simple tracker certificate, ex-dividends. Bonus certificates are built with a zero strike call and a long down-and-out put.[26]

Let's recall the characteristics of a down-and-out put option: it's like a normal put, which protects the investor when the underlying asset declines in value, but it ceases to exist (in trading slang the option "dies") once the price of the underlying asset reaches a certain

---

[25] Note that because the construction of a bonus certificate requires dividends or yield to purchase the down-and-out put, the zero-strike call's price must be lower than the spot price of the underlying asset at the issue date. In the example, the level has been set at 95% and the cost of the option equals that level for illustration purposes.

[26] The second way to build a bonus certificate is a short down-and-in put (i.e. with a strike of 115% of spot and a barrier at 75% of spot) plus a long call at 115% of spot plus a money-market investment. This is the way the Swiss tax authorities treat bonus certificates, basing their calculation of the theoretical bond floor on the money-market part.

barrier[27] (the knock-out barrier). The down-and-out put option is therefore much cheaper than a classical plain vanilla put option.

In order to be able to buy the down-and-out put and at the same time issue the bonus certificate at par with the underlying asset (which is standard practice in the market), it is necessary to take some value from somewhere. Where the bonus certificate's underlying asset is a stock or a stock index, then it is necessary to use *dividends* (if the underlying asset is a stock index, then it must be an excess return index) to purchase the down-and-out put. Where it's a commodity index or other asset class index, it must be an excess return index and the *yield* is used. Otherwise, it's not possible to issue the bonus certificate at par with the underlying asset.

The dividends or yield used to purchase the down-and-out put represent the cost of the protection. In the case of stocks, using the dividends to purchase the barrier has the advantage of being consistent with an uncertain bullish view. If the situation deteriorates, then stock prices and dividends would surely fall and the protection comes in handy (if chosen high enough).

A structurer can vary four main parameters to parameterize a bonus certificate. Those are:

- the level of the participation;
- the level of the bonus;
- the level of the barrier; and
- the maturity.

Other features include caps, worst-of, Asian tails, lock-ins, etc. But the points above are the key to structuring the right product for a given client or market view. Each of the parameters influences the others. Let's go through them one by one.

*The level of participation.* This can be decreased in order to raise the bonus, lower the barrier or shorten the maturity. In the extreme, it can be lowered to zero above the bonus level, effectively placing a cap. Figure 3.11 shows an example where the participation above the bonus has been lowered to 25% in order to raise the bonus by 10% to 25%.

*The level of the bonus.* This can be decreased to raise the participation, lower the barrier or shorten the maturity. Figure 3.12 shows an example where the bonus has been lowered to zero in order to lower the barrier (increase the buffer) to 65% from 75% of spot.

*The level of the barrier.* The level of the barrier can be increased to raise the participation, raise the bonus or shorten the maturity. In an extreme case, the barrier can be removed entirely, increasing the participation to the maximum, thus obtaining another type of product, the outperformance certificate.[28] Figure 3.13 shows an example where an increase (i.e. a reduction in the buffer) of 5% in the barrier allowed an increase in the participation to 175%.

*The maturity.* Always shorten the maturity as much as reasonably possible without destroying the purpose of the product. The longer the maturity, the higher the chances that a negative event occurs and the barrier gets hit. In general, each addition of a time unit

---

[27] The down-and-out put of the bonus certificate is effectively the opposite of the down-and-in put of the barrier reverse convertible. However, while with the barrier reverse convertible, the down-and-in put is sold short, with the bonus certificate, the down-and-out put is bought.

[28] See page 67.

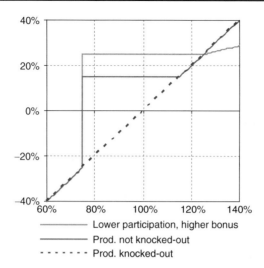

**Figure 3.11** Payoff 10: lower participation, higher bonus

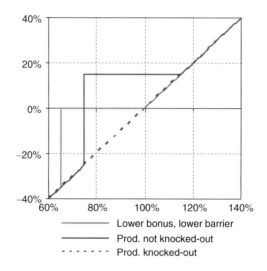

**Figure 3.12** Payoff 11: lower bonus, higher barrier

(a month, a year...) brings less benefit to the product than the previous one. For example, if a product has a barrier of 75% (buffer of 25%) for a maturity of 2 years, adding one year might lower the barrier to 60% (buffer of 40%), but adding two years would only lower it to 52% (buffer of 48%). The question for the investor is then whether the addition of one year is worth 8% more protection. Also, if the initial decision was to go for a high bonus, it will take more time to get it if the maturity is long. A bonus certificate on stocks or indices should have a maturity between one and two years. As a rule of thumb, avoid investments in bonus certificates with maturities of more than three years, remaining preferably within a range of one to two years.

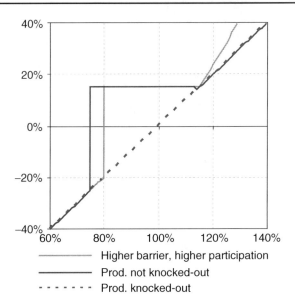

**Figure 3.13**   Payoff 12: lower barrier, higher participation

### 3.3.3   Twin-win certificates

Twin-win certificates are a special version of the bonus certificate. Instead of a bonus level, a positive participation to the downside of the underlying asset is bought, hence the name, twin-win. The investor wins when the underlying asset rises, but also when it falls. Where is the risk, then? There is still the barrier to the downside. Once it's breached, the twin-win transforms itself into a classical tracker certificate and any positive downside participation is lost. From a construction point of view, the twin-win is identical to the bonus certificate with the addition of another down-and-out put in addition to the already existing one. The elements are therefore: long zero strike call + 2 * down-and-out put.

Figure 3.14 shows that the flat bonus line that characterizes a classical bonus certificate has been replaced with a positive participation when the underlying asset falls. The strike

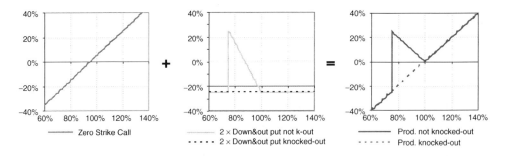

**Figure 3.14**   Payoff 13: twin-win certificate construction

of the down-and-out put option is often selected to be at-the-money. Otherwise, the same construction parameters as those for the classical bonus certificate apply: lowering or capping the upside participation can be used to set a deeper barrier, etc.

A twin-win certificate is a useful alternative to the classical bonus certificate when the future development of the underlying asset is not foreseeable at all, or where an otherwise long-only portfolio might profit from this structure, rather than lose, if the markets decrease moderately. It is very important to place the knock-out barrier at a level where one can be fairly certain that a knock-out will not occur. Absolute certainty of not being knocked out and thus incurring negative performance with twin-win certificates cannot be economically reached, but losing the positive performance of a twin-win through a knock-out when markets crash a little too much is the worst thing that can happen with this type of instrument. So as an investor, always optimize the barrier first! Place a cap to the upside participation if it seems necessary in order to lower the barrier even further.

### 3.3.4 Airbag certificates

Airbag certificates participate in the upside performance of an underlying asset and have a certain amount of downside protection down to which level the investor doesn't lose any of his capital. In other words, as long as the underlying asset doesn't lose more than a predefined level, the capital is 100% protected. That level is called the airbag, named after the automobile safety system. As in a car, where the airbag protects and reduces the pain in the event of an accident, the financial airbag dampens the effect of a negative performance of the underlying asset at maturity. The level of the airbag is determined at the issue of the product and placed relatively far below the spot level of the underlying asset, typically between 85% and 70% of the spot price. If the underlying asset falls below the airbag's level, the product starts to lose in value with a certain amount of leverage that depends on the level of the airbag: the greater the buffer from the airbag, the higher the leverage from that point downwards. In negative markets, however, the airbag's performance will always stay above that of the underlying asset, unless that asset falls to zero, in which case both performances will be equal.[29] As opposed to the bonus certificate or the twin-win certificate, airbags are built *without barriers* that could be knocked-out in case of adverse market conditions. The product consists of three plain vanilla European-style options:

- The upside is provided by a long at-the-money call.
- The downside and the airbag are constructed by a ratio call spread: a long zero-strike call plus a short call with the strike at the height of the airbag. The ratio of the call spread to the long at-the-money call depends on the level of the airbag and determines the amount of leverage discussed above.

In the classical case where the airbag's upside performance starts at 100% of spot, the downside leverage must always equal 100% divided by the level of the airbag. Figure 3.15 shows the construction steps.

---

[29] Not considering any dividends or yield.

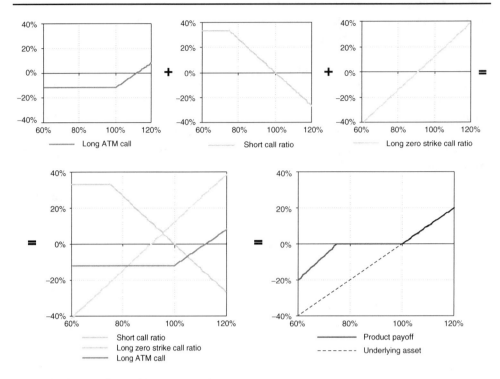

**Figure 3.15**  Payoff 14: airbag construction

In the example above, the airbag level has been set to 75%, protecting the investor against the first 25% losses.[30] Thus, the three components of the product would be:

- 1.33 * long zero-strike call;
- 1.33 * short call strike 75%;
- 1 * long at-the-money call.[31]

Similar to the bonus certificates, the protection is paid for by either the dividends (in case of stocks) or yield (in other cases). Airbag certificates often appear less attractive than bonus certificates, because the buffer of an airbag is smaller than for a comparable bonus certificate. There is a big difference, though: as previously mentioned, the airbag protection doesn't knock-out. In a bonus certificate, once the barrier is knocked-out, even if the underlying asset recovers to a level above the barrier but stays below the strike, the investor incurs a loss. With an airbag certificate, a recovery above the strike of the short call means that the product has reached the protection zone again. In addition, with an airbag certificate,

---

[30] Calculated on 30 June with underlying asset Allianz SE, maturity of 2 years, dividend yield of 5.25% and interest rate in EUR at 5.20%. Volatility was assumed to be flat at 30%. Note that as for the bonus certificate, the zero strike call has been drawn on the chart according to its value at the issue date including dividends, as they are necessary for the construction of the product. In this case, the values for the individual legs are $\sim -12\%$ for the long at-the-money call, 33% for the short call and $\sim 91\%$ for the zero-strike call.

[31] The second way to construct this airbag certificate would be: long ATM call + short 1.33 [1/0.75] puts with strike at 75% + money market.

the value of the product always stays at or above that of the underlying asset, even in sharp decreases. To put it another way, the protection of an airbag is smaller than one of a comparable bonus certificate because it is worth more, all other things held equal. That being said, the fact that many investors have a preference for bonus certificates may be a signal that the greater value of the airbag is not recognized by investors. Many go automatically for the bigger protection (in percentage) if their anticipated scenario is that the barrier of the bonus certificate will not be breached. This may explain why the bonus certificates are so popular and airbag certificates are relatively scarce.

As with so many structured products including an option component, an airbag's final payoff is reached only at maturity. For most of the product's life, the protection is only partially reflected in the product's secondary market price. It is mainly for this reason that it's advisable to keep the maturity short. From a statistical point of view, it is extremely unlikely that an asset (in particular a stock or a stock index with an average volatility of 15%) will trade within a range from 0% to 30% below the current spot price in three or four years time, which is the typical amount of protection an airbag offers. Either the asset's price will be far above or far below that range, in which case a direct investment or a capital protection would have made better investments respectively. If an airbag cannot be constructed with satisfying conditions with a maturity of at most two years,[32] then the addition of one or more of the following features may improve the product's characteristics:

1. Cap the product by selling an additional out-of-the-money call. This may be especially appealing for risk-averse investors with a target expected return. Strike the additional call at the level at which the investor reaches his target return. Figure 3.16 shows how the airbag level from Figure 3.15 has been lowered to 65% of spot by means of the sale of an additional call struck at 140% of spot, effectively forming a cap. The maximum return would be 20% p.a. since the product has been constructed with a maturity of two years. The scale has been extended in order to see that, despite the downside leverage (here ~1.54% (1/65%)), the product's payoff stays above the underlying asset until it reaches zero.

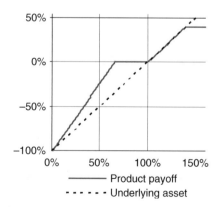

**Figure 3.16**   Payoff 15: capped airbag

---

[32] Implying 2 yearly dividends for stocks.

2. Use a worst-of feature including a second asset to lower the airbag through monetizing the imperfect correlation between the two assets. Do this only if the expected scenario is that the correlation between the two assets will stay stable or rise throughout the life of the product, or if both assets are expected to rise.

3. Raise the strike of the at-the-money call for example by 5% to 105% of spot. Note that where the asset's performance is positive (which should after all be the expected scenario), the airbag's performance is reduced by the difference between the spot at issue and the strike. In the case above, if the spot price of the asset had risen from 100% to 125% at maturity, the performance of the airbag would only be +20%. In the example, raising the call strike to 105% lowers the airbag level by 2.5%.

4. Lower the upside participation to 90% or 80%. This doesn't add much value though, and should only be used as a means of fine-tuning.

If none of these features allows the design of a satisfactory product, then the asset doesn't yield enough dividends (in case of stocks or stock indices) or the interest rate is too low, or the volatility parameters are adverse.

*Dos & Don'ts*

- Use airbags when the expected scenario is bullish for the underlying asset, but moderate setbacks are possible in the medium term.
- Don't worry too much about the price of the underlying asset falling slightly below the level of the airbag as the loss will likely be of minor nature.
- Don't be fooled by the relatively low level of the protection when comparing an airbag to a bonus certificate. Both types of protection are bought with exactly the same amount of money and therefore are worth the same. A 20% buffer on an airbag certificate may well be worth the same as a 40% buffer on a bonus certificate, because the latter can simply disappear on a knock-out event, while the former stays active until the maturity of the product.
- Do construct airbags when it is likely that yields or dividends are high and/or will drop in the foreseeable future. Airbags start to "look good" with dividends starting from 4% p.a. and above. Remember, however, that the expected scenario must be that the asset outperforms the dividends or yield in order to be profitable.
- Do note that in the case of the classic airbag with three options, the investor may profit from a high skew[33] between the short call struck at the airbag level and the long at-the-money strike. Although the skew has a relatively small influence on pricing, it should be taken into consideration.
- Don't cap the airbag when the skew is too high, because the added value of the short out-of-the money call will be comparatively low.

### 3.3.5 Turbo certificates[34]

Turbo certificates are capped participation products, which have no protection but generally have a leverage of two times between the spot price of an underlying asset and a cap. The

---

[33] See volatility skew in Section 4.1.

[34] The neutral name for the turbo certificate would be the capped outperformance certificate. As that appellation is rather long and little known, the author has chosen turbo as the standard name in this book. Other common names include speeder and booster.

construction is achieved by means of a long zero strike call, a long at-the-money call, and two short out-of-the-money calls. The product's constituents can effectively be considered as two call spreads with different strike levels.

Turbo certificates can be replicated even by non-professional financial participants on the listed option market relatively easily (Figure 3.17). This is valid for any asset, but will be described for stocks by means of an example about Nestlé. One can hold (or buy) the stock, buy an at-the-money call and sell two out-of the money calls for every stock owned. The strike level of the short calls is determined by searching for the call strike that costs half the premium of the at-the-money long call's cost. Let's illustrate the procedure with numbers.

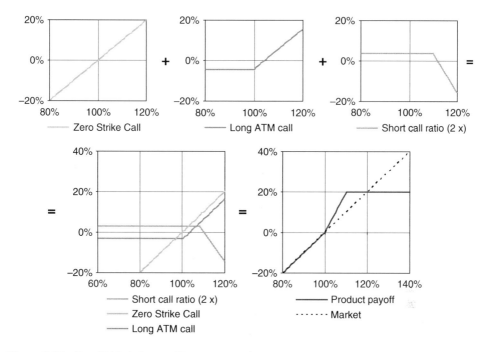

**Figure 3.17** Payoff 16: turbo certificate construction

Suppose an investor wants to replicate the turbo's payoff on Nestlé for CHF 1 million with a maturity of six months. On 30 June 2008, Nestlé was trading at a spot price of 46.12,[35] and the price levels of exchange-traded options for December 2008 expiries are listed in Table 3.15.

The differences between the bid and the ask prices seem quite large at first glance. However, the spread on the two options needed for the product must not always be paid in full. Placing limits slightly higher than the mid for buys and slightly lower than the mid for sells minimizes execution slippage and usually works perfectly well on the listed exchange. To realize the desired payoff, the investor would purchase 21 500 shares of Nestlé at 46.12

---

[35] The stock had just split 10:1 on that date.

**Table 3.15**  Nestlé listed options

| Strike | Bid | Ask |
|--------|------|------|
| **44** | 4.07 | 4.54 |
| **45** | 3.45 | 3.87 |
| **46** | 2.88 | 3.26 |
| **47** | 2.37 | 2.71 |
| **48** | 1.92 | 2.22 |
| **49** | 1.53 | 1.81 |
| **50** | 1.21 | 1.45 |

Source: Bloomberg

(worth CHF 991 580), buy 2150 calls[36] with strike 46 at ~3.10 (worth CHF 66 650) and sell 4300 calls with strike 49 at ~1.60 (worth CHF 68 800). The payoff (rounded) for the constructed product at maturity is as shown in Figure 3.18.

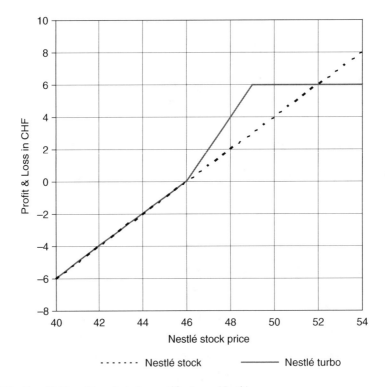

**Figure 3.18**  Payoff 17: self-made turbo certificate on Nestlé

If Nestlé trades between 46 and 49 at the expiry of the options, the investor makes double the profit he would have made by simply holding the shares. His maximum return is CHF

---

[36] One option controls 10 shares.

5.88 per share, or 12.8% for $4\frac{1}{2}$ months, which is achieved when the stock reaches CHF 49. However, the turbo will remain more profitable for the investor even if the stock rises to 52.10. Only above that level will the stock outperform the turbo. The fact that the stock was purchased at 42.12 as well as the slight difference in the premium of both options implies that the investor will lose 10 cents less than the stock if the performance at maturity is negative. Note that in this example, no dividends are expected to be paid by Nestlé until after expiry. If dividends are paid, the structure looks more attractive, since the stock is expected to drop by its amount on the ex-dividend date and that fact will be discounted in the option's prices.

The turbo certificate is best used when the expected scenario for the underlying asset is moderately bullish with falling volatility, for instance after a substantial drop and expecting a short-term rebound. Usually, this product is structured with a maturity from 3–9 months. The disadvantage for the investor lies in the fact that the high participation – which, in its standard version, amounts to 200% of the underlying asset upside performance – is realized only at maturity. During the lifetime of the product and in particular at the issue date, the participation may be less than 100%, which has caused disappointment for many an investor in the past. The turbo certificate is seldom used nowadays.

*Dos and don'ts*

- The best scenario to structure a turbo certificate is when the volatility is high and the skew is low. This makes the out-of-the money calls sold short worth more. The forecast for the stock must be positive but range bound.
- Structuring the product with less than 200% participation between spot and cap is possible but its attractiveness is reduced when the skew is negative. For instance, a turbo with 150% participation would have a long at-the-money call ratio of 0.5 and 1.5 short calls out-of-the money. Reducing the leverage between the strikes is one way to increase the cap. On the Nestlé example, reducing the leverage to 150% would have increased the cap to ca. CHF 52 and the max return to CHF 9, but if the stock was trading at CHF 49 at expiry, the gain for the investor would only be 150%*(49 − 46) = CHF 4.5 as compared to 200%*(49 − 46) = CHF 6 in the double leverage version. Always choose the cap in consideration of the expected scenario and for the maturity of the product.
- As the structure's maturity is rather short, timing is essential when issuing the product.

### 3.3.6 Outperformance certificates

Outperformance certificates are used by investors when the outlook for the underlying asset is strongly bullish. This product is mostly used with single stocks and can be considered the most aggressive (and thus risky) of the classical structured products, with the exception of warrants. The construction is as follows: long zero-strike call and a ratio of long at-the-money calls, the ratio depending on the level of dividends or yield used to finance the calls (Figure 3.19).

In this structure, the forecasted dividends are used to buy at-the-money calls. Hence, the structure is only possible with dividend paying stocks or on excess return indices. The two factors needed to structure the product efficiently are a low volatility and a high dividend yield. The forecasted scenario must be that the stock's performance will be strong enough

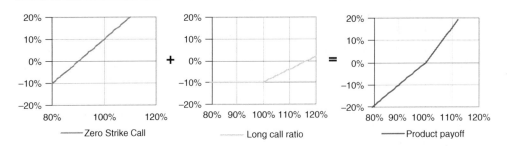

**Figure 3.19**  Payoff 18: outperformance certificate construction

to outperform the upcoming dividends. The trick is to include as many dividends in the structure as possible and to use a long maturity even though the forecasted rise in the stock's price is only seen as a short-term movement. The expiry date of the product should be set shortly after the furthest dividend date that will be included in the product. That way, the time value of the call is minimized with respect to the amount of dividends paid during the lifetime of the product. The calls will quickly rise in value with the performance, and the product can still be sold with high profit after a few months.

Suppose the following scenario: An investor thinks that, after a long period of a sideways trending market, a stock will perform strongly in the next 3 to 6 months. The stock pays 5% dividend yield on an annual basis. The next dividend is due in 10 months. The volatility is rather low due to the inactivity in the stock and therefore calls are rather cheap. A quick calculation yields the following results:

- The one-year zero-strike call is worth 95.25%.
- A one-year ATM call is worth 6%.

The certificate's upside participation would be approximately 180% at maturity:

$$100\% + \left[ \frac{(100\% - 95.25\%)}{6\%} \right] \cong 180\%$$

Now, the investor sees the upside in the stock only for the next 3–6 months, not one year, so why a one-year maturity? The answer is simple: the next dividend is 10 months away and the structure cannot be done without including at least one dividend in the lifetime of the product.

The investor's interest is also to know how the structure behaves during its lifetime. Adding the deltas from the two option legs gives:

$$100\% + \frac{80\%}{2} \cong 140\%$$

This means that the outperformance certificate's participation from day 1 will be 140%, i.e. for each percent that the stock rises, the certificate will rise by 1.40%.

Note that the calculation above is not strictly correct mathematically speaking. The delta of the zero-strike call is not 100%, but approximately 95.25% and the exact delta of the ATM call is around 43%. But as a rule of thumb, the participation at the issue date is approximately

100% plus half the amount over 100%. This way the investor, even without complex calculation instruments, can quickly evaluate the participation of the outperformance certificate on day 1.

If the stock rises by 20% in the forecasted period, the certificate will appreciate roughly[37] by 20% * 1.4 = 28%.

Let's go back to the investor's scenario of a strong rise in the stock within the next few months. It might be interesting to modify the structure to extract more value out of the forecasted dividends to increase the product's potential. Suppose we increase the maturity to 2 years and 10 months, including three dividends into the structure:

- The 2 year 10 month zero strike call is worth 87.6%.
- The 2 year 10 month ATM call is worth 8.5%.
- The certificate's upside participation would be approximately 246% at maturity:

$$100\% + \left[ \frac{(100\% - 87.6\%)}{8.5\%} \right] \cong 246\%$$

The delta is in this case would be around $100 + (246/2) \approx 170\%$. Now the certificate will rise by ca. 1.7% for each percent that the underlying stock gains at the issue date. If the investor's scenario materializes and the stock rises 20% within the next 3–6 months, he can sell the structure. The certificate would be worth roughly 100% + 20% * 1.7 = 134%. The investor gains 34% while the stock rises by 20%, a nice outperformance.

It is important to realize that during the lifetime of the product, the delta works both ways. Should the stock drop by 1%, then the certificate would also drop by 1.7%.[38] Lengthening the maturity not only increases the upside participation, it increases also the risk of the structure. Considering this important fact, it can be stated that the stronger the opinion of the investor *or* the higher the risk appetite of the investor, the longer the maturity and the more future dividends can be included.

---

[37] All other things staying equal, not taking into account the rise in the delta (which would be positive for the product), nor the time value decay of the ATM call option (which would be negative).

[38] In the next chapters, it will be demonstrated in more detail how the products behave during their lifetimes.

# 4

# Behavior of Structured Products During their Lifetime

As has just been shown with the Outperformance certificate (Section 3.3.6), the final payoff of a structured product does not say much about the behavior, or *mark-to-market* price, of a structured product during its lifetime. At the issue date and in the first few months of their lives, the prices of most structured products deviate substantially from their final payoffs at maturity for a given change in price of the underlying asset. The variation of some key factors, like the passing of time, the implied volatility, the risk-free interest rate or, in turbulent times, the issuers' funding rate[1] can strongly influence a product's price. A first step toward understanding these effects is to go through an explanation of some of the most important valuation and risk measures of structured products in general. An understanding of these factors is a prerequisite to elaborating on the behavior of products during their lifetime. After that we will examine how and why varying these factors affects the price of some example products.

Although the examples are specific to the products shown in the section, the general behavioral principles can be extrapolated to products that are similar in construction. The goal for the reader is to get a general idea about how a change in a parameter can affect the mark-to-market price of a product.

Note that the examples of this section have been calculated using a standard model, without volatility skew and other risk adjustment parameters like gap risks, bid-ask spreads, bending and shifts, etc. Hence, the examples, while being representative of the general value evolution of a product during its lifetime, may actually vary from the live prices of similar products observed in the market.

## 4.1 MAIN VALUATION AND RISK MEASURES

### 4.1.1 Volatility

Of all the factors influencing a structured product, volatility is probably the most important as it is central in the valuation of options. Let's define volatility in a simple and easy-to-understand way:

Volatility is a measure of the magnitude of price fluctuations around their mean over a given period of time, for a particular asset.

Consider Figure 4.1.

---

[1] The funding rate designates the rate at which a financial institution would issue a bond. Higher rated companies (AA- and above) typically have a low funding rate, usually below the Swap rate, while lower rated companies have a higher funding rate, typically above the Swap rate.

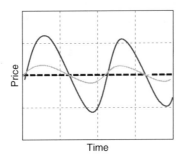

**Figure 4.1**   High and low volatility

Both wavy lines represent an asset with the same mean, which is represented by the dotted black line. The darker line has variations of large magnitudes and its volatility is high. The lighter line has variations of low magnitudes around its mean and its volatility is low. Hence, volatility is a measure for risk according to most investors. Highly volatile assets have a high risk, while assets with low volatility have low risk.[2]

A simple but good example to illustrate the above is to compare two assets: a government bond and a stock index (Figure 4.2).

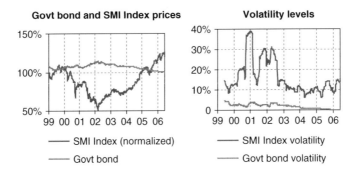

**Figure 4.2**   Price risk and volatility of two different assets
*Source:* Bloomberg

On the left-hand chart, it can be seen that the government bond price has small fluctuations, and they tend to become smaller as the bond matures in June 2007; the line is practically straight in the last year and tends towards zero. Any economic event such as, for example, interest rate fluctuations, has a smaller impact on the bond's price as it matures. Its volatility drops steadily as its duration diminishes (right-hand chart). It is a low volatility asset, which at the end of its life can be considered as the risk-free asset. On the other hand, the stock index has much larger variations and is a risky asset. Figure 4.3 plots the variations around the mean for both assets. It's clear that the stock index experiences much higher price variations than the government bond and that the variations are not constant. The standard deviation, which is the square root of the variations around the mean, is the

---

[2] It will be shown in the second part of the book that "risk" can also be defined through other ratios and concepts.

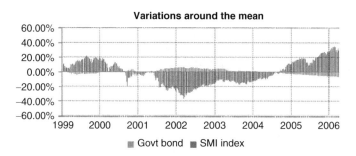

**Figure 4.3**   Government bond and stock index volatility
*Source:* Bloomberg, own calculations

common measure used for determining risk. A quick calculation of the standard deviation yields a result of 3.4% for the bond and 17.5% for the stock index. This signifies that if the deviations are evenly (normally) distributed, roughly 68% of all the deviations will be within +/−3.4% and +/−17.5% of their respective means, while 95% of all deviations will fall within ranges twice as large (+/−6.8% for the bond and +/−35% for the SMI).

In practice, one differentiates between historical and implied volatility. Historical volatility can be observed from an asset's past movements and can be mathematically calculated. On the other hand, the implied volatility denotes the future level of volatility. Let's define it formally:

Implied volatility is the market's expectation of the volatility of a given asset for a given period in the future.

The implied volatility is the major unknown parameter when pricing options. It must be guessed. The historical volatility helps in forecasting the implied volatility, but other factors must be taken into account: is the market situation expected to be fairly tranquil, or are major events probable or already foreseeable? In a crisis, the volatility will increase; when all is "business as usual", volatility falls. The combination of the historical volatility calculations with the forecasts by the market participants results in the implied volatility.

The trivial example of the bond and the stock index leads to the general characteristics of volatility for an asset:

- it spikes when market crashes;
- it reverts back towards its mean;
- it may experience longer periods of high or low levels; and
- it is usually negatively correlated with the underlying asset return.

There are two conclusions to draw from this short analysis and they are crucial for structured products:

- Volatility on a financial asset is not constant. Its level depends on the time window over which it is measured.
- Volatility on a financial asset never falls to zero and generally does not rise beyond a certain limit. It is usually mean reverting.

The level of implied volatility is defined by the market participants, which for the most part are the major financial institutions' traders.

Similar products, including options – especially exotic options – can have features that differ from one issuer to another even if structured simultaneously. For instance, the coupons of two barrier reverse convertibles might have different levels, or the barrier of one bonus certificate may be lower than the other. The reason is often that one trader pricing the embedded exotic option in the product is "guessing" or forecasting a different volatility level than the trader at another issuer. Therefore, there is no "right price" at any given point in time for any structured product, including options. The price that fits one trader might not fit the other. Other parameters can also have a similar effect on the product's price: forecasted dividends, the issuers' funding rate, the positions the trader holds on his trading books, can all have an effect, but the implied volatility is often the most important factor.

### 4.1.2  Implied volatility skew

It has been shown that volatility is not constant over time. In addition, implied volatility varies with the strike price for any given expiry. This phenomenon is called the skew (also sometimes referred to as the smile, or half-smile):

The skew refers to the volatility difference between options on the same asset with the same time to maturity but at different strike prices.

This can easily be observed in the stock market. Figure 4.4 plots the implied volatilities on the Eurostoxx50 index as of July 2008 for one-month (solid lines) and 18-month (dashed lines) options. The spot price of the index was at 3312.

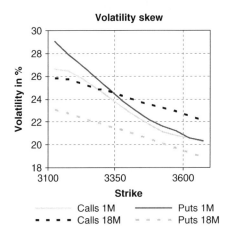

**Figure 4.4**  Volatility skew example on the Eurostoxx50 index
*Source:* Bloomberg, own calculations

In the theory developed by Black & Scholes (1973), a single volatility was assumed for any given period. Actually, there exists only one single historical volatility for an asset measured over a given period. However, for implied volatility, it can be observed from

Figure 4.4 that for different strikes expiring on the same date, several volatilities are traded simultaneously.

At first glance, it doesn't seem obvious that there should be several implied volatilities on the same asset. At the end of the day, there will be only one historical volatility that is mathematically correct. So what could be the reasons why the market forecasts and trades on several different levels of implied volatility?

One possible explanation is the imbalance between supply and demand. Many institutional investors like to write calls on existing equity portfolios and hedge downside risks with out-of-the-money puts. In other words, there is chronic oversupply of out-of-the-money call options and chronic excess demand for out-of-the-money put options. This particular behavior observed for a majority of investors has been the subject of extensive studies by behavioral finance specialists such as Kahneman and Tversky (2007).[3]

Another explanation is the historically asymmetrical price trend of equities. Prices fall faster and harder in crashes than they rise in bull markets. This is why it appears more likely for an out-of-the-money put option to ultimately end in-the-money than for an out-of-the-money call option to end up in-the-money as a result of strong price gains. Professional traders (market makers) price this fact in and "shift" their offers and bids on the market, thus creating the skew.

In the stock market, a high skew denotes that lower strikes have a much higher volatility than higher strikes. Selling calls in order to finance the purchase of puts to hedge a portfolio becomes unattractive. High skews appear most often in times of crisis, when institutional investors scramble to buy puts. A high skew in stock options is sometimes also a preliminary sign that a crisis is imminent or expected.

For structured products, the skew can have a major impact. For instance, the short out-of-the money call options in the turbo certificate described in Section 3.3.5 will be worth less if the skew is high, reducing the upside of the product. However, a high skew favors the coupon of a barrier reverse convertible.

### 4.1.3 Volatility term structure

The historical volatility varies with the period over which it is measured. This is true both for the historical and for the implied volatility. Looking at the market, empirical observations show that the implied volatility varies with the maturity. This phenomenon is called term structure.

The term structure can be positively sloped, negatively sloped, or humped. A positively sloped term structure means that short dated options have lower implied volatilities than longer dated options. It is called the "normal" term structure. In the stock market, it is usually the case when markets behave quietly. A negatively sloped "inverted" term structure means the opposite: longer dated options have a lower volatility than shorter ones. Figure 4.5 plots the term structure of at-the-money options on the Eurostoxx50 index as of July 2008, at a time when the subprime crisis was already having a strong effect on the stock market.

The positive, "normal" term structure expresses the opinion that uncertainty gradually rises with time to maturity: the longer the remaining time to maturity, the greater the likelihood that an event (crisis, war, weak corporate results, bankruptcy, takeovers, etc.) will cause volatility to increase. An investor should consider this as a risk premium an option bears

---

[3] "Choices, Values and Frames" by D. Kahneman & A. Tversky, 2007

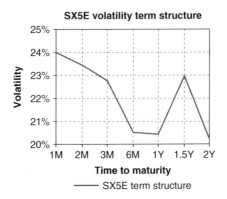

**Figure 4.5**  Volatility term structure of options
*Source:* Bloomberg, own calculations

for the longer maturity. It's a little like weather forecasts. The forecast accuracy for one day is usually high: it will rain or not with a certain probability, and this probability is pretty precise. However, forecasting the weather for three weeks ahead is more difficult. The certainty of the forecast diminishes. In other words, one can still forecast rain or sunshine with a probability, but the confidence in this probability is low. With an option, this uncertainty due to time is worth a premium. Hence, the rising term structures in normal market conditions.

When the term structure is inverted, it is usually because a disruptive event has just happened or is in the process of happening. The short-term uncertainty is high, but market participants expect it to normalize in the long run. A good example is any crisis that might be thought of: the internet bubble, 9/11, the subprime crisis and following credit crunch. In those times, the short-term volatility of nearly all asset classes spiked to incredibly high levels, whereas the longer dated volatilities, while certainly higher than usual, only rose slightly in comparison.

This shows another attribute of volatility: the short-term volatility is itself more volatile than the long-term volatility. In other words, the short-term volatility reacts more strongly to events than long-term volatility.

The term structure is also a key element when structuring or investing in products. It may make sense to shorten the maturity of a short volatility product if the short-term volatility is high.

Combining the skew with the term structure on a single graphic gives the *implied volatility surface*, as represented in Figure 4.6 below.

### 4.1.4  Delta

The delta is one of the "Greeks"[4] which each quantify a specific aspect of the risk of an option. Let's define the delta formally:

---

[4] The "Greeks" are selected Greek letters used in derivative finance to symbolize the risk measures of options. The most important are: delta, gamma, vega (though not actually a Greek letter), theta and rho. More "Greeks" have been developed with the ongoing development of derivative models. Please see www.wikipedia.org or other sources for more information on this topic.

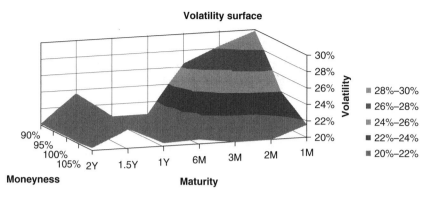

**Figure 4.6** Volatility surface example (Eurostoxx50 index, July 2008)
*Source:* Bloomberg, own representation

The delta measures the price sensitivity of an option for a given change in the underlying asset's price.

In other words, it shows how much an option's price will rise or fall if the price of the underlying changes. For example, if a share is worth CHF 100 and the call option with a delta of 40% is worth CHF 5, the value of the call option will increase to approximately[5] CHF 5.40 if the share gains CHF 1 (eight-fold leverage).

The delta is always positive for call options and negative for put options. The more an option is in-the-money, the higher the delta tends to be. If the call remains at the money, the delta hovers around the 0.5 (or 50%) mark. If the call shifts to in-the-money, the delta tends towards one and if it shifts to out-of-the-money, the delta tends towards zero. Figure 4.7

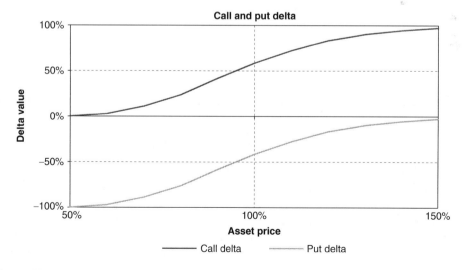

**Figure 4.7** Delta of an option

---

[5] The gamma should not be neglected when the price variations are large.

plots the delta for a call and put option on a stock index as a function of its price. The time to maturity has been set at one year. Dividends and the interest rate have a small influence on the delta, which is why their values are not exactly at 50% when the price is at 100%.[6]

Figure 4.8 shows the delta of a one-year call option as a function of its moneyness[7] and time to expiration. The in-the-money call option (top line) has a strike of 100% and the asset's price is set at 110% for the whole lifetime, therefore the call is 10% in-the-money and its delta starts at 73%. The out-of-the-money call option (bottom line) has a strike of 100%, the asset's price has been set to 90%, the call being therefore 10% out-of-the-money, and its delta starts at 43%. It can be observed that the deltas do not vary much initially. Only after approximately 70% of the time to maturity has expired do the deltas begin to move in their respective directions.

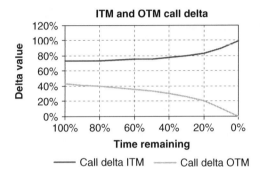

**Figure 4.8**   Delta as a function of time and strike

This behavior of the delta is the main reason why structured products do not behave as implied by their final payoff diagrams during their lifetime. At maturity, the delta of an option is binary: either the option lies in-the-money and its delta is 1 (or −1 for puts) or it is out-of-the-money and its delta is zero (for both calls and puts). This characteristic gives the final payoff diagram lines of products at maturity (straight lines with sharp angles). However, during their lifetimes, the options' delta is (mainly) a function of time and spot price. The product behaves according to the sum of the embedded options' deltas, and on the payoff diagram, this translates into the smooth lines as will be seen in the next section.

## 4.2   CAPITAL GUARANTEE

In this section, the behavior of a classical capital guaranteed product during its lifetime is analyzed. Let's begin by restating a few characteristics of the product. The most important variables are the interest rate and the volatility of the underlying risky asset. The product is constructed with a zero coupon bond and a long call option. It has been shown how the combination of these two financial assets results in the payoff diagram at maturity. Let's now add a line representing the payoff at the *issue date* and combine both on a new diagram.

---

[6] Dividends and interest rates influence the forward price of the underlying asset. The delta should be exactly 50% at-the-money forward.
[7] "Moneyness" denotes how far in- or out-of-the-money an option is.

### 4.2.1 Spot price variations for classical capital guaranteed products

A capital guaranteed product is constructed according to the data shown in Table 4.1 for illustration purposes.

**Table 4.1**  Sample capital guaranteed product

| | |
|---|---|
| Underlying risky asset | Eurostoxx50 Index |
| Maturity | 4 years |
| Implied volatility | 23% |
| Asset's dividend yield (p.a.) | 4.0% |
| Interest rate level (4 year swap rate, p.a.) | 4.5% |
| Capital guarantee level | 100% |
| Participation | 100% |

Source: Bloomberg, own calculations

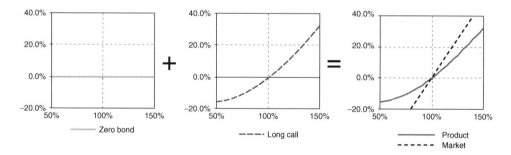

**Figure 4.9**  Payoff 19: capital guaranteed construction at issue date

The leftmost diagram representing the zero coupon bond has now a level of 0% and is represented by a horizontal line, as its final value is independent of any market movements. In fact, the cost of the zero-coupon bond with the data of Table 4.1 amounts to approximately 84%. But since the vertical scale represents the P&L of the investor at the time the chart is plotted, its level must be its fair value minus acquisition costs, which amounts to 0%. By the way, 84% is the so-called *bond floor*. It represents the amount of money that must be placed at the risk-free rate on launch date in order to get back 100% at maturity. Being independent from the performance of the risky asset, the zero coupon bond thus warrants the capital guarantee in the product.

The observation of the middle diagram representing the long call option shows that the straight line with a kink, typical of a call at maturity, is now a smooth, convex line. It starts at approximately −16% below par on the left-hand side of the diagram and rises slowly but steadily to attain a slope not quite reaching that of the underlying asset at the rightmost point on the graphic.[8] The cost of a plain vanilla call option on the Eurostoxx50 with the data of Table 4.1 is 16%. The line represents the value of the option at the issue date, four years prior to maturity. It warrants the participation to the positive performance of the index.

---

[8] Whenever smooth lines can be observed in a payoff diagram including an option, it means that there is still some time to maturity. In other words, the embedded option may consist of time value and intrinsic value (i.e. strike< spot for a call option, in-the-money) or of time value only (i.e. strike > spot for a call option, out-of-the-money).

The combination of the two diagrams gives the payoff at issue date of the product, as a function of the spot price of the underlying risky asset. It looks quite different from the payoff at maturity, which was described in Section 3.1: Capital guaranteed products. If both lines are plotted, payoff at maturity and payoff at issue date, the picture becomes even clearer:

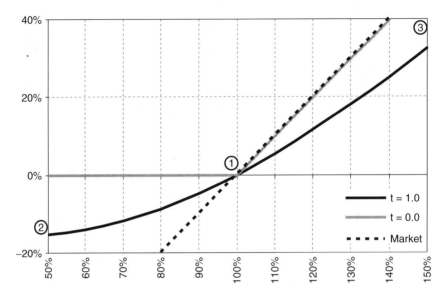

**Figure 4.10**  Payoff 20: capital guarantee price as a function of spot price

Three main points can be observed on Figure 4.10:[9]

*Point 1:* in the middle of the graph, the payoff line crosses the horizontal axis at the spot. Indeed, the price of the product at issue almost always equals 100% of the underlying asset's spot price. The sum of the parts (bond plus call) equals the total investment.

*Point 2:* going left from the middle, the line drops below the capital guarantee level, but flattens until becoming practically horizontal. It tends to the bond floor, as the call loses almost all value, until practically only the present value of the zero coupon bond remains.

*Point 3:* Going right from the middle, the line rises slowly at first and its slope gradually steepens, but not at the same rate as the payoff at maturity line. The call gains in intrinsic value, but gradually loses its time value.[10] At the far right, the call is so deep in-the-money that practically no time value is left. Yet the value of the product is still far below the payoff line at maturity. The explanation for this phenomenon lies in the time left until maturity of the zero-coupon bond: it has still to accrue its interest. In other words, the zero-coupon bond price of 84% must gradually rise to 100% in the four years it needs to reach its maturity.

---

[9] The small "t" in the key stands for time remaining. t = 1.0 signifies that 100% of the time until maturity remains, in this case, four years. t = 0 signifies that 0% time to maturity remains. This notation will be standard for all the graphics in this section.

[10] The time value of a plain vanilla option is greatest when spot price equals strike price.

The steepness of the slope also indicates the delta of a product, which in turn indicates the *momentary participation* (or risk exposure) in the performance of the underlying asset: a line rising at 45° indicates a delta of 100%. To determine the exact delta of the product, a tangent line to the selected point on the curve can be drawn. Its constant slope represents the delta of the product at that point. A vertical line indicates a point where the participation is infinite: it is usually a point where a knock-in or knock-out barrier is set, or where a digital option's payoff switches from 0% to 100% (not the case with classical capital guaranteed products).

The most important conclusions are that the investor who buys a capital guaranteed product with a medium-to-long time to maturity should be aware that his capital is only guaranteed at maturity, and not before. Furthermore, the participation of the product in the performance of the underlying asset *at inception* is lower than stated on the term-sheet of the product. For the vast majority of classical capital guaranteed products, the participation at inception hovers around 40% to 60% of the participation at maturity as stated on the term-sheet.[11] A good rule of thumb is to divide the stated participation of the product by 2 to estimate its behavior in the first months of its life.[12]

The investor must also be aware that the capital guarantee is only valid if the product is bought at par. A product purchased at 110% when it is capital guaranteed at 100% will guarantee only approximately 91% of the investor's capital. Purchasing a capital guaranteed product below par may guarantee more than 100% of the investor's capital. However, with most products, in order to be able to do this, the spot price will be below the strike price, which means that the underlying asset must first rise by the amount of strike minus spot for the product to begin participating at the set rate. So unless the investor wants to buy a zero-coupon bond, it is usually not a good idea to purchase a capital guaranteed product trading around its bond floor.

Last but not least, it is important for the investor to realize that the capital guarantee level is fixed for the lifetime of the product.[13] Suppose that the capital guarantee is fixed at 100% of spot for a maturity of 4 years as in the example above, and the spot climbs to 180% within the first year. The capital guarantee becomes quite useless, unless the investor is ready to lose the 80% gains. Especially for investors who have to report on a yearly basis (i.e. portfolio managers, pension funds...), long-term capital guaranteed products must be implemented with caution. For those investors it is sometimes advisable to shorten the maturity and accept less than full upside participation or a full capital guarantee.

It has been stated previously that the most important criteria for a capital guaranteed product are the volatility and the interest rate. In the next sections, these two variables will be shifted together with the passage of time to measure the effect on the product in Table 4.1. Measuring the variation in these three key parameters during the lifetime of the product will allow the investor to get a feeling about how it reacts on a mark-to-market valuation basis.

---

[11] There are exceptions: for instance, Shark notes have very low deltas at their inception date, around 15% to 25%. The delta of capped capital guaranteed products also typically ranges only between 20% and 30%.

[12] This rule of thumb is only valid for uncapped capital guaranteed products, where the strike of the embedded call is around 100% of the spot price. If the strike is substantially lower than the spot, the participation at inception will be higher. If it is substantially higher, the inverse will be the case.

[13] Unless the product features so-called *lock-up* levels, which raise the capital guarantee if the underlying asset reaches a predefined level.

### 4.2.2  Variations in the volatility

Volatility[14] is the second most important factor influencing the embedded value of the call option of the capital guaranteed product, coming just after the changes in the price of the underlying asset itself. It has, however, no influence on the bond part. Since this product category has generally a long-term maturity, even small shifts in the volatility can mean large price variations. In the example in Table 4.1, the product has an embedded 4-year maturity long call with a volatility of 23% at the issue date. Suppose the volatility rises 1 point of percentage to 24% immediately after the issue date. What is the effect on the call? It rises by about 0.66%. So all other things remaining equal, the product's price will rise from 100% to 100.66%.

A change in the price of 0.66% is not very large, and investors might not even notice. But then 1 point in volatility is not a large difference either. With bigger changes in the volatility, the price variation becomes more noticeable. For instance, what happens to the price of the product when the volatility rises from 23% to 30%, or to 35%? And is the price variation of the product linear, or is it dependent on the level of the spot price of the underlying asset? Is the effect the same if the remaining time to maturity is 4 years or 2 years? What if the product's time to maturity is near? These are questions that an asset or portfolio manager should be able to answer, if not mathematically, then at least intuitively, if he wants to manage his assets in a professional manner. Let's review these questions one at a time with the help of some diagrams.

*Price as a function of maturity*

Figure 4.11 plots the mark-to-market value of the product example from Table 4.1 as a function of the remaining time to maturity and the underlying asset's spot price. It is

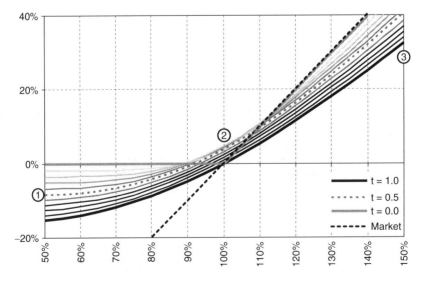

**Figure 4.11**  Payoff 21: capital guarantee price as a function of spot and time to maturity

---

[14] A change in the price of an option for a shift of the volatility is denoted by the symbol vega.

assumed that the purchase price was 100% at issue date. The thick lines bottom and top are the calculated prices at issue and maturity respectively. Starting from the thick line at the bottom, each thin line draws the price of the product with 10% less time to maturity. For instance, the thin dark line nearest the thick dark line has 90% of the time to maturity left, which is 3.6 years; the next line has 80% (3.2 years) time to maturity left etc. The systematic continues until the lightest line nearest the thick light line, which has 10% (0.4 years) time to maturity left. For clarity, the line where 50% of the time has passed is plotted in thick light dots. The legend only describes four elements: market, at issue, with 50% time remaining and at maturity.

Let's analyze the diagram step by step. First, let it be said that all the parameters (volatility, yield...) except time to maturity remain constant. There are several points of interest for the investor: when the product is far out-of-the-money (point 1), at-the-money (point 2) and deep in-the-money (point 3).

*Point 1:* when the embedded call is far out-of-the-money, the product tends to its bond floor. The call is practically worthless. As time elapses, the product's price gradually increases to the thick top payoff line at maturity. Note that with 100% or 90% of the original time remaining to maturity (in our case four years), even at −50% performance, the line is not totally flat. With close to four years until maturity remaining, the call is still worth a small amount and the delta may still be between 5% and 10%. However, with only 10% or 20% of the original time remaining, the line is much flatter; the embedded call is already almost worthless if the Eurostoxx50 loses 25% of its value. This is explained by the characteristic of the time value: if one day after the issue date the index lost 50%, it is still possible that it will regain this[15] during the three years and 364 days that remain. However, if the index lost 25% in the first three years and nine months, it is very unlikely that that 25% will be recovered in just the three months remaining until maturity.

*Point 2:* this is the at-the-money point for the embedded call. It is important for the investor to know that all other factors holding equal, the passage of time is beneficial for the product at the beginning of the product's life. This is because the time value[16] lost on the call is smaller than the interest gained on the zero-coupon bond in the first years of the product. Figure 4.12 shows the case in our example: the price increase of the bond is almost linear, increasing 3.8% in value in the first year, while the call decreases at a slower rate of approximately 1.6% in the same time. The bond's increase in value is greater than the call's decrease in value until approximately three-quarters of the time to maturity has elapsed. In our case, this difference peaks at around 4.6%, one year prior to maturity.

Afterwards, once the time value of the call starts to decrease at a faster rate than the interest from the bond accrues, the value of the product converges again to the centre line of the payoff at maturity. This rule holds for the great majority of products where the interest rate level of the underlying bond is medium to high but not for extremely low levels, like JPY bonds.

*Point 3:* at this point, the product's embedded call is deep in-the-money. The slopes of the lines have practically reached that of the payoff at maturity, but virtually all time value in the call is gone. The underperformance of the product during its lifetime compared

---

[15] Actually, if the market loses 50%, it has to recover by 100% to return to its initial level.
[16] The time value of an option is denoted by the Greek letter theta ($\Theta$)

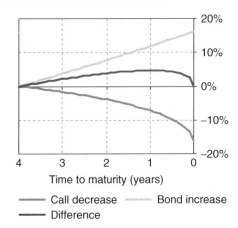

**Figure 4.12**   Call time value decrease as a function of time

to its value at maturity is due to the zero-coupon bond, which still has to accumulate the interest. With the passage of time, the product's value slowly tends toward the thick payoff line at maturity. As previously mentioned, at this point the capital guarantee becomes practically useless since the 50% that was gained previously can easily be lost again. In addition, the delta has increased to between 90% and 100% from its initial value of roughly 50%, thus increasing the participation in the price of the underlying asset, here the Eurostoxx50.

*Implied volatility increase*

Let's now suppose that the implied volatility rises by a large measure, say by 10 points from 23% to 33%.[17] What happens to the mark-to-market price of the product?

Figure 4.13 depicts similar lines as Figure 4.12, each showing 10% less time to maturity remaining. With an implied volatility of 33%, the lines have become steeper and the product has gained in value. Because the embedded call option is bought ("long"), the product is long volatility and any increase in implied volatility after the product has been issued has an overall positive effect.

*Point 1:* as the call is far out-of-the-money, a variation in the implied volatility has very little effect. The volatility only affects the time value left in the option, and at a performance of −50%, there is scarcely any time value left. The price of the product is influenced mainly by the bond component. Nevertheless, with such a large increase in implied volatility, the product's value at issue is still 2.2% better than with the original implied volatility level of Figure 4.13 at the −50% market performance point.

*Point 2:* the effect of a change in the implied volatility is greatest at-the-money. The product has gained almost 6.5% with no movement in the Eurostoxx50 index just after the issue

---

[17] A 10-point volatility increase for a 4-year option is rare. The large increase shown in the example exaggerates the behavior of the product for illustrative purposes. Smaller volatility movements will have the same effects as depicted here, albeit to a lesser degree.

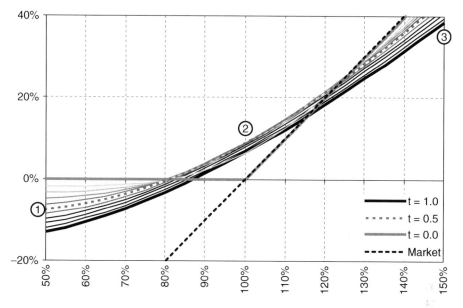

**Figure 4.13** Payoff 22: impact of volatility increase on capital guarantee

date (thick bottom line, t=1.0). Also noteworthy is that the index can fall by over 10% before the mark-to-market price declines below par. This is a nice feature of capital guaranteed equity (or equity index) products for investors: because the implied volatility has a tendency to rise when prices fall, a decline in value of the underlying asset is partly offset by a gain in the implied volatility of the option. Note that the lines have bunched closer together. This is because losses due to time decay are smaller early in the life of the option priced at a high implied volatility than they are for one priced at a low implied volatility.

*Point 3:* as previously mentioned, there is little time value left in the call option when it's deep in-the-money, hence a change in the implied volatility has but a small effect.

### Decrease in implied volatility

Suppose that the implied volatility for the product described in Table 4.1 decreases by 10 points to 13% from 23%. What are the effects on the product?

As expected, the product's value decreases. The inverse reasoning from that used in Figure 4.13 can be applied. At point 1, virtually all time value has already gone by the time the index dropped by 40% immediately after issue and by 20% when close to maturity. Without any change in the spot price, the mark-to-market value of the product has dropped by over 6% at point 2. At point 3, the call is composed only of intrinsic value, and the delta of the product approaches 1 (or 100%). Bear in mind that one of the ideal conditions for issuing a capital guaranteed product is low implied volatility and that the implied volatility generally does not fall below a certain threshold. Therefore, if the timing of the issue has been well orchestrated and the implied volatility was already low, the falling implied volatility scenario, although it may still occur, should have only mild consequences.

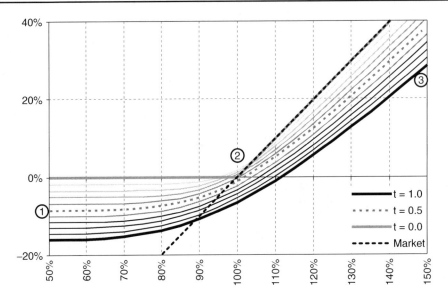

**Figure 4.14**  Payoff 23: impact of implied volatility decrease on capital guarantee

### 4.2.3  Variations in the interest rate

The interest rate level is the factor influencing the price of the embedded zero-coupon bond. It has also an effect on the price of the call,[18] but this is of less consequence than the massive impact it can have on the bond price.

Fundamentally, when interest rates rise, bond prices fall and vice versa. Of all bonds, zero-coupon bonds have the greatest sensitivity to a change in interest rate, as their duration[19] is equal to the full remaining time to maturity. Considering that most capital guaranteed products consist of about 80% or more (depending on construction and time to maturity) zero-coupon bond, any change in interest rate has a major effect on the product.

*Interest rate increase*

In the initial example of Table 4.1 on page 79, the interest rate at inception was set at 4.5% per annum. Figure 4.15 depicts the effects of a shift in the interest rate level to 6.5%.

Bad news; the whole product has dropped significantly in value. The zero-coupon bond value decreases at all points on the graph linearly (horizontal shift of the bond component), while the call option is influenced to a variable degree, based on its moneyness. Looking at the three points pictured on the diagram, the following conclusions can be drawn:

*Point 1:* the influence of the interest rate shift on the product is greatest here, where the call is far out-of-the-money. Since at this point it is solely the bond that determines the

---

[18] The sensitivity of the price of an option for a change in the interest rate is measured by the Greek letter rho ($\rho$)
[19] The duration of a bond is the weighted average maturity of a bond's cash flows. Since a zero-coupon bond pays only one cash-flow at maturity, its duration always equals its maturity.

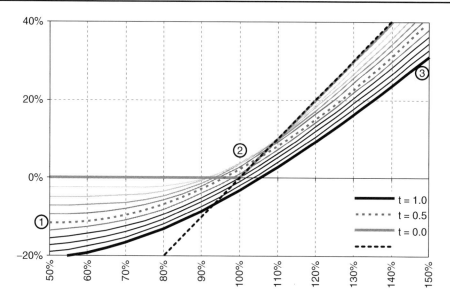

**Figure 4.15**   Payoff 24: impact of interest rate increase on capital guarantee

product's price, the price difference of the bond due to the shift in the interest rate is fully reflected in the product. On the issue date (thick dark bottom line), the price of the product has decreased by over 5%. Again, this is a theoretical case, as it is unlikely that, immediately after issue, the underlying asset would drop by 50% and interest rates rise by 200 basis points. The case nevertheless illustrates well the impact of an interest rate rise in a capital guaranteed product when the call of the embedded product is virtually worthless.

It is important to note that *the bond floor is now lower* than it was at the inception of the product. It is a common misconception that a capital guaranteed product cannot fall below its bond floor at issue. In the worst-case scenario (strongly falling underlying asset price plus an interest rate rise with a long time left until maturity), the product's mark-to-market price can fall below the initial assumed lowest possible price. Especially in times of hyperinflation (not seen for decades, granted, but possible nonetheless), long-term capital guaranteed products can fare poorly.

*Point 2:* at the strike price of the call, the value of the product has also decreased, by approximately 3% on the issue date. The impact is smaller than at point 1 because here the value of the product consists of approximately 17% calls and "only" 83% bonds. Moreover, the price of the call increases the value of the product by about 3%, partly offsetting the −6% of the bond part.[20]

*Point 3:* at 50% positive market performance, the weight of the bond component has decreased further, as the call option has gained in intrinsic value. The call now represents over 40% of the product. The impact of the interest rate change is more positive for the call as well. The price decrease of the bond is nearly offset by the price increase of the call. The product's value drops by only 1%.

---

[20] $(17\% * 2.7\%) + (83\% * (-7.2\%)) \cong -3\%$

*Interest rate decrease*

Exactly the opposite is true when interest rates fall. The product generally gains in value, and the lines tend to converge, especially at-the-money. Time value becomes less important (as the bond part has already made a good part of its expected gains), and the bond floor has generally risen.

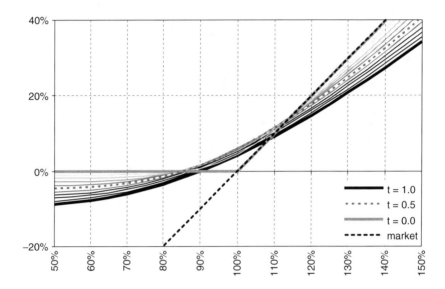

**Figure 4.16**   Payoff 25: impact of interest rate decrease on capital guarantee

*Conclusions*

- Shifts in implied volatility influence the capital guaranteed product most when at-the-money.
- An increase in volatility tends to increase the value of the product.
- A positive shift in interest rates lowers the value of the product most when the embedded call is out-of-the-money.
- When the call is deep in-the-money, an interest rate shift has less impact.
- Everything else held equal, the passing of time (without movement on the spot) is positive for the value of the product over time, since the time value lost on the call is, with most products, more than offset by the gain in the zero bond value.


## 4.3   YIELD ENHANCEMENT

In this section, the behavior of a classical yield enhancement product during its lifetime is examined. Yield enhancement products are mainly influenced by the implied volatility of the underlying asset, but other less important factors also contribute. The behavior of yield enhancement products will be illustrated (by means of an example with a knock-in reverse convertible on an index). It is constructed with a zero-coupon bond and a short down-and-in put option. The process is similar to the analysis of the capital guaranteed product, shifting variables and plotting the lines on a diagram. The data shown in Table 4.2 will be used.

**Table 4.2**   Sample knock-in reverse convertible

| | |
|---|---|
| Underlying risky asset | Eurostoxx50 Index |
| Maturity | 1 year |
| Implied volatility | 23% |
| Asset's dividend yield (p.a.) | 4.0% |
| Interest rate level (1 year swap rate, p.a.) | 4.5% |
| Barrier level (in % of spot) | 75% |
| Coupon | 10.4% |

Source: Bloomberg, own calculations

The influence factors are shown in Table 4.3, in order of importance.

**Table 4.3**   Knock-in reverse convertible influence factors

| | Factors | | | | |
|---|---|---|---|---|---|
| Factor's tendency | 1. Spot price | 2. Implied volatility | 3. Implied correlation[21] | 4. Interest rate | 5. Dividends |
| Up | Product's price increases | Product's price declines | Product's price increases | Product's price declines | Product's price declines |
| Down | Product's price declines | Product's price increases | Product's price declines | Product's price increases | Product's price increases |
| | | | Impact | | |
| | Maximum | High | Medium – low | Low | Low |

*Spot price:* a lower spot price means the down-and-in put option is more likely to touch the barrier, annihilating the conditional capital guarantee.

*Volatility:* the embedded down-and-in put option is short, therefore a rising volatility is negative for the product. A higher volatility implies that the chances of touching the barrier increase.

*Correlation:* if the product features a "worst-of" option, based on multiple underlying assets (e.g. two or more stocks), a rising correlation is positive for the product, as the risk declines that one asset could significantly underperform the other(s), thus making the embedded short option less expensive.

*Interest rates:* rising interest rates will lower the price of the embedded bond and also lower the price of the down-and-in put which is held short. However, the effect is greater on the bond.

---

[21] For yield enhancement products with a "worst-of" feature.

*Dividends:* small influence, as the product has usually a short maturity. A lower dividend means a decrease in the price of the option, which is held short, raising the price of the product. Note that dividends generally fall when the stock price has decreased by a significant amount. A stock price movement has a far greater negative influence on the price of the product than a reduction in dividend has a positive one.

### 4.3.1 Variation in the spot price

The example of Table 4.2 is plotted in Figure 4.17. The mark-to-market price of the product is shown in relation to the spot price and remaining time to maturity. Each line plots the value of the product with 10% less time to maturity remaining, starting with the thick dark line at the bottom (t = 1.0 = 100% = 1 year), followed by the thin lines (t = 0.9 = 90% = 10 months and 24 days) from dark to light gray, etc. down to the thick light upper line (t = 0.0 = 0% = maturity). The horizontal axis represents the price of the underlying asset (here the Eurostoxx50 index) normalized. The vertical axis is the profit and loss the investor incurs at the different spot prices and maturities.

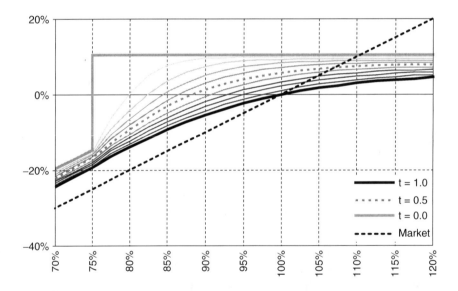

**Figure 4.17**   Payoff 26: reverse convertible as a function of spot and time to maturity

The following conclusions can be derived from Figure 4.17:

On the issue date, the product behaves more bond-like when the underlying asset rises and like the asset itself when it falls: the payoff line flattens (the delta diminishes) when the performance is positive and the product's price tends to the present value of the capital plus the coupon. The lines steepen (the delta increases) when the asset declines in value and the price of the product tends to the price of the asset plus the present value of the coupon.

It is important to note that on the issue date (thick dark bottom line) the price evolution of the product as a function of the spot price is smooth, even at the knock-in level. It behaves as if there were no barrier at all. However, as the maturity draws nearer, the smoothness disappears around the knock-in level (set at 75% of spot) and a "gap" develops. Here occurs a rare phenomenon: the delta of the product takes on values above 1![22] In theory, it can even take on extremely large values, like 5 (i.e. 500%) or even 10 (i.e. 1000%). This means that while the underlying asset gains or loses 1%, the product can rise or decline by 5% or 10% respectively. In fact, the product develops a leverage to the underlying asset as a function of the distance between the spot price and the barrier and the remaining time to maturity: the payoff lines become steeper and tend to a vertical asymptote the lower those two values become.

This price behavior of the product in this example is easily explained to the nonprofessional investor. As long as the barrier of 75% has not been breached, the investor receives back his full capital plus the coupon. However, if the barrier has been breached and the stock price stays below the strike of the option, the product is redeemed for a cash amount equal to the invested capital minus the negative performance of the Eurostoxx50 plus the coupon. Hence, the final payoff of the product can change dramatically when the barrier is touched. If this happens with a small amount of time left to expiry, the effect will be larger than it would be with a lot of time left to maturity; the more time is left to maturity, the more time the underlying asset would have to move back above the strike, making the option go out-of-the-money. If the spot price of the Eurostoxx50 is very close to the barrier and the maturity is near, the bank that issued the product does not know how much it will have to pay back to the investor. Will the barrier hold or not? The bank's models will indicate to the traders at one point that the chances are the barrier will not be touched and, a short time later, with only a small variation in the spot's price to the downside, that the chances are the barrier will indeed be breached. The bank's trader has to account for the change in probability by buying or selling the Eurostoxx50 Index in the market to hedge his position and change the mark-to-market price of the product accordingly. Since the redemption amount of the product will vary by more[23] than the change in the price of the underlying asset, the delta rises above 1 (or above 100%).

The point where the barrier is breached is an inflection point where the product transforms itself into another form: the knock-in reverse convertible becomes a reverse convertible. The knock-in disappears, along with the conditional capital guarantee. The payoff diagram changes to a shape similar to that of Figure 3.5 page 44. The barrier feature means that the capital is guaranteed until it is breached, in this case until the Eurostoxx50 index falls by 25% or more. This "conditional insurance" doesn't come for free. A similar reverse convertible without the knock-in feature would have yielded a coupon about 3% higher.

One more word about the delta of the Eurostoxx50 knock-in reverse convertible before going on to the next topic: at the issue date, the delta of the product is approximately 34%. In other words, this means that, on issue, the chance of the embedded down-and-in put option ending in-the-money is roughly 34%. What does that tell the investor? That the chance of losing part of his capital due to a decline in price of the Eurostoxx50 by 25% or more within the lifetime of the product (1 year) is 34%. Even though that statement is not strictly correct from a modeling point of view because of the path-dependency of the barrier option, empirical evidence[24] observed over the last 10 years suggests that barriers are breached far more often than implied by the "large" protection buffer. This is easily forgotten in bull

---

[22] Otherwise said, above 100%

[23] In this case by +/−25% of the total notional amount.

[24] See the back-tested yield enhancement products in Section 12.3.

markets when some representatives, investment advisors or investors marketed or invested in knock-in reverse convertibles as if they were bonds, which clearly they are not. The vast majority of the yield enhancement products have a delta to the underlying risky asset between 40% and 30% which, while making them less risky than the risky asset itself, certainly does not qualify them as a bond.

### 4.3.2   Variation in the implied volatility

*Increase in implied volatility*

Volatility is the second most important variable affecting the price of yield enhancement products after spot price variations. The reason for the sensitivity of this category of products to volatility is the large weight the short put[25] takes in the product's construction. Let's take the parameters from Table 4.2 on the Eurostoxx50 and shift the volatility from 23% to 33%, implying a sharp drop in the stock market (Figure 4.18).

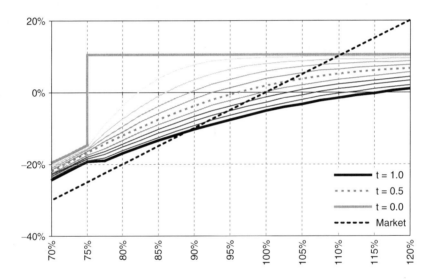

**Figure 4.18**   Payoff 27: impact of implied volatility increase on reverse convertible

Compared to Figure 4.17, the lines are generally lower for a comparable spot price. Below the barrier, there is no noticeable difference. The mark-to-market line on the issue date (thick dark bottom line) has dropped in value. At the spot price, the value of the product has lost about 5%. Let's suppose that the market has declined by say, 10% in the same time that the volatility increased (now looking at the 90% point on the horizontal axis), the product has lost... also 10%! This is the curse of typical yield enhancement products on equities like the example on the Eurostoxx50. The most important negative effects tend to cumulate and decrease the value of the product by more than many otherwise assume.

It has just been stated above that the delta at issue of the product was 34%, implying that a 1% move in the Eurostoxx50 would be reflected by a 0.34% price change in the product.

---

[25] Down-and-in put in our example.

Now a 10% drop in the Eurostoxx50 index shows a value decrease of similar amplitude in the price of the product, implying a delta of 100%. Isn't that a contradiction? The answer is no, because the delta of the product changes with changing market conditions. First, the delta increases due to the drop in the index.[26] The model assumes that the knock-in becomes more probable, and the delta rises accordingly. Second, the increase in implied volatility increases the delta further, because the model assumes a yet higher chance of a knock-in happening. In fact, the delta rises to approximately 49%.

Consequently, the shift in implied volatility causes a 5% decline in price, and the market decline, through the product's delta, causes the remaining 5% drop in value. In this particular case, the investor, who thought he was investing in a rather conservative product, quickly finds himself in possession of an equity-only product in adverse market conditions. This makes life harder for investors in yield enhancement products. Just when it is needed, the conditional capital protection is not effective. In fact, a conditional capital protection constructed by means of a barrier is effective only when the product is close to maturity. Looking at the thin light lines on the diagram representing respectively 10% and 20% time to maturity, it can indeed be observed that the barrier starts to "grip" and tends towards the thick top line of the payoff at maturity. In fact, with only 10% time left to maturity, the product is still just 7.7% in positive territory when the market has decreased by 10% and the implied volatility has increased by 10 percentage points.

*Decrease in implied volatility*

Figure 4.19 plots the mark-to-market price of the barrier reverse convertible defined in Table 4.2 but with the implied volatility reduced to 13% from 23%.

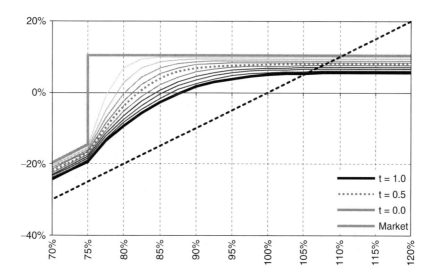

**Figure 4.19** Payoff 28: impact of volatility decrease on reverse convertible

---

[26] This, the change of the delta for a change in the spot price, is called the gamma.

Generally, the lines are clustered more tightly together and are leveled out everywhere except near and below the barrier. As a consequence, the price of the product is less sensitive to variations in the spot price except near the barrier, where the fall in value is more abrupt. Comparing Figure 4.19 to Figure 4.18, it is interesting to note that the 10 point reduction of the implied volatility has also moved the market price of the product by 5% (albeit in the other direction) at the issue date. This implies a linear relationship between changes in implied volatility and the change in price at the 100% spot price level. However, any further upside is limited due to the time value of money: the bond part of the product needs to accrue its interest for the price of the product to converge to the thick light upper line representing maturity. In other words, with a much lower implied volatility, the delta of the product tends rapidly towards zero if the spot price stays at 100% or moves beyond.

*Dos & don'ts*

The conclusions an investor can draw from this section are:

- Do invest in yield enhancement products when the implied volatility is already high or expected to drop. Interest rates have a relatively low impact compared to implied volatility, unless the product has a very long maturity.
- Do time the product carefully; don't fall into the habit of always investing in 1-year products. Sometimes a six- or nine-month product will fit a portfolio better or its conditions will be more attractive. Sometimes a 3-year product will also be more attractive. There is no reason except habit to invest always in yield enhancement products with 1-year time to maturity. In fact, it's a bad habit of the bank's issuing "factories" that have no incentive to do otherwise: they do not know their clients' portfolios and they do not care about whether the volatility will rise or fall. Their only goal is to place as much volume as possible.[27] Therefore, they have found a consensus by issuing 1-year products, which has become a kind of standard in the industry.[28]

### 4.3.3  Variation in the implied correlation

Implied correlation becomes a factor for structured products when more than one underlying asset is used to construct them. All kinds of products nowadays are based on multiple assets, be they in the form of capital guaranteed, yield enhancement or participation. This section is only valid for yield enhancement products with multiple underlying assets featuring "worst-of" options. All the conclusions presented in this section are also inversely valid for "best-of"[29] options. Let's begin by defining implied correlation in the context of structured products based on multiple assets:

---

[27] This is not strictly true, as some product representatives or specialists do indeed propose products which they personally think will perform. But for the great majority of cases, the products are simply issued without further analysis. Some products are even optimized to "look attractive", either from a barrier or a coupon point of view.

[28] In Switzerland mainly. In Germany for instance, the maturity variation of the yield enhancement products issued is actually greater, because the majority of products consists of discount certificates, which are much easier to issue because they do not have any bond component. Tax issues also matter.

[29] The "best-of" feature in an option with several underlying assets where the best performing asset to determine the final payoff at maturity is selected, or, in case of "best-of" barrier options, only the best performer can trigger the barrier.

Implied correlation expresses the level of linear relationship between two assets within a given period of time, which is implied by the prices observed in the market.

Thus the price of two assets with an implied correlation of 1 (or 100%) should evolve in perfect symmetry, while an implied correlation of −1 (or −100%) implies that their prices will diverge in total asymmetry; while one rises 1%, the other falls 1%. An implied correlation of zero implies that both assets follow their courses without one influencing the other.

The value in the implied correlation of two assets is often extracted and reflected in higher coupons or bigger discounts with the "worst-of" feature. In times of low implied volatility, the issuers often resort to the value inherent in the implied correlation to maintain double-digit coupons in their reverse convertibles. Thus were created the "worst-of" two, three, four and five stocks. The proliferation of multiple-asset worst-of products in clients' portfolios without a clear understanding of the associated risk has contributed to the deterioration of structured products' image in the financial world during the 2008 crisis.

A change to the example in Table 4.2 defined on page 89 needs to be made to show the effect of correlation in a product by adding at least one underlying asset. Single stocks will be used to avoid confusing the results with the FX effects, which would come from using indices labeled in different currencies. Let's assume that an investor would like to invest CHF 2 million into two stocks, Roche and Zürich Financial Services (ZFS). He ponders between the following two choices:

- Invest CHF 1 million in each of two single barrier reverse convertibles on each stock.
- Invest the whole CHF 2 million into a worst-of barrier reverse convertible.

Table 4.4 gives an overview of the characteristics of the products.[30]

**Table 4.4** Implied correlation impact on reverse convertible

| | |
|---|---|
| Underlying risky asset 1 | Roche |
| Underlying risky asset 2 | Zürich Financial Services |
| Maturity | 1 year |
| Implied volatility asset 1 | 25% |
| Implied volatility asset 2 | 30% |
| Dividend yield asset 1 | 3% |
| Dividend yield asset 2 | 5.9% |
| Correlation (implied) | 53% |
| Interest rate level (1 year swap rate, p.a.) | 3.28% |
| Barrier level (in % of spot) | 70% |
| *Coupon on Roche (single RC)* | *7.50%* |
| *Coupon on ZFS (single RC)* | *10%* |
| *Coupon on "worst-of" Roche/ZFS* | *13%* |
| Price (for all three products) | 100% |

Source: Bloomberg, own calculations

---

[30] All the examples above with reverse convertibles can be applied to discount certificates as well.

A quick calculation yields the difference in expected revenue at maturity for the two variants:

1. CHF 1 million in each single product: 1 million * (7.5% + 10%) = CHF 175 000.
2. CHF 2 million in the worst-of: 2 million * 13% = CHF 260 000.

The difference of CHF 85 000 (or 4.25% on the CHF 2 million) can be defined as the value extracted from the imperfect correlation. In exchange for this, the investor bears the risk of having to take the worst performer of Roche and ZFS for the whole CHF 2 million (concentration of risk as mentioned in the example of Table 3.7).

With a "normal" implied correlation of 53%, the price of the "worst-of" product would be 100%. Let's shift the correlation to 80% and to 20%, to imply higher and lower correlated assets (Table 4.5).

**Table 4.5**   Correlation shifts

| Correlation level | Price of the product |
| --- | --- |
| 80% | 101% |
| 20% | 99.40% |

Source: Bloomberg

Hence, a relatively large shift in the implied correlation does affect the price of the product to a certain degree, but to a lesser extent than shifts in implied volatility or spot price as seen earlier. While this is true for a product whose payoff depends on the worst of two stocks, other products with worst-of three, five, 10 or more stocks will have a greater sensitivity to implied correlation. The more underlying assets are included in the product, the more important it becomes to consider the expected correlation scenario.

A tentative conclusion would state that an expected rising correlation is beneficial for existing products featuring a "worst-of" option. Their mark-to-market price will rise slightly due to the increase in correlation. This fact has to be weighed against another one: in the stock market, correlation usually rises when the market in general declines. On occasions when the market crashes, it's not unusual to see huge spikes in the implied correlation, as all the underlying stocks are sold off regardless of their valuation or sector. The decrease in the spot price combined with the probably higher implied volatility will more than offset any gains derived from higher implied correlation. On the other hand, it is not advisable to invest in products with "worst-of" features when the implied correlation is already high, because when it reverts to the normal historical level, the mark-to-market price of the product will have lost some value. The case for worst-of options thus appears rather slim, to be used, if at all, only in very specific expected scenarios such as sideways trending markets.

*Implied correlation and number of assets*

It was mentioned in Section 3.2.2 that it is better to avoid yield enhancement products with "worst-of" features where the number of underlying assets is too high. The advice was to limit the number to a strict minimum of two, maybe three, assets. To illustrate this point, Table 4.6 gives an idea of the increase in the coupon of an additional asset in the case of

**Table 4.6**  Decreasing value of implied correlation for additional assets #1

| Underlying risky assets | 1 to 5 stocks | |
|---|---|---|
| Maturity | 1 year | |
| Implied volatility | 25% | |
| Dividend yield | 2.8% | |
| Interest rate level (1 year swap rate, p.a.) | 3.0% | |
| Barrier level (in % of spot) | 70% | |
| Correlation | 50% | Difference |
| Coupon for a product on one asset | 7.25% | - |
| Coupon for a product on two assets | 10.10% | +2.85% |
| Coupon for a product on three assets | 12.2% | +2.10% |
| Coupon for a product on four assets | 14% | +1.8% |
| Coupon for a product on five assets | 15% | +1% |
| Price (for all products) | 100% | |

Source: Bloomberg, own calculations

a barrier reverse convertible. Hypothetical stocks with the same volatility, dividend yield and currency are used in order to avoid confusing the source of the added coupon with other factors. The resulting coupon is calculated for each additional stock in the product. Each additional stock has a volatility of 25%, and a dividend yield of 2.8%. The implied correlation of all the equities is assumed at 50%.

The above results are different if the implied correlation is set at another level. The added value for each additional asset rises with lower correlation. Table 4.7 shows the coupon levels reached by using truly uncorrelated assets (correlation of 0%), which admittedly are rather difficult to find.[31]

**Table 4.7**  Decreasing value of implied correlation for additional assets #2

| Coupon for a product on one asset | 7.25% | Difference |
|---|---|---|
| Coupon for a product on two assets | 11% | +3.75% |
| Coupon for a product on three assets | 14.3% | +3.3% |
| Coupon for a product on four assets | 17.4% | +3.1% |
| Coupon for a product on five assets | 19.4% | +2% |

Source: Bloomberg, own calculations

The rate at which the coupons increase is much higher, as each additional asset included in the structure has more value in the implied correlation than in the example of Table 4.6 where the implied correlation was set to 50%.

The same exercise can be made with generally higher, say 80%, implied correlations (Table 4.8), reflecting a correlation spike or assets of the same industry sector (say financials).

Apart from the fact that the coupon levels are generally much lower than in Table 4.7, the increase in the coupon for each additional asset has shrunk to practically a negligible

---

[31] Note that correlation, similar to volatility, changes over time. Two uncorrelated (or even negatively correlated) assets at a given point in time may positively correlate at a future date. A good example for this is the commodity sector, which had a slightly negative correlation to equities during 2007, but started to correlate more strongly with the deepening of the financial crisis in 2008.

**Table 4.8** Decreasing value of implied correlation for additional assets #3

| | | Difference |
|---|---|---|
| Coupon for a product on one asset | 7.25% | |
| Coupon for a product on two assets | 9.2% | +1.95% |
| Coupon for a product on three assets | 10.2% | +1% |
| Coupon for a product on four assets | 11.2% | +1% |
| Coupon for a product on five assets | 11.6% | +0.4% |

Source: Bloomberg, own calculations

amount. In the author's view, it is not worth taking on the risk of including an additional asset, especially if it is a stock with an average 25% volatility, for a 1% or 2% additional coupon. The risk associated with the additional stock is simply not worth it.

*Conclusion*

From three assets onwards, there is little added value to the coupon, unless the correlation is very low or negative. Even if that were the case, the concentration risk associated with the worst-of feature must be considered. This proves the point made in the previous section about keeping the "worst-of" feature, if included at all, to a minimum of assets, as each additional one adds less value but more risk to the product and the portfolio in general.

Another aspect of correlation in structured products with the worst-of feature is the difficulty it creates for a portfolio manager in managing the effective exposure of the product to an industry sector or to an asset class altogether. Consider the following product: a worst-of reverse convertible on ABB/Roche/UBS, yielding an 18% coupon, with remaining maturity is 9 months. The stock nearest to the barrier is UBS with 22% remaining barrier, which was set at 70% from spot (protection buffer of 30%) at inception of the product. How should the portfolio manager allocate the product? To bonds because it is still conditionally capital protected,[32] to financial stocks because UBS is the stock nearest the barrier, or to a yet to be determined split according to the delta or some other risk measure? With classical portfolio management tools as they exist in private banking as of today, the software often dating back to the 1970s, it is usually not possible to make a proper allocation. Most issuers also do not provide any risk figures of the products they issue,[33] making the split classification even harder. For the private banking client, who invests heavily in structured product with "worst-of" features, the overview of the portfolio can quickly become quite difficult.

## 4.4  PARTICIPATION PRODUCTS

As the range of participation products is very large, involving a multitude of structures and variations, the detailed examples will be concentrated on a particular structure, the *bonus certificate*. Other products, such as the turbo certificate, the airbag certificate and the outperformance certificate, will be described in less detail.

---

[32] No, certainly not!

[33] EFG FP is one exception to the industry, with extensive product risk reports on their website.

Apart from the spot price, the main factors influencing participation products are often the implied volatility and the dividend yield (for stocks) or the interest rate (for excess return indices on commodities for example). For stocks, the dividend yield is essential. Without it, some products like the bonus certificate or the outperformance certificate could not be structured.[34]

### 4.4.1  Bonus certificate

The bonus certificate is a widespread structure among private banking clients whose mark-to-market price evolution is little understood by many investors. Let's first of all clarify one important fact: the delta of the classic bonus certificate at the issue date is approximately 1 (or 100%), for the upside *as well as for the downside*! The term-sheet shows the investor the payoff at maturity; more often than not, he thinks that the product behaves (more or less) like the lines with kinks shown on it. Well, no product's mark-to-market valuation differs to a wider degree from its payoff at maturity than the bonus certificate. This fact has caused many an investor to be disappointed, especially when the representative or the investment advisor had not properly explained the risk parameters. Let's first state the factors which influence the price of the product (Table 4.9).

**Table 4.9**  Factors influencing bonus certificate

| | Factors | | | | |
|---|---|---|---|---|---|
| Factors' tendency | 1. Spot price | 2. Implied volatility | 3. Implied correlation[35] | 4. Interest rate | 5. Dividend yield |
| Up | Product's price increases | Depends | Product's price increases | Product's price declines | Product's price declines |
| Down | Product's price declines | Depends | Product's price declines | Product's price increases | Product's price increases |
| | | | Impact | | |
| | Maximum | Depends-high | Medium-low | Low | Medium |

*Spot price:* a lower spot price means the down-and-out put option is more likely to break the barrier, annihilating both the conditional capital guarantee and any potential bonus.

*Implied volatility:* the embedded down-and-out put option is held short, therefore an increase in implied volatility after the issue date is generally negative for the product. Depending on the time left until maturity and the relation of the spot price to the strike and barrier, a rising volatility can have either a strong negative or a slight positive effect.

---

[34] At least, not as they are known by investors, with the strike set at the spot of the underlying asset or higher. It would be possible to structure a bonus certificate on a stock paying no dividends with a strike *below* the spot, but the structure wouldn't look very attractive to many investors.
[35] For yield enhancement product with "worst-of" feature.

*Correlation:* if the product features a "worst-of" option, based on multiple underlying assets (e.g. multiple stocks), a rising implied correlation helps the product, as the risk lessens that one asset could significantly underperform the other(s).

*Interest rates:* rising interest rates will lower the price of the embedded bond and also lower the price of the down-and-in put which is held short. The effect is greater on the bond, though.

*Dividends:* since the dividends are used in order to purchase the down-and-out put, thus determining the bonus and barrier levels, any increase in dividends after the product has been issued is negative for the product. The opposite is true for a decrease in dividends after the issue date.

### 4.4.2  Variations in the spot price

Movements in the spot price have the highest impact on the product, as with most – if not all – products. As previously, a product's price evolution will be illustrated by means of an example. The rationale behind it is an investor who is bullish on European stocks in general for the medium term, but with some doubts about the economy. He is ready to give up the dividends on the stocks to buy some protection, but would like a return at least as high as the risk-free interest rate in case the stocks don't perform as he thinks they will. A sharp decline seems out of the question but, at worst, he is ready to accept a loss. The bonus certificate he considers is described in Table 4.10, from which the data are used for the calculations in the payoff diagrams that follow.

**Table 4.10**   Sample bonus certificate

| | |
|---|---|
| Underlying risky asset | Eurostoxx50 |
| Maturity | 2 years |
| Implied volatility asset | 23% |
| Dividend yield asset | 4.0% |
| Interest rate level (2 year swap rate, p.a.) | 4.5% |
| Barrier level (in % of spot) | 65% |
| Bonus level | 9% |
| Participation | 100% |
| Price | 100% |

Source: Bloomberg, own calculations

The 2-year period corresponds to the investor's medium term view, and the 9% bonus at maturity amounts exactly to 4.5% p.a. The 65% barrier seems solid enough as no crash or bear market scenario is forecast. The uncapped upside participation of 100% leaves the door open for a high return in case the forecast scenario materializes.

Figure 4.20 depicts the behavior of the product as a function of the underlying asset's spot price and time to maturity with the same procedure as in the previous examples, i.e. each line represents a remaining time to maturity starting with t = 1 (or 100%) for the full remaining maturity (2 years) down to t = 0 for the maturity.

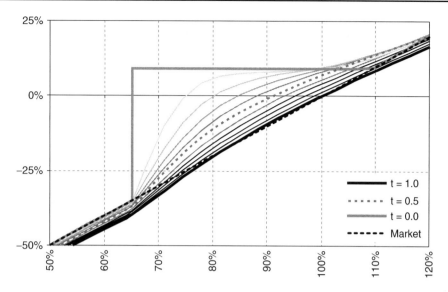

**Figure 4.20**   Payoff 29: bonus certificate price as a function of spot and time to maturity

The thick light straight top line shows that the investor will get a minimum return on his investment of 9% at maturity (the bonus level) as long as the Eurostoxx50 index never declines below the preset barrier of 65% of the initial spot price. Should the barrier be breached, the bonus certificate is transformed into a simple participation certificate: the conditional capital guarantee and the bonus disappear and the product's payoff would fall back to the level of the dotted black line of the market.

The striking element of Figure 4.20 is the price evolution of the product at the issue date (thick dark bottom line). It's nearly a 45° straight line following the market line. In other words, the bonus and the barrier have virtually no effect at the inception of the product. This phenomenon is what disappointed most investors who were shown only the payoff at maturity and subscribed to bonus certificates when they became popular in the early 2000s. As the stock market crashed after the bursting of the internet and biotech bubble and declined further with the 9/11 terror attacks, the protection mechanism of the bonus certificate didn't seem to function. The mark-to-market valuations were dropping as fast – or even faster on many occasions – than the market itself. What many investors ignored at the time is that the protection does not "grip" until most of the product's lifetime has passed. In fact, as mentioned earlier, the delta of the bonus certificate at inception is nearly 1, implying a full participation both to the upside and to the downside. With the passing of time, the mark-to-market price of the product tends more and more towards the payoff line at maturity, but it is only in the last 20% or so of remaining time[36] that the product really starts to behave like the final payoff line, as can be observed in Figure 4.20.

The unfavorable behavior of the product during its lifetime for the investor can also be explained in a more intuitive way. Remember that the product is built with a long zero-strike

---

[36] Top two thin lines on the diagram.

call and a long down-and-out put option, the latter providing the bonus and the barrier. Also keep in mind that the down-and-out put option is financed solely by the expected discounted dividends (for stocks and stock indices; interest rate for other excess return indices like commodity indices) for the whole lifetime of the product. Now, how high are the discounted dividends? In the example above, the dividend yield per annum is set at 4%. Considering the maturity of two years, this accounts for roughly 8%. So at its inception, the product consists of 92% of a zero-strike call and 8% of a down-and-out put option. Knowing this, what would be a reasonable assumption of the product's behavior when the market declines by, say, 10%? Well, it would decline by −9.2%, plus or minus whatever the remaining 8% of the down-and-out put would still be worth. But the down-and-out put cannot have increased that much in value, because if the market fell by 10%, the chances are greater that it will be knocked out[37] and "die" and this fact offsets the gain in intrinsic value the option has accumulated with the market decline.[38] On the other hand, if the market increased by 10%, the down-and-out put will be about at-the-money, losing intrinsic value, but the chances are also lower that it will be knocked out, since the spot is now 10% further away from the barrier. So overall, the down-and-out put option doesn't gain or lose too much yet, with so much time to maturity still remaining, and the product's change in value with market movements is practically only determined by the value of the zero-strike call.

### Conclusion

The down-and-out put, the sole element giving the bonus and the protection to the product, contributes little to the product price development at inception. Both features start to become apparent only once about 80% of the time to maturity has passed.

### Dos & don'ts

- As an investor, keep the maturity of the bonus certificate as *short* as possible; no one likes to wait for four and a half years to get the bonus and protection finally going.
- Also, the longer the maturity, the lower the chance that the underlying asset remains within the range defined by the barrier and the bonus level. Remember that the bonus certificate outperforms the underlying asset *only* when it trades within this range. If it trades lower, the barrier has been knocked out and the bonus certificate transforms into a normal certificate, but the investor loses any dividends or yield. On the other hand, if it trades higher, the dividends that were used to purchase the down-and-out option become useless, and the bonus certificate tracks the underlying asset's positive performance ex-dividends. Only when the underlying asset stays between the bonus and the barrier does the bonus certificate outperform the asset. In most instances that should be the real goal of this structured product.
- As an investor, consider carefully if the level of the barrier matches an expected worst-case scenario for the given time frame. Remember that the embedded down-and-out put isn't worth much, at least at inception of the product. The investor has to choose to emphasize one parameter of the three: bonus, barrier or participation. If in doubt, always choose

---

[37] Remember that we are still talking about the product at its issue date, with the full time to maturity that has yet to expire.

[38] The put would now be 19% in-the-money, having a strike of 109% of spot to begin with.

to lower the barrier instead of increasing the bonus or the participation. The chance that the Eurostoxx50 ends between 100% and 109% in two years time, as in our example, is rather small. It is much more likely that the index will trade higher or lower than those two numbers. If it trades higher, no harm done: the bonus and barrier were just useless. However, if it trades lower, then the last thing the investor wants is for the barrier to be touched and the option knocked out! So better put a 5% extra barrier versus a 10% more bonus or participation.

Note that as the maturity draws nearer, the delta of the product behaves wildly if the spot is around the barrier.[39] The product builds up leverage as the barrier approaches.

### 4.4.3   Variations in the implied volatility

The bonus certificate contains only a few percent of a down-and-out put option, but even a moderate change in implied volatility can have a measurable effect on the product. As with practically all structured products featuring a barrier, there is no absolute rule as to how a shift in implied volatility affects the bonus certificate. Many factors have to be taken into consideration, but usually a good indication is that the longer the maturity, the bigger the influence of the implied volatility on the product as a whole.

At the issue date of the product, it is best that the implied volatility is high, as the pricing model used to determine the product's parameters assumes a greater chance that a knock-out will occur than with a lower implied volatility. Hence, with a higher implied volatility, more protection can be bought, as the barrier can be set at a lower level, all other parameters of the product remaining constant.

As a general rule, once the product has been issued, the best thing for the product's mark-to-market valuation is to see a decline in implied volatility. However, there are some times in the life of the product where even a higher implied volatility can be positive for the product's valuation.

*Increase in implied volatility*

Figure 4.21 shows the effect on the secondary market price of the bonus certificate of Table 4.10 when the implied volatility increases from 23% to 33%.

When comparing Figure 4.21 to Figure 4.20, it can be seen that the mark-to-market valuation lines have a less pronounced curvature, tending less quickly towards the payoff at maturity (top thick line) especially around point 1. The product's bonus has less of an effect prior to maturity. The issuer's pricing model assumes a higher chance of a knock-in happening, thus decreasing the product's theoretical value – especially near the barrier – for all remaining maturities. At the spot price of 100%, the bonus certificate has lost about 4%.

However, looking at point 2 where the down-and-in option has been struck, a slight increase in the mark-to-market value of the product for selected maturities is noticeable. From 60% remaining time to maturity onwards, the product's value seems to have increased. This can be explained by the fact that the passing of time added more value to the down-and-out put than the increase of implied volatility subtracted. In other words, the

---

[39] At this point, the behavior of the bonus certificate is in fact almost identical to the barrier reverse convertible or the barrier discount certificate when they are close to maturity and to the barrier.

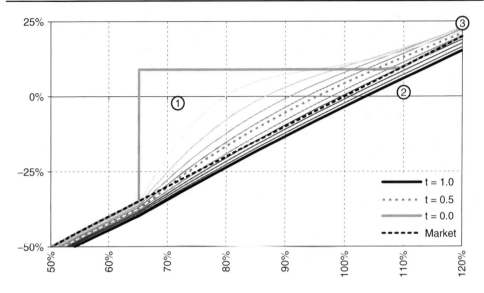

**Figure 4.21**  Payoff 30: impact of implied volatility increase on bonus certificate

model assumes that at this distance from the knock-out point, and with so little time remaining to maturity, the increase in implied volatility is insufficient to significantly increase the chance of a knock-out. The model thus assumes that the barrier will hold. But the fact is that an increase in implied volatility also works to the upside. So since the model assumes a nearly safe downside with an upside that is open, an increase in volatility can only be profitable, thus increasing the value of the product as a whole. The same reasoning can be held at higher spot levels (point 3).

*Decrease in implied volatility*

The exact opposite reasoning to an increase in implied volatility can be applied to a decrease.

In Figure 4.22, the volatility has been reduced from 23% to 13%. The lines are more sinuous, their curvature (concavity) is more pronounced, and they tend generally more towards the payoff at maturity. At the strike of the product (point 2, 109% of spot), the mark-to-market value tends to be slightly lower than with 23% volatility in our Eurostoxx50 index example. At point 3, above the strike of the down-and-out put, the product's decrease in value compared to Figure 4.20 is significant. The option quickly loses its value as it moves away from its strike and the value of the bonus certificate tends to the price of the zero-strike call, which is worth the spot price of the index minus any discounted dividends.

Note that, below the barrier, the implied volatility has no more influence at all. In all the three payoff diagrams, the lines are straight 45° lines. There is no more volatility value in the bonus certificate once a knock-out has occurred, as the down-and-out put option "dies". As a matter of fact, all the lines are situated well below the market line, finally converging with it, which means that the bonus certificate trades below the market value of the index. This is attributable to the fact that once a knock-out has occurred, the bonus certificate

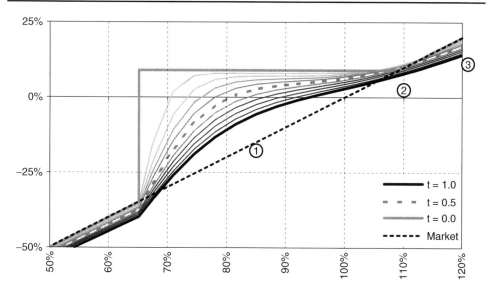

**Figure 4.22**    Payoff 31: impact of implied volatility decrease on bonus certificate

becomes a simple certificate (without dividends, which are lost to the investor). Due to the time value of money,[40] the certificate catches up with the index as its maturity approaches.

*Conclusion*

A bonus certificate behaves like its underlying asset at the issue date and catches up with its payoff at maturity only shortly before the expiry of the product. A high volatility yields better conditions when issued but rising implied volatility during the product's life worsens its mark-to-market valuation. As a general conclusion, a word of warning must be stated at this point. The above example is one among hundreds of thousands of possibilities for constructing a bonus certificate. A "classical" example was chosen to represent an average product, which has similar characteristics to those seen in many new issues from leading investment and global banks. However, some of the conclusions drawn from the current example might not hold for other bonus certificates constructed with different barriers, bonus or participation levels, and different time to maturity or with different implied volatility characteristics.

### 4.4.4    Variation in the dividends/yield

Bonus certificates cannot be constructed in the classical way without the underlying asset paying a dividend or yielding interest. For the sake of simplicity, only the effects of changes in the dividend on a stock-based bonus certificate will be described, bearing in mind that similar rules apply for yield variations as well.

---

[40] In the above example, the calculations were made assuming constant continuous dividends.

The dividend level and payment date are the key to the construction of the bonus certificate because they strongly influence the value of the zero-strike call on the underlying stock: the higher the dividend yield, the lower its forward price, the lower the barrier of the down-and-out put can be placed. To get a feeling for how much a one percent change in the dividend influences the barrier of the bonus certificate, let's take the example of Table 4.10 on page 100 and vary the dividend yield of the Eurostoxx50 index between 1% and 7%. Figure 4.23 shows the level of protection that each dividend level can buy. While 35% protection was possible with the original 4% dividend yield, this level falls to 27% when the dividend is halved to 2% and rises to 39% when increased to 6%. The curve of Figure 4.23 is concave, which is explained by the fact that the amount of dividends needed for each higher level of protection increases, and dividends are assumed to remain constant. The cost increase of the option comes from the pricing model, which assumes increasingly lower chances of the option being knocked out with each lower barrier. At the limit, the down-and-out put tends to the price of the plain vanilla put option. In the Eurostoxx50 example of Table 4.10 the price would amount to ca. 17% of spot. In other words, if a 17% dividend yield were available, the barrier could be lowered to zero percent of spot. The bonus certificate would then be equal to a capital protected product, albeit constructed with a zero strike call and a long put instead of the classic zero bond plus at-the-money call.

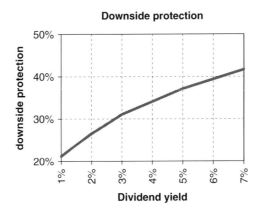

**Figure 4.23** Level of downside protection as a function of dividend yield
*Source:* Bloomberg, own calculations

The levels in Figure 4.23 are valid in practice for dividend yields above 2%. Dividends below that level usually do not result in attractive products in practice even if in theory a reasonable barrier could be achieved, the main reason being structuring costs. The mentioned levels may differ strongly for products with different bonus levels and maturities. Bonus or participation levels have the same tendency to increase with rising dividend yields and vice versa.

This paragraph focuses on the importance of the payment date of the dividend for the bonus certificate structure. Figure 4.24 shows bonus levels for bonus certificates on two different underlying assets, the Eurostoxx50 index and Swiss Re, with a level of protection of 40%, which could have been traded as of 25 April 2008 for maturities ranging from

2.5 to 3.5 years.[41] On that day, for instance, a bonus certificate on the Eurostoxx50 with maturity February 2011 would pay a bonus of 118.7%. The interesting observation is the sharp increase in bonus levels for products expiring between February and June 2011 in the Eurostoxx50 index and the absence of prices for products on Swiss Re for that period. This phenomenon has its roots in the dividend payment dates. The majority of the stocks included in the Eurostoxx50 index pay their dividends between those two dates. The inclusion of the dividends allows the structurer of the product to invest more money into the down-and-out put option, which is reflected in the higher bonus.[42]

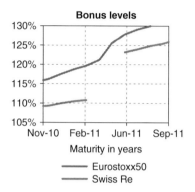

**Figure 4.24**  Bonus level examples as a function of maturity (start April 08)
*Source:* UBS, own calculations

The absence of prices for the Swiss Re products is due to the dividend payment date as well. In the past years, the company paid an annual dividend at the end of April or beginning of May. The issuer of the product cannot be absolutely sure on which exact date the company will pay its dividend in the future. Since the issuer takes the dividend risk on his trading books, he would rather not issue a product in which the dividend is included in his pricing, only to see that it is paid out a few weeks later than forecast, after the product has expired. The product sheets that UBS and other issuers send out are indicative. In practice, if an investor absolutely wants a product to expire on the dividend day, he will probably get it priced. However, the trader is likely to exclude the dividend when he calculates the fair value of the product because he will not want to take the risk,[43] so it is to be expected that the product will have poor parameters compared to one expiring a month later.

### 4.4.5  Variations in implied correlation

Several payoff formulas can be imagined for bonus certificates based on multiple underlying assets:

---

[41] Some issuers, in this case UBS, communicate on a daily basis indicative bonus certificates on a range of stocks and stock indices to their institutional clients in order to give them a global picture about the possible variants that could be structured.

[42] One could also have lowered the barrier or increased the participation.

[43] Believe it or not, most derivative traders are risk-averse.

- barrier triggered on the worst-of asset, participation on the basket;
- barrier triggered on the worst-of asset, participation on the worst-of;
- barrier triggered on the worst-of asset, participation on the basket as long as the barrier hasn't been triggered, participation on the worst-of asset after a knock-event;
- barrier triggered on the basket, participation on the basket;
- barrier triggered on the best-of, participation on the basket;
- etc.

The value extracted from the implied correlation in "worst-of" structures can be used to enhance or reduce the four main parameters: higher participation or bonus level, lower barrier or shorter time to maturity. In worst-of types, an increase in implied correlation is almost always positive for secondary market prices. In best-of types, the reverse is true. While including several assets in the product to extract the value of the implied correlation in "worst-of" types can dramatically enhance the payoff at maturity, a change in the implied correlation has a limited impact on the price of bonus certificates compared to variations in the volatility.

It is always difficult for the simple investor to gauge which parameter should be the beneficiary of the implied correlation value, or if it should be used at all. If in doubt, worst-of features shouldn't be included. If they are, the extracted value should usually be used to set a more conservative barrier or a shorter maturity. Here as well, the rule of maximal two assets in a worst-of structure should be respected.

## 4.5   OTHER PARTICIPATION PRODUCTS

### 4.5.1   Tracker certificates

Tracker certificates come in two forms: total return trackers and excess return trackers. The total return tracker, assuming no costs, will always track its underlying asset on a 1:1 basis. Excess return tracker certificates are usually issued below the spot price of the underlying asset. They catch up the spot price over time as dividends or interest rates reduce the price of the underlying asset. As tracker certificates have no optionality embedded, any change in implied volatility of the underlying asset has no influence on the secondary price of the product.

One factor that theoretically has an influence on excess return certificates based on dividend paying stocks is a change in realized or expected dividends. At the time of issue, the expected dividends for the lifetime of the tracker are discounted, and subtracted from the spot price. The expected dividends are thus incorporated as a fixed amount in the issue price of the tracker and, no matter what, the tracker will pay back 100% of the spot price at maturity. The dividend risk lies thus with the issuer and not with the certificate holder. Should the dividend payment on an underlying asset be reduced or completely eliminated, the loss is borne by the issuer. Conversely, any increase in dividends will accrue to the benefit of the issuer.

As a tentative conclusion, it could be stated that if an investor expects falling dividends in the future, he or she should "lock-in" any future dividends with an excess return tracker certificate purchased at a discount. There are, however, several problems with this reasoning.

- First, one can assume that traders are at least as well informed as any investor, and the market already discounts lower future dividends in the price of the certificate. The investor therefore has to expect a sharper decrease in dividends than the market already discounts for this trade to make sense.
- Second, it might not be a good idea to use the tracker certificate as a structure to bet on falling stock dividends. Generally, investors see it as a weakness if corporations reduce or skip their dividends, and the stock prices will probably fall. Therefore, despite being right in locking-in high dividends, the investor will still probably have a loss due to the fall in spot price.
- Third, continuing the line of thought from the second point, the investor might be better off spending the high expected dividends on either protection or outright downside performance. A possible structure would be a *short* total return tracker with stop-loss,[44] or a capped twin-win structure, or any other structure with downside participation.

### 4.5.2 Twin-win certificates

The mark-to-market value of twin-win certificates behaves similarly to that of bonus certificates. One small difference is the greater gap that develops when the product is close to maturity and the spot price is just above the barrier. The twin-win certificate usually has a higher level of absolute upside performance up to the lower barrier when the spot price declines, all other things staying equal. Therefore, the gap becomes bigger. For changes in the other variables, the same reasoning as described in Section 4.4.1 applies.

### 4.5.3 Airbag certificates

The behavior of airbag certificates is similar to that of bonus certificates in the sense that the protection only begins to become apparent shortly before maturity. The main difference is that no gap due to a barrier influences the secondary market price. A follow-up on the construction example of Figure 3.15 (page 62) on Allianz SE is represented in Table 4.11. The airbag had a maturity of two years, 25% protection and 100% participation. The downside leverage from 75% of spot price and lower amounts to 1.33.[45]

**Table 4.11**  Example of airbag certificate

| | |
|---|---|
| Underlying asset | Allianz SE |
| Maturity | 2 years |
| Upside participation | 100% |
| Airbag level | 25% |
| Downside leverage from Airbag level | 133% |

---

[44] A short tracker behaves exactly inverse to the tracker. Should the underlying asset fall by 20%, the short tracker gains 20%. The short tracker must have a stop-loss, as there is no way of making the purchaser put more money into the certificate (otherwise said, a structured product cannot become a margin-call product like a future). For example, if the underlying asset increased by 120%, without a stop-loss, the short tracker's value would become −20%.

[45] $\frac{100\%}{1-25\%} \simeq 133\%$

Figure 4.25 plots the profit and loss of the product as a function of the spot price and the time to maturity left.

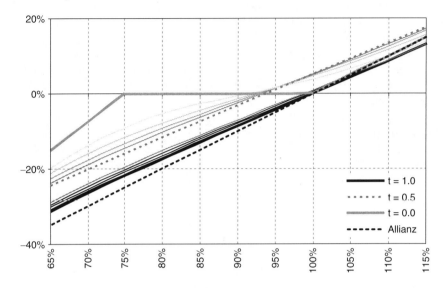

**Figure 4.25**  Payoff 32: airbag certificate price as a function of spot and time to maturity
*Source:* Bloomberg, own calculations

As anticipated, the protection only starts to have an effect close to the maturity of the product (top two thin lines representing 10% and 20% remaining time to maturity respectively). However, one characteristic of the diagram calls for explanation: why is there a sudden jump in price between 60% and 50% time remaining? The reason is a dividend payment, which occurs within this time window. Contrary to the examples on the Eurostoxx50 index, where the dividends are treated as continuous in this book,[46] Allianz paid an annual dividend in May. Relative to the price of the stock, the airbag's value will therefore increase by the dividend amount paid out on the dividend's ex-date.[47] The second dividend of this 2-year structure takes place in the last months of the life of the product, which is why the 10% remaining lifetime line is still so far away from the payoff at maturity.

Implied volatility has a lesser influence on airbag certificates because the long at-the-money call and short in-the-money call ratio partially offset each other's price variation. Again, the dividend yield is the factor that makes the airbag certificate attractive. In the example, 25% stable protection (to contrast with protection that could be knocked-out) was bought with 10.5% dividends.

### 4.5.4   Turbo certificates

Turbo certificates were popular short-term structures in 2003–2004, before the barrier products overwhelmed the market and captured the investors' attention. The double participation between the spot price and the cap combined with the short maturity attracted

---

[46] Which is not strictly correct as has been stated in Section 4.4.4, but which helps to simplify the calculations of the examples considerably.
[47] Note that the dotted black line representing the Allianz stock is ex-dividend.

many investors, but the product disappointed when it became clear that timing was essential to exit the product with an outperformance measured against the underlying asset. The problem was once more related to misunderstanding the product's functioning during its lifetime.[48] The investor had a scenario in mind about the underlying asset, most of the time a stock. Should the stock price rise 10% within six months, he would make 20% (not more, but that was sufficient). A 10 percent gain within six months was, for a conservative stock, a hefty performance. Thus, some good money could be made from lazy conservative large caps like Roche, Nestlé or Allianz over a short period. But, most of the time, the turbo certificate did not deliver on its promise. Either the stock did not perform at all, the product ended with a negative performance (having no downside protection whatsoever), or the stock outperformed the investor's scenario and the product didn't even keep up with the stock's performance, much less outperform it. Figure 4.26 shows an example for Nestlé with a maturity of 6 months. No dividends are included, hence no jumps in the product's mark-to-market value as a function of the time remaining until maturity, contrary to the example of the airbag on Allianz SE seen previously. The initial price was CHF 46.00. With the volatility on the strike date (7 July 2008) of 22.5% for the at-the-money call and 19.5% for the out-of-the-money calls,[49] the product yielded double the upside stock performance up to a price of CHF 49.00. In other words, should the stock rise by 6.5% (+CHF 3.00), the performance of the product would be 13% (+CHF 6.00).

**Table 4.12**   Example of a turbo certificate

| Underlying asset | Nestlé AG |
| --- | --- |
| Maturity | 6 months |
| Strike | CHF 46.00 (100%) |
| Cap | CHF 49.00 (106.5%) |
| Max performance | CHF 6.00 (+13%) |

Figure 4.26 plots the profit and loss (in CHF for once) as a function of the spot price.

Figure 4.26 shows again one defining characteristic of structured products that include optionality: the product's behavior at inception diverges strongly from the payoff at maturity as long as time value is left in the embedded options. With the maturity of the product approaching, the valuation of the product will begin to tend toward the final payoff at maturity. But it is only during the last 30% of the product's life that the "turbo" actually has an effect on the valuation of the product. This fact has disappointed many investors, as the product underperformed if the stock rose sharply in the first few months after the product was created.

To understand why the product underperforms the underlying asset in the first half of its life, its delta has to be analyzed. At inception, the delta of the example is 78%. This is due to the construction of the product: long zero strike call, long at-the-money call[50] and short two out-of-the-money calls.[51] The sum of the deltas of the individual options falls as the spot price rises at inception. Let's illustrate this: Figure 4.27 plots the delta of the turbo certificate from Figure 4.26 as a function of Nestlé's spot price and the time to maturity.

---

[48] Maybe the product's behavior during its life hadn't been well explained either.
[49] Implying a slight skew.
[50] Giving the double participation between the at-the-money strike and the cap.
[51] Defining the cap.

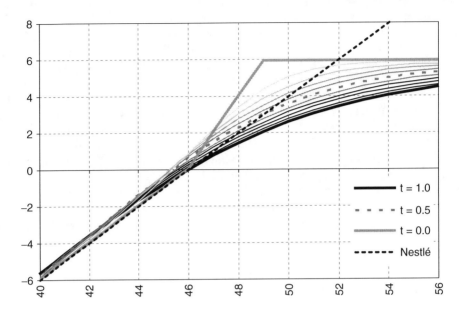

**Figure 4.26** Payoff 33: turbo certificate price as a function of spot and time to maturity
*Source:* Bloomberg, own calculations

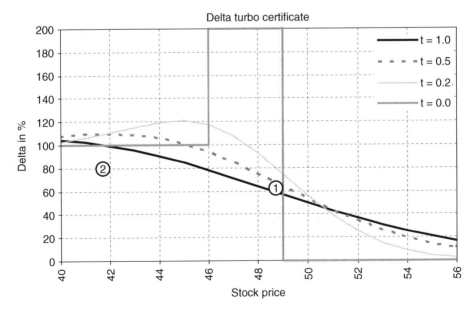

**Figure 4.27** Turbo certificate delta as a function of spot and time to maturity
*Source:* Bloomberg, own calculations

As can be seen from on the thick curved line representing the delta on the issue date, the value at the issue price of CHF 46.00 is 78% (point 1 on the diagram). This is calculated as shown in Table 4.13.

**Table 4.13**  Turbo certificate delta calculation

| | |
|---|---|
| Delta zero-strike call (1×) | 100% |
| Delta at-the-money call (1×) | 56% |
| Delta out-of-the-money call (-2×) | −78% |
| Total | 78% |

Source: Bloomberg

Should Nestlé's price decline (in the direction of point 2), the delta will gradually rise towards 100%. In fact, since there is no protection to the downside, the product tends to move in symmetry with the stock. Should the stock rise, the delta of the zero-strike call will stay constant near 1, while the delta of the at-the-money call rises steadily from 56% at inception. However, at the same time, the two short call deltas also rise, but at a faster combined speed than the single long call. Since the calls are held short, their deltas are negative and are subtracted from the positive deltas. Consequently, the total delta of the product declines steadily with a rising spot, tending towards zero (point 3). This price behavior carries on until shortly before maturity. While at half way to maturity (dotted line) the turbo effect still cannot be felt, at 20% remaining time (top thin line) the delta rises above 100% around the strike price of the at-the-money call. Finally at maturity (straight thick line), the delta's level amounts to one of the following three levels:

- 100% when the spot is below the strike of the at-the-money call (symmetrical price movement between the stock and the turbo certificate);
- 200% when the spot is between the at-the-money strike and the cap (the turbo zone where the performance of the product is double that of the stock); or
- zero when the spot is above the cap.

The turbo certificate is dependent on one more important factor: the skew of the volatility for a given maturity. At the issue date, the steeper the skew, the less attractive the turbo certificate becomes. With a steep skew, the out-of-the money call options are worth less, and their strike has to be lowered, implying lower maximum potential returns. Table 4.14 gives an indication of the strike levels for different levels of skewness for the turbo certificate on Nestlé:

**Table 4.14**  Skew Impact on turbo certificate cap level

| Skew | Implied OTM Strike | Max performance |
|---|---|---|
| Original: 22.5% ATM – 19.5% OTM | 49 | CHF 3.00/13% |
| High: 22.5% ATM – 17.5% OTM | 48.15 | CHF 2.15/9.3% |
| Low (flat): 22.5% ATM – 22.5% OTM | 50.05 | CHF 4.05/17.6% |

Source: Bloomberg, own calculations

Remember that the sale of the two out-of-the money call options finances the purchase of the long at-the money call option: to keep the 200% performance between the strike and the cap, the strike of the former has to be set such that its cost is one half that of the latter. It is therefore useful to have a look at the whole volatility surface[52] of the underlying asset. It might be that for six months' expiry the skew is very steep, but for three or nine months, it is not. The investor has to evaluate the pros and cons of shifting the maturity forward or backward. Maybe the underlying stock reports its yearly results in exactly six months' time and that is the reason for a steeper skew for that maturity. Hence, it might be worth while to keep the 6-month maturity for the product and accept less favorable conditions due to the adverse skew. It is up to the investor, or for that matter his advisor, to determine which parameters are best for his product.

### 4.5.5   Outperformance certificates

The outperformance certificate can be synthetically replicated by holding the underlying stock, buying a predetermined ratio of at-the-money calls, and shorting the future dividends for the lifetime of the product. The discounted value of the future dividends pays for the extra calls. The higher the dividends and the more dividends included, the higher the ratio. The other main variables are again spot price followed by implied volatility. Only the effect on price due to movement in spot price is depicted here. To illustrate the behavior of the product, a simple example is represented in Table 4.15.

**Table 4.15**   Sample outperformance certificate

| | |
|---|---|
| Underlying risky asset | BASF |
| Maturity | 670 days (2 years 10 months) |
| Implied volatility ATM | 26% |
| Dividend yield asset | 5.10% |
| Dividend payment dates (2) | 9 months/21 months |
| Interest rate level (2-year swap rate, p.a.) | 5.14% |
| Outperformance leverage | 65% |
| Price | EUR 42.00 (100% of spot) |

Suppose an investor is strongly bullish on BASF in the short to medium term. BASF pays an impressive annual dividend of over 5%. Despite a heightened implied volatility level, the investor considers buying an outperformance certificate. The upside participation would amount to 165%, implying a leverage of 0.65, or 65%. The next dividend is due in nine months and the investor would like to include two dividends. The bank's representative advises him to limit the maturity to 2 years 10 months to save two months' time value on the at-the-money call. In effect, the two months after the second dividend payment do not add value to the strategy, even having a slightly negative effect.[53] The representative further argues that the additional one month beyond the second dividend payment date is

---

[52] The volatility surface of an underlying asset denotes its various volatility levels for different strikes and different maturities. Option traders combine all the strikes and maturities on a 3D graph, forming a surface. It is also referred to as "local vol" in the traders' lingo.

[53] It reduces the leverage by 5% to 60%.

to make sure the trader will include both dividends in his pricing. A maturity of 2 years 9 months might fall directly on the dividend date, a risk the trader hedging the product on the issuer's proprietary books is loath to take. The investor mentions he would like to be able to sell the product before maturity if his scenario materializes without underperforming the stock. Figure 4.28 plots the profit and loss in EUR the investor would make as a function of BASF's stock price and the time to maturity of the product.

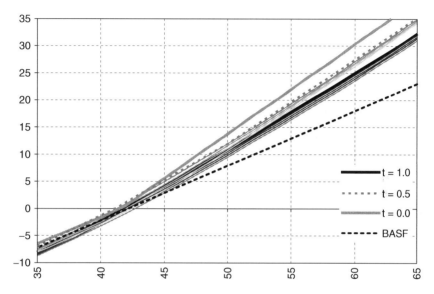

**Figure 4.28**   Payoff 34: outperformance certificate price as a function of spot and time to maturity

   The good news for the investor is that any upside price movement of the stock is reflected by a factor over 1 in the product. He can sell the product prior to the final maturity and achieve an outperformance versus the stock if his scenario materializes. The delta at the issue date is $100\% + (65\% \times 54\%) = 135\%$. That is slightly more than half the leverage at maturity. On the upside, the delta will increase with the passage of time or, if the spot price rises, enhance the outperformance of the product as compared to the stock. On the downside, the delta rapidly falls when the stock falls, but the product will still underperform the stock because of the leverage. Note that the lines from $t = 1.0$ to $t = 0.1$ jump at the time when BASF pays the dividends as did those in Figure 4.25 (the airbag certificate on Allianz).

# 5

# Common Special Features of Structured Products

## 5.1 QUANTO OPTIONS

When an investor buys a stock or any risky asset based in a foreign currency, he incurs an additional foreign exchange risk. In fact, another risk-return component is added to his portfolio. More often than not, investors do not actively decide whether they want to take the currency risk, but neglect it. This can lead to massive underperformances in a portfolio, as we will see later in this section. Structured products can help reduce the currency risk in a portfolio by embedding a currency hedge within the product. Of course, any investor could hedge the currency by himself. However, practice shows that it is seldom implemented with precision and in a cost-effective way in self-directed private banking portfolios. Sometimes, currency hedges are not implemented at all for various reasons: the lack of liquidity, no market access and no time or know how.

### 5.1.1 A practical example and definitions

A quanto option is a type of derivative in which the underlying asset is denominated in one currency, but the instrument itself is settled in another currency at a predefined fixed rate. Hence, an investor can have exposure to a foreign asset, but without the corresponding exchange rate risk. The term "quanto" originates from "quantity adjusted option". To illustrate how exchange rate variations affect investments, the example below looks at the case of an investor whose reference currency is EUR and who invests in IBM, a USD-based stock.

The investor bought an IBM share in late 2001 for USD 63.90. At the time, the EUR/USD exchange rate was 0.9875, so one share cost the investor EUR 64.73. In July 2008, six-and-a-half years later, the share price had risen by more than 85% to USD 119.50.[1] Because the dollar has lost a lot of ground against the euro in those years, the EUR investor did not benefit from the share's performance to a large degree. Were he to sell the shares and exchange the proceeds today at a EUR/USD spot rate of 1.5700, he would receive EUR 76.11. After currency adjustments, his performance would therefore be only 18%, which looks very poor compared to the 85% the USD-based investor would have made.

This trivial example shows how important it is to consider currency swings within a portfolio. Another example would be a hedge against inflation through investments in commodities. Since raw materials such as gold or oil are all traded in USD, the main price drivers for a EUR-based investor will be the EUR/USD exchange rate followed by macro political events, speculation and, to a lesser extent, inflation. Eliminating the exchange rate risk will remove one potential undesirable factor from the investment.

---

[1] Not taking any dividends into account.

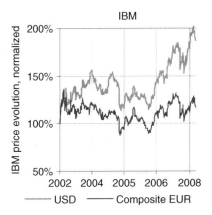

**Figure 5.1**  Stock performance as a function of currency
*Source:* Bloomberg, own calculations

Two ways exist of dealing with exchange rates when issuing structured products that are labeled in another currency than its underlying constituents:

- quanto (quantity adjusted option); and
- compo (composite).

Let's define the two terms formally:

Quanto is the term for a product labeled in a different currency than its underlying asset(s) in which exchange rate risk is **excluded**; currency fluctuations do not affect the product performance.

The formula for calculating performance for quanto products is:

$$\text{Nominal}^* \sum_{i=1}^{n} \left[ W_i * \frac{\text{Asset}_{i,\ \text{Final}}}{\text{Asset}_{i,\ \text{Initial}}} \right]$$

with $W_i$ the weighting of the Asset$_i$.

This is nothing other than the formula for calculating the performance of an asset without considering FX movements, as if the asset was labeled in the reference currency of an investor. Note that the formula says nothing about the costs of the quanto option. Now let us define composite:

Composite is the term for a product labeled in a different currency than its underlying asset(s) in which exchange rate risk is **included**; currency fluctuations affect the product performance.

In the case of *composite* products, potential gains or losses in the underlying asset have to be adjusted to reflect any exchange rate fluctuations (as in the example of the IBM share). The formula for calculating composite product performance is:

$$\text{Nominal}^* \sum_{i=1}^{n} \left[ W_i * \frac{\text{Asset}_{i,\ \text{Final}}}{\text{Asset}_{i,\ \text{Initial}}} * \frac{\text{FX}_{i,\ \text{Initial}}}{\text{FX}_{i,\ \text{Final}}} \right]$$

As can be observed, a second fraction with the FX relative performance has been added to the formula. Table 5.1 shows an example of a currency-adjusted performance for each option. It uses the example of a tracker certificate on a basket of shares made up solely of USD denominated securities.

**Table 5.1** Example of a quanto performance calculation

|  | Quanto EUR | Composite EUR |
| --- | --- | --- |
| Purchase price (nominal) | EUR 100 | EUR 100 |
| EUR/USD exchange rate | 1.2500 | 1.2500 |
| Basket: initial value | USD 125 | USD 125 |
| Basket: final value | USD 150 | USD 150 |
| Performance USD 150−USD 125 | USD 25 | USD 25 |
| EUR/USD exchange rate | No impact | 1.3500 |
| Currency-adjusted performance | EUR 20 | EUR 11.10 |
|  | 100*(150/125) | 100*(150/125)*(1.25/1.35) |

The absolute quanto performance is expressed in EUR, not USD; for the composite option, performance has to be adjusted to reflect the current exchange rate. In this example as well, no cost for the currency hedge is assumed.

### 5.1.2 The cost of hedging exchange rate risk

The price of a quanto option depends mainly on the interest rates differential and on the correlation between the currency pair. Of course, volatility, maturity strike etc. are also key factors in determining the price of the option. However, the goal is to compare the price of a standard, plain vanilla option with an underlying asset in its base currency with the same option hedged in another currency.

As a rule of thumb, it is sufficient to remember that compared to a standard call option, a quanto call option will become *more expensive* if the interest level of the base currency of the underlying asset is *lower* than the currency in which the option is to be hedged. This is best seen through an example.

Suppose the following situation: a wealthy CHF-based investor is interested in the capital guaranteed product on the Eurostoxx50 of Table 4.1 (page 79). It was a 4-year product offering 100% capital guarantee and 100% participation in EUR. The investor would like to exclude the EUR/CHF currency risk from the product and he asks for a quanto CHF version. The interest rate levels of both currencies are:

- interest rate in EUR: 4.5%;
- interest rate in CHF: 2.5%.

The resulting product would have a participation of 50% instead of 100% in the EUR version. Alternatively, the capital guarantee level could be lowered to ca. 89% to keep the participation at 100%. To gauge roughly the reduction of the capital guarantee as a result of the quanto costs, the interest rate level difference can be multiplied by the years to maturity. This is mathematically not correct, but in the middle of a conversation with a client, the investment advisor does not always have the opportunity to open his laptop and perform model calculations. This rule of thumb helps indicate to the client whether the quanto product can be considered at all.

This example shows that, mainly due to the interest rate differential, the quanto option costs more than the plain vanilla option. How can this be explained? The reasons are inherent to the basic Black and Scholes option model, the base of all option calculations. Without developing the math behind the formula, suffice it to say that currencies with a relatively high interest rate tend to have low forwards, making hedges more expensive. However, when the situation is reversed, quanto options can offer a premium and lower product prices, offering better participation levels, shorter maturities or higher capital protection levels.

### 5.1.3  Impact on structured product prices

Imagine two identical tracker certificates on the same basket of stocks (Table 5.2). Let's suppose that around 60% of the underlying assets are denominated in USD. The remainder is made up of EUR, CHF, JPY and BRL securities. Both were composite products, one in USD, and one in EUR.

**Table 5.2**  Currency impact on composite products

| Currency | Compo USD | Compo EUR |
|---|---|---|
| **Issue price** | USD 100 | EUR 100 |
| **Ask price 22 May 2007** | 102.6 | 96.9 |
| **Change** | +USD 2.6 | −EUR 3.1 |
| **Conversion** | +EUR 1.9 | −USD 4.2 |
| **Difference** | EUR 5 | USD 6.8 |

Source: Julius Baer, own calculations

After approximately eight months, the tracker certificates achieved performance differences of EUR 5 or USD 6.80. In the same period, the EUR exchange rate advanced 5.5% from 1.2800 to 1.3500. The EUR product was hit by the weak dollar, while the USD product benefited from the EUR rise against the dollar. The example of Table 5.2 shows that, in sideways trending markets, the currency can have a huge impact on a composite product.

Commodities, being for a large part traded in USD on the international market, have an important relation to currency exchange rates. The example of Figure 5.2 compares the price evolution of two partially capital-protected products on gold: a quanto EUR product and a USD product.[2] The other conditions are identical, with one small exception: at the time of the issue the EUR product was denominated in a lower-yield currency, so the strike price was three percentage points higher than for the USD product.[3] As a result, the EUR product always lagged behind the USD certificate (see Figure 5.2). However, the investor was not exposed to USD exchange rate risk.

Figure 5.2 also shows a third light line which plots the price trend for a hypothetical composite EUR certificate, i.e. a EUR investor who effectively buys the USD version and accepts the exchange rate risk. This investment product was the worst performer for the EUR-based investor, because of the falling USD. A EUR investor would have been well

---

[2] The gold price is quoted in USD.

[3] At this time, the USD yield was higher than the EUR yield.

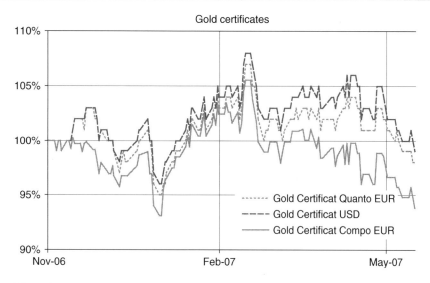

**Figure 5.2** Prices of quanto and composite gold certificate performance
*Source:* Bloomberg, own calculations

advised to purchase the EUR quanto product (even though it consistently lagged 3% behind the USD alternative), thereby avoiding exchange rate risk.

This last example shows how developed structured products can help in hedging currency risk in a portfolio. Of course, professional investors also resort to other types of hedges in a portfolio, like currency overlays. But for the single investor, such a hedge might be impractical due to size, length or complexity. Hence, the advice to hedge as much as possible the currency risk directly within the product through quanto options. It doesn't cost more (or less) than any other form of hedge and, in addition, it is possible to include quanto options in any type of structured product, from capital guarantee to participation.

At the end of the day, the investor has to decide whether to opt for performance determined solely by changes in the underlying or whether to include also exchange rate fluctuations. This section mainly illustrated the quanto feature through examples where an investor benefited from the currency hedge. Of course, a quanto option can have both positive and negative effects.

## 5.2 BARRIER OPTIONS

Barrier options, which have already been mentioned on several occasions, are present in barrier reverse convertibles and bonus certificates amongst other products. To define every kind of barrier option and the possible use for structured products would go beyond the scope of this book. There are, however, some elements in barrier options that an investor should know about, if only to be able to compare apples with apples.

Barrier options are commonly used in a number of structured products. However easy the basic description may be, barrier options are among the most complex exotic options in existence. Nevertheless, let's define barrier options formally:

Barrier options are exotic call or put options that include a barrier condition placed above or below the strike that, when crossed, either transforms the exotic option into a plain vanilla option ("in" barriers) or cancels it altogether ("out" barriers).

The barrier is therefore a transformation feature that modifies the option's payoff from an initial state into a final state. The final payoff cannot be determined with certainty until the maturity of the option.

### 5.2.1 Barrier option variations

Table 5.3 lists the eight possible barrier options.

**Table 5.3**  Barrier option types

| Option | Barrier | | Effect of barrier on payoff | |
|--------|---------|----------|----------------------|-------------|
|        | Type    | Location | Crossed              | Not crossed |
| **Call** | Up&Out   | Above spot | Worthless          | Plain vanilla call |
|          | Up&In    | Above spot | Plain vanilla call | Worthless          |
|          | Down&Out | Below spot | Worthless          | Plain vanilla call |
|          | Down&In  | Below spot | Plain vanilla call | Worthless          |
| **Put**  | Up&Out   | Above spot | Worthless          | Plain vanilla put  |
|          | Up&In    | Above spot | Plain vanilla put  | Worthless          |
|          | Down&Out | Below spot | Worthless          | Plain vanilla put  |
|          | Down&In  | Below spot | Plain vanilla put  | Worthless          |

In addition, each barrier option can have a so-called rebate,[4] which denotes a lump sum paid out to the buyer of the option at maturity when the barrier was crossed.

A few characteristics of barrier options:

- Barrier options are usually cheaper than plain vanilla options, because either the barrier must be crossed for the option to be worth something, or the option can suddenly become worthless.
- For "in" options, the longer the maturity, the more the option's price tends to the value of a plain vanilla option.
- For "out" options, the longer the maturity, the cheaper the option becomes, at the limit tending towards zero.
- For "in" barriers, the price of the option will tend to the price of a plain vanilla option the nearer the underlying asset's price will move to the barrier
- For "out" options, the price of the option will tend to zero the nearer the underlying asset's price will move to the barrier.

---

[4] As seen in the Shark note, which has an embedded up-and-out call where a rebate may be paid out should the underlying asset cross the barrier.

## 5.2.2 American and European barriers

Like a plain vanilla option, a barrier option comes in two main variants:

- *American style:* the option can be exercised any time; and
- *European style:* the option can only be exercised at maturity.

Every option embedded in a structured product is always European style. It cannot be exercised before the product's maturity; otherwise, the option should be detachable from the rest of the product. But what about the barrier itself? It also comes in two main variants:

- *American-style:* the underlying asset can knock the barrier any time during the life of the option, even intraday. This style is also called "continuous monitoring".
- *European-style:* the underlying asset can only knock the barrier at maturity.

The vast majority of structured products have American-style barriers. Why? Most probably, because the normal investor doesn't pay too much attention to the type of barrier, focusing on other factors in a product, such as a high coupon or a better participation. The type of the barrier is seldom mentioned in the title of the product, and is often considered a "technical detail". Let it be known here that the type, or style, of a barrier in a product is crucial. A down&in put with a European-style barrier will always be worth less that the same option with an American-style barrier, because the former can only be knocked-in at maturity. Hence, a barrier reverse convertible with a European-style barrier will feature a lower coupon that the same product with an American-style barrier. The same (reverse) reasoning applies to down&*out* puts; a down&out put with an American-style barrier can "die" anytime during its life, if the underlying asset crosses the barrier level. A similar down&out put with a European-style barrier will be worth more, because it will remain "alive" until the day of its maturity, no matter what. A bonus certificate with an American-style barrier will have a higher bonus or a deeper barrier than its counterpart with a European-style barrier, because the latter can only be knocked out at maturity. Product issuers like investment banks suffering from ferocious competition realized this fact rapidly and issued American-style barriers mainly because their product looked more attractive to the general public than products with European-style options. To illustrate this, let's calculate the difference between an American barrier versus the same product with a European barrier. For that purpose, several examples of "American-style" barrier products that have been shown in previous sections are recalculated using European-style barriers (Table 5.4).

**Table 5.4** Impact of changing an American into a European barrier option

| Example | American barrier (original) | European barrier |
|---|---|---|
| Shark note (Section 2.5) | Barrier 131.5% | *Barrier 123%* |
|  | Rebate 7.5% | Rebate 7.5% |
| Barrier reverse convertible on | Coupon: 10.4% | *Coupon: 8.6%* |
| Eurostoxx50 index (Table 4.2), | Barrier 75% | Barrier 75% |
| Bonus certificate on Eurostoxx50 | Bonus: 9% | *Bonus: 2.5%* |
| index (Table 4.10) | Barrier 65% | Barrier 65% |

The examples show how much a change from an American-style barrier to European style can do to a product. Is the reduction in barrier level, coupon or bonus justified? Certainly, at least from a modeling point of view. The second part of this book[5] illustrates how American style barriers have fared as compared to their European counterparts in the last ten years.

Instead of lowering the coupon of a reverse convertible or the bonus of a bonus certificate when changing the barrier style from American to European, an alternative is to raise the protective barrier to a level closer to the spot. The American barrier might then seem more secure, but it can be knocked anytime, even intraday, while the European barrier can only be knocked at maturity. Since market crashes are (not always, but) often followed by rebounds, the European-style option might weather the storm and finish unscathed, despite the fact that the underlying asset would trade for a while below the barrier.

### 5.2.3   Window barrier options

There is a middle ground between American and European barrier styles. Some products' barriers can be "hit" only between certain time-windows during the lifetime of the product. For example, the barrier of certain reverse convertibles can only be breached during the last three months of their one-year lifetime. Window barrier options are fairly rare in structured products, but occur from time to time.

For the investor, it might be worth comparing an American barrier option to a window barrier. Especially for the variant where the knock can only happen in the last remaining 30% period of the product's life but not before, the trader's models usually don't make such a large value difference between the two options. The investor, by choosing the window option and giving up a small value (in coupon, barrier level or participation, etc.) saves himself the risk of 70% of the lifetime of the product. Granted, the chances to be knocked are greatest during a product's last 30% of its lifetime, but an early knock may be avoided by a window barrier active only a few months prior to the product's maturity. Especially if the give-up in value is small, investors should consider window barrier options.

## 5.3   AUTOCALL AND CALLABLE OPTIONS

Structured products are increasingly being designed with what are known as autocall features. Such products generally carry an attribute such as "autocallable" or "with autocall provision" in their names. The word "autocall" is an abbreviation for "automatic call". Let's define the term formally:

Autocall is a feature where the issuer must redeem a product upon the occurrence of a predefined event. The feature can be set up such that the event can occur anytime or at a predefined date, at a predefined price.

If this event never occurs during the term of the product, the product runs until the predetermined expiry date. The event is often a price level the underlying asset has to reach at or within the predefined period.

In addition to *autocall* provisions, there is also what is known as *callable* provisions, whereby the issuer can *choose* whether to redeem the product on predetermined dates or

---

[5] Starting in Section 12.3.4.

allow it to run its course. The value of the callable feature is slightly greater than the autocallable, since the issuer reserves itself the right – but not the obligation – to redeem the product prior to its final maturity.

Investors generally receive better conditions, such as a higher coupon, when a product features an (auto) call provision compared to a product without that feature. The cost of the (auto) call for the investor is the uncertainty regarding the timing of the product's expiry.

### 5.3.1 Various autocall conditions

An autocall event can be observed either at any point during the term of the product (continuous), or on specific key dates (periodic, for example quarterly).

The classic example of an autocall event is when the underlying rises to a defined mark at a defined date. This mark can be set, for instance, at 105% of spot, at 100%, or even at 90% in some occurrences. In most cases, a predefined coupon is paid out at this mark, the invested capital is reimbursed, and the product is cancelled.

As the diversity of autocall products is huge, it is near impossible to depict them all. But as the concept is also difficult to grasp for common investors, we take a closer look at some common autocall structures.

### 5.3.2 Autocallable notes

Autocallable notes are fully capital guaranteed. The issuer redeems these classic autocall products if the underlying asset(s) closes above, for example, the 100% mark at one of the defined observation dates. Should this be the case, the investor receives 100% of the capital plus a coupon of x%, multiplied by the number of years the product has run to that date. If the product is unconditionally capital guaranteed, then its goal is often to beat an interest rate in order to enhance the returns of a fixed income portfolio. The potential coupon of x% can for instance be set at twice the swap rate. The risk is that the predefined condition will never be met during the term of the product, and the return on the product falls de facto to zero. Figure 5.3 shows how such a product's architecture functions during its term. The product example is based on the SMI index with a capital guarantee of 100% and the payment of a *cumulative* coupon of 6% per annum should the index close above 100% of its spot price at issue date during one of the four annual observation dates. The spot price of the SMI at issue was 7100 points.

In case the capital protection is linked to a condition, that condition is often a kick-in barrier, providing protection up to a specified spot level (for example 70% of spot). If the barrier is touched at any time during the term of the product (American barrier), the investor is short an *at-the-money put*. The product is then classified as yield enhancement by the SVSP under the name "express certificate". The following product would have been possible in July 2008, due to the high volatility of the underlying asset, the SMI index (Table 5.5).

The functioning of the express certificate is similar to the autocallable note, with the difference that the capital protection is conditional to the SMI not trading anytime below 55% of its initial value.

The loss of capital in case of a barrier breach amounts to the invested capital times 1 minus the negative performance of the SMI. For instance if the SMI breached the barrier

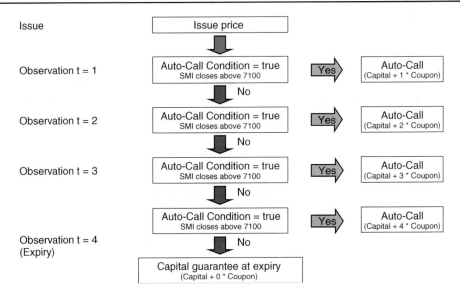

**Figure 5.3**  Payoff 35: autocallable note example

**Table 5.5**  Express certificate example

| | |
|---|---|
| Underlying asset | SMI index |
| Issue price | 100% |
| Spot at issue | 6670 |
| Maturity | 3 years |
| Observation dates | Annual, at each anniversary date |
| Early redemption condition | If at an annual observation date, the SMI closes above the initial spot price |
| Barrier | 55% of spot |
| Cumulative coupon | 15% |

Source: Bloomberg, own calculations

during the lifetime of the product (assuming an American type of barrier) and ended at, say, 4000 points, the redemption would be:

$$1\text{Mio} * \left[ 100\% + \frac{4000 - 6670}{6670} \right] \cong 600\,000$$

In theory, the graphical representation would also be possible, but it is very cumbersome to picture. One needs multiple graphs to represent all the possible outcomes. Figure 5.5 draws the possible outcomes of the express certificate of Table 5.5. The top line represents the hypothetical market price evolution of the SMI index (normalized at 100%), and the bottom line the barrier of 55%.

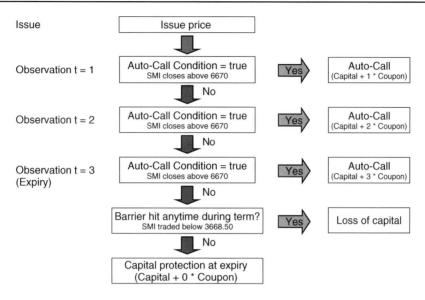

**Figure 5.4**   Payoff 36: express certificate example

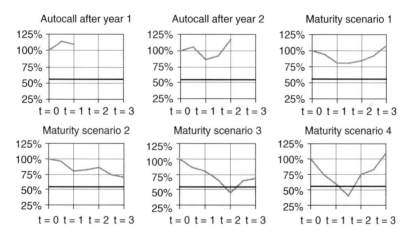

**Figure 5.5**   Payoff 37: alternative express certificate payoff representation

The first three graphs in Figure 5.5 represent the occurrences where the certificate is redeemed with profit (specifically at 115% after year 1, 130% after year 2 and 145% after year 3). Note that, in this example, the certificate outperformed the market on all occasions. Remember that the full coupon is paid even if the market closes only 0.01% above its initial level at an observation date. In the next graph, Maturity scenario 2, the product is redeemed at par, without any coupon because the index never traded above its initial spot price on an observation date, but it didn't breach the barrier either. Maturity scenario 3 redeems the product with a loss of capital because the barrier was breached in t = 2 and the index

finishes below its initial spot price. A rare scenario is Maturity scenario 4, where a breach of
the barrier occurs but a tremendous rally means the spot price of the index closes above its
initial mark at maturity. The certificate is redeemed at par plus the three cumulated coupons,
making the performance of this scenario identical to Maturity scenario 1.

The coupon difference between the Autocall note in Figure 5.3 (6%) and the Express
certificate above (15%) may shock. After all, 55% seems a secure enough barrier for an
index. Why is the note paying only a potential 6% p.a. when the certificate is paying 15%
p.a.? The answer lies in the long maturity, the high volatility and the American-style barrier.
At the pricing date, the SMI's volatility was quoted by Bloomberg at 26.75% (!). Taking only
a 20% volatility would have yielded only 9% coupon for the express certificate, but would
have barely affected the note that remained at 6%. It can be concluded that the certificate
is extremely sensitive to volatility (the higher the better), while it has little impact on the
note. This is reflected in the delta as well: the note has a delta of 13%, while the certificate
has 47%.

As mentioned, with autocallable certificates, investors should take into account that they
are rather *short* volatility. This means that they lose out in times of rising volatility as the
probability that the barrier is broken or touched increases. At the same time, the likelihood
that the underlying will surpass the 100% mark also increases. This has a less pronounced
impact, however, since the event is only significant on the predefined observation dates and
not on a continuous basis.

Why include an autocall feature in a product? Sometimes, the value inherent to the
autocall can make a product possible where it would not have been possible without. Since
a product's autocall is triggered when the underlying asset moves in favor of the product's
holder, it can be considered like a cap for the investor. Caps can have large values, and
either increase coupons, or lower barriers, or enable full capital guarantees. Including an
autocall into a product limits the investor's gain but can make the product possible to begin
with.

### 5.3.3 Autocall worst-of barrier reverse convertibles

These products on multiple underlying assets function in the same way as classical barrier
reverse convertibles, but are redeemed early in the event of an uptrend. In addition to
the features of a worst-of barrier reverse convertible as seen in Table 3.7, a *trigger level
activating the autocall* has been set. The autocall activates when all underlying assets trade
above the trigger level (e.g. at 105% of initial spot). So, if on any given day during the term
of the product the condition is fulfilled (autocall event), the autocall reverse convertible is
automatically redeemed at 100% of its nominal value *including the full coupon*, regardless
of whether or not the knock-in barrier was breached previously.

Figure 5.6 illustrates the case of a trigger barrier worst-of reverse convertible. If all the
stocks rise above the 105% hurdle, the product is redeemed immediately with full coupon.
In the example, the last stock to reach that level is Stock 2, which reaches it at the beginning
of month four. The product redeems at that time, including the coupon that would otherwise
have been paid over the full period of 12 months.

It was mentioned that correlation plays a significant role when using multiple underlying assets. On highly correlated assets, the probability of all three assets surpassing the
trigger level in rising markets is greater than on lower correlated ones. In other words,
the investor is *long* correlation and even stronger than with conventional worst-of barrier

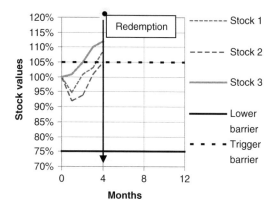

**Figure 5.6** Trigger worst-of reverse convertible

reverse convertibles. In order to capture the most value from an investment in an auto-callable worst-of barrier reverse convertible, the investor must have a specific scenario in mind. In graphical form, Figure 5.7 represents such an ideal scenario:

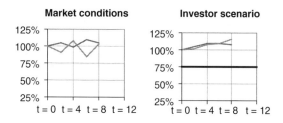

**Figure 5.7** Autocall market conditions and expected scenario

The two top lines each represent two assets. The black line on the second graph is a hypothetical barrier that the investor thinks will not be reached. The horizontal axis is labeled in months. On the left-hand side is graphically represented what the market anticipates: a high volatility and a low correlation (this information can be recovered from how the market prices the options on the two assets; however, no information about the trend of the market is possible). On the right-hand side is drawn the investor's anticipated scenario: he thinks that the volatility will drop and the correlation will rise. His view is not congruent with the markets. After a recent correction of the two assets, he thinks that a bottoming out with a rebound is possible, but is uncertain about the longer term. Investing in an autocallable barrier reverse convertible with a trigger level slightly above initial spot allows him to play this scenario best. If he is proven right, his two stocks will rebound and the product could be redeemed with full coupon after a few months or even weeks after it is issued. If not, well, he must hope that the barrier holds until maturity.

The autocall function can play an important role in the case of the construction of the worst-of barrier reverse convertible. Usually, yield enhancement products like the barrier reverse convertible (with or without a worst-of feature) are recommended by investment advisors and salespersons in "volatile but sideways tending markets". Such market scenarios are rather rare. In the last 10 years, volatile markets were either plunging or recovering fast. The author prefers to use yield enhancement products when the market is indeed volatile and has corrected, but the *expected scenario* is a recovery with falling volatility, while uncertainty persists. When using multiple assets and worst-of features, the correlation must be low or expected to increase. The addition of an autocall feature stating that if all underlying assets rise above a predefined trigger level set closely above the spot price at issue (e.g. 101% or 105%), enables investors to use this product type in other market conditions, like playing an expected (short) rebound in a bear market after a local bottoming out. One might even consider investing in bull markets, as long as all chosen underlying assets are forecast by the investor to rise by approximately the same amount. In that case, the autocall worst-of barrier reverse convertible might even outperform the bull market since it redeems after a short period (theoretically even the next day) with the full coupon, enabling the investor to reinvest the proceeds immediately. These are, however, marginal cases to be well thought over, as the timing would be essential for the strategy to work out.

### 5.3.4   Autocallable steepeners (interest rate based products)[6]

An autocall provision is especially effective with interest rate-based products. A so-called autocallable yield curve steepener is presented here. These instruments are ideally suited to investors who anticipate a steepening of the yield curve. Investors receive a high coupon if the spread between, for example, the 10-year constant maturity swap (CMS) and the 2-year CMS widens beyond a predefined value. If this point is reached, the product is *redeemed* at par plus a relative high coupon by the issuer. Figure 5.8 shows the yield curves of the US swap rates at different dates:

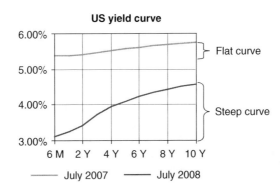

**Figure 5.8**   Flat and steep yield curve
*Source:* Bloomberg

In July 2007 the difference, or spread, between the 10-year and 2-year swap level was 5.75% − 5.41 = 0.34%, otherwise said the yield curve was pretty flat (top line). In July 2008 the same 10- minus 2-year spread amounted to 4.57% −3.41% = 1.16%, in other words the curve was steeper (bottom line). The investor betting on a steepening of the curve in July 2007 could have invested in the product described in Table 5.6.

---

[6] For more information about fixed income structures, see Section 7.2.

**Table 5.6**  Autocallable yield curve steepener example

| | |
|---|---|
| Product type | Autocallable capital guaranteed yield curve steepener |
| Underlying asset | Difference between the 10Y and 2Y US swap rate |
| Capital guarantee | 100% |
| Strike | 95 basis points |
| Maturity | 3 years |
| Observation dates | Annual, at each anniversary date |
| Early redemption condition (autocall) | If at an annual observation date, the 10–2 year swap spread quotes at or over the strike |
| Coupon in case of autocall (cumulative) | **10%** p.a. (includes previous years' missed coupons) |
| Issue price | 100% |

With this investment, if the steepness of the curve had reached the strike of 95 bps, the investor would have made a return of approximately double the yield he would have made had he invested in a bond instead. If that had not been the case within the first year, then a second and third chance to realize this rate of return would have been possible in the second or third year. As we can see in Figure 5.8, the strike would have been largely reached, and the product redeemed with a return of 10% after one year.

Only the autocallable provision allows this product to be designed with attractive coupons. If the issuer were unable to recall the product prior to maturity, then when the shape of the curve moved in the "wrong" direction from the issuer's perspective[7] its hedging costs would become enormous and the product conditions disadvantageous.

Autocallable steepeners are among the very interesting products that have totally bypassed the typical private banking clientele up to now. Yet they would enhance the diversification in a portfolio, they can become short-term investments if set up properly,[8] and the chance of outperforming normal bonds (or even stock markets, for that matter) are good to excellent. Over the last 10 years,[9] all an investor would have to do was to invest in steepeners at the beginning (or even in the middle) of a big crisis, or when the yield curve was rather flat. The strategy then consists of waiting for the central banks to lower short-term interest rates to dampen the effect of the crisis on the economy. Consequently the yield curve steepens and the product is redeemed to its maximum value, probably before its final maturity.

### 5.3.5  The value of the autocall: examples

An autocall provision adds a new dimension to the pricing of a product (i.e. one more variable) and it can basically be applied to the majority of products. Its inclusion thus creates a new range of capital protected, yield enhancement and participation products. While it is impossible to illustrate the consequences of an autocall for all products, it is still important to get a feeling of the effect it can have. In this section, the value of an autocall by means of two different examples will be shown.

---

[7] In this case if it steepened to above the strike.

[8] Thanks to the autocall.

[9] Probably even the last 20 years, but autocallable steepeners didn't exist back then.

*Shark notes with autocall*

The first example is based on a shark note on the TOPIX index in CHF quanto, with a term of two years.[10] Let's first look at a version without an autocall provision. For an identical fair value of 100%, there are two optimum combinations (Figure 5.9) of barrier and rebate:[11] a rebate of 6.25% pro rata with a high barrier of 128%, and a slightly lower rebate of 5.75% pro rata with a considerably lower barrier of 115% (both barriers are observed during the entire term and are therefore continuous).

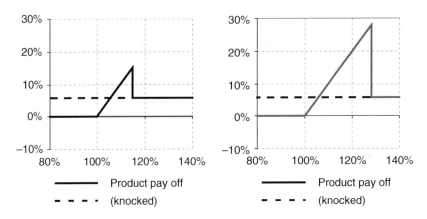

**Figure 5.9**  Payoff 38: Shark notes with rebate (left 115%/5.75%, right 128%/6.25%)

Table 5.7 shows the exact same products, but featuring an autocall provision.

**Table 5.7**  Autocall effect on a Shark note

|  | Version 1 | Version 2 |
| --- | --- | --- |
| Barrier | 115% | 128% |
| Without autocall | 5.75% | 6.25% |
| With autocall (pro rata basis) | 6.25% | 7.50% |

Source: redrawn from an e-mailed product idea sent by an investment bank

The autocall provision increases the rebate because it is above the risk-free interest rate and – in case of the autocall – has to be paid over a shorter period. In addition, the issuer's hedging costs are reduced due to the, on average, shorter term.

---

[10] This example combines the autocall and the quanto feature seen previously. Although the Topix index' base currency is the Japanese Yen, the quanto option eliminates all FX risk for a Swiss Franc-based investor.

[11] A rebate denotes the sum paid to the investor to compensate for a knock-out event on a barrier option, in this case the "up and out". Once a knock-out has occurred, the rebate becomes the value of the option at maturity.

*Autocall frequency and express certificates*

In the next example, we see an express certificate, also on the TOPIX in CHF quanto. This product has a term of three years, and the continuously observed barrier is set at 75%. Its parameters are otherwise similar to the express certificate shown in Table 5.5.

Table 5.8 shows the correlation between the number of autocall observation periods and the height of the coupon.

**Table 5.8**  Autocall frequency on an express certificate

| Autocall observation period | Coupon p.a. (*t) |
| --- | --- |
| Annually | 15.75% |
| Semi-annually | 16.00% |
| Quarterly | 16.25% |

Source: redrawn from an e-mailed product idea sent by an investment bank

The autocall benefit is evident here as well: The greater the number of observation periods, the higher the probability that the product will be redeemed sooner, and consequently the coupon (p.a.) increases as well.

In summary, it is clear that an autocall provision normally enhances the attractiveness of the product conditions. This is attributable to the fact that the autocall or call provision is in all cases triggered if the market trends *against* the issuers, effectively placing a cap on the product's performance for the investor.

The consequences for the clients are that following an (auto) call event they are able to reallocate their capital based on a current market assessment.

### 5.3.6  Factors influencing (auto) callability

Finally, yet importantly, it is useful to get a feeling about the different factors adding or deducting value from an (auto) call. The investor should consider these factors when faced with the decision about an investment. Note that the factors are stated for new products to be issued. For products already issued, the reasoning has to be reversed.

*Factors for discretionary callability by the issuer*

- *Interest rates:* the higher the rates, the more value in the callability.
- *Volatility:* the higher the volatility, the higher the value in the callability.
- *Correlation:* mixed influence factor, depends on the other factors and is of less relevance.
- *Credit spread of the issuer:* the higher, the more value in the callability.

The evolution of all these factors has an important significance for the secondary market price and on the call probability of the product. As a matter of fact, the product might not get called in some instances even when the price of the product is above par. This is because not only the underlying asset's price but also all the above named factors, and more important so, their forwards, are considered by the issuer whether to call the product or not.

*Factors for autocall on predefined condition*

The case for an autocall is similar to the callable, but with small differences: since the product will be certainly called if a predefined condition based solely on the level of the underlying asset(s) level is met, the *future evolution* of the other factors is of less relevance. For instance, the autocall has a higher value when the interest rates are high, as with the callable option, but the subsequent evolution of the yield curve is of little relevance to the product.

It is also worth mentioning that some products are impossible to structure with a discretionary callability feature but must use the autocall. For instance, a product on stock indices being redeemed at par plus coupon if all indices are above 90% of their spot price after one year, must be autocallable, and not callable. No issuer in his right mind would discretionary call a product where the spot trades 10% below its initial value.

### 5.3.7   When to invest in a callable or autocallable product?

There is no single straight answer to that question due to the wide diversity of the product range using (auto)callable options. As already said, the main risk of an (auto)callable product is the uncertainty about the time the capital plus eventual proceeds are redeemed. The investor is usually paid his money back when the market conditions don't allow for a reinvestment at the same conditions and remains invested when he could get better ones. In other words, the investor incurs *an increased reinvestment risk*. That risk is compensated by a higher expected return in the product when compared with a similar product without the (auto)call feature.

In general,[12] the compensation of the (auto)call would be sufficient when an investor expects, in order of importance:

- steady to slightly rising prices in the underlying asset (to allow reinvestment at roughly the same level);
- falling interest rates (ideally issue the product with a rather flat or even inverse yield curve);
- steady forward volatility (allows for reinvestments at same conditions if called);
- tightening credit spreads of the issuer.

When these conditions are met, it may be advantageous to use a callable feature. However, the conditions may change according to the product construction.

## 5.4   ROLLING PRODUCTS AND PRODUCTS WITHOUT FIXED MATURITY

A number of products are constructed around a predefined trading strategy of short to medium term, which is rolled automatically at regular time intervals. The product itself has no maturity, it is said to be *open-ended*.

---

[12] Some products will behave differently to the statement made here, due to their specific construction or market conditions. The bullet points attempt to reflect the scenarios needed for the classical majority of the products, based on the author's subjective and empiric experience.

The idea behind this type of product is the continuity in the strategy which, as often claimed by their inventors, should lead to an outperformance when measured against its underlying asset. Thus were created hundreds of recurring strategies. A good example is the so-called "buy-write" strategy, which consists of buying a stock or an index and writing short-term calls on it, either at-the-money or out-of-the money. In the structured product world, this strategy has translated into the *rolling discount certificate (RDC)*, in which a discount certificate strategy is implemented every month, quarter or year and rolled over without finite maturity date. Later, several exchanges created listed indices to track the "buy-write" or covered call strategy as well.[13] Figure 5.10 draws the sequential process for a hypothetical RDC. An analogous systematic is implemented in the covered call indices, on which tracker certificates have since been issued. The assumption in this example is that, for each period, a new certificate is issued at a 3%[14] discount to the actual market spot price for the duration of the period.

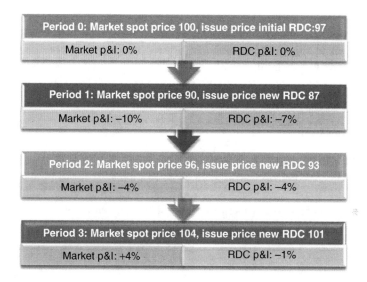

**Figure 5.10**   Rolling discount certificate performance example

The observation in the example illustrates the main drawback of the strategy: once the underlying asset has experienced a sharp correction followed by a rebound, the RDC takes several periods of stable markets to recover, due to the cap inherent to the product.

Other strategies, based on Price/Earnings ratios, dividend yield growth, seasonality or price appreciation, were packaged into certificates without fixed maturity, the strategy being implemented methodically. Indeed, behind every one of these strategies lies a precise mathematical formula that steers it.

---

[13] DAXplus covered call index (Bloomberg ticker: DXCC Index <go>), S&P500 buy-write index (Bloomberg ticker: BXM Index <go>), Eurostoxx50 buy-write index (Bloomberg ticker: SX5EBW Index <go>).

[14] The discount level is actually the variable of the RDC. In high volatile markets, the discount will be greater, while a low volatile environment will produce smaller discounts. The naïve assumption in the example is a constant level of volatility.

*Dos and don'ts*

What should an investor make of these products? As with the autocallable in the preceding section, there is no closed-end answer to this question. Every investor should make up his or her own mind about the product considered. One strategy might appeal to one investor, while being thought useless by his neighbor or colleague. The author would nevertheless like to express a few words of warning about rolling products and those without fixed maturity:

- Since the strategy will not change as it is mathematically defined, is it reasonable to assume that it will still perform adequately when important economic changes occur? When invested in one of these products, reconsider the investment on a period basis given the new market situation. Such products are often "forgotten" in a portfolio. They may not fit the overall strategy any more, or their risk profile has changed and the overall risk in a portfolio is being concentrated instead of being diversified.
- A mathematical trading strategy offered to the wide public usually has small chances of outperforming any other strategy. Too many investors trading it will shrink any "alpha"[15] down to zero. In principle, the author does not believe in systematically applying a derivative strategy without the consideration of the factors that influence the said strategy.
- Also, do not pay too much attention to the fine and glossy back-testing graphics many of these products usually show. Especially, in-sample[16] back-tested products usually show a fine pro-forma "track record", only to disappoint investors after the time they are effectively launched.
- In products without fixed maturity ("open ended" products), the costs inherent to the product have to be considered carefully. Many structured products use either the dividend yield or an interest rate to finance the embedded options. If no maturity has been fixed, then have a close look at the term-sheet where the dividends or interest rate are mentioned and see if it flows back partly or in full into the product and is not kept by the issuer.

## 5.5 CONDITIONAL AND ACCUMULATING COUPONS

### 5.5.1 Conditional coupons

Not all yield enhancement products guarantee the coupons. Some products link the payout of a coupon to a condition. For example, Credit Suisse has established a line of yield enhancement products resembling the callable reverse convertible, but with the coupon at risk. Credit Suisse uses the names Callable *yield* note for the guaranteed coupon products and Callable *return* note in products where the coupon is not guaranteed, but subject to the underlying asset(s) not breaking through a predefined barrier level. The latter structure will

---

[15] The term "Alpha" designates the outperformance a strategy extracts from the market in addition to any performance the market achieves by itself. The market performance is often named "Beta", and anything that a manager achieves above that is called "Alpha". True "Alpha" should be considered risk-adjusted and sustainable.
[16] In-sample back-test designates a performance that has been calculated on a data sample used also to define the strategy itself. In other words, the strategy has been approved as sound based on the good performance it delivered based on the past data. In-sample performances often don't live up to the past when the strategy goes live, "out of sample".

pay a relatively high coupon if the barrier, set well below the spot of the underlying asset(s), is not crossed during the lifetime of the product (American-style barrier). If the barrier is broken, not only does the investor experience a (partial) loss of capital, but the coupon is not paid out as well. Since the coupon is at risk, it is higher than a coupon of a comparable callable yield note. Let's look at a simplified table comparing the products (Table 5.9)

**Table 5.9** Coupon difference example between secure and at risk coupon

| Product | Coupon | Coupon p.a. (*t) |
| --- | --- | --- |
| Callable yield note | Guaranteed | 6% |
| Callable return note | At risk | 9% |

Source: redrawn from an e-mailed product idea from an investment bank (August 2008)

The difference in the coupon may vary according to the volatility, yield and correlation levels.

### 5.5.2  Accumulating coupons

Other products have *accumulating* coupon functions. The payout of the coupons is also linked to a condition, like the crossing of a certain strike at an observation date. If a coupon is missed out, it can be recovered if the condition is met later. The sum of the missed coupons is then paid out together. However, if the condition is never met, then no coupons are paid out at all. The yield curve steepener seen in Table 5.6 is a good example of a cumulating conditional coupon product.

How should an investor choose between a guaranteed and a conditional coupon? All things staying equal, the question could be answered by the investor's dependency on income. Does he need the coupon or can it be put at risk? If the coupon is needed, then better not put it at risk. The temptation to link the payout of a coupon to the barrier can become big if the investor is in any way of the opinion that the barrier will not be breached. The investor has to keep in mind that the actual probability that the underlying asset(s) trades below the barrier is usually larger than he would otherwise estimate, especially if the product features a worst-of option with an American-style barrier.

# 6
## Functionality Options of Structured Products

## 6.1 PHYSICAL OR CASH DELIVERY WITH EQUITY-BASED PRODUCTS

Products like the reverse convertible, the discount certificate, the bonus certificate, or any other product that is based on stocks can have different settlement types, depending on the issuer. For instance, when the barrier of a yield enhancement product has been knocked and the underlying asset's price finishes below the strike at maturity, there can be two possibilities:

- physical delivery (with residual paid out in cash); or
- cash settlement.

Both have the same economic value, but there are still some minor differences.

Physically-settled products deliver the shares only at the product's *redemption* date, which can on occasion be set weeks after the embedded option *expiry* date. Consequently, the investor stays exposed to the stock's risk, but may be unable to sell it, as he does not hold it yet. The drawback comes when the investor's view on the stock changes during the time when the product's option has expired, but the redemption is yet several days or weeks away. During that time, the stock can still lose value and the investor who sells it at the redemption date will trade it at a lesser price than the fixing price of the product's option at its expiry date. The only way to sell the stock would be to arrange a forward sale, which is seldom done for small sizes. This is one potential reason why a cash settlement should be preferred over a physical settlement. It depends on the amount of time the investor is "locked" with the stock at the end of the product's life. Some clients have restricted stock holding clauses, because of local regulations or otherwise. For these investors, a cash settlement is preferable.

Stock-based retail products are typically physically settled, which obviously corresponds to the preferences of the majority of investors. The only reason to choose physical over cash delivery comes from behavioral finance. Some investors have a tendency to not "take the loss" of a product ending with a negative performance, but want to wait until the delivered stock recovers. But since (as a general rule) the stock delivery of a physically-settled product has the same costs as the purchase of new stock position, the same portfolio effect of holding to the loss-bearing stock can be reached by purchasing the amount of stocks that would have been delivered otherwise in a cash settled product. The advantage being that if the investor didn't want to hold on to the loss-bearing stock any more, he would save the costs linked to the selling of that stock in a cash-settled product. Hence, under the mentioned conditions, cash settlement is preferable to physical settlement.

Underlying assets such as indices or commodities are never physically settled, as they cannot be delivered. The same goes for products with quanto options, as it is impossible to deliver a stock with the performance in another currency.

## 6.2   CLEAN PRICE AND DIRTY PRICE

Products featuring a guaranteed coupon may be quoted in two ways in the secondary market:

- clean, *excluding* accrued interest; or
- dirty, *including* accrued interest.

Clean and dirty are expressions that come from fixed income trading. Traders tend to think in terms of clean prices, because a change in the price of a bond then has an economic significance. If the price is dirty, then the price movement may be attributable to the paying of a coupon. It is important to know the difference, especially when considering investing into, selling or comparing a product with another. Most counterparties quote their products clean, but there are exceptions. Some counterparties offer their clients the choice to quote either clean or dirty, mixing their global offering and making comparisons difficult. Table 6.1 shows the quoted price difference of a clean and dirty reverse convertible with six months of accrued interest, a maturity of one year and a coupon level of 7%.

**Table 6.1**   Clean and dirty pricing conventions

| Product | Quotation | Price quote |
|---|---|---|
| Reverse convertible 1 | Clean | 100% |
| Reverse convertible 2 | Dirty | 103.5% |

Both products have the same economic value. Were an investor to buy the clean quoted product, he would still end up paying 103.5% because he has to pay the 3.5% accrued interest. There is no economic advantage for one or the other type of quotation.

## 6.3   LENDING VALUES

Structured products, being securitized and tradable financial instruments, have lending values like any other security. The level is usually determined by the credit department of the bank, and the level varies with the type of product, its maturity, its issuer and the underlying asset. Many products have no standard lending value, due to their exotic nature. Hence, they must be assessed on a case-by-case basis. As a rule, banks differentiate between capital guaranteed products and other products.

### 6.3.1   Capital protected products

The products can be considered relatively safe from a lending point of view if:

- the capital protection is above a certain threshold, say 90%;
- the maturity doesn't exceed a certain maturity, say 5 years;
- the issuer has a good rating, say minimum AA−; and
- the reference currency is any G7 currency.

Products with the above characteristics can be attributed a high lending value. A typical lending value for a product fitting these criteria rests in a range from 70% to 90%. Products with less than the set minimum guarantee are not considered capital guaranteed and fall into yield enhancement or participation category, or are assessed on a case-by-case basis. Capital guaranteed products with currencies (FX) as underlying assets score in the high end of the mentioned range, while equity and commodity products fall in the low end of that range. The level for fixed-income notes depends largely on the maturity and the issuer rating, short-term/high rated issuer products quoting in the high end of the range.

### 6.3.2    Yield enhancement and participation products

For both product categories, which tend to be mingled in the credit department's eyes, the criteria are more asset based. Conditional protection, even deep ones, have little influence over the lending value, as the bank considers worst-case scenarios as generally possible, which is consistent with the principle of prudence. Currency products usually have higher lending values than equities or commodities, ranging from 60% to 80%, because of their inherent lower volatility. For equity-based products, the lending rate is often the same as for the equity itself (50–60%). For equity baskets or equity index-based products, an average level might be in the range of 60–70%. Commodity products may have slightly lower rates, around 50–60%. Note that the 2008 credit crisis may have a restrictive effect on lending values in the future.

### 6.3.3    Lending value as a structuring feature

For an investor, the level of lending value might make a difference in the structuring of a given product. Basically, the investor has the choice between choosing an aggressive structure and a more conservative one plus taking leverage through the lending value of the product.

Suppose, for example, that an investor would like a bonus certificate on the HSI index. The calculations give a structure with 10% bonus level, a barrier at 70% of spot and 100% participation for a 2-year maturity. On the one hand, the investor would like a higher participation, akin to 150%, but on the other, he is loath to either raise the barrier or lower the bonus. Increasing the maturity is out of the question. After asking the credit department, the investment advisor informs the investor that the lending value would be maximum 60% for that structure. The investor chooses to leverage his portfolio to 50%, effectively gaining the wished-for 150% exposure to the HSI index. To generate 150% participation with the product would have meant reducing the bonus to zero and the barrier to 85% of spot, a rather unattractive structure.

Cases of investors leveraging their portfolios are common. By keeping the structure more conservative and leveraging the portfolio instead, part of the risk is shifted from the product to the wealth of the investor. The target upside participation of 150% is reached, the knock-in chances are lower since the barrier stays at 70% of spot, but should it not hold then the investor's loss is leveraged 150%. By adopting such a strategy, the investor risks margin calls and puts more than his total wealth at risk (unless other assets are available). While the wish of investors should be considered, the author generally discourages the use of leverage in a portfolio.

## 6.4  ISSUE MINIMUM/MAXIMUM SIZE AND LIQUIDITY

The size, or volume, of a product, measured in currency which an issuer needs for managing it efficiently, has usually a minimum and a maximum. The minimum is dictated by economics and the maximum (if applicable) by risk. The liquidity is difficult to ascertain for most products.

### 6.4.1  Minimum size

The issuer will only issue a product if it is economically reasonable for him. For most classic products, fixed costs play an important role: listing costs, ticket costs, back-office costs, computer calculation power, etc. determine the minimum amount an issuer will need to issue a product. If the issuer has a fully automated trading – quoting – booking process, the minimum issuing size will be small. It will be further reduced if the issuer's books are large, as some variable costs, such as index-license costs, are diluted.

Certain issuers will issue customized "flow" products such as discount certificates or bonus certificates for as little as CHF 50 000,[1] tendency dropping. Sometimes, issuers also issue products without any volume in order to gain market share, or because they hope for secondary market activity. Other issuers, who have only partially automated processes or a labor-intensive organization, will have much higher required minima going up to CHF 1 million for classical products.

The minimum size for a product therefore varies from issuer to issuer. It is in the investor's interest to subscribe or buy products from issuers who have low fixed and variable costs, as these are reflected in the product's price, all other criteria remaining the same. For instance, comparing two identical products of the reverse convertible type, one from an issuer with fixed costs of CHF 10 000 per issue and another one with negligible costs, will result in 1% less coupon if the issue size is CHF 1 million.

For complex products requiring a certain amount of financial engineering and customized trading, the minimum size may be much higher. Most fixed income products typically need 2–3 million in the reference currency of the product. Products on alternative asset classes like hedge funds[2] or commodities usually need 5–10 million. Finally, customized trading strategies requiring legal setup, new prospectus and complex customized derivatives may require 15–20 million.

### 6.4.2  Maximum size

The maximum volume that an issuer is willing to issue on a single product is determined by the issuer's risk management rules. The size of the product at issue date is written in the term-sheet, but can usually be increased at the leisure of the issuer any time.

An issuer will limit the size of a product when he deems that hedging costs may become too high. Especially for products featuring exotic barriers or digital payoffs, the so-called "gap" risk and potential loss can become unbearable if the liquidity of the underlying asset

---

[1] Or EUR, USD, GBP . . .

[2] While structured products on alternative asset classes like hedge funds and funds-of-hedge funds have been popular for some years, the author discourages such investments, mainly because of liquidity, transparency and cost reasons.

is low or deteriorates. Let's quickly remember how the hedging of a product functions. The product, a barrier reverse convertible on Sulzer Namen (a Swiss small cap stock), has an initial volume and delta of CHF 10 million and 40% respectively. This means that the issuer will buy the equivalent volume for CHF 4 million of Sulzer shares in the market. Sulzer daily volume expressed in CHF averages at around CHF 30 million per day. So the initial hedge already sums up to 13% of total daily volume. The issuer will buy more shares as the delta increases and sell them when it declines. Suppose now that, shortly prior to maturity, Sulzer trades close to the barrier, and that the delta rises to 200%.[3] The trader should hold for CHF 20 million worth of Sulzer shares. Now suddenly the shares recover and the delta of the product quickly falls back to 50%: the issuer has to sell CHF 15 million worth of stock within a fraction of a day! In such a situation, where 50% of the total daily volume is thrown into the market, the issuer might effectively provoke a "knock-out" of the option by moving the market himself. Should he do that, the delta of the product would immediately move back up to 100% once the option is "knocked", and the issuer should again buy CHF 5 million of stock, re-raising the price of the market and resulting in trading losses for the issuer as well as frustration for the investor. Figure 6.1 illustrates this example.

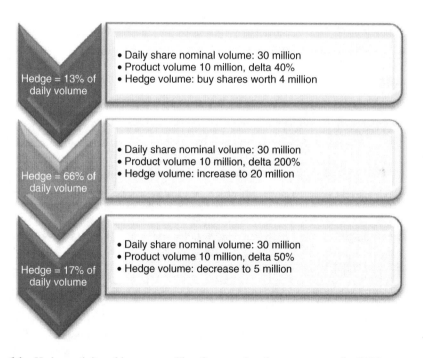

**Figure 6.1**   Hedge activity of issuers resulting from stock price movements (in CHF)

Hence, the issuer's risk management systems limit the maximum size to be issued according to the expected liquidity of the underlying asset. Other factors, like total trading book

---

[3] Deltas can rise above 100% when the underlying asset trades near the barrier and close to maturity of the option, see Section 4.3 for further details.

size and the knowledge of the existence of other barrier or digital products on the same asset with similar maturities might further influence the maximum volume of a product. Once a product is at full capacity, it is closed for new investments, and the issuer may quote a bid price only.

Some product types, like participation products without optionality, may have no limited size, as the hedging risk for the issuer is limited.

It becomes clear with the above example that a structured product is by no means a done deal for an issuer. The trading and hedging activities of the issuer must be correctly set up and professionally executed during the whole life of the product. Of course, the issuer expects to earn money on any structured products deal, but he cannot be certain of doing so at the issue date. In fact, with growing competition and the commoditization of some product types, the margins have become so slim that some issuers prefer to stay on the sidelines for "flow" products and concentrate on more complex or captive structures to generate their profit.

### 6.4.3  Liquidity

Liquidity has been a source of frustration for many investors. Fortunately, it has increased to an acceptable level in the recent past with more and more products listed on electronic exchanges. In Switzerland, Scoach, the exchange for securitized derivative products, and the Euwax in Stuttgart, Germany, had over 5000 and 160 000 (!) products listed as at end of April 2008 respectively, not including leverage products like warrants. A large part of the issues remains as private placements, however. The spreads on the products vary from country to country and from issuer to issuer. In Switzerland, the quoted bid–ask spread for most products amounts to 1%, but recently some issuers began to quote at 0.5%. In Germany, it ranges from 1% to as low as 0.1%, making the trading for some instruments worthwhile. These low spreads are only valid for small sizes, however. Larger sizes typically have larger spreads; small trades are often not hedged by traders, because most of the time one trade will negate another from a hedging point of view. The larger and broader the trading book, the less the trader will need to hedge, and the tighter he can quote the spreads. A large deal, on the other hand, is less likely to be matched by another, similar trade. Hence, the trader must hedge the deal in the market and here the much larger bid–ask spread of the volatility of the underlying asset is relevant.[4] The trader will quote the deal at either bid or ask volatility, depending on the side of the deal, but in any case, the spread is likely to be much larger than 0.1%, because his hedge costs will be defined by the larger spread.

The liquidity is in any case dependent on the issuer, since only the issuer will quote prices in the secondary market. This raises the question of price fairness. How can it be ascertained that the price of any given product is fairly quoted? This may prove difficult even for professionals. As already stated, there is no one "fair" price for all practitioners together. A price may seem fair to a trader but unfair to an investor. In addition, a price may seem fair to one trader but unfair to another, as their view on the price determination factors of the product differ. One way for the investor to get information about prices is to examine their

---

[4] The bid–ask spread in the option market is often quoted in volatility points. Even "liquid" listed options on indices like the Eurostoxx50 have a volatility spread ranging between 0.25% and 2% depending on strike and maturity. Translated into price bid–ask spread this amounts to roughly 2%, which is far wider than on the relevant future whose spread quotes at 0.02%.

"aggressiveness" in comparing a product from one issuer to similar products from others. Some structured products-related internet sites[5] help the investor to compare products of the same type. The comparison should be carefully studied, since a small difference in a single parameter might influence the price substantially. For instance, if the maturity of one product differs just a few weeks from another otherwise identical product, it might be that just in that time window a company pays a dividend, or an important economic decision is expected. The price comparison must then consider that fact.

For very large issues, say CHF 10 million and more, it is sometimes possible for a private banking or other buy-side representative talking to their sell-side investment banking counterparts to obtain bids for products being issued by other issuers. Suppose Issuer A has sold to Buyer X a product. After some time, Buyer X would like to sell the product back to Issuer A. For various reasons, both parties cannot agree to the price of the product. Buyer X may solicit prices from Issuer B or Issuer C to buy Issuer's A product. As long as the trader of Issuer B or C is happy to take Issuer's A credit risk on their books, they will quote a price to Buyer X, as long as the size is interesting enough for them. Let it be said that this "sell-back" competitive bidding process is rare, complex and time consuming. A lot of misprice feeling must be present to initiate, let alone conclude, it.

To summarize, the investor should take heed of the liquidity issue especially if his intention is to trade the product prior to its maturity. A comparison of the most common flow products for price fairness and spreads can be undertaken, but small details may become important. If the intention is to buy and hold until maturity, liquidity is of less importance.

## 6.5   FUNDING RATES AND COUNTERPARTY/CREDIT RISK

### 6.5.1   The issuer's funding rate

The funding rate, which is the rate at which an issuer refinances himself in the inter-bank market, has already been mentioned. The funding rate is essential in structured products, because it influences the yield of the bond component within a product. In a sense, the funding rate reflects the credit risk of the issuer, which in turn the investor perceives as the counterparty risk. Similar to fiduciary deposits, the investor bears the risk of the issuer going broke. Consequently, it is advisable to diversify the issuers in a portfolio.

By way of example, on 23 April 2008, in the midst of the subprime crisis, the author received from an American investment bank the following offer for a EUR curve steepener (see Table 6.2):

"For investors who expect a steeper EUR curve in the medium to long term, this simple trade idea now looks very attractive. The 15 year notes offers a high fixed coupon in the first 5 years, then a variable coupon of 3% *plus* leveraged exposure to the 2Y−10Y spread.

Please find below indicative terms *with a choice of issuers*."

Note that the author would not recommend a 15-year product in the first place, but this example shows how strongly the price of a product is influenced by the funding rate of the issuer. The coupon differences resulting from the different issuer are written in bold

---

[5] See Appendix G: issuer and product related websites.

**Table 6.2**  Indicative terms for a yield curve steepener with issuers of different ratings

| Issuer: | American investment bank[6] (Aa3/AA−) | European bank (Aa2/AA−) |
|---|---|---|
| Currency: | EUR | EUR |
| Coupon: | Y 1–5: **7%** | Y 1–5: **6.5%** |
| | Y 6–15: 3% **+10** × (10Y EUR CMS – 2Y EUR CMS), floored at zero | Y 6–15: 3% + **7** × (10Y EUR CMS – 2Y EUR CMS), floored at zero |
| Redemption at Maturity: | 100% | 100% |
| Maturity: | [ ] May 2023 | [ ] May 2023 |
| Issue Date: | [ ] May 2008 | [ ] May 2008 |
| Distribution: | Private placement only | Private placement only |

Source: own representation, redrawn from an investment bank e-mail offer

characters. The rating of the American issuer wasn't particularly low, although it was on negative watch from the rating agencies. But as of April 2008 in the subprime crisis, the funding rate of American investment banks were skyrocketing at Libor +100 up to +400, while some European banks still had funding rates of "only" Libor +30 or +50. Later in the crisis, the European banks also experienced rates of +100 to +400. The example shows that purely this factor is responsible for a fixed coupon difference for the 5 first years of 0.5% per annum (!) and a leverage difference of ×3 on the steepness of the EUR curve in the years 6 to 15.

Another even more striking example appeared just one day later, 24 April 2008, from another American investment bank, this time in grid form on callable daily range accruals:[7]

"LIBOR Range Accrual

Coupon is paid semi-annually, 30/360

Coupon is paid for the days when the 6-month LIBOR stays within the specified range

Callable semi-annually after one year"

Here as well, the choice of the issuer is essential for the investor: for a 7-year CDRAN with a 0% to 6% range, the difference in the coupon amounts to 1.65% per annum from "best" to "worst" issuer. Even more so, the differences between the two "best" AAA-rated issuers, US agencies[8] and the European bank, are still large, amounting to 0.26% per annum (Table 6.3).

Two conclusions can be drawn from these examples:

- Always be aware that the investor bears the risk of the issuer. When facing a decision whether to invest in a product or not, the credit – or counterparty – risk weighs heavier the longer the maturity of the product.

---

[6] Name of the issuer known to the author.

[7] See the complete product description on page 177.

[8] i.e. SLMA or Federal Home Loan Bank.

**Table 6.3**  Indicative terms for a range accrual with issuers of different ratings

| Issuer: | US Agencies (AAA) | | | American investment bank[9] (A1/A+) | | | European bank (AAA/Aaa) | | |
|---|---|---|---|---|---|---|---|---|---|
| Ranges | 0% – 6% | 0% – 6.5% | 0% – 7% | 0% – 6% | 0% – 6.5% | 0% – 7% | 0% – 6% | 0% – 6.5% | 0% – 7% |
| 7 year maturity Non-call 1 year | 5.85% | 5.34% | 5.00% | 7.50% | 6.85% | 6.41% | 6.11% | 6.74% | 5.22% |
| 10 year maturity Non-call 1 year | 7.24% | 6.48% | 5.93% | 9.24% | 8.27% | 7.56% | 7.53% | 6.76% | 6.17% |
| 15 year maturity Non-call 1 year | 8.89% | 7.81% | 7.01% | 11.27% | 9.91% | 8.90% | 9.19% | 8.10% | 7.28% |

Source: own representation, redrawn from an investment bank e-mail offer

- When asking several counterparties for prices on a given structure,[10] bear in mind that the possible price difference of the product given by the issuers can result purely from their funding level disparity and, hence, that the cheapest price is not often the best price if the counterparty risk is taken into account.

Today, funding rates have not only an impact on primary product prices, but also on the secondary market. The current funding rate of an issuer will be applied to all the products already issued, adjusting the price accordingly. Before the subprime crisis, this was not the case: all secondary market products were priced "Libor flat", meaning that the funding rate was only of relevance for the construction of the product, but afterwards the bid and ask prices were not "shifted" according to the funding rate the issuer's treasurer would apply. Note that, until the subprime crisis, the funding rate differences were also much smaller – give or take a few basis points for the major issuers – and had lower impacts on the price of products as a consequence. As the subprime crisis distorted their funding rates, some issuers had to scramble to update their secondary market prices. Some had this factor included in their models and the process went on smoothly. Others didn't and the representatives had to ask tradable prices at their trading desk per phone for every single trade, resulting in hectic trading, backlogs and disgruntled investors who had to wait for hours to get a trade executed, most of the time in a falling market. The price they got for their product was, of course, below their expectation because of the worse funding rate, adding to their frustration. The fact is, none of the investors were aware that the issuer's risk would take such large proportions, the issuers themselves weren't. What's for sure is that, before the subprime crisis, the investors were not or too little compensated for the counterparty risk they were taking, but now at least that risk is fairly priced into the products.

### 6.5.2  The counterparty/credit risk

What happens when an issuer declares bankruptcy? The recent case of the Lehman Brothers failure illustrates the effects on structured products. The first immediate consequence is the

---

[9] Name of the issuer known to the author.

[10] Procedure normally known as "competitive bidding", which is in a way similar to tendering.

inability to trade products. As soon as the firm was put under creditors' protection, all trading stopped. This was not only true for structured products, but also for OTCs, swaps, equities, bonds, accounts, etc. The second effect was the nomination of an administrator (in Lehman's case, PricewaterhouseCoopers, PWC) to take over control, thus changing the contact person for external business partners. An investor calling or mailing Lehman for information about a product was told that PWC would answer questions in the future. Lehman specialists (and indeed all employees) were forbidden to send out any communication. The third effect was that all securitized products were mingled with the rest of the assets that Lehman held. In the liquidation process, the ranking of the structured products was equal to senior unsecured bonds. For a product holder, this means that the value of his product is linked to the recovery value of the defaulted bonds. In the case of Lehman, that value was estimated at 60% in the first days after the bankruptcy declaration, but fell to ca. 20% and then < 10% in the following weeks. It will probably take years for PWC to settle all the claims and reimburse the product holders with a fraction of the worth the products would have otherwise.

Table 6.4 summarizes the ranking of structured products in the case of bankruptcy of a bank or a broker.

**Table 6.4**  Ranking of debt claims in case of bankruptcy (in Switzerland[11])

| 1st category | Administrator's expenses |
| | Salaries and insurance of employees |
| | Pensions |
| 2nd category | Social security |
| | Client's money on accounts (up to a certain maximal amount, varies by country) |
| | Private pension holdings |
| 3rd category | Senior unsecured bonds |
| | *Structured products* |
| | Loans |
| | Taxes |
| 4th category | Subordinated bonds |
| | Other subordinated debt |
| 5th category | Shareholders |

Source: Swiss Debt Enforcement and Bankruptcy Law (SchKG)

What can an investor do when he holds a product from a counterparty that fails? There are not many possibilities: either hold on to it until the recovery value is determined and paid back, or try to sell his product to other issuers willing to take the risk of the bankrupt firm. Needless to say, the price at which a third party is willing to take a bankrupt firm's paper is often way below the mark-to-market price it should have in normal conditions. With Lehman Brothers products, the few counterparties giving quotes indicated prices at around 15% of nominal value as of September 2008.

A major consequence of Lehman's demise is the loss of confidence by investors in structured products worldwide. From the beginning of the subprime crisis that evolved in a global

---

[11] The ranking may vary for other legislations. Different kinds of bankruptcy may lead to restructuring rather than liquidation of the assets.

credit crunch, many banks were fighting for sheer survival and had to be supported massively by central banks or were crash-sold to more solid financial institutes. Even rock-solid (it was thought) banks like Citigroup, UBS and Goldman Sachs had eventually to be kept afloat by government funds and/or guarantees. When whole economies like Iceland had to be nationalized and decades-old money houses like Citigroup, Fortis, RBS or Dexia were put under the umbrella of the state, investors' trust in banks was nigh zero. Who would now purchase a 5-year capital guaranteed product if the capital guarantee was linked to the issuer? Only two years ago,[12] the author received multiple comments from high-level bank managers that the dividend yield of some banks was quasi as certain as the coupons of government bonds (!). Now, banks that have accepted taxpayers' money are forced to diminish or skip dividend payments altogether, at least until they repay the government's funds. The main concern for the investor, the issuer's bankruptcy, will stay for years in investors' minds. Hence, banks must find a practical way to separate the issuer's risk from the products, analog to funds, which are protected in case the depositary bank fails. This can be achieved in several ways:

*SPV:* the issuer can create a Special Purpose Vehicle and fully fund the structure. The issuer risk would be solved, but other problems with this structure arise: high minimum volume, non-transparent and little trusted construction etc.

*Structured funds:* the structured products can be replicated in a fund structure, which protects the investor from the issuer's default. The problem here would be the single components within the fund, which are usually based on swaps. Costs are another weak point of these heavy structures.

*Global guarantee fund:* if all the major issuers were to create a guarantee fund whose sole purpose was to uphold the value of the products in case one of the issuers went broke, a major step would be accomplished in terms of regaining investors' confidence. It would be cheap, practical, global and recognized. Issuers, unite!

---

[12] September 2006.

# 7

# Foreign Exchange, Fixed Income and Commodity Products

## 7.1 FX-BASED STRUCTURES

Foreign exchange is the market where many exotic options were developed. Therefore, many options that have appeared in equity products only recently have been used in the FX market for much longer. A whole book by itself would be necessary to describe all the options that could be embedded into an FX-structured product. Although professionals use all kind of currency options,[1] structured products for private clients have had a less broad evolution, the main trend being concentrated on a few products which are being presented in this section. The focus will principally be on capital guaranteed and yield enhancement products.

Three attributes of the foreign exchange market make it attractive for investments in structured products:

1. It is the most liquid market in the world.
2. The spreads are minimal.
3. The volatility can be very low, at least when comparing it to equities.

This combination of attributes makes possible, for instance, very short maturity capital guaranteed products, which is not – or only seldom – viable in equities or commodities.

Although currencies and exchange rates are well known to investors, they are not always recognized as an asset class. There are, however, some arguments for considering them at a similar level as bonds or equities. The first and strongest argument is diversification. In a nutshell, an asset is of use to a portfolio if it has an expected return that is at least as high as a risk-free investment, and is not perfectly correlated with other assets (Woo, Koeva and Siourounis, 2006). FX does yield an interest (the interest rate differential between one currency and another), and is not correlated to a high degree to other asset classes. The second argument derives from the market characteristics: FX is one of the two markets (with fixed income) where trends are observable. This, a rather technical argument, opens to investors the opportunity to profit from those trends. The reasons behind the trends can all be different: political will to stabilize, appreciate or depreciate a currency against another one; hedging currency risk by industrial global players having a steady export or income stream of goods to or from a foreign country; or macroeconomic situations like trade surpluses or deficits. Many of the actors in the FX market are not trading for profit; as mentioned, a central bank may have an interest to support or depreciate its currency against another one. The central bank may not do this to make a profit, and it may even provoke an

---

[1] Mostly to hedge the value of an investment or of a production in a foreign country, e.g. Daimler hedging the USD revenues from its automobile sales in the USA.

artificial discrepancy between the two currencies. A sound strategy by the means of options, forwards or structured products is able to profit from this state.

As such, structured products, which base a strategy on the probable future evolution of foreign exchange rates between currencies, can be placed at the same level as products on equities, fixed income and commodities.

### 7.1.1 Conventions

It is always difficult for non-FX specialists to get used to the FX conventions. FX is the only asset class where basic options are priced on two assets: the reference currency and the alternative currency. As a result, a call on the reference currency equals to a put on the alternative currency. For instance, an EUR/USD call would be equivalent to a USD/EUR put. This may seem trivial to some, but to others it is not so obvious.

Suppose an investor's reference currency is the EUR. He is bullish on the USD and buys the greenback. The EUR quotes at 1.58 against the USD, meaning one EUR buys 1.58 USD.[2] Should that number become larger or smaller for him to make a profit? While some people will know immediately, others will struggle with pen and paper to come up with an answer. Another easier way to put the question would be whether the EUR has to rise or fall against the USD for him to make a profit. Of course, the EUR should fall, and the number 1.58 should fall as well, since to take his profit the investor will have to sell the USD back for Euros. The lower the number, the more EUR he can buy back with one USD. It becomes more complicated because of the quoting conventions. Americans have the tendency to quote everything from a USD perspective: the EUR/USD 1.58 from above becomes USD/EUR 0.6329, while Europeans quote most currencies from an EUR point of view. This can unsettle investors who sometimes see the quote and sometimes its reverse. The convention adopted here is the European one, where all currencies are quoted against the Euro with the exception of the USD.

The investor's main currency, which denotes the one in which the investor is based, will be called "reference" currency hereafter. The second currency will be called the "alternate" currency.

### 7.1.2 Theoretical and practical background

Current and future exchange rates are essentially influenced by the interest rates and inflation of the relevant economies. Irving Fisher described the equilibrium between exchange rates with the covered and uncovered interest rate parity, the latter being known as the International Fisher Effect. Aside from inflation effects, the *uncovered interest rate parity* in particular is quite significant for structuring currency products.

- The covered interest rate parity implies that an investment in a foreign currency, with concurrent hedging against exchange-rate risks, generates the same return as an investment in the domestic currency.
- The uncovered interest rate parity implies that if money is borrowed in countries with low interest rates and invested in countries with high ones, exchange-rate movements will effectively equalize the returns. In theory at least, this refutes the efficiency of carry trades.

---

[2] That was pretty close to the high the EUR reached against the USD in 2008.

In practice, neither the covered nor the uncovered interest rate parity holds. The above-mentioned carry trades, which are strategies that borrow in a low-yielding currency (i.e. the Japanese Yen or the Swiss Franc) and invest in high-yielding ones (i.e. the Euro or the USD, but also the Mexican Peso or the Russian Ruble) have been profitable investments for years, at least until the credit crisis came along in late 2008.

What is important for the investor to understand is that certain FX pairs, like those of the G7, have very low volatilities when compared to other asset classes like equities. Hence, it is possible to buy options at seemingly very low prices. Which product category needs low volatility to be structured efficiently? Capital guaranteed products. Moreover, the nominal interest rate differential between these currencies can offer very appealing opportunities to structure capital guaranteed products. If the yield of the reference currency is higher than the yield of the second currency, the forward price of the second currency will be much lower. Any at-the-money spot call will be considered as out-of-the-money forward by the trader's model and consequently cheap. Hence, since some FX calls have very low value due to low volatility and yield differential, very short-term capital guaranteed products could be structured.

FX is maybe the only asset class where 3-month capital guarantee products can be efficiently constructed. All other asset classes would require at least 1-year maturity. The investor considering an FX capital guaranteed structure should have the following risk-return profile:

- short term risk-averse;
- target holding period: 3 to 18 months;
- target (expected) return: X times the risk-free money-market rate, where X should lie between 1.5 and 2. Above 2, the probability of really getting the expected return drops dramatically, as the option must generate too much value for the little amount of time available and risks ending out-of the money because of too tight ranges or knock-out events.

Thus, the reasons for investing into FX capital guaranteed products are their features of full capital guarantee combined with low maturities on an asset class, which has the highest possible liquidity.[3]

### 7.1.3 FX tower note

*Description*

A tower note is a short-term capital guaranteed product, which is suitable for use as a money-market replacement. Typical tenors have a time-span of between three and 12 months. The payoff of the tower note is as follows.

At maturity, 100% of the capital is redeemed in the tower note reference currency, plus:

- a high coupon (i.e. twice the risk-free rate) if a currency pair (i.e. the EUR/USD) stayed within a certain range during the tenor;
- only a minimum or no coupon at all if the range was broken at any time during the lifetime.

---

[3] FX options have the tightest bid–ask spread of all asset classes.

A tower note is constructed with a double no-touch option on the exchange rate of the selected currency pair plus a money-market investment in the reference currency. The yield of the money market[4] serves to purchase the option. The double no touch option has two barriers, one above and the other below the current spot rate, which form the range. The option expires worthless if one of the barriers is touched during the lifetime of the option.

*Market expectation and risk*

The ideal scenario for implementing a tower note is a highly volatile environment in a currency pair where the volatility is expected to decrease and the exchange-rate fluctuations to remain range bound during the lifetime of the product. The main risk resides in unforeseen erratic exchange-rate movements: a single trade outside of the range will engender the second scenario with lower or no coupon payout.[5] Apart from the credit default of the issuer, the only risk incurred by the investor is the payout of a lower or no coupon at all. A tower note is therefore a fairly conservative instrument, whose aim is usually to enhance the yield of a short-term bond or money market portfolio.

*Example*

In the following example (Table 7.1), a 6-month 100% capital guaranteed tower note on the EUR/USD pays a coupon that is slightly less than double the 6-month Libor if the range is not broken and a minimum coupon of 1% p.a. otherwise.

**Table 7.1**  Example of an FX tower note product

| | |
|---|---|
| **Reference currency** | EUR |
| **Underlying exchange rate** | EUR/USD exchange rate |
| **Tenor** | 6 months |
| **Lower/upper range** | 1.5400–1.6200 |
| **Max coupon (p.a.)** | 7% (3.5% bullet) |
| **Min coupon (p.a.)** | 1% (0.5% bullet) |
| **Spot exchange rate** | 1.5800 |
| **6-month EURibor (p.a.)** | 4% (2% bullet) |

Figure 7.1 shows the returns on a 6-month basis, while the terms in Table 7.1 are based on annualized numbers. It is standard practice in the structured products industry to write numbers in annualized terms and show them graphically in absolute terms based on the tenor for short-term investments of less than one year.

In this example, it becomes clear why an FX tower note can be an alternative to a money-market investment. The capital is not at risk; only the yield can be either (quasi) doubled or entirely lost. The chance of receiving the higher coupon is a function of the width of the range and the time to maturity:

- The narrower the range, the lower the chance of a high coupon, due to the increased hit probability.

---

[4] Or part of it if the product pays a minimum coupon.
[5] Unless the range is constructed with European style barriers and the exchange rate fixes within the range at maturity. European range barriers are seldom used, though.

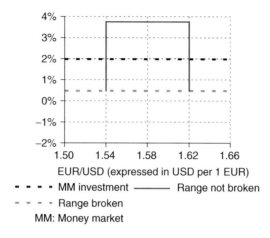

**Figure 7.1**  Payoff 39: FX tower note payoff example (double no touch)

- The longer the tenor, the lower the chance of a high coupon, due to the increased hit probability.

In addition, a high volatility will provide for large ranges.

*Dos & don'ts*

- Don't let the goal of the instrument get out of sight. If it's a money-market replacement type of goal, fix the product parameters accordingly. Trying to get four times the risk-free rate is not a money-market type of return. The high coupon will seem very attractive, but its chances of being paid at maturity will decrease considerably.
- Try a version where only one (upper or lower) barrier is embedded in the product: it would suit the view that a breakout in one direction is unlikely but still possible, while in the other it's quite certain that no break will occur. The product becomes a one-touch note (Figure 7.2).

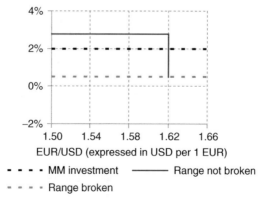

**Figure 7.2**  Payoff 40: Example of FX one-touch note

- Go for several short-term towers over a single one with longer maturity and multiple ranges that widen with time but do not reset the barriers around the spot. After each expiry, don't just roll the product into a new one, but reassess the situation.
- If the volatility is really high, expected to decrease and the investment horizon is longer than six months, use a longer-term product that resets the ranges on a monthly or quarterly basis around the spot. The product will profit from the lower volatility in the later months of its lifetime.
- Try using European-style barriers. The coupons will be considerably lower when compared to American-style barriers, but a spike in the exchange rate in one or the other direction with ensuing normalization will not annihilate the high coupon. Again, if the goal is money-market plus, maximize the chances of getting the high coupon, even if this means reducing its level to a few dozen pips over the risk-free rate. Always keep in mind the opportunity costs (i.e. Libor) and define the potential coupon accordingly.
- If European-style barriers diminish the maximum coupon by too much, try using central bank fixings instead. These fixings occur once a day and limit intraday risk. In the case of the example of Table 7.1, the central bank fixing would be that of the ECB.

### 7.1.4  FX (daily) range accruals

*Description*

Range accruals are better known in the interest rate structuring world, but widely used in the FX space as well. The difference is that when structured with an FX pair, these products usually have a short tenor, whereas interest rate range accruals are mostly long term.

FX range accruals are capital protected products similar to tower notes, but which pay a coupon whose level depends on the number of successful fixings. A successful fixing occurs if the underlying FX pair's exchange rate fixes within certain boundaries (ranges). When the observations are made daily,[6] the name of the product becomes an FX daily range accrual.

The product's maximum coupon is defined at inception and is reduced by fixings that occur outside of the range. The coupon calculation formula is:

$$\text{Coupon} = \text{Max coupon} * \frac{\text{Number of fixings within the range}}{\text{Number of total fixings}}$$

The variations of the FX range accrual are manifold. The range can have two boundaries, one upper and one lower, or only one (either above or below). It can feature a knock-out, after which the product's coupon doesn't accrue any more, even if the spot fixes again within the range. The range can remain constant or increase at predefined intervals. It can feature a reset of the range based on the spot after a predefined period. Alternatively, the coupon paid after each period can be a function of the previous coupon (ratchet feature).

*Market expectation and risk*

As with the tower note, the investor should expect a range bound exchange rate and possibly lower volatility. The risk of the FX range accrual is very low, because the probability of

---

[6] The great majority of the products have daily observations. See also CDRANs in Section 7.2.4.

the exchange rate staying within the predefined range in the beginning of the life of the product is high. Unless a dramatic unforeseen event leads to a breakout of the predefined boundaries shortly after the product's launch, a minimum coupon will always be paid out. The FX range accrual is less path-dependent than the tower note. All other things staying equal, a range accrual will feature a lower maximum coupon than a tower note due to the digital nature of the latter.

*Example*

A classical example of an FX range accrual to illustrate the payoff is shown in Table 7.2. It features a 90-day 100% capital guaranteed product with the EUR/USD as the underlying exchange rate, which pays a 1.58% maximum coupon if all the daily fixings occur within a range between 1.4500 and 1.5500 (0.0175% per day). The spot is currently at 1.5000, and an equivalent risk-free rate would yield 1.00%.

**Table 7.2**  Example of an FX range accrual product

| | |
|---|---|
| **Reference currency** | EUR |
| **Underlying exchange rate** | EUR/USD |
| **Tenor** | 3 months |
| **Lower/upper range** | 1.5500–1.4500 |
| **Max coupon (p.a.)** | 6.3% (1.58% bullet) |
| **Min coupon (p.a.)** | 0% |
| **Spot exchange rate** | 1.5000 |
| **6-month EURibor (p.a.)** | 4% (1% bullet) |

The payoff diagram of an FX range accrual is seldom represented otherwise than by an example of the FX pair trading in and out of the range with the according coupon calculation. This variant is illustrated in Figure 7.3, where the level of the coupon is shown as a function of the number of days the fixings remain within the range. The capital, which is paid back at maturity, is not shown on this representation.

The left-hand graphic shows a hypothetical EUR/USD exchange rate from the launch of the product until maturity. In this example, the fixings inside the range amounted to 56 days out of 90. The coupon paid out at maturity thus totaled:

$$\text{Coupon} = 1.58 \ * \ \frac{56}{90} = 0.9833\%$$

The right-hand graph reveals the number of days the fixings need to be within the range for the product to break even with a riskless money-market instrument. At close to 60 days, this represents two-thirds of the total time. The example nearly misses that number, which is in fact quite representative of the average FX range accrual. As mentioned, the first weeks practically always fix within the range, thus guaranteeing a minimal coupon, but afterwards, the drift of the exchange rate usually comes close to either the upper or the lower boundary, and then it's more a matter of chance than of forecast skill.

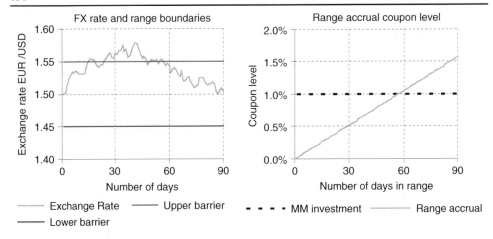

**Figure 7.3**  Payoff 41: FX range accrual payoff example

*Dos & don'ts*

- As FX is one of the few markets where trends can be empirically observed and traded (the other one being interest rates), use sloping barriers corresponding to the slope of the exchange rate trend. Use a regression analysis if necessary. This system will lower the chances of fixings occurring out of the range because of the drift of the trend.
- Don't try to play a trend reversal with an FX range accrual. It's the wrong instrument for such a strategy.

### 7.1.5   FX emerging market (EM) currency notes

It has been mentioned that G7 currency pairs have a relatively low volatility. In contrast, EM currencies have much higher volatilities. However, some EM currencies also have much higher yields compared to the highest yielding G7 currencies. Remember that at-the-money spot call options are cheaper the higher the yield differential of the currency pair, if the call is on the higher yielding currency. It is worthwhile explaining the reasoning behind this fact before elaborating on the possible FX EM structures in which an investor could invest.

*Carry trades*

An EM currency yield curve often trades at a higher level than one of the G7 countries, which means that placements in the former often produce better returns compared to placements in the latter. A carry trade exploits this rate difference by borrowing cheap money in Switzerland (CHF) or Japan (JPY) and placing it, for example, in Turkey (TRY) or Brazil (BRL) to generate a higher return.

This effect would be theoretically neutralized by a decline in the TRY and BRL exchange rates against the CHF. However, the picture is rather different in practice. Over the past few years, the TRY has been stable against the CHF, and the BRL has actually appreciated substantially. Other EM currencies show a similar picture.

*Impact on options: BRL/CHF example*

Figure 7.4 shows the exact same information in different forms. The left-hand chart plots the CHF/BRL forward. The slope of the curve is rising, which means that the market expects the BRL to weaken against the CHF; the investor may change CHF 1.0000 today for BRL 1.7400, or agree to a forward trade and receive BRL 1.9600 for the same CHF 1.0000 in 18 months. It is counter-intuitive for most equity investors to look at a rising curve that implies that the risky asset (here the BRL) is *weakening*. A more intuitive forward shape would be the one plotted in the figure on the right-hand side, which shows a BRL/CHF spot rate of 0.5750 and a forward rate of 0.5100. Here, the view is taken that an investor would have to spend CHF 0.5750 today to buy BRL 1.000 or that he needs only spend CHF 0.5100 for BRL 1.0000 if he agrees today to make the deal in 18 months. However, FX conventions have adopted the CHF/BRL standard. The BRL/CHF forward is lower due to the International Fisher Effect.

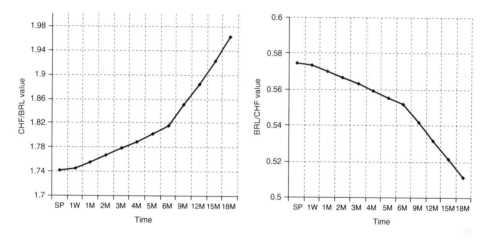

**Figure 7.4**   CHF/BRL (left) and BRL/CHF (right) forward curve

As a result, CHF/BRL at-the-money spot call options are very cheap. These call options bet on the BRL *strengthening* against the CHF (e.g. on the spot rate being lower than 1.7400 in 18 months' time). Yet the model calculating the option is based on the forward exchange rate, which is already at 1.9600 in 18 months (Table 7.3). Based on this information, the model assumes that the exercise price fixed on the spot rate at issue will be significantly out-of-the-money at expiry, and that the option has therefore high chances to expire worthless.

**Table 7.3**   The effect of forward rates on FX options

| Currency pairs | ATM spot option | 18 month forward | Premium |
| --- | --- | --- | --- |
| **CHF/BRL** | Call | 1.96 | 1.8% |
| **CHF/BRL** | Put | 1.96 | 9% |

By contrast, a put option on the BRL is extremely expensive because of the reverse logic.

*Examples of structured products*

Since investments in EM currencies carry a certain risk, the corresponding products are mostly structured with capital protection in the reference currency of the investor. The low call option costs allow short tenors with 100% capital protection at maturity and participation rates of 100% or even higher.

Three products with EM currencies as underlying assets and capital protection are considered in more detail below.

**Example 1:** Figure 7.5 is a popular payoff diagram of an emerging market currency note. The example used is an EUR/BRL with a maturity of 18 months.

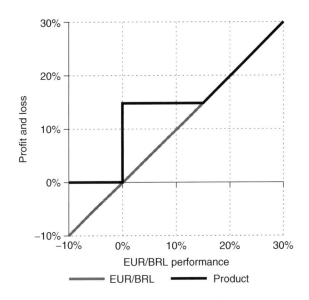

**Figure 7.5**   Payoff 42: example of digital emerging market currency note

**Table 7.4**   Digital emerging market currency note components

| Component | Approx. value | Effect |
|---|---|---|
| **Zero-coupon bond** | 94% | Guarantees the capital in EUR at maturity |
| **Digital call** | 5% | Pays 15% coupon if the BRL appreciates by a single pip against the EUR at maturity |
| **OTM plain vanilla call (strike 115%)** | 1% | Provides the upside participation for an appreciation of the BRL above 15% |

Source: Own calculations

The capital protection is guaranteed using an EUR-denominated zero-coupon bond. The product's positive performance is guaranteed by the use of digital and normal EUR/BRL call options. If the value of the BRL only rises minimally against the EUR at expiry, the digital option pays out a predefined premium, for example 15% as represented. An additional call option that is substantially out-of-the-money (usually set at 100% plus the level of the coupon, here 15%) ensures the extra participation in a positive exchange rate movement that would be higher than the digital option payout.

---

**Example 2:** instead of a digital option, a leveraged ratio of call options can also be bought on a currency. With this method, the participation in any outperformance of the BRL against the EUR rises above 100% (e.g. 200% as represented in Figure 7.6 and Table 7.5).

---

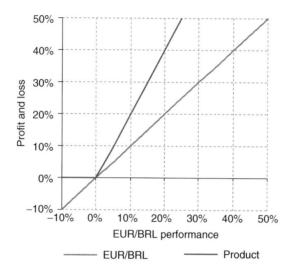

**Figure 7.6**   Payoff 43: example of leveraged emerging market currency note

**Table 7.5**   Leveraged emerging market currency note components

| Component | Approx. value | Effect |
|---|---|---|
| **Zero-coupon bond** | 94% | Guarantees the capital in EUR at maturity |
| **Call ratio (200%)** | 2×3% | Provides the 200% participation to the BRL appreciation against the EUR |

---

**Example 3:** another interesting structure pays a fixed coupon on a selected basket of currencies for every currency that outperforms the reference currency. The coupon is increased for each additional currency that posts a positive performance. This structure is usually called a "podium" note.

---

The following payoff (Figure 7.7) gives an example of five emerging market currencies against the EUR with a 2-year maturity. Imagine a basket consisting of Turkish Lira,

Mexican Peso, Indian Rupee, Indonesian Rupiah and Russian Ruble. If none of the mentioned currencies appreciates against the reference currency, i.e. the EUR, then only the capital is paid back at maturity. If one currency appreciates, then a 5% coupon is paid in addition to the capital. If two currencies appreciate, the coupon increases to 10%, and so on.

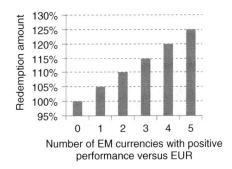

**Figure 7.7**   Payoff 44: example of a podium note

*Impact factors in EM currency pricing*

To illustrate the impact of the interest rate differential and volatility on product conditions, four new capital guaranteed structures are considered, this time with the CHF as reference currency (Table 7.6). All have a maturity of two years and have full capital protection at maturity as well as 100% participation above the digital call level.

**Table 7.6**   Effect of volatility and forward rates on emerging market currency notes

| Underlying currency pairs | Digital coupon | Condition |
| --- | --- | --- |
| **CHF/BRL** | 19% | BRL $\geq$ CHF |
| **CHF/INR** | 21% | INR $\geq$ CHF |
| **CHF/TRY** | 25% | TRY $\geq$ CHF |
| **Basket/CHF** | **27.5%** | **Basket $\geq$ CHF** |

The coupons are only paid when the condition is met. Table 7.7 provides information on the input used to calculate the digital options.

**Table 7.7**   Calculation details for Table 7.6

| Underlying currency pairs | $\Delta$ interest rate | (Fwd-spot)/spot | Volatility |
| --- | --- | --- | --- |
| **CHF/BRL** | 9.10 | $-15.04\%$ | 12.20% |
| **CHF/INR** | 4.95 | $-9.25\%$ | 7.40% |
| **CHF/TRY** | 16.45 | $-24.66\%$ | 17.50% |
| **Basket/CHF** | **10.17** | **$-16.32\%$** | **10.89%** |

The greater the interest rate differential, the better are the conditions for the digital option. The basket's imperfect correlation between the currency pairs means that the volatility is lower than the sum of the weighted individual volatilities, which has a positive impact on the coupon in addition to the interest rate differential.

*Dos & don'ts*

- Don't use a worst-of option when structuring an emerging market currency product replicating a carry trade (be it capital guaranteed or not), but try a *best-of* feature. For instance, a "three best out of four" trick, in which the worst performing currency is *not* considered in the calculation of the basket, can be used to significantly enhance the return of a basket. Choose four currencies that are not necessarily correlated one to another, e.g. one for each EM region in the world (South America, Eastern Europe, Middle East and Far East). The additional cost is low, because the call option on the basket is cheap.

### 7.1.6   FX reverse convertibles (dual currency note)

*Description*

A common product in private banking is the FX reverse convertible[7] on a currency pair. In essence, the building blocks of the product consist of a money-market investment in the reference currency and a short call on the reference currency. The payoff is summarized in two points:

- If, at maturity, the reference currency has weakened to below the strike against the alternative currency, the invested notional plus a coupon are redeemed in the reference currency.
- If the reference currency has strengthened to at or above the strike, the invested notional plus a coupon are redeemed in the alternative currency, with the invested notional converted at the strike level.

The coupon is paid in any case, but is converted at the strike level in the alternative currency if the exchange rate ends above it. Note that a discount can replace the coupon, transforming the FX reverse convertible into FX discount certificate.

An FX reverse convertible is practically equal to a stock or stock index reverse convertible; the maximum gain is capped by the level of the coupon, and the investor incurs losses if the currency exchange rate moves above the strike increased by the coupon. The coupon results from the combination of the yield from the money-market investment and the premium earned on the short call. The major difference between FX reverse convertibles and other asset class reverse convertibles is that the redemption occurs *always* at 100% of the invested capital, but the investor doesn't know in advance in which currency. FX reverse convertibles belong to the category of yield enhancement products.

The FX reverse convertible is usually an investment for very short periods, e.g. one to three months. Depending on the bank, it can be implemented on an individual basis for

---

[7] Generally known as "dual currency note" or "dual currency deposit".

as little as EUR 50 000.00 and some banks offer automated web-based systems to trade it quasi instantaneously. Price, execution and term-sheet in several languages are completed electronically within a matter of seconds. Most of the time, these products are not truly securitized. Their security number is often a bank-internal number, determined by the issuer of the product, and may not be transferrable. Mark-to-market data may also not be available, making FX reverse convertibles one of the few structured products that cannot be traded, or where trading is very difficult, during their lifetime. This didn't prevent the development of the popularity of the product, as many investment advisors saw in this product category an interesting alternative to low-yielding money-market investments for their clients. Given the very short tenors in FX reverse convertibles, this is not a big disadvantage.

*Market expectation and risk*

The optimal timing to enter an FX reverse convertible is when the volatility on the currency pair is high and expected to decrease while the exchange rate stabilizes. The risk is the conversion of the capital in the alternative currency to an unfavorable exchange rate. This instrument is therefore suitable only for investors who at the least envision the possibility of a conversion. The ideal case is an investor who is truly indifferent between two currencies.

An often-cited goal for the product is the investor who wants to achieve a higher interest than the money market rate of his reference currency. For investors who would rather avoid risking a conversion, this goal can be better achieved by other strategies, which do not embed a conversion risk of the capital in the alternative currency. With FX reverse convertibles, the reference currency rate may indeed be outperformed for several months in a row, but suddenly be converted when the alternate currency weakens beyond what would have been thought possible. This instrument typically generates many small gains that are annihilated by one huge loss on the last conversion if the investor considers the conversion a loss. One of the main advantages compared to other asset classes lies in the possibility of rollover trades in the alternative currency and therefore is not necessarily forced to take the loss out of the conversion.

*Example*

The FX reverse convertible is depicted with an example on the EUR/USD. Suppose an investor whose reference currency is the EUR, but who thinks that his base currency could weaken against the USD in the short term. He also owns some assets in the US, so he is relatively indifferent about which currency he holds. He decides to invest EUR 1 million in the FX reverse convertible shown in Table 7.8.

**Table 7.8**   Sample FX reverse convertible

| | |
|---|---|
| Spot EUR/USD | 1.5800 (USD per 1 EUR) |
| Strike | 1.5800 (at-the-money) |
| Tenor (maturity) | 1 month |
| Coupon (calculated) | 2.05% bullet, 24.6% p.a. |

The 24.6% per annum coupon seems huge. Here, the reinvestment risk has to be considered: to obtain this return over a whole year, the investor would have to invest in 12 FX

reverse convertibles all struck at-the-money, and never incur a loss on any of them. The probability of such a scenario is quite low; it would amount to roughly the same as betting that the flip of a coin would end on tails 12 times in a row and win. The simple fact of writing a per annum coupon in the product description bestows a framing element to the investment that sometimes misleads the investor into believing that enormous returns might be earned.

There is no standard in the industry about how the payoff may be depicted. As mentioned, the view may be taken from either the reference or the alternate currency: one variant is shown in Figure 7.8.

**Figure 7.8** Payoff 45: FX reverse convertible
*Source:* Bloomberg, own calculations

With this product, as long as the EUR doesn't rise above 1.5800 in one month's time, the investor gets back his EUR 1 million plus a coupon of 2.05% calculated for one month, which equals to EUR 20 500. His notional as well as the coupon will be converted into USD if the EUR/USD rises above 1.5800.

Let's now suppose the investor was wrong and the EUR did continue to strengthen against the USD. If after one month the EUR/USD exchange rate was quoted at 1.7000, what would the investor get back?

$$EUR\ 1\,000\,000 * 1.5800 + (EUR\ 1\,000\,000 * 1.5800 * 2.05\%) = USD\ 1\,612\,390$$

The notional as well as the coupon have been converted in USD at the strike level (1.5800). Note that in the scenario where the spot exchange rate rises to 1.7000, if the investor hadn't purchased the product, he would be able to convert his EUR at the 1.7000 rate, which would amount to USD 1 700 000, not counting any interest rate earned in EUR during that month. Herein rests the risk for the investor.

In the example above, investing in an EUR money-market instrument would yield only ~0.33% over the one-month period (ca. 4.03% p.a.). If the risk of receiving USD at an exchange rate of 1.5800 is acceptable for the investor, he can nicely outperform the money-market rate. By the way, the delta of the example is around 48%, meaning that the chance of having the EUR notional converted in USD lies at 48%.

The behavior of the FX reverse convertible defined in Table 7.8 is depicted in Figure 7.9. As the product is seldom traded (or valued) during its lifetime, the illustration remains largely theoretical.

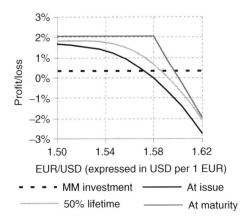

**Figure 7.9**  Payoff 46: FX reverse convertible price as a function of spot and time to maturity
*Source:* Bloomberg, own calculations

*Dos & don'ts*

- Don't invest in FX reverse convertibles if a conversion in the alternative currency cannot be sustained.
- Don't fall into the habit of rolling over the investment each time it expires on an automatic basis. Analyze the market and determine the expectations at each expiry date.
- Don't look at the level of the annualized coupon when considering a product with a short maturity. It may look extremely attractive, but is meaningless and will probably not be achieved. Consider instead the absolute level of premium: is it consistent with the risk of conversion?
- Before concluding a deal, try several strikes out- or in-the-money and have a look at the delta to judge the chances of whether or not it could be converted. Out-of-the-money strikes will obviously have a lower conversion probability.

### 7.1.7  FX barrier reverse convertibles

*Description and product example*

FX barrier reverse convertibles[8] have become very popular as well. The difference to the classical FX reverse convertible is that a predefined barrier must be broken for the product to be redeemed in the alternative currency. The construction of the product is thus a money-market investment in the reference currency plus a short up- (or down-) and-in call.

In comparison with the FX reverse convertible without barrier, the coupon of the barrier product is lower, all other parameters remaining the same. This is because the barrier decreases the chances that a conversion in the alternative currency will occur.

Resuming our FX reverse convertible example from Table 7.9, but adding a barrier at a level of 1.64 would decrease the coupon to 1.27%. The delta also diminishes to 36% (Figures 7.10 and 7.11).

---

[8] Often referred to as Barrier Dual Currency Deposits. Similar to barrier discount certificates.

**Table 7.9**   Sample FX barrier reverse convertible

| | |
|---|---|
| Spot EUR/USD | 1.5800 (USD per 1 EUR) |
| Strike | 1.5800 (at-the-money) |
| Barrier (up-and-in) | 1.6400 |
| Tenor (maturity) | 1 month |
| Coupon (calculated) | 1.27% (bullet) |

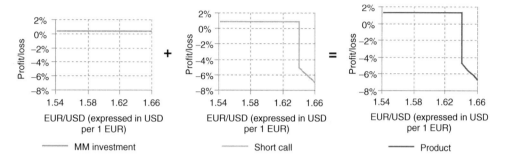

**Figure 7.10**   Payoff 47: FX barrier reverse convertible
*Source:* Bloomberg, own calculations

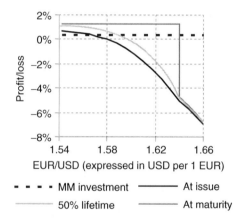

**Figure 7.11**   Payoff 48: FX barrier reverse convertible price as a function of spot and time to maturity
*Source:* Bloomberg, own calculation

*Dos and don'ts*

When should the investor use a barrier, and when not? As usual in the structured product world, the answer lies in the risk aversion of the investor. Basically, the question should rather be divided into the following sequence:

- How likely should the redemption of the product in the alternative currency be?
- If the product is going to be redeemed in the alternative currency, at what level (strike) should the redemption occur?

The first question relates to the delta of the product, meaning the risk associated to the embedded option actually ending in-the-money. The second question addresses the height of the conversion level if it should happen. Actually, the investor will be better off with a higher conversion level in the alternative currency should it occur. Indeed, a product with the same initial risk of ending in the alternative currency can be constructed in two ways:

- Setting the strike out-of-the money and not using a barrier.
- Setting the strike at-the-money and using a barrier.

Both products can have the same delta, and thus the same initial risk of ending in-the-money. However, if both options are to end in-the-money, the conversion into the alternative currency should be done at the strike of the call option of each product. This means different amounts of alternative currency paid back to the investor. Therefore, the investor's choice between a product featuring a higher (out-of-the-money) strike without a barrier and a lower (closer to the at-the-money) strike protected by a high (far out-of-the-money) barrier must be answered by his risk appetite to receiving the alternative currency in case of a conversion, combined with his own perception of the chance a conversion takes place. Hence the author's recommendation:

- When in doubt, always choose the product with an out-of-the-money strike instead of an at-the-money strike protected by a barrier.

The reason for this behavior is simple. Adverse exchange rate movements of low-to-medium amplitude are usually not big enough to cause a conversion with out-of-the-money strikes. Only large or very large movements will induce a conversion in the alternate currency. When such adverse swings happen, it is unlikely that even a high barrier will hold. The conversion level of the out-of-the-money strike is then more advantageous to the investor than the at-the-money strike.

## 7.2  FIXED INCOME STRUCTURES

If equity investments represent micro-economic bets, then fixed-income investments represent their macro-economic counterparts. The underlying assets of a fixed-income structure are mainly bonds and options on an economy's yield curve. As such, the performance of a product is linked to the accuracy of the forecast on an economy as a whole. For instance, a fixed-income product could bet on higher interest rates in the Euro-zone. Another example of a common private-banking fixed income structure has already been given with the auto-callable yield curve steepener as autocall options were described.[9] Fixed-income product variations are as numerous as FX or equity products. In private banking, however, they are seldom used, accounting for less than 10% of the total volume held. The reasons can be of diverse nature:

*Complexity:* inherently, yield products are more complex than equity or FX products. Few private investors realize the functioning of the yield curves and have little appetite for products that take more than two sentences to explain.

---

[9] On Section 5.3.4.

*Tracking:* common media such as television or newspapers mostly talk of stocks or currency exchange rates, but still little information is given about yields on a day-to-day basis. Products on assets that are difficult to track are less interesting for investors.

*Investor behavior:* most persons view fixed-income bonds as safe investments and do not consider speculating on them with "risky" structured products, despite the fact that most fixed-income products are capital guaranteed. There seems to be a preference to use equity- or FX-based products for "playing" with markets.

*Past experience:* at the beginning of the millennium, fixed income products had a popular phase, but many products met unfavorable market conditions and traded far below par despite being capital guaranteed, irking most investors.

Yet objectively, and from an economical point of view, there's no reason not to use fixed-income based products in private banking. Since the product's base has become so small, amounting to less than 10% of the total structured product market, only a few examples will be listed here. However, every investor should seriously consider fixed-income products in his investment universe, especially as a replacement for classical bonds when expecting higher yields for instance. There are many opportunities of enhancing the yield of a portfolio, and here the wording is not meant to be misleading. One of the major characteristics of fixed-income structures is their relatively low correlation to other asset classes. Short-term interest rate movements, which are to a large part determined by central banks, may be correlated to an economic cycle. However, the correlation of interest rates to equity, FX or commodity markets remains at a fairly low level, the more so for long-term rates. The imperfect correlation to the other asset classes makes fixed-income structures attractive from a diversification point of view.

A fixed-income product can be constructed in such a way that the expected returns are customized to the investor's need, as with other asset class products. Yet an important difference between fixed-income and, for instance, equity-based products is that fixed-income products usually increase the risk versus the underlying asset. Equity-based products usually reduce the risk versus the underlying asset by devising some sort of protection on the risky asset. Private banking fixed-income products are capital guaranteed by nature, even if non-capital guaranteed products exist. The underlying asset of fixed-income based products is often an interest rate level, which is by definition risk free. The structure tries to increase that rate by taking a risk of some sort, usually on the coupon payout probability. Hence, the investor is often confronted with a high (seemingly attractive) nominal coupon, which has only an uncertain, often low, probability of being paid to the investor. If the scenario around which the product is constructed materializes, the return is higher than on a comparable rate, and if not, then it is lower or can even trend to zero. To summarize, most fixed-income notes are capital protected where only the coupon is at risk.

Before going into the detail of products, and in order to guide the investor into the world of fixed-income structures, a first step consists of describing a yield curve and the possibilities it gives to a structurer for product ideas.

### 7.2.1   The yield curve, swap rates and the forward rates

Fixed income is generally assimilated to bonds. Bonds, in their classical form, have a fixed coupon level that is paid out at regular intervals, usually annually or semi-annually. Hence the name: every so often bondholders earn a fixed income paid out by the bond issuer – no risk and no fun at first glance. A second look will show a slightly more complex picture: not all coupon levels are the same, and bonds trade at different price levels – the yield differs from bond to bond. For instance, long-term bonds seldom have the same yield as short-term bonds. A plausible explanation for that fact is that investors have different views on the future evolution of interest rate levels. Investors may for instance think that rates are going to rise in the future and are unwilling to invest for the long term at the level of the short-term rate. Investors may also think that a short-term investment may be less risky than one for the long term. After all, even bonds default from time to time. In that case, investors will demand a higher yield for the long term than for the short term. The different level of bond yields as a function of their time to maturity forms the *yield curve*. It is usually represented either by the yields of the government bonds according to their maturity or by *swap rates*.

Swaps are bilateral contracts used by banks among themselves or between banks and their institutional clients to lend and borrow money. The swap rate is the level at which the lending and borrowing takes place. The liquidity of swap rates has increased beyond that of standard bonds, even government bonds. Hence, the swap rates are being used by traders as reference yield in their daily business. They are also more practical because of their standard maturities (ranging from three months to 30 years) and because they can be easily interpolated. On the contrary, fixed coupon bonds have a maturity that decreases every day and are less practical to work with. Swap rates yield generally the same interest as a comparable government bond investment, but can deviate quite strongly on occasion, such as during the subprime crisis that led to the credit crunch of 2008; swap rates traded much higher than the government bonds during that time. Unless they are specifically structured with physical bonds as underlying assets, fixed-income structured products are based on swap rates.

The yield curve can have many shapes: normal, flat, inverted, or humped. Figure 7.12 shows three different yield curve shapes as a function of their maturity which were observable on 9 September 2008: a "normal" rising yield curve of USD swap rates, an inverted Iceland Krona curve (ISK) and a humped (nearly flat) EUR curve.

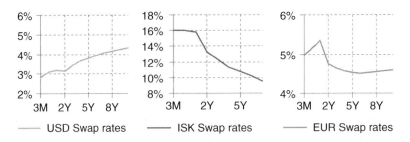

**Figure 7.12** Normal (USD), inverted (ISK) and humped (EUR) yield curves
*Source:* Bloomberg

Investors will be most familiar with the typical upward-sloping normal shape of the curve such as the one of the USD. It can be more or less steep. As can be guessed, the yield curve is not stable over time and experiences shifts with a changing macroeconomic environment. The most important types of curve shape changes are enumerated below, taking as a reference curve the USD swap rates of Figure 7.12.

1. *Shifts of parallel nature*, where the curve rises or falls over all maturities (Figure 7.13).

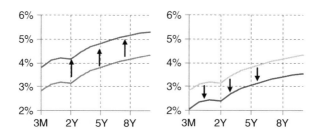

**Figure 7.13**   Upward shift (left) and downward shift (right)

   Shifts of parallel nature are often caused by general macroeconomic events or forecasts that affect a whole economy over a long period. For instance, a slowdown in growth across all industry groups combined with a money injection from central banks might provoke a downward parallel shift in the curve.
2. *Shifts pivoted around an axe*, where the slope of the curve either flattens or becomes steeper (Figure 7.14).

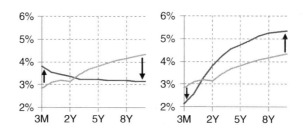

**Figure 7.14**   Pivot shift: flattening (left), steepening (right)

   There are various reasons why a yield curve might flatten or become steeper. In the case of a flattening curve, a rising short-term inflation combined with a strong demand for long duration bonds may be the cause. The curve may steepen when the central bank increases the short-term money supply but inflation is believed to pick up in the long term.
3. *Partial shifts, where only a part of the curve changes*. In that case, the curve can experience a bullish or bearish flattening, or a bullish or bearish steepening.

   Partial shifts are driven by events or expectations that affect either only the short or only the long term.

   In essence, the present shape, combined with the expectation about the yield curve's future shape is the fixed-income specialists' daily bread. Those two factors, along with the level of (un)certainty and the speed of the expected change (given the volatility, skew etc., of the options on interest rates) allows the structurer to think about new product opportunities.

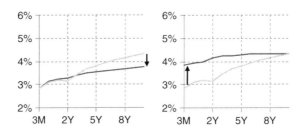

**Figure 7.15**  Examples of bullish flattening (left) and bearish flattening (right)
*Source:* Own representation

Another important factor in fixed income is the *rating* of the issuer. In the mentioned subprime crisis, the funding level[10] of the issuers has taken on major importance when calculating the price of a structured product. Usually, the funding level reflects the spread (which may be positive or negative) on top of the swap rate that the issuer uses for his products. Better-rated issuers (AA+ or AAA) usually have a lower funding rate than lower-rated ones (A or A-). This fact is reflected in the product's price, all other factors remaining equal. When credit spreads[11] widen, the difference in the funding rate of the various issuers can become huge, impacting interest-rate based products to a large extent mainly due to their long maturities. The investor is ultimately confronted with the choice of a better-rated issuer and a product with less attractive conditions, and a lower-rated issuer (implying a higher default risk) with more attractive product conditions.

When structuring interest-based products, an essential figure is the implied *forward rate*. In structuring, the forward rate is the level of a given maturity rate that is anticipated in the future. For example, the 6-month Libor[12] spot rate may be quoted 3% today, but the 6-month Libor *in 3 months* may be quoted 3.2% and the 6-month Libor *in one year* may be quoted at 3.7%. Hence, a product based on a stream of 6-month Libor rates for the next five years is sensitive to the implied 6-month forward rates. Any view that an investor takes on the future evolution of interest rates must consider the forward rather than the spot levels, as the pricing of an investment will be made on those forward rates, and not on the spot.

Does an implied forward rate for a future date $i$ correctly predict the actual spot rate at date $x$? The answer is no. Empirically, the forward rates are very bad at predicting the future. They are simply reflecting the view the market has about how the rates could be in the future, given current economic data and expectations. But since the market doesn't know the future (no one has a crystal ball), a new forward scenario pops up every day with fresh macro-economic news flow,[13] and the implied forward curves are changed by the market to take the latest news into account.

With this in mind, it is now easier to understand why interest-rate based products are perceived as complex by many private banking investors when compared to equity-based products. One has to consider the current shape of the yield curve, the implied forward

---

[10] The rate at which a bank or corporation refinances itself.

[11] The credit spread is the difference in yield between different bonds due to the quality of the issuer. It gives an indication about the solvency of the issuer. The higher the spread, the higher the chance of default.

[12] LIBOR: London Inter-Bank Offer Rate. The reference yield at which banks lend unsecured funds to other banks, to which the credit spread of the borrower, must be added.

[13] For instance the Consumer Price Index, or the Consumer Confidence Sentiment, or the Unemployment Rate, etc.

for each maturity, and combine these factors with one's forecast, not an easy feat for the average investor. Add to that the implied volatility of each point in the curve and eventual credit spreads, and the factors to consider become quite numerous and interdependent. To summarize, there are less underlying yield curves than there are stocks (there are only so many central banks), but each interest-rate based product seems more complex than a product on a single stock, because the product's price depends on the parameters and variations of the whole yield curve and not only on a single point of the curve. However, it will be shown shortly that the apparent complexity isn't that difficult to understand; indeed, some products depend only on the movements of a single point on the yield curve, while others take only two sentences to explain.

### 7.2.2  Categories of interest rate based products

Structured products based on interest rates need to be classified in a way other than the capital guarantee/yield enhancement/participation scheme. As mentioned, most products are capital guaranteed at maturity, being a major criterion of fixed-income investments. Instead, a classification based on the feature and the underlying index of the product is both common and intuitive: it allows one to quickly select the matching product to a forecasted scenario. Products can be divided in the following categories:

- range accruals;
- floating rate or CMS[14] notes;
- inflation-linked notes; and
- credit-linked products.

In addition, the *callable* feature is very popular among fixed-income notes and can be linked to any of the above-mentioned categories. For some products in each of these categories, the *path dependency* may play a major role in the final payout to the investor. Path-dependent notes are products based on an option strategy where the evolution of the underlying index (which is mostly the 3- or 6-month Libor) during the lifetime of the product plays an important role.

Others exist, but they are more seldom used in private banking and will not be mentioned here.[15]

*Range accrual* notes are products based on an interest rate index, mostly the 3- or 6-month Libor rate, which pays a high coupon if the index stays within two predefined ranges.

*Floating rate or CMS notes* are products based on one or several maturity points on the yield curve, which must behave in a certain way (increase or decrease, absolutely or relative to each other) for the product to pay a high coupon. A steepening or a flattening of the curve are often played with CMS notes.

*Inflation linked notes* are linked to inflation indices and are used to generate inflation-adjusted, or real returns. They are seldom used in their structured product form in private banking, as inflation-linked bonds already exist. However, inflation-linked bonds do not provide principal protection or indeed a floor, which inflation options can provide for.

---

[14] Constant Maturity Swap

[15] For a more complete list of products see the Interest Rate Handbook of derivatives from BNP Paribas or browse the issuers' internet sites.

*Credit linked products* have credit-default options on sovereign, corporate or private debt embedded. The well-known CDO[16] structures are part of this category. Products of this type are used when an investor expects credit spreads to shrink or to widen. Little known in private banking, they are not considered here. Credit-Linked Notes (CLOs) or First To Default (FTDs) notes are more common, but still rare.

### 7.2.3 Considerations for investing in interest-rate based products

Yield curve movements and changes in shape are an investor's main concern. The amplitude and the time over which the expected changes take place rank second and third is the level of risk with which the view should be played. The fixed-income product will be constructed around these three parameters, to which the credit risk of the issuer must be added. In essence, the investor should find an answer to the following three questions in order to find the product fitting his investment needs:

• How are the *current market conditions* (i.e. shape of the curve, forward rates and/or volatility)?
• What are the *expected scenarios* (i.e. awaiting a drop in short-term interest rates, or an inflation pick-up)?
• How likely is the scenario to materialize, and what happens if it does or doesn't?

For instance, if the curve and its forwards are currently flat or even slightly inverse and the investor expects the yield curve to assume its "normal" (rising) form again, i.e. to steepen as short-term rates decrease while long-term rates increase, an idea would be to invest in a product betting on a steepening of the yield curve. It could be based on the 10-year minus 2 year constant maturity swap rate as described in Section 5.3.4. Should the curve already be steep and expected to stay that way but volatility is expected to fall, a range accrual (callable or not) could be a possibility.

The following table summarizes some of the possible products in certain market environments. Some of the mentioned products will be explained by an example.

In addition, two factors have to be considered when structuring a fixed-income note. First, the risk/return profile of each client should be determined for the construction of the product, as a fixed-income product can be constructed aggressively or defensively. The risk profile for each separate product example below will be stated, but it has to be kept in mind that more or less aggressive variations can be structured. Second, as the quality of the issuer often determines to a large degree the conditions of a fixed-income product, the examples are assumed to have the best possible issuer (AAA).

### 7.2.4 Ratchet note

*Description*

A ratchet note pays a floating coupon usually linked to the 3- or 6-month Libor rate that is only allowed to increase by a certain amount per period. The value generated by the cap is

---

[16] Collaterized Debt Obligation.

**Table 7.10**  Selected fixed income products according to an investor's view

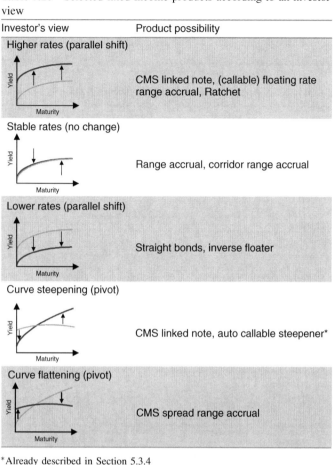

| Investor's view | Product possibility |
| --- | --- |
| Higher rates (parallel shift) | CMS linked note, (callable) floating rate range accrual, Ratchet |
| Stable rates (no change) | Range accrual, corridor range accrual |
| Lower rates (parallel shift) | Straight bonds, inverse floater |
| Curve steepening (pivot) | CMS linked note, auto callable steepener* |
| Curve flattening (pivot) | CMS spread range accrual |

*Already described in Section 5.3.4
*Source:* Own representation

reflected in a fixed premium added to each coupon. The product is fully capital guaranteed at maturity.

*Market expectation and risk*

A ratchet note is suitable for investors who think that the interest rates will rise, but less than implied by the forwards. Ideally, the yield curve is steep and volatility is high when the note is structured. Both factors have a high influence on the level of the cap and the fixed premium. After the note is issued, a flattening of the curve, a decrease in the volatility and a parallel shift downwards increase the mark-to-market price of the ratchet note.

The risk for the investor is small: unless the Libor rate becomes negative (which happens seldom), a coupon is paid each quarter. In addition, the coupon is higher than the normal Libor in the case of decreasing or stable rates. Only in the case where the rates rise rapidly (spike), the note underperforms and needs several quarters of stability to catch up.

*Example*

In Table 7.11, the note pays a quarterly coupon equal to the level of the 3-month EUR
Libor rate plus 30 basis points, but any increase in the coupon due to an increase of the
Libor rate from quarter to quarter is capped at 20 bps. Suppose the product had been issued
in December 2004. At this time, the 3-month Libor was at 2% and rose in the following
years to 4.25% before crashing down to 2.5% in the subprime/credit crisis. Table 7.12 and
Figure 7.16 illustrate the functioning as well as the hypothetical performance.

**Table 7.11**   Example of a ratchet note

| | |
|---|---|
| **Capital protection** | 100% |
| **Maturity** | 4 years |
| **Currency** | EUR |
| **Underlying instrument** | 3-month Libor (EURibor) |
| **Callability** | Non-callable |
| **Issuer** | AAA |
| **Coupon** | 3M EUR Libor + 30 bps, quarterly |
| **Cap (ratchet)** | 20 bps per quarter |

**Table 7.12**   Example of a ratchet note

| Date | Quarter | 3 m-Libor | Coupon |
|---|---|---|---|
| **Dec-04** | 0 | 2.00% | – |
| **Mar-05** | 1 | 2.00% | 2.30% |
| **Jun-05** | 2 | 2.00% | 2.30% |
| **Sep-05** | 3 | 2.00% | 2.30% |
| **Dec-05** | 4 | 2.25% | 2.50% |
| **Mar-06** | 5 | 2.50% | 2.70% |
| **Jun-06** | 6 | 2.75% | 2.90% |
| **Sep-06** | 7 | 3.00% | 3.10% |
| **Dec-06** | 8 | 3.50% | 3.30% |
| **Mar-07** | 9 | 3.75% | 3.50% |
| **Jun-07** | 10 | 4.00% | 3.70% |
| **Sep-07** | 11 | 4.00% | 3.90% |
| **Dec-07** | 12 | 4.00% | 4.10% |
| **Mar-08** | 13 | 4.00% | 4.30% |
| **Jun-08** | 14 | 4.00% | 4.30% |
| **Sep-08** | 15 | 4.25% | 4.50% |
| **Dec-08** | 16 | 2.50% | 2.80% |

Source: Bloomberg, own calculations

Despite the rather quick increase of the 3-month Libor rate during the life of the product, the quarterly coupons stay higher in all but four instances (from December 2006 to
September 2007). It caught up with the Libor in the following quarters of stable fixings.
This shows that a ratchet note can be a conservative (true) yield enhancement product even
in times when the interest rates are low. In the example, the simple average of the coupons
is approximately 16 basis points higher than the Libor fixings.

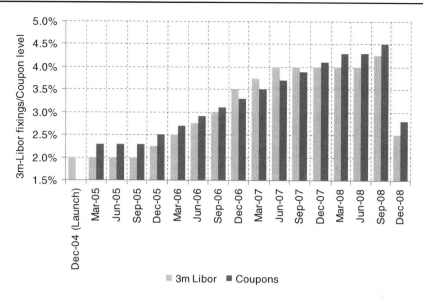

**Figure 7.16** Ratchet note historical performance
*Source:* Bloomberg, own calculations

*Dos and don'ts*

- A ratchet note is usually a very conservative instrument used to enhance *slightly* the yield of a bond portfolio. The target yield enhancement remains small most of the time, of the order of one fifth or less than the reference yield rate (here the 3-month Libor). Don't jeopardize the small yield enhancement by selecting an issuer that is not top notch.
- Always select the ratchet cap in relation to the coupon increase; it is best to have both numbers approximately at equal levels. It's useless to have a high cap but no premium, as it is to set the cap so low that a single rate increase for the whole lifetime of the product will have it underperforming.

## 7.2.5 (Callable) daily range accrual[17]

*Description*

A range accrual is an instrument where the coupon level is determined by how many days within a year a reference index fixes within a predetermined range. The level of the coupon is then calculated by the number of days where the index has fixed within the range divided by the total number of days. The possibility for a lower total yield on the investment (= cost) is compensated by an increase of the nominal coupon, which is often much higher than the risk-free rate and may look quite attractive at first glance. The range accrual can be compared to a bond where the coupon is put at risk.

---

[17] (C)DRAN.

The reference index is in most cases the 3- or 6-month Libor rate, but it could also be the 2-year or 10-year CMS. When the product is callable, the reference index is usually linked to the call frequency; a product callable every three months will have the 3-month Libor as reference index, while a semi-annual callable product will have the 6-month Libor as underlying. Callable range accruals are the most common fixed-income products in private banking.

A *callable* daily range accrual (CDRAN) adds to the product the feature that it can be called by the issuer at regular intervals. The fact that the product is callable by the issuer mitigates the value of the higher coupon. The title of a term-sheet often features an abbreviation like "10YNC3M", which means: "ten Year maturity, Non-Callable before three Months". Hence, the product may be redeemed already three months after it has been issued, even though its longest maturity is 10 years. This makes the reinvestment risk of the issuer one of the highest imaginable: if the reference index is well inside the range, the issuer will call the product, and the high coupon will have been paid only over a few months. The reverse situation, where the index fixes outside of the range, leaves the investor with a non-performing product where, in the extreme case, no coupon accrues for the remaining time to maturity. In that case, the product's mark-to-market value drops to the implicit bond floor. It is essential to see the level of the coupon in relation to the risk-free rate: a 12% coupon when the risk-free rate (swap rate) is at 3% will bear a high reinvestment risk as well as a high mark-to-market risk. Generally, the products with high relative coupons also have long or very long maturities. Ten or even 15-year maturity CDRANs were common products at the turn of the millennium. Those products not only bear the coupon and price risk, but the issuer risk also becomes significant.

*Market expectation and risk*

Range accruals can fit a number of market scenarios. The main element of this product type is the range concept. The investor must believe that the reference index stays within a range for a determined period. The range may have only an upper boundary, in which case it does not matter how low the rate falls, as long as it does not fix above it. Alternatively, the range may have only a lower boundary, in which case the rate should not fix below that boundary. Or else the range may consist of a corridor, having both an upper and a lower boundary. The range may be constant for the whole lifetime of the product (for example, an upper boundary of 4.5% for three years), or it may be incremental (for example, 4.25% in the first year, 4.5% in the second, and 4.75% in the third), or decreasing. Table 7.13 summarizes the type of ranges that fit different market expectations.

**Table 7.13**  Market expectations and type of range accruals

| Type of range | Market expectation |
|---|---|
| Upper boundary | Lower rates, flattening of the curve |
| Lower boundary | Higher rates |
| Corridor boundary | Stable rates, or rate movements as implied by the forwards |

Remember that the market expectation is taken on the implied forwards and not on the spot rates. The volatility should be high as the range accrual is issued. After the issue, a decrease in volatility is desirable. If the product is callable, the importance of the volatility is increased.

The issue is less clear concerning the forwards. The product can be structured in such a way that it deliberately trends against the forwards, if the investor's expected scenario is contrarian to them. This will guarantee a very high coupon (until the first call date if callable), because the model will assume that the chances are high that the daily fixings will be out of the range and no coupon will accumulate. However, should the forecast materialize and the forwards massively move into the investor's predicted direction, then the product will most certainly outperform any plain vanilla bond (or be called after the first call date and the investor will bear the reinvestment risk afterwards). Ideally, the product is structured thus that it would just slightly underperform the forwards so the actual yields come ever closer to the barrier without breaching them. If callable, the issuer will not call the product because his model will indicate that, based on the forwards, he should not call it; the received coupons outperform any money market or bond instrument.

The main risk is the fixing of the reference index outside of the boundary. In that case, the coupon ceases to accrue and the product will most likely be valued below par.

*Example*

Table 7.14 is an example of a callable daily range accrual (CDRAN) taken from Table 6.3:

**Table 7.14**   CDRAN example

| | |
|---|---|
| **Capital protection** | 100% |
| **Maturity** | 7 years |
| **Currency** | USD |
| **Underlying instrument** | 6-month LIBOR |
| **Interest rate range (boundary)** | 0%–7% |
| **Callability** | Semi-annually after 1 year |
| **Issuer** | US investment bank |
| **Coupon** | 6.41%, semi-annually |
| **Coupon accrual** | For every day the 6-month LIBOR stays within the range. |

Source: redrawn from an investment bank e-mailed offer

In this example, a 7.5% coupon accrues for every day the 6-month Libor stays within 0% and 7%. For each day that the 6-month Libor closes outside the range, the coupon stops accruing. Every six months, the accrued coupon is paid to the holders of the product. After one year, the issuer can call the product for the first time. If he chooses to do so, the issuer redeems the full capital plus the accrued coupon for the last six months. The product's functioning is best illustrated graphically (Figure 7.17).

Suppose the Libor fixing level at the product's issue date is 3.25%. In the first six months, no fixing occurred outside the range and the full coupon is paid (first black dot on the graphic):

$$6.41\% * \frac{180}{180} * \frac{1}{2} = 3.205\%$$

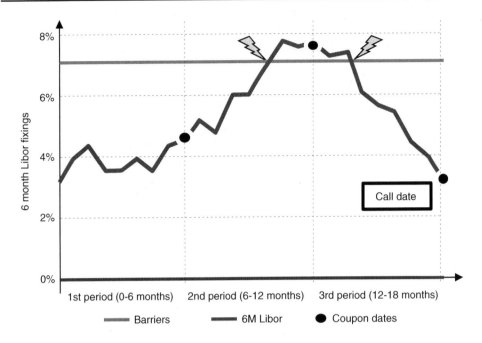

**Figure 7.17**   CDRAN graphical simulation

In the next six months, the Libor crosses the upper barrier after four months (120 days, first lightning bolt) and ends outside the barrier (second black dot). The coupon is paid for the days that the fixings occurred within the range, which amount to:

$$6.41\% * \frac{120}{180} * \frac{1}{2} = 2.137\%$$

The yearly coupon is thus 5.3420%. At this point, the issuer decides not to call the product. The trader's model will indicate a high chance that the next Libor fixings will be out of the range, and calling the product now would be uneconomical for the bank. Actually, the product's mark-to-market price will be below par.

In the third observation period, the Libor fixes outside the range for the first 1 month 20 days and falls back into it afterwards (130 days inside the range, starting from the point represented by the second lightning bolt). The coupon amounts to:

$$6.41\% * \frac{130}{180} * \frac{1}{2} = 2.315\%$$

At this point, the issuer decides to call the product and redeems it to 100% along with the last coupon. The issuer has no interest in continuing to pay a 6.41% coupon when the 6-month Libor fixes at 3.5%.[18]

---

[18] Other factors, like forward rates and volatilities, also weigh on the issuer's decision to call or not to call a product. For illustration purposes, these factors have not been considered here.

A common variant often used in rising yield curves is a step-up upper barrier level. Figure 7.18 shows a variant of the precedent CDRAN example, where the single 6% upper barrier over the whole lifetime of the product has been replaced by three individual barriers (Table 7.15)

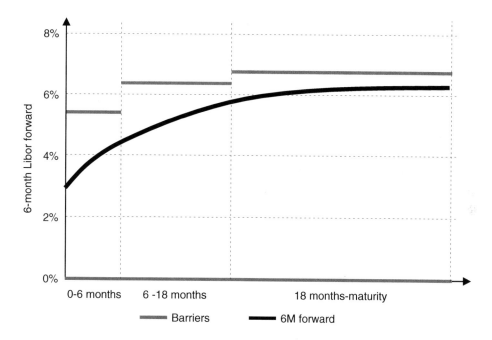

**Figure 7.18**   CDRAN variant with step-up barriers

**Table 7.15**   Individual CDRAN barrier example

| Time | Barrier level |
| --- | --- |
| **First six months** | 5.5% |
| **6–18 months** | 6.25% |
| **18 months–maturity** | 6.5% |

The structuring of the product in this way allows tailoring the barriers closer to a specific scenario. It also means that more value is extracted from the nearby barriers and shifted to the later ones. Note that the lower barrier in these examples always rests at 0%. While it is possible to raise it in order to generate higher coupons or higher upper barriers, the common thing to do in the past few years[19] was to keep it down there. However, it's perfectly sensible to set the lower barrier to levels above the 0% rate if the expected scenario warrants it and the value generated by the increase is worth it.

---

[19] 2006–2008.

*Dos and don'ts*

- A conservative investor should avoid selecting a range accrual with a call feature. It strongly raises the reinvestment risk.
- Always compare a (C)DRAN to a bond and its corresponding yield; never try to beat equity market expectations with a (C)DRAN.
- Keep the risk-free rate in mind when considering the coupon of a (C)DRAN. If it's more than twice as high, then there's a high risk embedded in the product, in the form of reinvestment risk and/or a long maturity.
- Try to keep the maturity of the product close to a preferred holding period. Do not invest in a 10-year product when the investment horizon is three years at most.
- To lower the reinvestment risk in callable products, set the first call date after one year and semi-annually thereafter. If in doubt, ask the structurer to present several examples of structures with different call dates to see the coupon difference.
- Since (C)DRANs are fixed-income products, keep the issuer's rating and refinancing rate in mind. A product issued by an AAA-rated institution will have apparently worse conditions than an A-rated one, but that will be only due to the default risk. Remember that the investor holding the product bears the risk of the issuer defaulting.

### 7.2.6   (Callable) inverse floater

*Description*

An inverse floater functions in the opposite way to a normal floating rate note. In a normal floater, the coupon is set at every observation date according to an index, for example, quarterly at the level of the 3-month Libor rate. The coupon of an inverse floater is set according to a *fixed rate minus a floating rate* of the type:

$$\text{Coupon}_i = \text{Fixed rate} - \text{3M Libor}$$

The lower the floating rate fixes on an observation date, the higher the coupon for the period $i$. Usually, the coupon level is floored at zero, in case the floating rate becomes higher than the fixed rate. If the product is callable, the issuer has the right (but not the obligation) to redeem the note at the first call date and on each subsequent call date after the first.

*Market expectation and risk*

A suitable scenario for an inverse floater is the expectation that the floating rate index will stay low or drop further while the forwards indicate that the market expects it to rise. The anticipation of a parallel downward shift of the whole curve also fits. If the view about a lower floating rate is very strong, the product can be built more aggressively by leveraging the formula by a factor, for example:

$$\text{Coupon}_i = \text{Fixed rate} - (2 * \text{3M Libor})$$

The higher the leverage factor, the higher the fixed rate level. The risk of the worst-case scenario, a zero-coupon, increases with the amount of leverage. If the floating rate rises instead of falling, the product's mark-to-market price is likely to decrease, at the extreme trading around its zero-bond floor. Note that if the rates increase, the bond floor will be lower than expected at the issue date of the product.

*Example*

The issuer often includes callability in inverse floaters. The following example (Table 7.16) illustrates the functioning of two inverse floater versions, the first non-callable for the whole period and the second callable semi-annually after one year. The hypothetical forecast is that the short-term rates (represented by the 6-month Libor) will decrease but that the forwards are currently flat.[20] Comparing the two variants will show the value of the callability.

**Table 7.16**   Example of a callable inverse floater

| | |
|---|---|
| **Capital protection** | 100% |
| **Maturity** | 5 years |
| **Currency** | EUR |
| **Underlying instrument** | 3-month LIBOR (5.25% at calculation date) |
| **Callability version 1** | Non-callable |
| **Callability version 2** | Semi-annually after 1 year |
| **Coupon version 1** | 13.10% – (2 × 6 M Libor), semi-annual |
| **Coupon version 2** | 14.80% – (2 × 6 M Libor), semi-annual |
| **Issuer** | European AA+ bank |

Source: own representation, redrawn from an investment bank e-mail indication for 29.9.2008

Without performing many mathematical calculations, it looks like the callability is not worth much: the difference of (14.80% – 13.10%) = 1.7% between the two versions seems small for the issuer to call the structure of version 2 after one year and semi-annually thereafter. The forwards, which predict that the chances to call the structure are low, yield little value to the callable option. In such a situation, it is questionable whether to implement a callable version, which cuts off potential gains for little value in return.

Table 7.17 illustrates the coupon flows of the non-callable version of the example above. The coupon is floored at zero.

**Table 7.17**   Inverse floater coupon payment illustration

| Year | 6-month Libor | Coupon$_i$ |
|---|---|---|
| **0 (Pricing date)** | 5.25% | – |
| 1 | 6.00% | 1.10% |
| 2 | 5.00% | 3.10% |
| 3 | 4.00% | 5.10% |
| 4 | 3.50% | 6.10% |
| 5 | 3.00% | 7.10% |

---

[20] Note that in an ideal scenario, the forwards would be rising.

In the first years, while the short-term rate increases significantly, the note pays a low coupon, as the expected scenario does not materialize. At the end of the product's life, however, the returns are significantly above the money-market rate. The inverse floater can fulfill its goal even if adverse conditions are met at the beginning of the product's life. Note that the callable version would probably have been called at the end of year three, leaving the investor with a significant underperformance.

*Dos and don'ts*

- Don't use the callable version unless very certain about the expected scenario and when it adds significant value to the possible payouts. The risk of underperforming the risk-free rate increases quickly with the slightest error.
- Keep the maturity preferably at a similar level as the maturity of a comparable investment that would be made into a plain vanilla bond.
- The higher the leverage, the higher the risk and the potential return. A leverage of 3 is more likely to produce rounds of either huge or zero coupons.
- To generate returns similar to bond yields but profit all the same from the expected lower rates, just set the leverage to 1.
- Don't forget to floor the coupon at zero: otherwise, the capital may be put at risk if the rates rise too high.

### 7.2.7 Snowball

Sometimes structurers come up with product names of their own devising which they think are self-explanatory and great marketing appellations, but which no one but themselves understand. The snowball, also known as the ratchet inverse floater, is such a case: although the name evokes some distant relation to the payoff once the latter is known, it's still a far cry to the real description of the product. In fact, the particularity of the snowball is its *path dependency*: the coupon of each period depends on the level of the previous coupon received.

*Description*

A typical private banking structure has a first-period guaranteed coupon fixed at a relatively high level; the structure is said to be front-loaded. In the following periods, the previous coupon is first incremented by a small factor and then deducted by an index (usually the Libor or a CMS). The payoff can thus be decomposed in two main features: the first is the inverse floater part in the form of fixed coupon − (X times floating rate) as seen in Section 7.2.6, and the second is the so-called snowball itself, which links the fixed coupon of the current period to the one of the precedent period.

A typical snowball payoff thus becomes:

1. [Coupon Period$_1$ : X%]
2. [Coupon Period$_{2 \rightarrow n}$ : Previous Coupon + Y% − Index]

In their large majority, snowballs are callable by the issuer after the first coupon payment, usually set after one year.

A snowball can be implemented in a number of variants. In the following examples, the first coupon is always fixed at X%, X% being a constant number that is usually twice as high as the risk-free rate.

- *CMS Snowball:* [Coupon$_i$ = [Previous coupon + Y% − 10YCMS], where 10YCMS denotes the 10-year constant maturity swap.
- *Snowrange:* $\left[\text{Coupon}_i = [\text{Previous coupon} + Y\%] * \frac{n}{N}\right]$, where $n$ denotes the number of days an index (i.e. the 6-month Libor) stays within a predefined range and $N$ the total number of days during the observation period. This structure combines the range accrual with the snowball.
- *Resetting snowball:* at certain observation dates, the coupon level is automatically reset at predefined levels. This helps to reduce somewhat the path-dependency of the product.
- *Thunderball:* [Coupon$_i$ = Gearing * (Previous coupon − Index)], where the structure's dependency on the previous coupon is increased by a gearing on the previous coupon. These structures tend to have a cap.
- *Snowbear:* [Coupon$_i$ = Previous coupon + Z * (Index − Fix)], where Z denotes a factor typically ranging from 2 to 10, depending on the aggressiveness of the structure. Snow-bears, also known as reverse snowballs, are instruments used to bet on a rate decrease.

*Market expectation and risk*

The market expectation and risk expressed here is for the normal snowball having the following formula:

1. [Coupon Period$_1$ : X%]
2. [Coupon Period$_{2 \to n}$ : Previous coupon + Y% − Index]

where Index denotes a 3- or 6-month Libor and X% and Y% are constants.

By linking each coupon to the previous one, the snowball becomes a riskier structure than the inverse floater: if only on a single period the coupon falls to zero, the following coupons are highly likely to all be set at zero. Knowing this, risk-averse investors should stay wary of snowballs, and investors considering this structure should be very convinced about their market expectation. The ideal scenario is a steep rising yield curve with the view that the market overestimates the increase in spot rates in the future. Investors who think that the short-term rates will stay flat or decrease can play their view with leverage in a snowball structure.

*Example*

Tables 7.18 and 7.19 demonstrate how a small rise in the Libor rates at the beginning of the life of the product can decrease the coupon of all the later years.

What is striking is the speed at which the coupon decreases. The rise of the Libor to 6% in year one reduced the coupon of the second year to a mere 5%, and the product never recovered from that blow. Even though the view of decreasing Libor rates proved to be true in the following years, the product yielded less than a normal floating rate bond. This example illustrates the strong path dependency and the timing risk associated with snowballs. Note that had the scenario of decreasing rates materialized immediately, the outperformance versus the Libor rate would have been substantial (Table 7.20).

**Table 7.18**  Example of a snowball

| | |
|---|---|
| **Capital protection** | 100% |
| **Maturity** | 5 years |
| **Currency** | EUR |
| **Underlying instrument** | 3-month LIBOR (5.25% at calculation date) |
| **Callability** | After 1 year |
| **Coupon** | Year 1: 8.5% Years 2–4: (Previous coupon + 2.5% − 6-month Libor), floored at 0% |
| **Issuer** | European AA+ bank |

**Table 7.19**  Calculation simulation #1 of the snowball coupon

| Year | 6-month Libor | Coupon$_i$ |
|---|---|---|
| 0 (Pricing date) | 5.25% | |
| 1 | 6.00% | 8.50% |
| 2 | 5.00% | 5.00% |
| 3 | 4.00% | 2.50% |
| 4 | 3.50% | 1.00% |
| 5 | 3.00% | 0.00% |

**Table 7.20**  Calculation simulation #2 of the snowball coupon

| Year | 6-month Libor | Coupon$_i$ |
|---|---|---|
| 0 (Pricing date) | 5.25% | |
| 1 | 4.50% | 8.50% |
| 2 | 3.50% | 6.50% |
| 3 | 3.00% | 5.50% |
| 4 | 2.50% | 5.00% |
| 5 | 2.00% | 5.00% |

*Dos and don'ts*

- Be as certain as can be with the expected scenario. Only one bad Libor fixing can be enough for the product to trade near its zero-bond floor until maturity.
- To reduce the risk of bad fixings, reduce the maturity. Don't go above five years, stay preferably below three years or even less. The first coupon will be substantially lower, but the volatility of the interest rates, particularly in the US, has risen dramatically over the last 10 years and the risk of an unforeseen event has become greater.
- Rather than maximizing the initial coupon, put some weight in the Y% factor of the formula (Previous coupon + Y% − Libor). If a coupon falls to zero at one point, the only chance of recovery is that Y%.

### 7.2.8 General fixed income dos & don'ts

- When taking a market view on a yield curve, don't look only at the level of the spot curve, but also consider the implied forward levels. For example, if an investor is bullish on the 10-year rate and takes a position accordingly without considering the forwards, the return on his investment might actually be below market average even if his view materializes and the 10-year rate rises. The investor should take a position only if he believes that the rate will increase by more than the forward implies.

- Set the goal of the investment beforehand. It helps when selecting the right structure. For instance, if the goal were to outperform a 3-year floating rate note, do not consider a 5-year product based on a 10-year swap rate. Rather, try to find a structure with the 3- or 6-month Libor as underlying rate and select a 3-year maturity.

- Always consider the rating of the issuer in the pricing of the product, and keep in mind that the holder of the product bears the default risk of the issuer. An issuer with a higher funding rate will show better conditions than one with a lower rate, solely due to the funding rate difference.

- The mark-to-market price of most fixed-income products depends on a plethora of factors that are difficult to grasp for a private investor. Although a secondary market transaction is always possible, start with the expectation of holding a fixed-income product until its maturity.

- When using the callable feature, where the issuer can redeem the product at will on certain observation dates, select the first call date in relation to the longest possible maturity of the product. It's all right to have the product callable for the first time after three months if the maturity is not longer than three years, but if the maturity is longer, the first call date should be set after six months at the earliest. Remember that while the call feature increases the nominal coupon level, the issuer will always call the product when the investor would outperform the market.

# 7.3  COMMODITY STRUCTURES

There are several ways to define commodities: they can be defined as a good or a service whose broad availability and standardization focus on price and eliminate the value of a brand; or the term may refer to physical products which can be purchased by individuals in the market (i.e. flour, gasoline or memory chips). In a private banking context, a fitting definition of commodities would be:

A commodity is a tangible or intangible material of standardized quality, which is traded on a commodity exchange in lots of standardized quantity.

A tangible material may refer to wheat, crude oil or other physical materials, while an intangible material denotes non-physical matter like electricity or $CO_2$. The standardized quality signifies that it is of no importance what company delivers or produces the material, because its specifications are identical. The material must be tradable on a commodity exchange – for example the CBOT, CME or LME[21] – in order to differentiate it from other

---

[21] Chicago Board of Trade, Chicago Mercantile Exchange, London Metal Exchange.

asset classes like equity. Finally, the standardized quantity allows the trading in equal lots (i.e. bushel of wheat or barrel of crude oil), which is an important factor for liquidity.

Commodities are considered as risky and volatile investments and were shunned by private banking investors for a long time. Yet they have certain attributes that make them attractive to implement in portfolios:

1. They never "go broke", in the sense that no commodity will ever be handed out for free and as such they possess a minimum worth.
2. They show a low (albeit fluctuating) correlation to other assets like equities, bonds or FX.
3. Some commodities may act as a substitute for others; for instance if soybean meal becomes too expensive, cattle feed is produced from corn or barley instead. Commodities therefore have a relatively high correlation among themselves, at least on a medium term.

These attributes, especially the low average correlation to other asset classes, are useful to diversify a portfolio. For most investors, the difficulty is to find an investment vehicle that efficiently tracks the performance of the selected commodity which, as will be shown shortly, is anything but an easy task.

Commodities are the oldest traded products on earth. They were "rediscovered" in private banking only in 2004–2005, when Goldman Sachs launched a broad campaign encouraging investors to buy their GSCI[22]-based products. The campaign proved a great success, as global commodities soared, led by crude oil. Since then, nearly every major investment bank has developed its own commodity offering, each one claiming to have the better product and methodology than the others. A host of new commodity indices has emerged in less than two years, and it is increasingly difficult both for the individual and professional investor to keep up-to-date their knowledge of each index particularity and construction parameters. However, it is the author's strong conviction that structured products are a very good, if not the best, vehicle to invest in commodities. Since commodity investments are anything than trivial, an introduction to their characteristics is helpful before going into product details and available instruments.

### 7.3.1 Commodity investors and first generation indices

The main players in commodity markets are the professionals: refiners for oil, jewelers for gold, crushers for soybeans, etc. These major market actors usually have the knowledge necessary to deal with the physical commodity and actively use futures to hedge their physical goods, not shunning physical delivery. Professionals prefer the two classical ways to get exposure to commodities: by buying them physically or through future contracts. A physical purchase occurs when a cattle food producer buys barley and soybeans directly at a farm cooperative, or when a biofuel refiner buys the corn necessary for his plant from silo storage. Professionals can also choose to buy futures and hold them until maturity to take delivery of the physical goods in one of the standard delivery locations specified in the contract. Unlike equity futures, which are cash settled, commodity futures are physically settled.

---

[22] Goldman Sachs Commodity Index

For the private-banking investor, a physical investment is out of the question.[23] First, no private person would like to get 200 metric tons of wheat or soybeans delivered to a South Dakota silo (or anywhere else) and, second, no private bank has the infrastructure or expertise to deal with physical delivery. That's the main reason why private investors are very seldom allowed to trade commodity futures at their bank. If an investor forgets to close or roll his position in futures by the first day's notice,[24] physical delivery might actually occur. Note that as a consequence of not being able to hold a commodity physically, it is impossible for a private investor to track its *spot* price.

Physical and future investments being impractical, private-banking investors have turned to funds or *index-based* products. A commodity index is itself based on futures, but an investment bank or other professional manager, who rolls the futures on a timely basis and takes upon itself any physical delivery risk, manages it. Table 7.21 shows the oldest and first generation of commodity indices.

**Table 7.21**   First generation "beta" commodity index selection

| Index name | Inception date | Specifics |
|---|---|---|
| **Reuters-Jefferies-CRB** | 1957 | Equally weighted (no rebalancing), soft commodity-heavy, front-month future rollovers. |
| **GSCI, now S&P GSCI** | 1992 | Energy-heavy, front-month future rollovers, yearly rebalancing. |
| **DJAIG** | 1998 | Diversified (capped weights), front-month future rollovers, yearly rebalancing. |
| **RICI** | 1999 | Broad, diversified, front-month future rollovers, monthly reweighting. |

First generation indices were subsequently called "beta" indices, to differentiate them from indices developed later that were built using advanced technologies. A commodity index is *per se* non-investable. The index purely represents an aggregated calculation made on one or several commodities. When it became clear to the index providers that a broader clientele wanted to invest in commodities, investment banks developed models to trade these indices and offer products based on them. The front runner was Goldman Sachs, who offered to track the performance of the GSCI first with OTC, then with securitized products. Goldman subsequently licensed the GSCI to other banks, and the index became the global benchmark for commodities with billions of investments based on it.[25] On the other hand, although the oldest of the beta indices, the CRB index was never conceived to be investable and few or no products used it as their underlying.

To summarize, the path to investing into commodities for private-banking investors is as shown in Figure 7.19.

---

[23] Except for gold and other precious metals that banks can offer to hold physically in a safe.

[24] A date before the future's maturity date from which a long future holder can exercise his right to deliver the contract physically at one of the designated locations.

[25] Goldman sold the GSCI family to S&P in 2007 who subsequently rebranded it S&P GSCI.

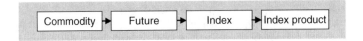

**Figure 7.19**   Building blocks for a commodity index-based product
*Source:* own representation

Products based on the first generation of indices mentioned above share one common characteristic, which could not be avoided in the past but can be optimized in today's more evolved markets: all are based on the *front-month roll* mechanism. They invest in the nearest future and, when it is close to expiry, the invested exposure is rolled into the next future available. Periodically, and especially in the years 2006–2007, the first generation indices' performance suffered from markets trading in strong *contango*. To understand the consequences of the front-month roll mechanism in commodity indices, a description of the commodity future market is necessary.

### 7.3.2   Contango, backwardation and the commodity future curve

For any commodity, there is a future price for each future expiry date. The aggregation of the future prices forms the commodity future, or forward curve. It compares with the forward yield curve, in the sense that it reflects the forecast of the market for future price levels. Note that also in commodities, future prices are seldom a good predictor of future spot prices; they purely reflect what the market *thinks* future spot prices will be, given actual market data. Dozens of variables other than supply and demand influence the shape of a future commodity curve. Just to cite a few: seasonality (crop dates in soft commodities, US driving or heating season for oil, barbecue season for pork bellies); shipping availability and cost; port strikes; terrorist attacks on pipelines and other disruptive events; storage availability; refining capacity; long- and short-term weather patterns; political interference such as import or export taxes and subsidies; US biofuel act; embargoes or country-internal price manipulation or fixing; subsidies; etc.

So what is the use of the current future curve, if it's not good at predicting the future spot price in any case? Similar to the interest rates curves, they are used by professionals to hedge, speculators to bet, and ... investment banks to price derivatives.

Figure 7.20 on West Texas Intermediate crude oil (WTI) clearly illustrates the poor forecast value of the future *spot* price by the future curve. Both curves are based on the same commodity, but at different times, with an interval of one year. The bottom line shows the future curve as of April 2007, and the top line as of April 2008. From April 2007 to April 2008, WTI crude oil for the nearest month delivery (June) rose from USD 65 to USD 116 a barrel. However, in April 2007, the future price for June 2008 deliveries traded at just USD 71, underestimating the future spot price by about USD 45. Such a large difference is not unusual in commodities, which have a higher volatility than equities on average.

The crude oil case also illustrates another important point. Drawn on individual scales, the shapes of the curves become more pronounced (Figure 7.21).

In April 2007 (left-hand chart), the WTI future prices were rising with time in the first months, until December 2008. The shape of the curve is said to be in *contango* (each future further out on the curve is more expensive than the previous). From December 2008 onwards, each subsequent delivery month is cheaper than the previous one. That part of

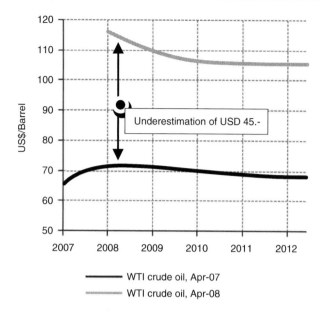

**Figure 7.20** WTI crude oil future curves
*Source:* Bloomberg

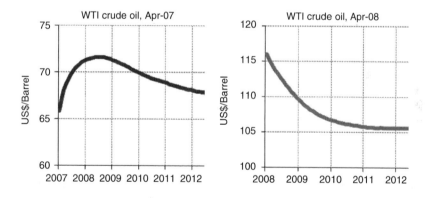

**Figure 7.21** Contango (left) and backwardation (right) commodity curves
*Source:* Bloomberg, own representation

the curve shape is said to be in *backwardation*. In April 2008 (right-hand chart), the whole curve was in strong backwardation.

A contango situation can also be translated as high inventory levels or a surplus of supply. Put another way, if inventories are high, then buyers will pay a premium to the seller for deferring the delivery of the commodity until a later period. This can be interpreted as an over-supplied market.

A backwardation situation, otherwise known as an inverted market, occurs in the physical market when there is a low inventory level or shortage of supply, i.e. a tight market. In such a situation, buyers tend to bid a premium for early delivery to secure their requirements in preference to deferred contracts where the supply will not become available until a future date. If investors are willing to pay such a premium to hold the physical asset, the underlying commodity has a so-called convenience yield. The greater the possibility that shortages will occur during the life of the futures contract, the higher the convenience yield and the higher the backwardation.

Humped curves, where the first months are in contango and the longer-dated contracts are in backwardation, occur when abundant material is available in the short term, but tightness is awaited in the longer term. The whole curve of the left-hand chart of Figure 7.21 is an example of a humped curve. U-shaped curves can happen as well for the reverse reasons.

The following example illustrates a contango situation in numbers. Suppose that a professional investor has bought 100 contracts of a commodity by way of futures, which are worth 10 per contract, exactly at the same level as the spot. Imagine that the future now expires and that the spot hasn't moved (it's still worth 10), but the next (front-month) future is trading at 11: he sells his current position for 100*10 = 1000. However, he can only buy 1000/11 = ~91 new contracts. If that situation repeats itself in the following rollover months, the investment shrinks in value without the spot moving. Figure 7.22 illustrates the example with the line representing the WTI crude oil future curve.

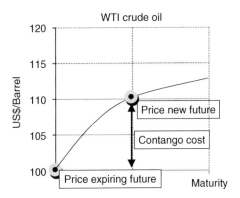

**Figure 7.22**   Contango illustration

### 7.3.3   Curve shape impact on first-generation "beta" commodity indices

A commodity index is split into three types (Table 7.22):

• The *spot* index tracks the spot prices of the underlying commodity and does not include roll effects. A spot index is non-investable.
• The *excess return* index takes the value of the spot index and adds the (positive or negative) roll yield to its performance when a rollover from an expiring future into a new one takes place.
• The *total return* index takes the value of the excess return index and additionally considers the returns generated by an interest.[26]

---

[26] Since the indices are constructed by means of futures and futures are bought on margin, the capital can be placed on the money market to earn an interest for the time of the investment.

**Table 7.22**   Commodity index types

| Index type | Performance components |
| --- | --- |
| **Spot index** | Price |
| **Excess return index** | Price + roll yield |
| **Total return index** | Price + roll yield + interest |

The difference in the performances of the three index types is best illustrated graphically (Figure 7.23).

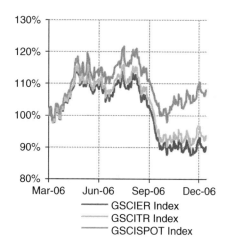

**Figure 7.23**   Value evolution of excess, total and spot return indices
*Source:* Bloomberg, own representation

Figure 7.23 shows three Goldman Sachs Commodity indices[27] between March and December 2006. All three indices track exactly the same 24 commodities. As the majority of them were trading in contango at that time, the spot return (top line) is higher than the excess and total return. When this is the case, *roll costs* occur on every roll date, since the closing of the expiring futures yield less than the cost of the opening of the new ones. If the curves had been in backwardation, roll *returns* would have occurred for the reverse reason. The excess return index (bottom line line) always underperforms the total return index (middle line) by the risk-free interest rate.

### 7.3.4   Contango and backwardation impact on structured products

Let's assume two tracker certificates, the first tracking gold and the second copper. The certificates are based on the S&P GSCI gold and S&P GSCI copper excess return indices as underlying assets. Suppose that gold is trading in contango, whereas copper is trading

---

[27] Now S&P GSCI Index

in backwardation, a market situation that occurred in January 2006. In order to measure the effect of the rollover taking place when an expiring future is rolled into the next one, the certificates' performances are compared to their respective front-month rolling futures. While excess return indices include roll costs and returns, futures do not. Since neither the future nor the excess return index includes yield returns, any difference in the performance can thus be attributed to the rollover effect.

Figure 7.24 compares the gold futures performance with the development of the certificate based on the excess return index. As gold is in contango, each subsequent contract is more expensive than the previous one. Thus, fewer contracts can be bought, and the certificate underperforms the future. The difference of more than 10 percent in less than a year is attributed to the rollover cost; the investor achieves what is called a *negative roll yield*.

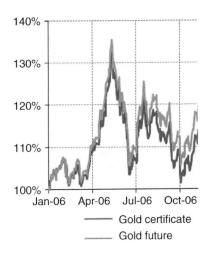

**Figure 7.24** Value of a certificate on gold (contango situation)
*Source:* Bloomberg, own representation

The situation is the opposite for the copper certificate (Figure 7.25). As copper is in backwardation the investor achieves a *positive roll yield*. The positive roll effect leads to an outperformance of the certificate against the futures curve.

The gold and copper examples show the importance of considering the term structure when analyzing or structuring products on commodities. Yet the examples shown seem relatively harmless. More extreme examples exist for first-generation index-based products when the curve's contango is greater. For instance in natural gas, the first-to-next month contango in 2006–007 amounted to 4% per month on average. An investor purchasing an index tracker based on the S&P GSCI Nat Gas index (or any other front-month based index) and holding it for a year would have seen his investment drop in value by a stunning 48% purely because of the negative roll yield.

The commodity future curves are not constant in their shape (see the WTI example of Figure 7.21). The positive roll yield of the copper certificate can rapidly become negative if the curve changes from backwardated to contangoed.

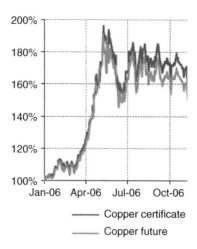

**Figure 7.25**   Value of a certificate on copper (backwardation situation)
*Source:* Bloomberg, own representation

### 7.3.5   Second generation "beta enhanced" commodity indices

With the first generation of indices like the S&P GSCI, the DJ AIG or the RICI index, there
was no alternative to front-month investments until the second generation of commodity
indices was created. These were subsequently named "beta enhanced", to account for their
advanced technology in terms of rollover and rebalancing mechanisms. As investments
in commodities soared with Goldman's initiative, professional investors and other investment banking specialists thought about solving the contango problem and began developing
new indices. This was in part possible because many future contracts experienced a sharp
increase in liquidity. The first generation indices were front-month based for a reason: lack of
liquidity in the contracts at the back-end of the curve. With a growing investor base as well
as increased hedge-fund activity, futures with longer maturities became more suitable for
integrating into an index. Thus were developed the "beta enhanced" indices, a new breed of
commodity indices that take an exposure on parts or the entire future curve instead of just
the front month. A host of sub-indices, based on the commodity sectors or on individual
commodities, became available at the same time. Figure 7.26 shows the performance of a
selection of both "beta" and "beta enhanced" indices.

The methodology of the mentioned indices is quite diverse. This book's scope is not such
that they can all be described, but two are described succinctly below. Suffice it to say that
each one has its particular single commodity weighting and rebalancing engine, as well as its
own future roll mechanism. But it is important for the investor to know that the performances
vary considerably from one index to another, as can be observed in Figure 7.26. A difference
of over 30% in annual performance divides the best from the worst performers on a five-year
basis. Figure 7.27 shows the constituents and weights of two indices from Figure 7.26: the
best (Deutsche Bank Liquid Commodity Mean Reversion Index) and the worst (Dow Jones
AIG Index) performer. The DJ AIG Index has obviously a much broader diversification than
the DBLCI-MR, and yet it performed poorly in comparison. The main reason behind this is
the rebalancing engine of the Deutsche Bank index, which uses an advanced systematic that

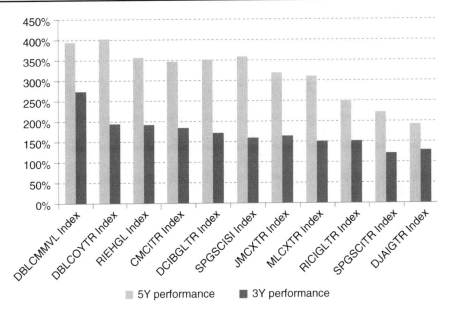

**Figure 7.26**  Selection of commodity indices, performance as of August 2008
*Source:* Bloomberg, own representation

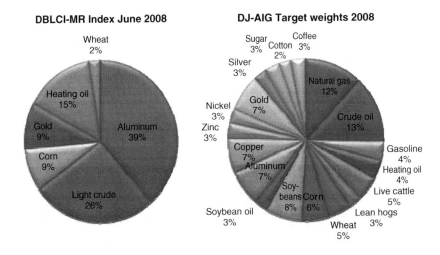

**Figure 7.27**  Deutsche Bank Mean Reversion™ Index and Dow Jones AIG™ Index weights

the DJ AIG does not implement. For the investor, this knowledge is of utmost importance; although the first generation indices are best known, they have not been the best performers in the recent past by far, partly because they rely on "old" mechanisms. Since the "new" mechanisms are relatively complex, they are also difficult to track for the investor.

In addition, the ranking is not constant; depending on the construction of the index, its rebalancing, the curve shape and evolution, its volatility etc., the outperforming index of today may be the underperforming one tomorrow. It must be said that the long-term performance of most second generation indices is often a pro-forma performance. Most have been created in the recent past, and their five-year performance remains theoretical, relying on the weightings and future rollover mechanisms of the back-test period. While back-testing is a useful method when considering investments, there's no guarantee that any thus calculated (out)performance will continue in the future. However, the message to the investor at this point is that the selection of the correct index has a major performance impact. The complexity of comparing all the indices with their weighting, rebalancing and investment mechanisms to the outlook on the different commodities is difficult, to say the least. One sensible approach is to divide one's commodity investment into several tranches allocated to different indices, if the volume allows it. In commodities, as in other asset classes, diversification is a key element to the portfolio performance. That way, the risk of stumbling exactly on the worst possible index is mitigated.

### 7.3.6  Commodity sub-indices

Like equities, which are split into industry sectors,[28] commodities are distinguished in four main categories (Table 7.23).

**Table 7.23**  Commodity categories and major components

| Category | Major components |
| --- | --- |
| **Energy** | Crude oil, refined oil products (heating oil, diesel, gasoline...), natural gas, ethanol |
| **Precious metals** | Gold, silver, platinum, palladium |
| **Industrial metals** | Copper, aluminum, lead, zinc, nickel, iron ore, ... |
| **Soft commodities** | Wheat, corn, soybeans, soy oil, soy meal, sugar, coffee, cocoa, rough rice, palm oil, FCOJ, live cattle, lean hogs, cotton... |

The commodity indices cited in Figure 7.26 are global commodity indices, each one attempting to optimize the performance of the market as a whole. To gain an exposure on a commodity sector or a single commodity, a sector or single commodity index must be selected. Not all of the global indices are organized in sector or single indices. Some do not offer exposure to the less liquid commodities, like frozen concentrated orange juice (FCOJ). In addition, the performance ranking of the different sub-index providers differs from the global indices. Figures 7.28 and 7.29 shows the UBS CMCI Agricultural index and the Deutsche Bank DBLCI Agricultural index, two agricultural sub-indices from the named index families that are described in more detail in Section 7.3.7.

---

[28] The Global Industry Classification Standard splits equities into 10 main sectors: energy, materials, industrials, consumer discretionary, consumer staples, health care, financials, information technology, telecommunication services and utilities.

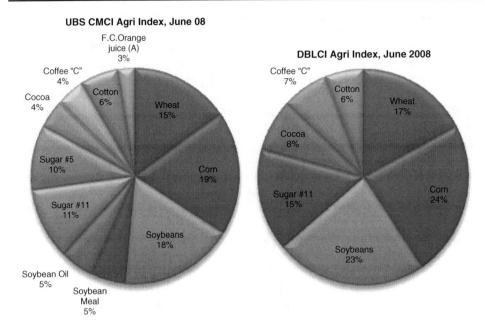

**Figure 7.28** Commodity sub-index examples from UBS and Deutsche Bank

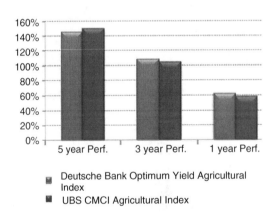

**Figure 7.29** Performance of commodity sub-indices (as of June 2008)
*Source:* Bloomberg

Both indices have similar performances, but their composition varies to some extent.

### 7.3.7 Particular index families

As mentioned, in order to give an overview of the diversity in the construction and the methodology of commodity indices, two "beta enhanced" index families will be described in more detail: those of Deutsche Bank and UBS.

Deutsche Bank was one of the first investment banks to issue a second-generation index on a broad basis in February 2003: the Deutsche Bank Liquid Commodity Index.[29] It tracks only six commodities – light crude oil, heating oil, gold, aluminum, corn and wheat – which are all very liquid. Its two main features, mean-reversion and roll optimization, solved the main problems encountered in the "front-month only" first-generation of indices. Since its inception, it has shown a very good performance record, albeit the long-term volatility remains relatively high, around 20% p.a.[30] The high liquidity of the included commodities means that costs and spreads are kept low for any structured products. However, due to the complexity of the construction, it remains difficult to explain both the current weighting and the performance to a private-banking investor, as both the weighting and the tenor change constantly. In addition, the index looks as if it were quite concentrated in terms of risk, tracking only six commodities. Still, it remains one of the best-performing commodity index families, with many new sub-indices and strategies having been developed around the initial concept.

Figure 7.30 shows the commodities included in the index at two different dates. It gives a hint about how the index-rebalancing engine functions: in just nine months, the weightings have been largely reshuffled.[31] In contrast to first generation indices which are rebalanced on a yearly basis, the DBLCI-MR index is actively (mathematically) managed on a monthly basis. As of 2008, the DBLCI has been divided into many sector and single commodity sub-indices.

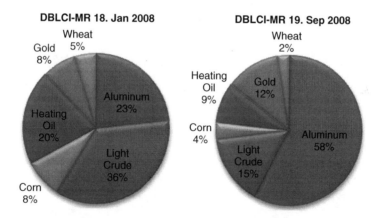

**Figure 7.30**    Deutsche Bank Liquid Commodity index – mean reversion
*Source:* index.db.com

In contrast, UBS has developed a very large and unique palette of commodity indices of the second generation: the CMCI, or Constant Maturity Commodity Index family. The

---

[29] DBLCI-MR™.

[30] Source: Bloomberg, 400 day historical volatility.

[31] In addition, look at the left-hand pie chart of Figure 7.27, which gives an intermediate status of the index between the dates mentioned in Figure 7.30. During the nine months covered by the three charts, the weight of aluminum in the index has subsequently increased from 23% to 39% to 58%.

weighting and rebalancing of the index family is based on the economic value of a commodity (CPI and PPI) in major economies and the consumption in USD terms of that commodity. In addition, caps and liquidity determine maximal weights. UBS calculates several indices on single commodities that allow investors to take positions globally or on individual points of the forward curve. The particularity of the CMCI is that the exposure thus taken stays at a fixed maturity on the term structure. In other words, the exposure does not mature and needs to be rolled at the expiry of the future contract, but is rolled on a continuous basis, hence its name. This is very practical for sophisticated investors who want to actively manage single commodity investments, and take positions on the forward curve in order to optimize the roll yield or take a view on a particular point.

Figure 7.31 illustrates the concept of constant maturity; the left-hand chart shows a traditional investment in which an initially implemented exposure gradually matures until it reaches the expiry of the future contract and has to be rolled in one block. The right-hand figure shows the constant maturity methodology: small batches of the total exposure are rolled on a daily basis into the next available contract, so the whole investment never deviates from the initial selected forward contract. The advantage of this methodology is principally lower costs in contango situations as the slope of a typical contango is steeper in the front months than in the higher maturity months. In backwardated curves, a positive roll yield is also generated. The CMCI family offers the possibility to invest at several points on the forward curve; investments on the three month, six month, one year, two year, etc. points on the curve are possible. The main advantage for the investor is the diversification of his investment along the commodity forward curve.

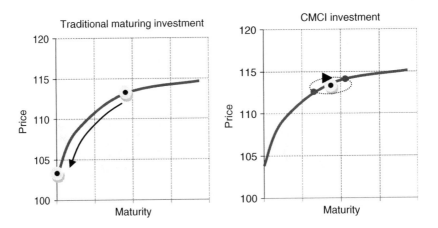

**Figure 7.31**  Constant maturity illustration

The long-term volatility of the CMCI is lower than the DBLCI-MR index, around 15%.[32] The CMCI family offers one of the widest available choices for structuring commodity products.

---

[32] Source: Bloomberg, 400-day historical volatility, June 2008.

### 7.3.8 Choosing an appropriate second-generation index

One of the main drivers for investment banks to offer new commodity indices was to lure investors in captive products. Actually, each investment bank can only issue products on its own index family. For instance, as of 2008 Deutsche Bank cannot issue a product based on CMCI, and UBS cannot issue a DBLCI certificate, since neither licenses its indices to other banks and each prefers to market their proprietarily developed indices. It can be assumed that the margins for the issuers are high, although there is no available data on that matter. Yet these high margins are to be weighed against the benefit of the performance of this new breed of indices. Any investor should be happy to pay a 1% or even 2% annual fee, if the chosen index outperforms the next best by 5% per annum. Compared to commodity funds, which often have a total expense ratio of over 2% and where the performance depends on the success of the fund manager (who may well buy the mentioned indices in one form or another), this seems like a bargain.

Hence, the choice of the index is the first element to structure a commodity product. The selection should not only be made on the index's past performance, which is no guarantee of future results in any case, but be determined by a number of factors, some of which are:

- the forecast for the market;
- the exposure of the index to the desired commodity;
- the roll methodology;
- the rebalancing methodology;
- the rating of the issuer;
- the capability of the issuer to issue the desired structure; and
- the costs.

The assessment and weighting of these points in order to select the optimal index may seem daunting. However, practice shows that most points solve themselves if one proceeds through elimination and common sense. For instance, if an investor would like to take an exposure on soft commodities only, the choice of indices already falls to approximately 10, the remaining global indices having no sub-sector offer. Further, if the rating of the issuer must be AA- or better, that number shrinks to circa five. Looking at the CRR <go> function of Bloomberg shows that the three best performers already fit these criteria, being tied in a nutshell in terms of performance (Table 7.24).[33]

**Table 7.24** Second generation commodity index selection

| Index | Name | 12 month performance |
|-------|------|---------------------|
| **JMCXAGTR** | JPMorgan Commodity Curve Agri Index | 52.43% |
| **DBLCYTAG** | Deutsche Bank Liquid Agri Index | 51.34% |
| **CMAGTR** | UBS Bloomberg CMCI Agri Index | 51.15% |

Source: Bloomberg

---

[33] Source: Bloomberg, 28th of April 2008.

From there on, it's a matter of technicalities and preferences; can the issuer provide the desired structure? Is the single commodity weighting adequate? Is it broad enough or should it rather be concentrated on the majors? Is the position on the forward curve in line with expectations? Is an active management of the curve allocation desired or not? And so on. Answering these questions will quickly point out the ideal index on which to base the product. This part is best discussed with product specialists, as they have in principle the tools and the knowledge to provide the best possible advice.

### 7.3.9 Product recommendations

In theory at least, the full range of products including all kind of exotic options is possible in commodities as well. In practice, however, several factors limit the practical use of exotics. Since many structured products have longer dated maturities, the liquidity of the underlying commodity future on which the index is based might be rather thin. Crude oil futures may be liquid for up to five years maturity, but soft commodities like wheat or soybeans are seldom traded beyond the next harvest. This influences the spread of the forward price. In addition, listed optionality in the longer-dated maturities is practically nonexistent, making the determination of the implied volatility used to price the product's option a random guess from the trader. The trader will take a large margin to avoid being caught on the wrong side of the deal – to the detriment of the investor. Also, the longer the maturity, the bigger the risks of hedging gaps,[34] which again increases the implied hedge costs.

Hence, sensible advice is to include as few options as possible in commodity products, and to avoid exotics, like barrier options. The possible benefit of multiple options (like spreads, caps, etc.) or worst-of features is most of the time annihilated by the prohibitive costs and safety margins the trader or the issuer includes in the pricing.

### 7.3.10 Dos and don'ts for commodity capital guarantee

Capital guaranteed products are notoriously difficult to structure efficiently on commodities, mainly because of the high volatility, entailing long maturities as well as large volatility and forward spreads. Some recommendations:

- To reduce the volatility overall, use global commodity indices instead of sub-sectors or individual commodities.
- To reduce volatility further, use an index with a low historical volatility if the choice of the index is still pending. That index will most certainly have a partial exposure to the back-end of the forward curve, as it is less volatile than the front-end.
- To reduce the volatility spread, take an index on which commodity products with embedded options already exist on a large scale. Traders will take a lower volatility spread on an index on which they already have an option exposure.
- If possible, reduce the time to maturity, as this helps reduce the spread taken on the forward.
- Avoid caps, asianing, and any other exotic or additional option component. Settle for a lower participation instead.

---

[34] Mainly due to trading limits, see below.

- Finally, yet importantly, take the shape of the forward curve into account. If the chosen index is front-end weighted, the long call will be less expensive with a curve in backwardation. In the issuer's calculation model, the call, which is at-the-money spot, will be out-of-the money forward. See an example on crude oil with Figure 7.32.

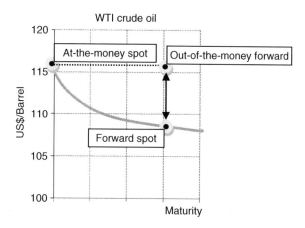

**Figure 7.32** Forward call value with a backwardated curve

### 7.3.11 Dos and don'ts for commodity yield enhancement

At first sight, yield enhancement commodity products like the reverse convertible or barrier reverse convertible often look attractive to the private-banking investor. However, behind the "great looking" conditions featuring high coupons and low barriers are sometimes hidden some rather questionable tricks the investor should know about. Some comments:

- Choosing an index with predominantly front-end exposure will increase the coupon or deepen the discount for reverse convertibles and discount certificates respectively. Due to the higher volatility at the front-end, the short option embedded is worth more, yielding a higher premium.
- A global index will yield less coupon/discount than a single commodity, but investors should take into account the benefit of diversification.
- When the forward curve is in contango and the index heavily front-month weighed, roll costs will be high! Barriers will be effectively closer to the spot than assumed. All other things remaining equal, the negative roll yield will drive the price of the product down, closer to the barrier.
- Frequently, worst-of options are used in yield enhancement commodity products. In commodities as well as in other asset classes, the investor must pay close attention to where the value comes from. Usually, one component yields all the value, the others being there just for show. A known example is the one-year worst-of gold/crude oil/natural gas reverse convertible based on the front-month with a 50% barrier. Suppose that natural gas trades at "only" a 2.5% contango per month (which is low compared to the 4% seen previously), a one year 50% barrier is being "eaten up" fast, and is effectively set at ... 20% below spot, not such a large margin if one considers the volatility of natural

gas. The benefit from the correlation between the other two components is negligible in comparison. Choosing an index that is exposed to the back-end of the curve (where the contango is flatter and the volatility is lower) will produce a product with worse looking conditions. However, this structure will be far closer to reality than the disguised front-end product with its high barrier.

- Due to the preceding point, as well as for the liquidity and trading spread reasons mentioned above, it is advisable not to use barriers at all until the market becomes more transparent and liquid.

### 7.3.12 Dos and don'ts for commodity participation

The same conclusions and recommendations as for yield enhancement products apply for participation products. Keep optionality simple and short term. The author recommends avoiding investing into longer-dated bonus certificates or airbag certificates for the same reasons not to invest in longer-dated yield enhancement products. In fact, unless the investor is very well informed about the functioning of the commodity markets and the available indices as well as their functioning and methodology, the author's recommendation is to take a view on the asset class as a whole, select the appropriate total return index, and invest in a tracker certificate. For any investor who is not totally risk averse, this is probably the most efficient way to gain exposure to commodities. Keep in mind that the indices of the new generation are themselves actively managed, both in terms of the individual commodity rebalancing as well as the future position on the curve.

Other investment vehicles like funds or exchange-traded commodities (ETCs) exist. However, these vehicles are seldom based on a second-generation index investment methodology, unless they are managed in a discretionary way. If so, the questions of the manager's skill and his benchmark as well as costs arise. Still today, many commodity funds have a first-generation index as benchmark. They would probably not fare so well when measured against a second-generation index, both in terms of performance and volatility.

### 7.3.13 Commodity conclusions

It is now time to draw some conclusions for the investor:

- It's difficult to gain exposure through physical delivery or future contracts, hence, commodity index certificates are good investment vehicles for private banking purposes.
- Most important in commodity exposure is the choice of the right index. This decision alone may already account for over 50% of the performance.
- The choice of the index will be based on its broadness, liquidity, roll methodology, rebalancing factors and curve positioning. The structuring capabilities of the issuer become important only if the structure is other than a simple delta one product.
- The investor should decide whether the exposure should be global, or limited to a category or even a single commodity exposure.
- Optionality, if necessary, is to be kept simple, using plain vanilla options, and maturities should be medium to short.

One last comment about commodities: many exchanges have daily trading limits beyond which it is not possible to buy or sell. In wheat, for instance, the daily limit is 50 c/bu, calculated from the close of the previous day. In corn, the limit is 30 c/bu. When a commodity reaches the upper or lower limit, it is said to be trading "limit up" or "limit down". These limits have been set by the exchanges to dampen the effects of a hypothetical crash (both to the upside and the downside), giving time for the market participants to reassess the situation and limiting the overall volatility. The trading stops once a limit is reached and resumes for that day only if the market reverses its course. For the private banking investor, as well as for the rest of the market participants, these limit rules can have some unwanted consequences. A situation might arise when the commodity in question is limit down for several days, and no investor holding a product will be able to sell it until the market has found its equilibrium again, as the investment bank having issued the product would not be able to unhedge its positions. For products on several commodities, this situation will arise more often than products on single commodities. Investment banks attempt to ease this situation by trying to proxy-hedge[35] in some situations, but if the whole market is locked at its limits, even they will not be able to fill the orders.

---

[35] Action of hedging one open position with another underlying asset. Both assets must be strongly correlated for the hedge to be effective.

# Recent Developments

## 8.1 CUSTOMIZED INDEX PRODUCTS

### 8.1.1 The index becomes a commodity

Every investor knows indices. In the field of equities, the Dow Jones Industrial is probably the best known index worldwide. The SMI™, DAX™, CAC™, and FTSE™ will also ring a bell among financial practitioners, and commodity indices have already been discussed at length. The public also knows inflation or jobless rate indices. Less commonly known are the MSCI World™ or the Citigroup Global Fixed Income™ indices, which are used by professional asset managers as global benchmarks. Then there are indices like the Baltic Freight™ or Sustainability™ Index and hundreds more of which few have probably heard about. Today there seems to be an index for just about everything that can be tracked, a theme, a trading strategy, an asset or a purpose. In fact, the number of indices created in the last two years has increased exponentially as every bank or broker has multiplied its marketing efforts for the new ones they created. Just to cite a few popular examples, dozens of global water, infrastructure and power supply indices have seen the day since 2006. Let's take a step back and analyze how and why this multitude of indices has been created.

With the evolution of computing power, electronic trading, and straight-through processes in their trading and operation departments, the investment banks were able to develop very flexible tools which they made accessible to their clients. It started years ago with so-called institutional *portfolio trades*. Institutional investors like pension, mutual or hedge funds held large or super-large portfolios, of which the equity allocation could be considered as stock baskets. These included dozens or hundreds of stocks, often listed on different exchanges. While the equity portfolios were more or less static in their composition, the overall asset allocation weight between cash, bonds, stocks, commodities and alternatives varied according to the fund's model. When the manager decided to change the asset allocation of the portfolio, say reduce the equity quota by 5%, instead of entering dozens or potentially hundreds of sell orders for each individual stock, a single order was issued to the broker. The composition of the portfolio was known and kept electronically by the investment bank (often acting as depositary as well); the order was handled as a basket or portfolio trade, and just by entering the amount to change and pressing the button, the dozens or hundreds of sell orders were triggered by the computer.

As more and more of these portfolio trades were set up, whole machineries were developed to keep track of the portfolios, their performance, risk, and mark-to-market value. Portfolio trading became so common at the majority of investment banks that it became a commodity. Needless to say, the investment banks use portfolio trading for routing the buy and sell orders of their own model portfolios. Over time, in order to differentiate each other from the competition, some brokers and banks found that quoting the mark-to-market value of the portfolio on an information system like Reuters or Bloomberg would help their clients keep better track of them. It was then just a matter of registering the name to transform the basket of stocks into an index.

Basically, the index creation offer was a means to enhance the equity cash business where margins are pitifully thin. This opportunity met a demand from institutional investors using the core/satellite[1] portfolio approach and from the growing client base of structured products distributors. As already mentioned, it is not possible to invest directly into an index, but an investment vehicle like a certificate on an index will do the job perfectly. Banks also had an interest in increasing the value of their research departments. Hence, a multitude of index certificates that "securitize" the research department top stock picks through an index certificate have been issued to give investors the opportunity of participating in those picks.

Today, nearly any financial participant, even private investors,[2] can ask a bank to set up a customized index. The index can be global, industry-specific, theme-oriented or just about anything the investor can think of. There are, however, certain rules to observe in order to make the customized index worth its name.

### 8.1.2 Index general rules

An index has a few characteristics that should be upheld and that differentiate it from other investments like funds or hedge funds:

- it focuses on one strategy with certain rules;
- the rules of the strategy are stable over time; and
- the rules of the strategy are transparent.

As a rule, an index does not switch strategies on a continuous or a discretionary basis. It follows one strategy, which may be either static or active. An example of a *static* index strategy is, for example the investment into the 20 European stocks with the highest earnings growth momentum with quarterly reviews. An example of a *dynamic* index strategy is, for example, the investment into the 20 European stocks with the highest earnings growth momentum (same as the static index) *unless* the average global European earnings momentum turns negative at which point the index sheds its stock positions and invests into money-market instruments, quarterly reviewed. Once the rules are set, they should remain stable over time, especially if the goal of the index is to entice others to invest in its strategy. The strategy should be timeless, and not be limited to a certain market condition or to the willingness of a manager to pursue it.

The rules defining an index should be transparent. This does not necessarily mean that they are accessible to the public. The index provider can keep them accessible only to licensees, who pay a fee to be allowed to issue products with the name of the index included in the product. The licensee, often an investment bank, can then hedge the product according to the index strategy on a rebalancing date. If the rules are not transparent, the investment bank cannot hedge itself properly when a rebalancing takes place and will probably not even want to issue products on the index. For private investors (and for that matter all non-licensee

---

[1] A portfolio management method where the core (essential) part of the portfolio is set up with liquid and cheap instruments, like exchange-traded funds on indices, forming the beta "$\beta$" of the portfolio. That part of the portfolio seldom moves. The satellites are positions where the portfolio manager expects to generate alpha "$\alpha$", like actively managed single stocks, or funds, or passive managed instruments giving the portfolio a style or a tilt. The satellites trade more often.

[2] Provided they have the minimum amount necessary.

potential investors), a transparent and accessible set of rules is practical and attractive, as is the availability of the current holdings (or at least the top 10 holdings).

### 8.1.3 Considerations for creating an index

The creation of an index must bring an advantage to its originator. For instance, an independent asset manager may wish to offer his clients a means to follow self-developed rigorous rule-based strategy. An index set up and calculated on a daily basis by his bank helps him keep his clients informed. An asset manager with large and complex rule-based equity portfolios may wish to simplify the performance calculation including the numerous corporate actions (splits, dividends, mergers. . .) of the portfolio. The bank calculating the index includes all this and reflects the information in the performance.

Nowadays, numerous products can be issued on customized indices by the bank providing an individual index service and acting as index calculation agent. For instance, the independent asset manager could issue a bonus certificate or a capital guaranteed product on the rigorous strategy index. If the purpose of the index is the offering of structured products on that index, the index calculation agent may offer the indexing service for free as long as the product(s) generate enough trading volume. While the volume needed for an investment bank to offer an indexing service varies, a minimum of CHF 15/EUR 10 millions for classic indices should be observed. For more complex indexes, involving assets with a lower liquidity or that are more difficult to access, CHF 50/EUR 35 millions are required. The only way to determine the exact cost of creating a customized index is to discuss the topic with the bank.

Another advantage of an index is that the rules keep the investment strategy focused. This is a major advantage versus a plain basket certificate, which is by definition a static investment where the selected underlying assets do not change once the basket has been set. However, this feature can also be realized by the issuance of a dynamic certificate with objective investment criteria, as mentioned in Section 3.3.1.

Last but not least, an index has a non-negligible marketing potential. In the eyes of an investor, an index stands for seriousness, stability and timelessness. It is superior to a strategy fund from a branding view for all but the most renowned funds, as it represents unbiased neutrality. It has certainly superior marketing potential than a static or objectively rule-based basket.

### 8.1.4 Dos and don'ts

To summarize, the major reasons for or against creating a customized index are listed below.

- Don't create an index on a whim. Indices have their costs and are among the financial instruments with the longest possible horizon, namely perpetual. Consider the costs versus the benefits.
- Create an index with transparent, clear and timeless rules.
- Create an index when the purpose is a combination of marketing, building a track record and product-creation on the underlying assets. Make sure that the volume can be gathered.
- If not enough volume for products can be found, revert to an objectively rule-based dynamic certificate, which can be issued with a smaller size.

- Consider the option of creating an index versus an actively managed certificate (see below).

## 8.2   ACTIVELY MANAGED CERTIFICATES

Actively managed certificates (AMC) have already been briefly discussed at the end of Chapter 3. However, the possibilities of this investment form are so encompassing that it warrants a whole chapter to itself. In order to situate the AMC correctly in the certificate universe, Table 8.1 recaps the possible certificate forms.

**Table 8.1**   The three certificate forms

| Name | Feature | Asset rebalancing |
|------|---------|-------------------|
| **Tracker certificate** | Static underlying assets | None |
| **Objectively rule-based certificate** | Dynamic underlying assets | Mathematic |
| **AMC** | Dynamic underlying assets | Discretionary |

The AMC is the most flexible investment form of all certificates and, indeed, of all structured products. The initial underlying assets can be exchanged for others on a discretionary basis. This is the major difference between this and the rule-based certificate where a mathematical formula regulates the investments.

### 8.2.1   AMC history

In July 2006, the Swiss Federal Banking Commission (SFBC)[3] issued a paper changing the practice for issuing structured products. Before that, single structured products with dynamic asset allocation had to be submitted to the SFBC for approval, especially if the dynamic strategy potentially conflicted with the Collective Investment Schemes Act (CISA).[4] The July 2006 paper changed this practice, clearly excluding structured products from the CISA with the effect of largely deregulating them. In theory, from that point onwards, a structured product could have any discretionary strategy. Nothing much happened until a communication from the SWX (now SIX) in April 2007 allowed the listing at the exchange for "actively managed certificates with discretionary management". Since then, the AMC form has known a tremendous development among professionals.

### 8.2.2   AMC construction

The rules are few and the possibilities are quasi limitless. In its basic form, the AMC is a tracker certificate, securitized as any other structured product. The AMC has three participants: the Investment Advisor (IA), the issuer and the investor (Figure 8.1). In some cases, the IA and the investor are the same entity. The IA can be compared to a fund

---

[3] Eidgenössische Bankenkomission, (EBK).
[4] Kollektivanlagegesetz (KAG).

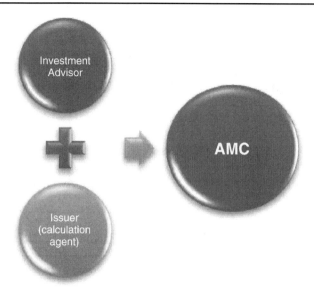

**Figure 8.1**   AMC components

manager: he determines the strategy and the investments made within the certificate. The IA also triggers and transmits the buy and sell orders to the issuer. The issuer (in reality the calculation agent) executes the trades transmitted by the IA and he provides the listing, secondary market price, etc. In short, the issuer acts as the administrator to the product. The AMC construction looks pretty much like a fund setup. In fact, AMCs are competing with funds to a large extent.

### 8.2.3   The investment advisor

The role of the investment advisor is to determine the strategy of the AMC. As such, the IA can theoretically be any financial participant (Table 8.2).

**Table 8.2**   Potential investment advisors

| Institution | Acting through |
| --- | --- |
| Bank | Employee or committee of research department |
| Independent asset manager | Asset manager himself |
| Hedge-fund company | Fund manager himself |
| Trust | Trustee |
| Private individual | Must act through a bank with separate agreement |

One of the most interested groups should be the independent asset managers. These small companies, commonly only composed of one or two individuals, manage their client's assets, which are often spread across a dozen depositary banks. When the independent asset manager switches one asset (i.e. a stock) for another for his discretionary mandates, he must give the order to several banks individually. An AMC would help solve that problem. The AMC can be deposited at all the managers' banks and include all the discretionary assets. When changing his asset allocation, the manger issues a single order to the AMC issuer. The change is reflected in the price of the AMC for all the clients of the independent asset manager.

The IA enjoys a wide freedom in the asset allocation within the AMC. An IA can rebalance or change the asset allocation of an AMC at any time (even intraday) or on preset dates (i.e. on the third Friday of every month, or quarterly ...), depending how the AMC has been set up initially. In theory, he could use derivatives, including OTC options, swaps or futures. He can park part or all of the assets in cash.

However free the IA might be, it is nevertheless recommended to define a clear strategy and stick to it, if only for marketing reasons. It is also a good idea to benchmark the AMC against a recognized index. For instance, if the AMC's goal is to beat the Eurostoxx50 index using only ethical European stocks, then benchmark it against the total return Eurostoxx50 index.

### 8.2.4  AMC characteristics and mutual funds

Although an AMC is not a mutual fund, both investment vehicles are often compared because of their similar characteristics. There are some major differences, though. What makes the AMC so attractive is its flexibility. In order to issue an AMC, a minimum of CHF 10 million notional investment is needed. This compares to ca. CHF 30 million for private-labeled funds and CHF 50 million for a full-fledged mutual fund. An AMC does not need lengthy registrations[5] and it can be launched as soon as the IA and the issuer are ready. The strategy within the AMC can be loosely defined, for instance "Growth stocks worldwide", or "Agricultural commodities". The IA can choose to sell some assets short, or decide to take leverage. Indeed the AMC can be structured like a hedge fund, with a global leverage far above the typical 130/30[6] found in the mutual fund industry. An AMC can invest in multiple asset classes. It all depends on the initial setup of the product. All these possibilities make the AMC a fund-like investment vehicle with more flexibility.

**Table 8.3**  Differences between an AMC and funds

|                 | AMC                          | Mutual fund                       |
| --------------- | ---------------------------- | --------------------------------- |
| **CISA**        | Excluded                     | Included                          |
| **Leverage**    | Theoretically unlimited      | Limited Max 130/30                |
| **Short positions** | Theoretically unlimited  | Limited                           |
| **Registration**| Not needed                   | Mandatory                         |
| **Seed money**  | Ca. CHF 10 m or equivalent   | Ca. 30 m/50 m or equivalent       |
| **Liquidity**   | Intraday                     | End-of-day basis with deadlines   |

Source: SFBX, SIX, own representation

A big difference between a mutual fund and an AMC is that the latter does not enjoy the investor protection given by the CISA. A fund must implement the strategy it follows and invest the investor's cash in the selected assets, and pool them in a common fund deposit.

---

[5] In Switzerland, the delay to register a fund at the Swiss Federal Banking Commission can take up to six months.
[6] Refers to the maximum long and short exposure a fund manager can take: up to 130% long and 30% short.

An AMC must track the performance of the IA's strategy by reflecting it in the AMC's secondary market price, but its issuer is not legally bound to invest the investor's cash into the selected assets. In other words, the issuer is not obliged to execute physically the orders it gets from the IA, which in turn means that should the issuer default, there is no common investment pool from which investors can recover their investments. This extreme scenario will only happen in case the issuer files for bankruptcy.

## 8.3   ELECTRONIC TRADING PLATFORMS

For a long time, structured products were issued only when the volume of subscriptions reached a minimum amount. The exact number varied depending on the type of the product, but around CHF/EUR/USD 1 million was usually enough to launch the issue. As the number of new products grew exponentially, major issuers were confronted with rising problems in handling the increased flow, especially in the secondary market. Much of the administration tasks as well as trading were done manually, and frequent errors occurred on term-sheets, trade confirmations and in the settlement instructions. The number of employees necessary to handle the ever-growing amount of issues rose proportionally, which consequently kept the cost for launching a product high.

At some point, leading institutions in the structured products business like UBS decided that an automation of specific markets was a necessary step to take the business to the next level. Internet and intranet technology had advanced to a point where reliable and fast applications allowed the trading, settlement and term-sheet production to be fully automated through the web. At UBS, the first market tackled was FX. Of all asset classes, FX was best suited for automation. It has a limited amount of currency pairs and a few standard structures that are widely used by investors. UBS decided to develop an electronic platform it later named "FX Investor", allowing its investment advisors to directly access a limited range of FX products electronically, through its intranet. The FX Investor offers two dozen FX pair combinations and half a dozen basic structures, like dual currency deposits with or without barriers and various capital guaranteed FX products (like one-touch or range accrual notes). Once a UBS investment advisor was trained and proficient with the electronic trading system, he could trade FX structured products directly through the firm's intranet.

This was a major breakthrough for the structured product business, because it integrates the whole value chain within one tool. Intermediary resources like the back-office, mid-office, settlement and sales desks could be allocated to other tasks. Thus, the cost of issuing one product drops from some thousands of CHF to a few dozen CHF. Consequently, the economically minimum amount required to issue a new FX product drops to CHF 50 000 or equivalent. The electronic platform enables an investment advisor to structure an FX product "live", through just a few clicks on his mouse. With a little training, products can be structured within two minutes, while the investor is on the other end of the phone or even sitting beside his advisor. Products become "tailor-made" once more, structured to fit every investor's portfolio on an individual basis. Indicative or final term-sheets in PDF format are available to download, print, or to send by e-mail a few seconds later, in six languages if necessary.

Besides lower costs, another major advantage of the electronic trading platforms is that investment advisors take over the role of the structurers. This in itself removes a major bottleneck in the conveyance of knowledge from the structurers to the investment advisors.

By structuring the products themselves, the investment advisors assimilate the knowledge faster and remember it longer than they otherwise would. No amount of presentations, training and teaching replaces the do-it-yourself experience. The value chain becomes shorter and more efficient, because the multiple back and forth telephone calls between the investor, his investment advisor, the structurer and the trader become unnecessary.

### 8.3.1 Available trading platforms

After the success of electronic trading on the FX market with internal investment advisors, UBS decided to make the platform available for third party users. External asset managers and other medium- or small-sized private banks could apply for login access and structure products for their clients. This proved again a success, as the externals could better serve their clients and UBS experienced additional business flows.

Equities were the second market where electronic platforms were later developed (Table 8.4). UBS, but also Vontobel and EFG Financial Products, launched platforms that could be accessed by third parties. The platforms of these providers differ in many aspects (available products and underlying assets, speed to calculate a product, minimum issues, listing, secondary market and so forth), but have a single common goal: to implement products quickly and efficiently. Similar to the FX platform, the equity tools allow its user the structuring and trading of structured products within a few minutes, faster than in some plain vanilla bond, fund or equity markets.

**Table 8.4** Available electronic trading platforms (as of February 2009)

| Name | Issuer | Web Address |
|---|---|---|
| **FX Investor** | UBS | www.ubs.com/fxinvestor |
| **Equity Investor** | UBS | www.ubs.com/equityinvestor |
| **Deritrade** | Vontobel | www.deritrade.ch |
| **Constructor** | EFG FP | services.efgfp.com |

(All these websites require logins and passwords.)

Table 8.5 summarizes the pros and cons of issuing new products via electronic trading platforms against the classical way of offering "off the shelf" products with a subscription period.

**Table 8.5** E-trading versus classical structuring

| Feature | E-trading | "Off the shelf" with subscription period |
|---|---|---|
| **Fixing (trading)** | Instantaneous | Predefined date, often set weeks in the future |
| **Structuring parameters** | Individual | Identical |
| **Volumes necessary to launch structure** | Low (e.g. EUR 50 000) | High (e.g. EUR 1 000 000) |
| **Choice of underlying assets** | Limited | Unlimited |
| **Choice of structures** | Limited | Unlimited |
| **Issuing costs** | Low | High |

The major limitations in electronic trading to date are the limited choice of underlying assets (between 110 and 250 stocks and stock indices) and the relatively thin choice of structures from which to choose. For instance, none of the platforms available as of February 2009 offered twin-win certificates or shark notes. Neither fixed income (e.g. range accruals) nor commodity assets were available. However, the platform providers strive to enhance their offerings and improve the user-friendliness of their graphical user interfaces. Overall, the author is convinced that these e-trading platforms are the first step toward what the future of the structured product market will look like. As the products can be structured to the liking of each individual, it is probable that an atomization of the products will take place: no more large "one size fits all" issues, but many small-size issues, individually parameterized.

Since products can be electronically structured for very small amounts, the long and tedious secondary market products searches become to a certain degree unnecessary. Previously, to satisfy an investor's need, and if that investor had not the necessary notional to issue a new product, an advisor had to consult multiple issuer websites to find a fitting product. With today's available tools, the needs of the investor can be satisfied within a few minutes. Of course, it's not always that easy: the underlying asset, the currency, the payoff, etc., may not be electronically available, in which case the advisor will still have to search for a secondary market product. Moreover, the advisor may already have several products of the e-trading platform issuer and not want to take any more of its credit risk for his clients.

The advantages still far outweigh the disadvantages, so it is likely that many investment advisors would like to profit from the advantages offered by e-trading platforms. It is in any case worthwhile trying them out.

### 8.3.2 Who can have access?

Although only a few clicks are necessary to construct and trade a standard product, most e-trading platform providers are restrictive with trading access. Private persons are generally not authorized, and only selected financial counterparties are granted access.

Reasons for not granting access to private persons are understandable: there's no way an issuer could know if the person was trading within the limits of his wealth, unless the e-trading platform were coupled with the investor's bank account, which is currently not the case. A careless investor not aware of his limits could engage with products for far more wealth than he possessed. Potential losses reaching higher than the investor's total wealth would be passed on to the issuer.

For financial entities, the reasons for granting or not granting access are more technical in nature. Those entities that do not have their own structured product-issuing program (the so-called pure "buy-side", which purchases the products from other issuers) are usually granted access. For instance, external independent asset managers and small private banks are the primary business partners that the e-trading providers seek to gain as clients. It is in the interest of the e-trading platform providers to bring as many third-party partners as possible to issue their products through their platform. Not only does the third-party entity provide additional and regular business to the issuer's trading books, but also the persons operating the tool become used to it and become captive clients. Those competitors that issue products themselves will likely not be allowed access to the e-trading platforms, because they could try to arbitrage the trading books of the platform's issuer. The volatility surface, which is the "secret" parameter influencing each trader's product prices, would be visible to a competing issuer and the latter could theoretically use that information to his advantage.

### 8.3.3  Conclusion

Electronic platforms will take a growing place in the future of structured product trading. It is likely that additional issuers to those mentioned above will offer such tools in the coming years when they begin to feel the increased competition from those who offer them already. The available product types and underlying assets will keep growing. It is a relatively simple thing for an issuer to add a new underlying asset or payoff once the system is set up and running. The whole value chain profits from e-trading, from the issuer to the final investor. It remains to be seen how fast the business will evolve, but unless the present financial crisis takes away all means from the banks, e-trading platforms should be first priority for issuers.

# Part II
## Structured Products in a Portfolio Context

# 9
# Introduction to Part II

The way most structured products are produced, recommended and implemented in private banking today is, in the author's view, not optimal to say the least. Many market participants perceive the products as individual investments and seldom go beyond checking whether the underlying asset(s) in the product fits an existing client's portfolio. In addition, empirical observation shows that clients tend to stick to a specific type of structure and asset class once they are used to investing in it. Consequently, financial advisors recommend that type of structure more often (they may also have developed the habit themselves) as it becomes easier to convince the client to invest in it. For instance, a common request received by structured product specialists looks like:

"Please structure a product (i.e. a reverse convertible) with one year maturity, 30% protection and three Eurostoxx50 stocks, highest possible coupon."

What happens? Usually, the structurer will take the three stocks with the lowest correlation, the highest volatility and the biggest dividend yield to select the underlying assets of the product. In other words, he will optimize the coupon given the universe restriction (here the Eurostoxx50). The structurer has no indication in what portfolio the structure will be embedded or whether the stocks would be optimal for it. Taking a step back to consider the structure, the request implied a reverse convertible without naming it. It is questionable if the reverse convertible is the optimal choice for the client, or if it resulted from the habit of investing in this type of product, and, if so, whether that habit was that of the client himself, or of the financial advisor. At other times, requests are formulated with even less precision:

"I have received new funds from a conservative client, and I would like to know what you would recommend for capital guaranteed products at the moment."

Little or nothing is said about any preferred holding period, existing positions, expected return, etc. Unfortunately, the reaction of the specialist is all too often to recommend whichever capital guaranteed product the bank currently has in subscription without inquiring further about its fit in the client's portfolio.

The drawbacks of this behavior are evident: wrong or ill-fitting products are placed into portfolios because of habit, and too little information and research about the portfolio. The portfolio's risk is not analyzed properly, and the performance as well as the client's satisfaction may suffer accordingly.

What the author proposes in Part II of this book is a practical methodology for using structured products as an integral part of modern portfolio management. The idea is simple: combine the economic forecasts (reflecting the view of an investor or an analyst) with the structuring factors (which determine the products' characteristics), while respecting the investor's preferences in terms of investment style. Figure 9.1 summarizes the approach graphically.

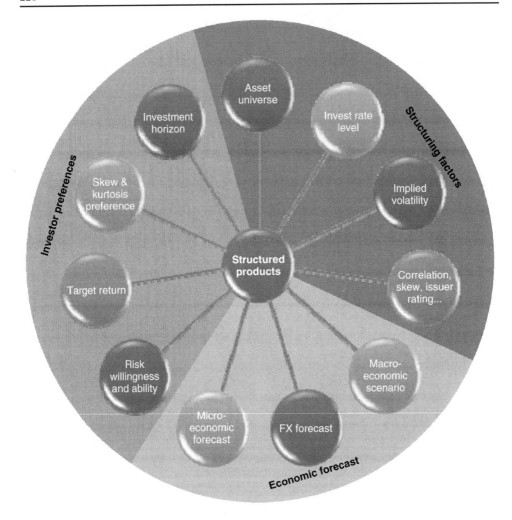

**Figure 9.1**  Integral structuring

Rather than an opportunistic implementation of the products, the proposed methodology integrates structured products into the portfolio from the start. The economic forecast, which may come from the research department of the investor's home bank, is used by structuring specialists to suggest optimal products of different categories. Investment advisors, having determined the investment preferences of their clients, can select or construct the products accordingly. The preferences include the already widely-known parameters of risk and return, but also new measures that consider an investment's return skew and kurtosis, which are higher central moments of the return distribution.[1] The investor's investment horizon is also an important factor to consider. Structured products, which allow parameterizing time to maturity, can provide investors with the ideal investment instrument.

---

[1] Explained in Section 10.1.

Traditionally, standard portfolios in private banking are split into risk classes, ranging from "Income" to "Growth", the former being the least risky and the latter bearing the highest risk. Investors are allocated an investment style corresponding to their profile. Young, aggressive investors with long investment horizons usually prefer "Growth" portfolios, while older, more settled investors prefer "Income" portfolios. Risk classes such as Income and Growth, as well as several classes in-between those mentioned, are determined by taking the volatility of the assets as a proxy for risk. A major problem in this respect is the volatility of the volatility of certain asset classes, in particular stocks. As seen previously, the volatility, and hence the risk, of an asset is anything but constant. The volatility fluctuations can cause major risk imbalances in portfolios, especially in times of stress such as market crashes, which become more frequent with globalization.

Portfolios consist of asset classes such as bonds, equities and "alternative investments", the latter being more often than not a pot-pourri of hedge funds, commodities, real estate, private equity, etc. The investor's investment preferences are reflected in the portfolios only through the expected return and volatility of the invested assets. The alternative investments especially can include all kinds of return distributions,[2] often with little consideration given to the investor's preferences. This can be troublesome for portfolio managers, who are often confronted with a dilemma: how can the expected return of a portfolio be increased when the risk (volatility) of many asset classes is too high to allow an investment? That dilemma can be solved by the concept of integral structuring. An asset with an unfitting expected return distribution shape can be implemented in the form of a structured product, whose own return distribution shape supplants the one of the asset. In other words, the risk of an asset becomes partly irrelevant, as it is taken over by the risk of the product.

Hence, the first novelty proposed here is that, thanks to the derivatives embedded in structured products, any basic asset's risk (i.e. its expected return distribution) can be shaped at will. If structured products are considered from the start of the investment process, classic asset classes become interchangeable to a large degree. The shape of the return distribution is driven by the choice of the *type* of structured product. This stands in contrast to classical portfolios, where the shape of the distribution is given by the selection of the underlying assets themselves. In other words, the option combination that is used within the structured product, rather than the asset itself, determines the risk of the investment. This is an important characteristic to consider with structured products, because portfolios that would otherwise have only limited access to some asset classes can be diversified. For instance, a pure bond portfolio can be mixed with a capital guaranteed product on an FX pair, a yield curve shape or a stock index. The risk of the bond portfolio, which is traditionally concentrated around yield, duration and credit risks, is thus diversified to other asset classes, possibly enhancing the return of the portfolio.

The second novelty proposed, which derives from the first, is that portfolios include enhanced risk parameters such as the higher central moments of the return distribution characteristics of the assets and products, namely skew and kurtosis, which should ultimately lead to a higher investor satisfaction.

Before the new ideas are developed, it would be useful, as a first step, to describe in detail the concept of return distributions, followed by the current landscape in terms of portfolio management.

---

[2] For instance, hedge funds have different return distributions than commodities, which in turn are different from real estate, etc.

# 10

# Classical Theory and Structured Products

The classical investment approach still used by the majority of portfolio or asset managers in private banking is Modern Portfolio Theory (MPT), which was developed by Markowitz in 1952, and the Capital Asset Pricing Model (CAPM), developed later by Treynor and Sharpe who built on Markowitz' work. After these two important concepts have been summarized, Fama's (1971) Efficient Market Hypothesis (EMH) as well as Behavioral Finance in general will be described. These theories and their practical applications will be useful when developing the concept aimed at integrating the use of structured products in a portfolio. The central concept around which the MPT and the CAPM are built is the notion of a normal return distribution of the returns of the financial assets considered. Since the concept of a return distribution is a central element of the theory developed later in this book, it is timely to describe it here in greater depth.

## 10.1 DISTRIBUTION OF RETURNS SHAPES

Let's start by defining a distribution of returns:

A distribution of returns is a probability distribution, identifying the probability an asset has of generating returns within particular (predefined) intervals. It is represented in the form of a histogram, which is a graphical display of tabulated frequencies in the form of bars. The area, not the height, of the bars denotes the value of an interval.

Figure 10.1 shows an example of a histogram.

An asset – for example a stock, or an index like the Eurostoxx50 – held over a period of one year, could have many possible returns: it could double in value or lose 50% but, on average, it is more likely that it will rise by 5% or 10%. In a distribution of returns, the possible returns are classified into ranges (i.e. ... from $\geq -10$ to $< 0\%$, from $\geq 0\%$ to $< +10\%$, from $\geq +10\%$ to $< +20\% ...$). The probabilities of returns are then calculated (either from historical or from expected future data) for each range. In Figure 10.1, weekly historical data over the last 10 years have been used to calculate the frequencies of returns of each range. Ordering the ranges from lowest to highest, it is possible to represent an area in graphical form as shown in Figure 10.1. In theory, to be absolutely accurate, either the ranges should always have the same interval width (i.e. in regular increments of 5% or 10%) or, where the ranges have different increments, the horizontal scale should be adapted for wider or narrower ranges (i.e. the width of an interval of 10% should be double that of an interval of 5%). For practical reasons, most of the histograms showing return distributions here have increments of 10%, *except* for returns above 50% or below −50%, which are aggregated in a single interval of the same width. While this is statistically not strictly correct, the readability of the graphics is improved, without distorting the reality too much.

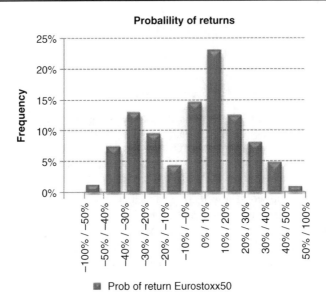

**Figure 10.1**  Sample histogram (yearly return probabilities of the Eurostoxx50, 1998–2008)
Source: Bloomberg, own calculations

### 10.1.1  The normal distribution of returns

A normal distribution is characterized by its symmetrical bell-shaped curve. It has a *mean
return* of μ (pronounced "mù") and a *standard deviation* of σ (pronounced "sigma"). Calculating the average return of an asset over a given number of periods (i.e. weekly, monthly
or yearly) will generate the expected mean return μ of that asset over the selected period.
The standard deviation is a measure of dispersion around the mean of the distribution and is
often taken as a proxy for risk. In finance, the standard deviation is a synonym for volatility.
If the measured returns of an asset are closely clustered around its mean, then its standard
deviation, or volatility, is small. If the returns diverge widely from its mean, then it is large.
As an example, consider the following set of values:[1] {2,2,12,12} and {6,6,8,8,}. Both sets
have an average of seven, but the former has a volatility of five while the latter amounts
only to one. In finance, the volatility is usually expressed in percent per annum as will be
described in the example further below.

Holding a position in an asset whose returns are normally distributed has a ~68% chance
of returning the mean return μ + / − σ (between μ − σ and μ + σ, centre section) for a
one-year holding period as indicated in Figure 10.2. Due to the symmetry of the distribution,
the chances of receiving a return that is either larger or smaller than μ are equal. In 95% of
all occurrences, the returns will be within two standard deviations[2] (between μ − 2σ and
μ + 2σ, sections either side of the middle section).

---

[1] Each set represents a population.
[2] For simplicity's sake, the term volatility will be used going forward.

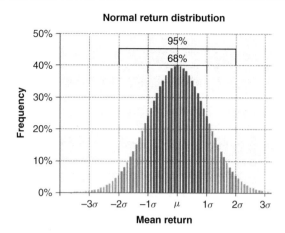

**Figure 10.2**  The normal distribution

For instance, an investor holding a position in a stock with a yearly mean (expected) return of 6% and a volatility of 15%,[3] will have a 68% chance that the return will be between −9% and +21% and a 95% chance of a return between −24% and +36%.

With intervals tending towards infinitesimal widths, the return distribution can be considered as a probability density function. As in Figure 10.2, the *area* under the bell-shaped[4] curve denotes the probability of the returns. In those cases, the graphical representation can be visualized by a line following the top of the intervals, as will be the case in the next few examples.

### 10.1.2  Other distribution of return shapes

For those readers not familiar with the concept of a return distribution, please read Appendix B.

In theory, the assumption that returns are normally distributed is practical, but in reality very few assets actually behave this way. Empirical observations for equities in particular have shown that distribution of returns are often characterized by left- or right-skewed distributions, so-called fat tails, and either leptokurtic (pointy) or platykurtic (flat) distributions. A lot of math is necessary to calculate the skew or the kurtosis of a distribution and will not be discussed here, but some distribution types must be described briefly in order that we can proceed.

A *skewed distribution* denotes a bias of the returns to either the upside or the downside.[5] In other words, a positive skewed distribution is more likely to generate returns above the mean (the mean is greater than the median, which is in turn greater than the mode), while a negatively skewed distribution is more likely to generate returns below the mean (the mean is lower than the median, which in turn is lower than the mode). Mathematically, the skew of a distribution is defined as its third central moment (the first being the mean, the second the

---

[3] These risk/return levels have characteristics similar to the stock market in general.

[4] Also called the "Gaussian" curve, from the German mathematician Carl Friedrich Gauss.

[5] The definition of skew in the context of the distribution presented here is different from the notion of skew in the volatility of options presented earlier.

variance), with a value of zero for a normal distribution. A distribution with a skew of 0.5 will be slightly skewed to the right, while a value of −2 will indicate a strong skew to the left.

The *kurtosis of a distribution* denotes the tallness or flatness of the distribution. In other words, kurtosis tells if the deviations from the mean will be tightly packed around it (high kurtosis, also called leptokurtic) or spread wide (flat kurtosis, also called platykurtic). The kurtosis is defined as the fourth central moment of a distribution, with a value of three in a normal distribution. A value of five will denote a strong leptokurtosis (pointy distribution), while a value of two will denote a flat one.

Both the skew and the kurtosis will be explained at length in the following section, as they are essential concepts for the implementation of structured products in portfolios. Figure 10.3 shows skewed distributions.

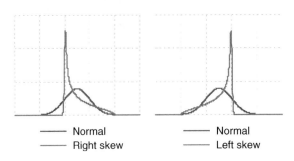

**Figure 10.3**   Skewed distribution examples
Source: Matlab

The left-hand graph shows a positive or right-skewed distribution of returns (the normal distribution is shown for comparison purposes). It has an overhang to the right, with a long right tail, the left tail of the distribution being cut off. With a right-skewed distribution, the chances are greater of generating a lower return than with a normal distribution, but that drawback is offset by the fact that negative returns are to a large part excluded. The right-hand graph shows a negative skewed distribution. It has an overhang to the left with a long left tail, and this time the right side of the distribution is cut off. In this type of return distribution, the average return is higher than in normal distributions, but it has in turn the disadvantage that large losses are possible, and the upside is capped.

Figure 10.4 shows a leptokurtic distribution with a fat left tail, a platykurtic, and a bimodal distribution:

The left-hand graph shows a fat tail to the left of the distribution, which happens when the asset has extremely high or low returns far more often than would be assumed in a normal distribution. A stock where the probability is 9% for the returns to be below $\mu - 2\sigma$ and 7% to be above $\mu + 2\sigma$ has fat tails. In a normal distribution, that probability is approximately 2.5% on either side. The center graphic shows a platykurtic distribution. Finally, the right-hand graph shows a bimodal distribution, cutting off the tails so that large positive or large negative returns are not possible but much of the distribution's frequencies are concentrated on the left and on the right edge of the distribution.

Structured products that contain options (i.e. all except trackers) usually attempt to *concentrate* the distribution of returns of the underlying asset somewhere. A concentration of returns may be achieved either by cutting off the distribution points beyond a certain limit

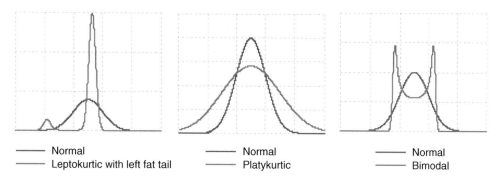

| Normal | Normal | Normal |
| Leptokurtic with left fat tail | Platykurtic | Bimodal |

**Figure 10.4**  Leptokurtic (left), platykurtic (center) and bimodal distribution examples
Source: Matlab

or by shaping the product in a way that enhances the chances of receiving a certain (range of) return(s). The area of concentration depends on the product type. It will be shown which product concentrates the returns at what point.

## 10.2  CLASSICAL PORTFOLIO MANAGEMENT THEORIES

### 10.2.1  Modern portfolio theory (MPT)

Simply put, MPT states that rational investors will diversify their portfolios to reduce their risk (Markowitz, 1952). Each asset has an expected return and a risk, where the (historical) volatility is used as a measure for risk. The expected return is also derived from historical data. Because the assets are imperfectly correlated to each other, diversifying a portfolio over several assets will reduce the risk or increase the return. Combining the assets' expected return and risk with consideration given to their correlation matrix can be represented as a surface, which represents all possible portfolios, and whose upper edge is referred to as the *efficient frontier*. The efficient frontier is defined as the set of portfolios that maximize expected returns for given levels of risk. The model assumes that investors are risk-averse, meaning that given two assets which offer the same expected return, they will prefer the less risky one. Hence, all investors should form portfolios that are placed on the efficient frontier and not below. It is theoretically impossible to achieve portfolios above the efficient frontier (Figure 10.5).

Highly risk-averse investors will tend to the left of the curve (portfolio 1), while less risk-averse ones seeking higher returns will tend to the right (portfolio 2). In other words, to achieve higher returns, higher risk must be accepted. Portfolio 3 would be inefficient, because a portfolio with higher return and equal risk or equal return and lower risk could be achieved.

MPT is built around three important assumptions:

- That the investors are rational and risk-averse.
- That the expected returns of the assets are normally distributed around their mean.
- That an investor will judge an asset purely on its expected return and its volatility (risk). No preference is made as to the skew or the kurtosis of the distribution, which represent the third and fourth central moment of the distribution respectively.

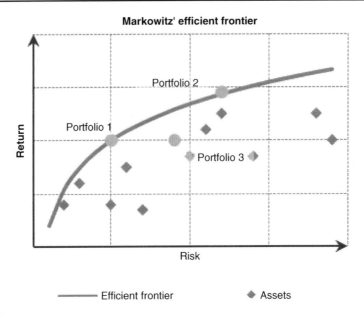

**Figure 10.5   MPT**

### 10.2.2   The capital asset pricing model

The CAPM (Sharpe, 1964) is a model used to estimate an asset's rate of return (i.e. price) if added to an existing portfolio given its non-diversifiable, or systematic, risk. In the CAPM, the measure of the risk of any asset or portfolio is given by its beta ($\beta$), which measures the sensitivity of that asset to the market. If in equilibrium, all assets will have the same return after adjustment for risk. In other words, an individual asset's reward-to-risk ratio divided by its beta will be equal to the market's reward-to-risk ratio. Excess returns, commonly called outperformance, are risk-adjusted returns that a manager or investment advisor may generate through skill. Excess returns are symbolized by the letter alpha ($\alpha$).

These are the main assumptions of the CAPM:

- That investors seek to maximize utility;
- That investors are rational and risk averse;
- That the asset's returns are normally distributed;
- That the variance of returns is an appropriate measure for risk.

### 10.2.3   The efficient market hypothesis

Eugène Fama (1971) developed the EMH in its weak, semi-strong and strong forms. The theory states that the prices of financial assets reflect all information and that no outperformance can be generated from past data analysis. Any new information will instantly move the price of the asset, but it cannot be foreseen in the present. Hence, it's impossible to outperform the market consistently except through luck.

- In its weak form, the EMH states that an analysis of the historical prices of a financial asset will not lead to an excess return. However, fundamental analysis may produce consistent excess returns.
- In its semi-strong form, the theory states that all publicly-available information is immediately reflected in the asset's price. Therefore, no consistent excess returns can be generated by fundamental analysis any more.
- In its strong form, the theory holds that the price of a financial asset reflects not only public but also private and insider information so that, in principle, no one can generate excess returns in the long run.

### 10.2.4   Classical theory and practice

Even without considering structured products, there are several major question marks around the application of the classical theories in practical investments. These criticisms have been described in several academic studies and given birth to new developments in the field of money management.

- The MPT assumes that the distribution of the asset's returns is normal.

However, many empirical studies suggest that the market is not normally distributed. "Fat tails", denoting the observed fact that large variations in the market, especially to the downside, happen more frequently than a normal distribution would suggest, are a good example. On several occasions, empirical examples of non-normal return distributions are also represented in this book: Figures 10.1, 13.3 and 13.4[6] depict non-normal distributions.

- Investors are not (always) rational and they do not always have all available market information.

The market participants as a whole might take rational decisions, but at the level of the individual, investors do not always do so. Proof of this exists in the innumerable portfolios that are badly diversified, overleveraged or underinvested.

The EMH and MPT both assume that all assets are fairly priced since all the relevant information for their price determination should be known by all the market participants. These are supposed to react instantly to news and adjust the market price of any asset. What actually happens is that professional traders usually act instantly, but non-professional investors often act without knowing the latest piece of news. The speed at which the professional traders get new information, be it macro- or microeconomic, is far greater than for private investors. This is especially true for wealthy private clients who are not chained to their Bloomberg or Reuters terminal 24 hours a day. It is also the case for investment advisors, who frequently have no more information than what's available on the internet and who have all sorts of administrative work to do in addition to advising their clients. Professional traders can react faster to new information, profit from arbitrage opportunities, etc, which private investors generally are not in a position to do. Their faster analysis of the new data effectively allows them to move the price of an asset to a point where that piece of information is reflected in the market price of that asset. By doing so, the traders lift or hit

---

[6] More examples are presented in Chapter 12.

all the limits the other investors have placed above or below that new price. The outcome is that the professional trader sold above or bought below the new fair value and other investors sold below or bought above that price. Indeed, if Fama's EMH hypothesis were applicable in practice, the whole hedge fund industry would probably never have flourished as it did prior to the credit crisis of 2008.

The EMH remains very theoretical in any of its forms. It may well be that at some times a given market is efficient in its strong form, becomes gradually more and more inefficient and then returns to efficiency at a later stage. The level of efficiency of a market in the present or past does not necessarily mean it will stay at the same level of efficiency in the future.

For structured products, the market is certainly not efficient to all participants, as will be demonstrated in a moment. However, this does not mean that a systematic outperformance versus the underlying assets can be generated with structured products by analyzing their past performance. Yet the elimination of inefficiencies in the pricing of the structured products as well as the gaining of expertise by investors does lead to better performance.

- The MPT and CAPM assume that investors will only consider the expected return and the risk of an asset for their choice to invest. They will be indifferent to other parameters, like the higher moments (i.e. skew or kurtosis) of the distribution. Their utility function can be described as a quadratic utility function.[7]

This assumption is critical with regard to the inclusion of structured products in the portfolio management process, as will be shown later. The normal distribution in the MPT and CAPM implies that the upside risk is identical to the downside risk and that upside surprises are considered as risky as downside surprises. In practice, however, empirical observations as well as studies show that many investors prefer upside volatility to downside volatility. In other words, they are more concerned about downside risk than upside risk. Yet another way of putting it is that preservation of capital is often more important than outperformance of a given market. Especially in private banking, mention is often made of the "worst-case scenario", which is to be avoided, while the "best case scenario" is seldom considered or less emphasized.

## 10.3 CLASSICAL THEORY AND STRUCTURED PRODUCTS

### 10.3.1 The EMH and structured products

A simple test will invalidate the EMH in all its forms for structured products in the primary market. Let us define a simple product and ask five investment banks to price it (Table 10.1).

The responses of the banks ranged from 14.0% to 15.2%. Even taking the difference of the funding rate of the selected institutions at the time of the pricing into account didn't justify such a large difference in the coupon. The traders who priced the structure simply do not have the same view on the exotic option embedded in the product. The price difference might come from a divergent view in the implied volatility, in the expected dividend yields or in the correlation. Alternatively, the mathematical models used to calculate the product's

---

[7] A quadratic utility function denotes a polynomial function of the second degree with two parameters of the type $f(x) = ax^2 + bx + c$

**Table 10.1**  EMH product test

| Instrument type | Multi-barrier reverse convertible |
|---|---|
| Underlying assets | Roche, ABB |
| Maturity | 1 year |
| Issue price | 100% |
| Barrier, in % of spot price | 70% |
| Coupon level (annual) | ??? |

price with the trader's input are not the same. This exercise can be performed on any other structured product and yield similar results. Note that the coupon-level range in the example above will be different depending on the day that one conducts the survey. In "fast" markets, it will be wider, in steady markets narrower.

The more complex the structure, the greater the differences become. In 12 years of practice, the author has never experienced more than two investment banks showing similar prices for a given structure. Hence, without acting through a competitive bid process to price an exotic structure, the primary market for structured products is inefficient, as there is never a single price at a given moment in time. Even if past information were reflected in the pricing, future information necessary for completing the calculation of a structured product like implied volatility, projected dividend as well as their exact payout dates, etc. is uncertain. An investor who seeks prices from several issuers is likely to outperform an investor who buys products only from one issuer. The EMH was published for the first time in 1971, at a time when derivatives were still in their cradle.

The secondary market's efficiency is much more difficult to assess in practice due to the differences in the structures and live information. It is rare to find two identical structures even among the hundreds of thousands that exist. Since only a fraction of the products in existence is listed on exchanges, the comparison becomes even more difficult. On the internet, prices are often shown with a 15-minute delay. Moreover, arbitrage in structured products is not possible since it is not possible to short a structured product. In addition, it is only the issuer, who may bend the price at will, who determines the price of the structure.[8] The combination of these factors makes the structured product market if not inefficient, then at least difficult for the common investor. It is difficult to ascertain that the product bought through competitive bidding at inception will be fairly priced when selling it later. The reader will perhaps feel a contradiction between what the author states here and Section 2.5.10 (Reading a term-sheet) Secondary market. The message to the reader is that there is always a secondary market, but it is unclear and difficult to prove whether or not the price reflects all information. Sometimes, even the absence of the issuer's head trader from his desk is enough to distort the price of a product. While this is seldom the case with common – simple – products, that fact has to be considered with complex products.

The price calculation process of common structured products remains a mystery for most private investors. They are built using proprietary, often secret, mathematical models that few understand completely. This does not mean that structured products are particularly risky, but their inherent complexity makes the price behavior difficult for the average private investor to understand. It is relatively easy to read a payoff diagram, but it becomes

---

[8] Price bending is more the case with warrants than with structured products.

extremely complex to judge how a structured product price should react to new information influencing a construction element of that product. The most important factors, like
variations in the volatility or the interest rate, have been discussed previously.[9] Yet even
the top investment banks, acting as issuers, don't always foresee that some particular bit of
information can influence the price of their own products. Proof of this came when the funding spreads were only considered in the secondary market prices of some issuers' products
once the subprime crisis was well under way, after their funding spreads had already risen
substantially. Consequently, the issuers were bidding too much for their products in the secondary market for some time, for once in the favor of the investors. Another example is the
evolution of the trading models: Yesterday, traders used models based on a volatility surface.
Today, the traders use the "local vol" models. Tomorrow, who can say? All this leads to
the conclusion that an investor whose expertise of structured products is superior will likely
outperform one with a lower understanding, as he will be more able to judge the fit into his
portfolio, assess the real risks, determine if the price is correct, etc. The author himself has
experienced cases where investors shunned products that were badly mispriced *in their favor*,
with the argument that the payoff wasn't attractive enough. On the other hand, some products the author has seen were clearly very expensive and yet they were heavily subscribed
despite the specialists' advice to the contrary. In conclusion, the EMH doesn't hold (yet) in
structured products mainly because of a generalized lack of information and know-how.

### 10.3.2 MPT, CAPM and structured products

Because the distribution of returns for structured products is often skewed,[10] the CAPM
and MPT, based solely on mean and standard deviation, will not correctly measure return
and risk. Leland (1999) showed that the classical beta ($\beta$) in the CAPM does not correctly
measure the risk of a portfolio when using options, and that the alpha ($\alpha$) consequently does
not correctly measure outperformance. Pursuant, other commonly-used risk/return metrics,
like the Sharpe ratio, which also do not take into consideration the higher central moments of
the distribution (skew and kurtosis), fail to produce correct results when applied to portfolios
including options (Leland, 1999; Leggio and Lien, 2008).

Brennan (1979) and He and Leland (1993) further showed that an investor must have a
utility function which includes the skewness of the distribution of returns and that skewness
is positively valued by the market. Therefore, the mean and variance on which MPT is
built are not enough to create an "optimal" portfolio, as the higher central moments of the
distribution are left out. There exists an implicit market for skewness and kurtosis, and
maybe even some as yet undetected even higher moments. Buying skewness reduces the
mean of returns while also reducing the risk. It creates a convex function of the market
payoff. Dubil (2008) shows that the chosen type of convexity that is bought (i.e. protecting
the portfolio through either long puts, put spreads or collars[11]), has a significant impact on
the portfolio's return and risk. Some of the tested strategies outperform others, among other
reasons because of the bid-ask spread and the skew in the option stock market.[12] Selling

---

[9] See Chapter 4 Behavior of structured products during their lifetime.
[10] Or outright truncated, except for tracker certificates which do not have any optionality included.
[11] A collar designates a combination strategy using two options: long put (usually at- or out-of-the-money) plus
short call (usually out-of-the-money). The premium of the short call reduces the cost of the long put.
[12] Dubil's results are based on the S&P500 index over a period of 40 years.

skewness increases the mean return while adding [tail] risk to the portfolio. It creates a concave function of the market payoff.

Kurtosis, the fourth central moment of a distribution, also influences the return and risk of a portfolio. Since it measures the concentration of the returns around the mean, a high kurtosis (leptokurtosis) gives an asset a higher probability of reaching that mean. For that reason, investors should be willing to pay a higher premium for assets whose distribution is strongly leptokurtic, if the mean of those assets meets their target. If the returns are normally distributed, both the left (downside) and the right (upside) tails are slim. There have been few studies about the kurtosis of assets and the preferences of investors.

Mean, variance, skew and kurtosis vary with time. Depending on the population sample, all central moments will yield significantly different results. There exists a long-term average for any given asset, but the sampling period typically extends over dozens of years, far longer than a private banking investor's average investment horizon. In private banking, investment advisors report at least annually to their clients. In itself, that fact is an enticement to recommend short-term products. The absolute longest practical investment horizon may reach up to 8–10 years, but products considered as long-term investments seldom exceed five years, which represents some sort of time barrier beyond which investors rarely want to commit their assets. It must be said that the average age of a private banking investor is relatively advanced, about 60 years. This partially explains why a majority of investors in private banking have little interest in investing in 10-year structures: they might pass on prior to the product's maturity. Whatever the reasons, even if the longest-dated structured products might expire in 10 years, the average product's life in private banking, based on volume, is at just about one year.[13] Hence, the average central moments of the return distribution of any structured product of medium time to maturity will have a significant deviation from the long-term average central moments for the same product.

Hosts of new measures have been developed to take the skew and kurtosis into account when measuring risk, performance, alpha, etc. Without expanding too much on them here, a few include Leland's beta "B" and alpha "A", the Sortino ratio and the Upside Potential ratio. Although they may be more accurate and technically superior, these new developments have seldom been broadly used throughout private banking.

## 10.4  CONCLUSION

The EMH cannot be applied to structured products, which remains a fairly opaque market for the basic investor. Specialists are needed to find the "fairest" price of a structure, and to determine if it complies with MiFID.[14] Neither MPT nor CAPM can be efficiently applied when a portfolio includes structured products with strongly asymmetric payoffs. In addition, expected return and risk, the two parameters used in private banking, do not sufficiently describe the investor's preferences. Performance and risk indicators like the Sharpe ratio and the CAPM's $\beta$ produce wrong results when applied to portfolios with strongly skewed

---

[13] This stands in contrast to the municipal market, in which cities or state regions refinance their debt by the means of very long-term structured products, typically with a maturity of ten to thirty years. This type of refinancing has been heavily criticized lately.

[14] *Markets in Financial Instruments Directive*, a EU directive regulating the distribution of financial instruments, providing investor protection, market practice, best execution, etc.

distributions. Skewness and kurtosis both have a price, but it is difficult to determine and hinges on the preferences of each individual investor.

Structured products enhance an investor's ability to manage his portfolio, not only in terms of expected return, but also in terms of downside risk and upside potential, by shaping the return distribution of the investments. However, the higher central moments of the distribution, skew and kurtosis, have a high chance of varying with time, as the typical holding period is relatively low. Although investors unconsciously build their own portfolio distributions by investing in several types of assets, only the expected mean and the variance (as a proxy for risk) are considered by the majority of the private banks. In some cases, other measures, like the value at risk, shortfall risk, etc., are used, which are good measures for determining the left side of the return distribution. Nevertheless, despite new measures having been recently developed to analyze and optimize portfolios, the author has never experienced any form of approach that reconciles the investors' preferences towards gains *and* losses in terms of return distributions with the effective return distribution of his portfolio.

# — 11 —
# Structured Solution Proposal

## 11.1 PREFERRED DISTRIBUTION OF RETURN INVESTMENT PROCESS

The addition of plain vanilla options to a portfolio provides the opportunity for investors to define their own, personalized distribution of returns to a certain degree. Furthermore, structured products with embedded exotic options allow investors to define their return distribution even more precisely, effectively widening their portfolio management possibilities. In fact, structured products provide an investor with a means to parameterize the desired distribution of returns of his portfolio in terms of expected return, volatility of return, skew and kurtosis. However, finding out an investor's desired distribution of returns isn't a trivial undertaking. Several questions arise:

- How does one determine what the preferred distribution of returns looks like?
- Should it be left, right, or not skewed? Platy-, lepto- or mesokurtic?
- How much skewness/kurtosis should be bought or sold and at what price?
- Are there special situations in which it is desirable to buy or sell skewness?
- Is it timely and possible to implement the selected strategy?
- What type of product is likely to have the desired distribution?
- Can the implemented strategy be measured?

These questions seem daunting; few common private banking measures exist to parameterize, implement and measure the distribution of returns of a portfolio beyond the classical mean-variance optimizations. A private investor seldom has the means to calculate this type of data. And yet, due to the assets included in their portfolios, each investor already *implicitly* implements his own distribution. Doing so with little more than "gut feeling" may or may not meet a desired set of criteria, but it is ultimately crucial for achieving an investor's goal. Then again, how does an investor know and implement his preferred distribution? The finance industry has made portfolio optimization using mean and variance a standard, but left out the skew and kurtosis optimization to a large extent. One may assume that structured products offer a means to specify and optimize all four factors according to the investor's preferences, but as yet no recipe has shown how to do so.

In order to come up with a practical solution that answers the above questions, the author proposes a methodical process in seven steps (four initial and three constant reviews):

1. Build a framework to categorize risk, skew and kurtosis of assets.[1] For portfolio management, standard return distribution classes will be determined in order to enable the construction of discretionary mandate types.

---

[1] The framework is discussed and set up on page 238 and finalized with product categories on page 299.

2. Determine an investor's investment preferences in terms of expected return, risk, skew and kurtosis. This will be accomplished by means of a *questionnaire*,[2] which will also gather information about the investor's holding period, age, cash flow needs, etc. The preferences will determine the shape of the distribution of returns that should be implemented in his portfolio.
3. Determine the expected return, risk, skew and kurtosis of structured products[3] as well as classical asset classes. The combination of the return distributions of the classical assets and structured products will be the asset universe from which the portfolios are built.
4. Construct the portfolio by selecting the appropriate product types according to the investor's preferences.[4] For discretionary portfolio mandates, implement the portfolios determined in point 2 with appropriate products from point 3.

These first four steps (Figure 11.1) should ensure that the correct instruments and vehicles are used for each investor's expectations and preferences. However, systematically implementing products with embedded derivatives does not necessarily add value to a portfolio when the risk-and-return measures are applied correctly and when the options are fairly priced. It is also intuitive that certain investments have a greater chance of success than others depending on factors such as the general economic situation, the scenario forecast by research, etc.

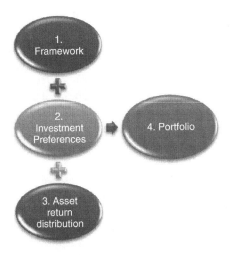

**Figure 11.1** Portfolio construction concept

Hence, after a portfolio construction process has been established, a constant review process must be implemented in order to take into account the current market conditions

---

[2] See Section 11.4.
[3] As it is neither possible nor practical to process calculations for all possible structures, a few standard products of the different types will be selected: capital guaranteed, yield enhancement and participation. Only stock and stock index products will be considered, and the currency will be limited mainly to the EUR with some products calculated in CHF. The testing of the products starts in Chapter 12.
[4] See Chapter 13.

and the expected micro- and macroeconomic forecasts as stipulated in Figure 9.1 on page 220. Several steps should be implemented to fine tune the selected instruments. These steps principally appeal to the skill of specialists in the field of research, analysis and structured products.

5. Determine the asset class weights in the portfolio according to the forecast macro- and microeconomic scenarios, as would be done in a classical portfolio.

6. Consider implementing the envisioned investments with structured products as well as direct investments in their underlying assets. In terms of structuring parameters, assess the cheapness or richness as well as the outlook for volatility, yields, etc. Products that would have been previously deemed as fitting an investor's profile but not attractive to implement at a given point in time are not considered if the structuring parameters and conditions are adverse at the chosen moment.

7. Determine the exact payoff and lifetime of selected products. In other words, fine-tune the parameters for each product.

Steps 5 to 7 allow the seamless integration of this process for all investment vehicle types (Figure 11.2). Step 5 is self-explaining: over- or underweight whole asset classes, sectors, single assets, etc. according to the forecast. As previously mentioned, derivatives in general, and structured products in particular, allow investors to exchange one asset class for another without changing the distribution of returns in the portfolio. Steps 6 and 7 are necessary to judge whether the conditions are optimal at any given time to invest in a structured product that fits the desired return distribution.

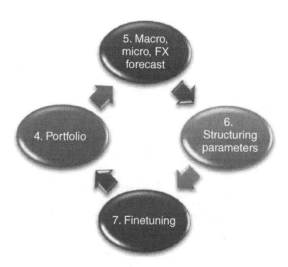

**Figure 11.2**   Portfolio constant review process

The last three steps will not be discussed further in this book, as they apply to practical situations involving multiple factors, persons and scenarios.

## 11.2 DISTRIBUTION CLASSES: THE RETURN DISTRIBUTION CUBE

The first step of the portfolio construction concept consists in elaborating a comprehensive framework for classifying the return distribution shapes. To that end, classes of return distributions will be determined. In order to keep the framework relatively simple but accurate nonetheless, three risk categories (low, medium and high) are combined with three classes of skewness and kurtosis respectively,[5] totaling 27 classes ($3^3$). Table 11.1 summarizes the classes in tabular form, while Figure 11.3, dubbed the "return distribution Cube", represents the framework in a graphical outline.

**Table 11.1**  Universe of return distribution classes

| Return distribution class | Risk | Skew | Kurt. |
|---|---|---|---|
| 1 | Low | Left | Flat |
| 2 | Low | Left | Medium |
| 3 | Low | Left | High |
| 4 | Low | None | Flat |
| . . . | . . . | . . . | . . . |
| 26 | High | Right | Medium |
| 27 | High | Right | Flat |

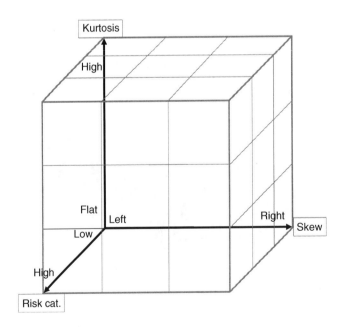

**Figure 11.3**  The return distribution Cube

---

[5] The risk classes are defined as low, medium and high risk. The skewness classes are left, none or right. Kurtosis classes are high (pointy), normal or flat (which equals to lepto-, meso-, and platykurtic respectively).

Although the Cube totals 27 classes, some will never be used while others may be impossible to reach. No one in his right mind would, for instance, willingly invest in a high-risk left-skewed and flat kurtosis return distribution. It would leave the door open to frequent large losses, all the while keeping the positive returns capped. This type of return distribution would almost certainly produce negative results over time. As such, it can be dismissed from the framework. In fact, it is intuitive that any type of distribution that combines a left skew with a flat kurtosis would be undesirable. On the other hand, it would probably be difficult to implement a low risk right-skewed, low kurtosis distribution, even if it were desirable. A medium or high risk, right skewed, flat kurtosis distribution would also be tricky to achieve. Hence, some extreme return distributions should be outright excluded from the framework as unachievable and some can be dismissed as inferior relative to others. The original universe of 27 classes is therefore reduced to about 10 that are achievable and desirable from an investor's point of view (Table 11.2).

**Table 11.2**  Achievable and desirable return distribution classes

| Return distribution class | Risk | Skew | Kurt. |
|---|---|---|---|
| **1** | Low | Right | High |
| **2** | Low | Right | Medium |
| **3** | Medium | Left | High |
| **4** | Medium | None | Flat |
| **5** | Medium | None | Medium |
| **6** | Medium | None | High |
| **7** | Medium | Right | Medium |
| **8** | Medium | Right | High |
| **9** | High | None | Flat |
| **10** | High | Right | Medium |

A low-risk oriented investor has to opt for a right-skewed distribution since he cannot or will not bear losses. The kurtosis will be high or medium at best; a flat kurtosis, although desirable in combination with a right skew, will be nigh impossible to achieve.

An investor who is ready to accept a medium level of risk will have the choice of investing in left, no, or right skewed distributions. If the skew is to the left, the kurtosis must be as high as possible. If there's no skew preference, then the kurtosis can be anything, depending on the investor's target return. With medium-risk and a right skew, a flat kurtosis is certainly desirable, but probably also difficult to achieve.

A risk-seeking investor had better not implement a left-skewed distribution, but should keep it neutral or to the right. The kurtosis is again dependent on the investor's style and preferences, but will most of the time be either flat or medium, as high-risk investors are likely to want a high probability of being positively surprised (uncapped upside potential).

The classification framework as represented by the Cube will be used later to classify the underlying assets and products according to their return distributions. Section 11.3 addresses the second point of the portfolio construction concept, which is the investor's preferences in terms of return distribution.

## 11.3   AN INVESTOR'S UTILITY (VALUE) CURVE

Which investor wants what type of investments? Who is able to bear losses and who isn't? Is the behavior of an investor stable in all market situations, or does he change his strategy as the market goes? In order to select the right form of investment, the right payoff and this for the right duration, it is necessary to have information about the investor's preferences. In theory, this is called an individual's *utility curve*. In financial practice, utility curves are seldom constructed, because they require highly mathematical skills to transform the psychology of an investor into a formula applicable to financial markets. However, advances in the field of *behavioral finance* have led to the development of *value functions (curves)* which, while also possible to represent through mathematical formulas, are more intuitive. For the sake of simplicity, let's assume that a utility curve equals a value function. In financial markets, the utility curve of an investor depends on a multitude of factors: his level of satisfaction (what is his target return?), his willingness and ability to accept risk, his age, investment experience, etc. Some forms of investments will have a higher utility than others for a given investor. For instance, a retired person living on his investment income will not necessarily invest in equities or equity options even if he were bullish on those investments because they may seem too risky for him. Hence, there exists a portfolio with which each investor will be optimally satisfied in terms of investments but which varies from person to person according to return distribution preferences.

Logic and experience confirm that a satisfied investor is more likely to remain with his banking institution, continue to use the presented services, and invest in the offered products. Unsatisfied investors will leave over time, become distrustful of the services and products, or squabble about fees at the very least. This will ultimately be to the detriment of the investment advisor, but is perfectly understandable behavior from an investor's point of view. Therefore, the ultimate goal of the investment advisor is to keep his client happy with the service. In order to maximize his chances of achieving that goal, he must know as much as possible about the investor's utility curve and construct his portfolio so that it satisfies the investor's criteria to a high degree. That goal should be upheld at all times. The investment advisor has also one particular restriction – he must report to his client at least on an annual basis, a standard practice in the industry.

### 11.3.1   The prospect theory

Prospect Theory (PT) was developed in 1979 by two pioneers of behavioral finance, D. Kahneman and A. Tversky and studies the choices that individuals make when faced with decisions involving risk. The theory holds that most persons are risk-averse when facing a choice involving gains, but become risk-seeking when faced with losses. Individuals do not necessarily demonstrate mathematically rational behavior, but their choices are perfectly rational to them. The theory also highlights the differences of the choices when an identical prospect[6] is framed differently. The framing effect is best demonstrated by the "Asian disease problem":[7]

---

[6] A prospect was initially represented by a lottery ticket. It can be more generally defined by the chance (represented by a probability) of gaining or losing an amount or an object.
[7] Kahneman and Tversky, (2007) *Choices, Values and Frames*, originally published 1981.

Imagine that the US is preparing for the outbreak of an unusual Asian disease, which is expected to kill 600 people. Two alternative proposals to combat the problem have been proposed. Assume that the exact scientific estimates of the consequences of the catastrophe are the following:

- *If Program A is adopted, 200 lives will be saved.*
- *If Program B is adopted, there is a 1/3 probability that 600 people will be saved, and a 2/3 probability that no people will be saved.*

Out of 152 subjects, 72% opted for the sure Program A and 28% for the unsure variant B. A second group of 155 subjects was presented a set of two different programs:

- *If program C is adopted, 400 people will die.*
- *If Program D is adopted, there is a 1/3 probability that that nobody will die and a 2/3 probability that no people will be saved.*

The results showed that 78% preferred Program D and 22% preferred Program C. Although Program A is identical to C and Program B is identical to D from a mathematical approach, the preferences are reversed. The results are influenced by the point of view from which the problem is described. The first group perceived the problem from a positive (gain) point of view, while the second one perceived it from a negative (loss) point of view.

The PT further assumes that private investors, taken as individuals, are not likely to see the final wealth they are able to gather, but rather view the gains and losses measured as from a certain reference point. The theory furthermore demonstrates that an investor's value function is steeper for losses than for gains, implying loss aversion. In other words, gains and losses of the same magnitude do not have the same influence on investment decisions. Losses hurt more than gains, a typical emotion found in the majority of investors in private banking. Figure 11.4 summarizes the PT's value function.

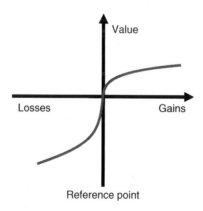

**Figure 11.4**   An illustration of a value function
*Source:* redrawn from Kahneman and Tversky, *Choices, Values and Frames*, 2007

If the reference point (the origin of the graph) represents the wealth status quo, then it is assumed that most investors have a certain target return beyond which the expectation of gaining more has little value. The investor's value function flattens above the point where the target return has been reached (value line to the right of the reference point). However, when facing choices involving losses, the slope of the value function steepens. Individuals are likely to become rather risk seeking. This behavior is best illustrated through another example, which was again presented to two different groups of subjects:[8]

- *Group 1: In addition to whatever you own, you have been given 1000. You are now asked to choose between*

$$A : 50\% \ chances \ of \ +1000$$

$$B : +500 \ for \ sure$$

- *Group 2: In addition to whatever you own, you have been given 2000. You are now asked to choose between*

$$C : 50\% \ chances \ of \ -1000$$

$$D : -500 \ for \ sure$$

The results showed that 84% of Group 1 preferred choice B, while 69% of Group 2 preferred choice C. Yet, in this example, on a purely mathematical level, A = C and B = D. The preferences of the subjects are reversed. The preferences of the example imply that, when making an investment decision, investorswill be risk averse when choosing between gains and risk seeking when choosing between losses. Let's replace this important concept in the context of the financial world from an investing point of view: suppose an investor whose investment preferences are aligned with the PT value function has the choice between three assets:

A. Lower than acceptable expected return with a low dispersion range.
B. Acceptable expected return with a medium dispersion range.
C. Higher than acceptable expected return with a high dispersion range.

This investor is highly likely to choose asset B. Asset A doesn't meet his target expected return and therefore doesn't qualify. The investor accepts or even looks for more risk in order to increase the expected return to the minimum acceptable. Asset C's return exceeds his target, but he will get little satisfaction from it, as it implies a higher risk he is not willing to take. In PT, each additional unit of risk over the investor's target return carries a higher weight than an additional unit of revenue does in terms of the investor's satisfaction. Therefore, an investment advisor should recommend a portfolio that has a high probability of closely matching the investor's target return; otherwise, the risks he takes will not be rewarded by additional client satisfaction. Exceeding the target return for his client will earn him little thanks while producing losses because of excessive risks will certainly lead to problems. Asset B is the one that minimizes the investor's risk while meeting his target expected return.

Sometime later, the investor is confronted with a loss: the previously chosen asset has lost a significant amount of value against all expectations. Moreover, the outlook

---

[8] Kahneman, D. and Tversky, A. (2007) *Choices, Values and Frames*, Originally published in 1979.

for his chosen asset is bleak. He has now the choice between the following investments:

A. Hold the asset with a bleak prospect and a medium dispersion range.
B. Switch to an asset with matching expected return and medium dispersion range.
C. Switch to an asset with lower than acceptable returns and low dispersion.
D. Switch to an asset with higher than acceptable return and high dispersion.

In this case the investor is likely to choose either A or D: A because of what is called the
"endowment effect", a situation where a subject is loath to give up something he owns,
or D because it is the only one which will give him a reasonable chance to get back into
positive territory. In choice D, the investor's stance towards risk has moved to risk-seeking
from previously risk-averse. Conversely, the endowment effect can be explained through
another example: imagine a person who owns a coin collection worth 2000 at list price. If
a numismatist offered him 2000 for the collection, the owner would probably not sell it.
If the numismatist were to offer to sell the person the same collection again for 1800, he
probably would not buy it either. The same can be observed for wine: imagine a person
who bought a dozen bottles of wine a few years ago for 25. The bottles are now worth 250,
and the person drinks a bottle from time to time, but he would neither sell them for the
250 list price, nor purchase additional bottles at that price, even though he likes them. In
the same way, choice A leads some investors to carry loss-making investments over long
periods of time, either until a break-even is finally reached or exasperation finally makes
the investor realize his loss. The latter is often enforced by the product's maturity.

The author recently experienced a situation which illustrates the behavior as described
above. It was in the first quarter of 2008, as the subprime debacle reached its full magnitude
and many financial stocks previously thought solid and well-managed were beaten down
to lows not seen since the 2000–2003 bear market. By then nearly all the worst-of barrier
reverse convertibles[9] with embedded financial stocks breached their barriers. When the
breach happened, the products were trading largely under their par value, between −20%
and −30%, depending on where the barriers were placed for each product. The reaction
of many clients as they were confronted with this mark-to-market value – representing not
only a potential loss but also the loss of the conditional capital guarantee linked to the
barrier – was to switch their knocked-in barrier reverse convertibles into another type of
product: the bonus certificate. A typical trade at that time was to sell the knocked-in product
at a loss, select the financial stock that broke the barrier, and structure a new bonus certificate
with a fresh 30% protection and a bonus of near 20%, the new product maturing in 18 to 24
months. Some investors thought to cap the bonus certificate at the level where they invested
in the barrier reverse convertible to begin with in order to raise the bonus further, again to
be able to recoup their losses. The switch was mostly done for three reasons:

1. The bonus certificate, with its open-ended upside potential (or high bonus) had the
   potential to recover the losses engendered by the barrier reverse convertible.
2. The volatility was already extremely high; a bonus certificate has better conditions when
   issued in a high volatility environment.

---

[9] As well as barrier discount certificates, express certificates, etc.

3. The financial stocks had already fallen by an amount that was considered virtually impossible only a few months before. It was more than improbable that they would fall by
   the same amount again.

Reason 2 is a valid technical observation, while reason 3 is a subjective market expectation
by each individual investor. However, reason 1 represents the change of behavior towards
risk of the investor. He becomes risk-seeking to increase the chance that he recovers his
losses. Everything else held equal, the bonus certificate, with its near-one delta, represents a
riskier investment type than the worst-of barrier reverse convertible that the investor opted
for in the first place.[10]

It was also possible to observe that the reaction of private banking investors facing losses
in the subprime crisis was much stronger than during the bull market where everything went
well. As long as no barriers were breached and the coupons plus the invested notional were
paid back at maturity, few investors cared about whether they underperformed the market
or not, or what risks they were actually taking. The investment advisor recommended a new
product, and it was done without too many questions being asked. However, when the barriers of the reverse convertibles and then of the bonus certificates began to be breached, the
investment advisors were suddenly faced with lots of disgruntled investors who demanded
explanations and solutions to the problem of positions which were losing over one percent
per day on a continuous basis. Unfortunately, there were few options left at that point.

Until now, the behavior of many investors has seemed to confirm the utility function as
proposed by Kahneman and Tversky, at least in the private banking universe. As previously
mentioned, another important aspect of the PT is that the decision about an investment is
also likely to be dependent on how it is framed. If the reference point is defined such that
an outcome is viewed as a gain, then the resulting value function will be concave.[11] In
that case, investors will be risk averse. Conversely, if the reference point is defined such
that the outcome is viewed as a loss, the value function will be convex and investors will
become risk seeking.[12] A look at private banking investors' holdings in structured products
in Europe shows that roughly 60%−70% hold yield enhancement products, 15%−25% hold
participation products and 10%−20% hold capital guaranteed products.[13] This distribution,
which strongly favors the yield enhancement products, confirms the PT. The framing of the
investment is such that the private banking client will be offered a coupon that matches
or even exceeds his expected return, and conditional protection that seems very safe at
first glance. The investor will see that payoff as a gain (high expected return, with little
apparent associated risk) and will agree to cap his returns. His decision to invest in a probably left-skewed, high-kurtosis return distribution has been triggered by the framing of the
investment description, which satisfies what he thought was his expected return and risk
at first glance. Was the investment description correctly framed? Were the risks associated
with the product correctly assessed? When persons have to give a weight to a probability,
Kahneman and Tversky found that they often overweight values with a low probability,
but that *"the simplification of prospects in the editing phase can lead the individual to dis-
card events of extreme low probability"* ... *"Because people are limited in their ability to*

---

[10] This is not strictly true but applicable to most products: a yield enhancement product usually carries less risk
than a participation product, although it depends on each product's construction parameters.
[11] Right side of Figure 11.4.
[12] Left side of Figure 11.4.
[13] Source: author's own estimates, June 2008. Not considering leverage products (warrants).

*comprehend and evaluate extreme probabilities, highly unlikely events are either ignored or overweighted...*[14]

Figure 11.5 pictures a typical weighting function. The dotted line gives the theoretical (mathematical) weight that a subject should attribute to a stated probability if he was perfectly rational. The solid line represents the weight individuals effectively assign to stated probabilities. Due to the risk-averseness, most subjects would underweight the rational probabilities. Actually, few people would accept the wager of winning or losing 1000 with an equal 50% chance of each outcome. Most would accept such a wager only if the chances were 55% in their favor or higher.

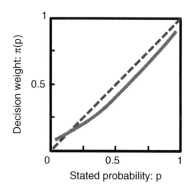

**Figure 11.5**   A typical weighting function
*Source:* redrawn from Kahneman and Tverksy, 2007

The higher weighting given to the low probabilities is shown at the point where the solid line is above the dotted line. Subjects especially tend to overweight prospects where the amounts that can be gained would change their lifestyle. This explains why people play the lottery: despite the fact that the expected return is extremely negative (the more so considering taxes), the prospect of winning millions induces many to play. At the extremes, the solid line fails, as the prospects are either neglected as too improbable (lower left), or assumed to be certain (upper right).

Coming back to the framing of the worst-of reverse convertible, should the same product be presented differently, the investor might not be so eager to invest. Instead of the high coupon and conservative barrier, the investment advisor could mention the chance, on average, of one stock breaking through the barrier[15] and the resulting possible loss. In addition, the concentration of risk in the worst-of barrier reverse convertibles due to the embedded short correlation position should be mentioned. The investor would get an altogether different picture of the product, sensing the potential losses, and perhaps opt for another – perhaps a capital guaranteed structure instead.

Prospect Theory yields very useful insights about the investor's probable behavior. More than any mathematical formula, the knowledge of (the shape of) an investor's value function can be used by investors and investment advisors alike to determine which investments are

---

[14] Kahneman, D. and Tversky, A. (2007). *Choices, Values and Frames* Originally published in 1979.

[15] As previously mentioned, the chance of a barrier breakthrough is represented by the delta of the product.

necessary to build a portfolio that implements a preferred return distribution. The two parties have a common interest in sharing that information. It enables the advisor to offer his client a more personalized service, which is likely to increase the investor's level of satisfaction. Hence, the next step consists in constructing a tool that will gather that information from the investor.

## 11.4  QUESTIONNAIRE

Several aspects of private banking investors' behavior must be considered in the construction of a tool that is able to determine an investor's preferred distribution of returns.

- His general behavior when facing an investment decision that is strongly dependent on the framing of the proposal.
- Not only mean and variance, but also skew and kurtosis are key to a successful parameterization (Figure 11.6).
- Other factors like investment horizon, age, risk tolerance, etc. also influence the decisions and shift the shape of the preferred return distribution.

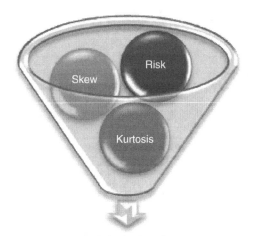

Individual distribution of returns

**Figure 11.6**  The main return distribution investment factors

Implementing the theory in practice is a difficult undertaking. Financial practitioners have a range of knowledge that extends from expert to neophyte, and finding a way to extract accurate information from clients about their investment value functions or utility curves with a standard tool is shaky at best. What follows is an attempt to capture some information through the means of a Questionnaire, which is composed of three parts:

- *Part 1:*  Expected return and volatility (defining the risk).
- *Part 2:*  Adjustments for volatility, skew and kurtosis.
- *Part 3:*  Adjustment for personal information.

The first part determines the risk tolerance of the investor. The answers to Questions 1 to 3 will establish a starting volatility capital. The answers to the second part adjust that starting volatility capital with consideration given to the investor's skewness and kurtosis preferences. The third part further adjusts the volatility, skewness and kurtosis based on detailed personal information. The Questionnaire is available for *personal use* at the end of the book.[16]

### 11.4.1  Questionnaire part 1: expected return and volatility

These two factors have been extensively researched, are known among investors ("no risk, no fun") and are relatively easy to measure. An existing technique consists of asking a series of questions where the investor must choose between a riskless asset with a relatively low expected return and a riskier asset yielding an expected higher return. The choices the investor makes will determine the level of risk he is willing to bear. The level of the expected returns for both the risky and the riskless asset depends on the reference currency. In the following example, it is assumed to be the Euro.

"In the following situations, when facing a choice between two assets, would you choose the riskless one, or the risky one?"

1. The riskless asset has an expected return of +4% with no dispersion range, while the risky asset has an expected return of +7% with a dispersion ranging from 0% to +14%
   a. I choose the riskless asset (go to question 3)
   b. I choose the risky asset (go to question 2)
2. The riskless asset has an expected return of 4% with no dispersion range, while the risky asset has an expected return of 7% with a dispersion ranging from −4% to +19%
   a. I choose the riskless asset (go to question 3)
   b. I choose the risky asset (go to part 2, question 4)
3. The riskless asset has an expected return of 4% with no dispersion range, while the risky asset has an expected return of 11% with a dispersion ranging from −4% to +19%
   a. I choose the riskless asset (got to part 3, question 11)
   b. I choose the risky asset (go to part 2, question 4)

### 11.4.2  Questionnaire part 2: adjustments for volatility, skew and kurtosis

The next step consists of determining the skew and kurtosis preferences of the investor who would like to hold risky assets. For those who do not even consider holding risky assets (answers 1a followed by 3a), the second part of the questionnaire is useless and can be skipped.

Concerning skewness, remember that assets with return distributions skewed to the right generally have a cost, while distributions skewed to the left generally generate a premium.[17] This doesn't necessarily mean that left-skewed distributions generate higher returns on average, though. The questionnaire should also gather information about preferences for *truncated* distributions to the left or to the right. It will determine whether or not the

---

[16] See Appendix C: Questionnaire.

[17] Right-skewed distributions usually cut off the distribution somewhere to the left, where the returns would otherwise be strongly negative. Insurance must be *bought* to implement this cut, and it bears a cost. The reverse is true for left-skewed distributions.

investor is ready to accept positive or negative fat tails. Since it would be extremely difficult to quantify skewness, the results will be limited to three global categories:

- left-skewed;
- right-skewed; and
- no skew preference

Information about skewness preferences will be extracted through two question types:

- questions about left- or right-truncated distributions; and
- questions about left- or right skewed distributions

The same procedure will be applied to gather preferences about kurtosis. The questions will aim at gathering this information in three global categories:

- high kurtosis;
- flat kurtosis; and
- no kurtosis preference (normal kurtosis).

Note that the answer to one question might give information about the investor's preferences for volatility, skew and kurtosis all at once.

Follows the questions (continued from question 3 on page 247 on expected return and volatility):

4. Would you be willing to reduce the expected return of your portfolio to protect it against market corrections or crashes?
   a. No (skip to question 5)
   b. I would be willing to reduce it by less than 1% annually
   c. I would be willing to reduce it by up to 3% annually
   d. I would be willing to reduce it by up to 5% annually
   e. I would be willing to reduce it by more than 5% annually
   f.
5. If you had to choose, which correction would you like to be protected against?
   a. The first −10%
   b. A correction between −10% and −30%
   c. A correction starting from −20%
   d.
6. Would you be willing to cap your maximum return? You will receive a premium in compensation, but large gains in the markets will be lost for you.
   a. No
   b. Yes
   c.
7. Would you be willing to cap your maximum return in order to receive a premium and buy protection against medium market corrections (−20% to −50%)? The protection vanishes with larger corrections.
   a. No
   b. Yes

8. Would you be willing to forego dividends or yield in order to buy protection against medium market corrections (−20% to −50%)? The protection vanishes with larger corrections.
   a. No
   b. Yes
9. Would you be willing to forego dividends or yield in order to buy leverage?
   a. Yes
   b. No
10. If you had the choice between two assets, both with an expected return closely matching your target but one with a small dispersion (chances are you can't gain much more, but you won't lose much either), and another with a greater dispersion (chances are that you will either gain more or lose more), which one would you choose?
    a. I would choose the one with the smaller dispersion.
    b. I would choose the one with the larger dispersion.

### 11.4.3 Questionnaire part 3: investor's personal information

Further adjustments have to be made in order to crosscheck the validity of the answers of Parts 1 and 2. In addition to the investor's risk *willingness*, central information about risk *ability* is asked in question 13.

11. On average, for how long do you usually invest?
    a. A year or less
    b. Between one and three years
    c. Up to five years
    d. Over 5 years: . . . . . . . . . . . . . . .
12. In which asset categories do you invest the largest part of your capital? (multiple answers possible)
    a. Investment grade bonds (funds)
    b. FX
    c. Derivatives (warrants, options or futures)
    d. Structured products
    e. Funds-of-hedge-funds
    f. Single stocks
    g. Cash or money-market
    h. Emerging market bonds (funds)
    i. Commodities
    j. Mutual funds
    k. Others (please state)
13. What are the annual cash flows you require or need from your investments?
    a. None
    b. Between 1% and 4% of the invested capital
    c. Between 4% and 8% of the invested capital
    d. Over 8% of the invested capital
14. Please state your age
    a. Below 30
    b. 30–45
    c. 46–60
    d. Over 60

### 11.4.4   Answer evaluation

*Part 1: questions 1–3*

An analysis of the results will show that an investor choosing 1(a)/3(a) will be strongly risk averse and has a low target return. He will aim for capital preservation with minimum volatility. An investor choosing 1(a)/3(b) shows loss aversion but has a higher target return and will invest in risky assets if his target can be met but losses limited. An investor choosing 1(b)/2(a)/3(a) is ready to give away the safe yield for the chance to get a higher return and is even willing to incur a small loss if the opportunity warrants it. An investor choosing 1(b)/2(b) does not shun losses and clearly has a higher target than the riskless asset. He can be considered as the most risk-seeking investor. An investor choosing 1(b)/2(a)/3(b) will invest in risky assets as long as the risks relative to the expected return are deemed acceptable. When the risk increases, he will exit the risky asset. Table 11.3 ranks the investor's answers from safest to riskiest:

**Table 11.3**   Question 1–3 ranking

| Category | Result |
|---|---|
| 1 | 1(a)/3(a) |
| 2 | 1(a)/3(b) |
| 3 | 1(b)/2(a)/3(a) |
| 4 | 1(b)/2(a)/3(b) |
| 5 | 1(b)/2(b) |

The five results represent the risk class into which an investor can be classified. Portfolio managers will have recognized typical model portfolios ranging from "Income" to "Growth". The results can be quantified in terms of volatility ranges (Table 11.4). The average of each range will be used to build the *starting volatility capital*, which will later be adjusted by the answers to the questions of Parts 2 and 3:

**Table 11.4**   Volatility averages and starting capital

| Category | Range | Volatility average (starting volatility capital) |
|---|---|---|
| 1 | Volatility of less than 7% p.a. | 5% |
| 2 | Volatility between 7% and 11% p.a. | 9% |
| 3 | Volatility between 11% and 17% p.a. | 14% |
| 4 | Volatility between 17% and 25% p.a. | 21% |
| 5 | Volatility over 25% p.a. | 27% |

The results should be considered over the whole portfolio, not only over parts of it. In order to simplify the process for illustration purposes, the first two categories will be grouped into a single one named "low risk", and the last two named "high risk", leaving the middle one alone as "medium risk", totaling three categories (Table 11.5).[18]

---

[18] The risk classes correspond to those selected in Table 11.2.

**Table 11.5** Portfolio risk categories

|  | Low risk | Medium risk | High risk |
| --- | --- | --- | --- |
| **Category** | 1 & 2 | 3 | 4 & 5 |
| **Volatility range** | 5%–11% | 11%–17% | 17% & above |

*Part 2: questions 4–10*

Questions 4 to 10 introduce adjustments for skewness and kurtosis preferences and raise or lower the starting volatility capital (Tables 11.6–11.12). Skew starts with a base value of zero and kurtosis starts with three.[19] The adjustments for volatility, skewness and kurtosis should be added or subtracted to their respective starting capital determined in the first part of the questionnaire. Adjustments for volatility are given in percentage points in the columns labeled "Risk". For skew and kurtosis, the adjustments are expressed in decimals. Note that the resulting mathematical numbers will be eventually interpreted as "left", "no" or "right" skew and "high", "medium" or "low" kurtosis.

**Table 11.6** Attributed points for question 4

| Answer question 4 | Risk | Skew | Kurt. |
| --- | --- | --- | --- |
| **a** | 0% | −0.3 | −0.2 |
| **b** | 0% | +0.1 | – |
| **c** | −1% | +0.3 | +0.1 |
| **d** | −2% | +0.6 | +0.2 |
| **e** | −3% | +1.0 | +0.4 |

Paying for protection is equivalent to cutting the distribution off somewhere to the left, effectively skewing it to the right while reducing the expected mean return by the paid amount. The higher the premium paid, the higher the skew becomes. The volatility of returns also diminishes with higher premiums paid. As for the kurtosis, it rises with rising premiums. Since a higher premium buys better protection, a higher proportion of the distribution of returns will be concentrated to the right of the protection level.

**Table 11.7** Attributed points for question 5

| Answer question 5 | Risk | Skew | Kurt. |
| --- | --- | --- | --- |
| **a** | 0% | −0.1 | – |
| **b** | 0% | – | – |
| **c** | −1% | +0.3 | +0.1 |

This question addresses the negative "fat tails" which are empirically observed in financial markets, especially stock markets. If only the first 10% losses are protected (answer a), the

---

[19] A normal distribution has a kurtosis of three, which represents the default number.

distribution will be less right-skewed than assumed in question four. If the protection was bought from a lower level but covers the entire left tail, the distribution will tend to be right-skewed and leptokurtic.

**Table 11.8**   Attributed points for question 6

| Answer question 6 | Risk | Skew | Kurt. |
|---|---|---|---|
| a | 0% | — | — |
| b | 0% | −1.0 | +0.7 |

Capping the maximum return generates a premium, but strongly skews the distribution to the left, effectively truncating it at the level of the cap. The kurtosis is positively affected, as all the distribution is concentrated at or below the cap. Capping the distribution does not necessarily have an impact on the volatility.

**Table 11.9**   Attributed points for question 7

| Answer question 7 | Risk | Skew | Kurt. |
|---|---|---|---|
| a | 0% | — | — |
| b | −1% | −0.7 | +0.7 |

As in question 6, the cap cuts the distribution off somewhere on the right side. The conditional protection, which vanishes when the market crashes, is weaker than the cap and does not prevent any extreme tail risk, hence the negative overall skew bias. The kurtosis naturally rises for the same reason as in question 6.

**Table 11.10**   Attributed points for question 8

| Answer question 8 | Risk | Skew | Kurt. |
|---|---|---|---|
| a | 0% | — | — |
| b | 0% | +0.2 | +0.2 |

Foregoing yield or dividends in order to purchase protection conditional to the market not falling by more than a certain amount slightly skews the distribution to the right, but leaves both tails open. It does not necessarily influence the volatility. As long as the protection holds, the kurtosis will be positively affected.

**Table 11.11**   Attributed points for question 9

| Answer question 9 | Risk. | Skew | Kurt. |
|---|---|---|---|
| a | 0% | — | — |
| b | +2% | +0.1 | −0.2 |

Using dividends or yield to purchase upside leverage has little impact on skew, but reduces the kurtosis as both upside and downside returns are spread wider. The returns are highly likely to be more volatile as well, increasing the volatility substantially.

**Table 11.12** Attributed points for question 10

| Answer question 10 | Risk | Skew | Kurt. |
|---|---|---|---|
| **a** | −2% | − | +0.5 |
| **b** | +2% | − | −0.5 |

The concentration or dispersion of the returns around a target, here the expected return, strongly affects the kurtosis. When they are rather concentrated, the kurtosis rises, and the volatility is usually reduced as compared to normally distributed return. By contrast, widely spread returns engender platykurtic and volatile distributions eventually building "fat tails".

### Part 3: questions 11–14

As for questions 4–10, questions 11 to 14 further adjust the volatility, skew and kurtosis. The questions in this last part of the questionnaire focus on the personal situation of the investor (Tables 11.13–11.16).

**Table 11.13** Attributed points for question 11

| Answer question 11 | Risk | Skew | Kurt. |
|---|---|---|---|
| **a** | −2% | − | − |
| **b** | 0% | − | − |
| **c** | +1% | − | − |
| **d** | +2% | − | − |

The evaluation of the point attribution for the question about the investment horizon is tricky. Most professional practitioners use the mantra "the longer the time horizon, the more risk can be loaded into a portfolio", as over time the value of the assets will rise at some hypothetical long-term average rate. This mantra has not always worked during the last 10

**Table 11.14** Attributed points for question 12

| Answer question 12 | Risk | Skew | Kurt. |
|---|---|---|---|
| **a** | −1% | − | +0.2 |
| **b** | −1% | − | − |
| **c** | +8% | − | − |
| **d** | −1% | − | +0.1 |
| **e** | −2% | − | − |
| **f** | +3% | − | −0.2 |
| **g** | −3% | − | +0.3 |
| **h** | +2% | − | − |
| **i** | +4% | − | −0.3 |
| **j** | −1% | − | − |
| **k** | . . . | . . . | . . . |

years, at least for most stock markets. A simple look at the historical performance of some of the major indices, not to mention single stocks, will suffice to confirm this statement. Nevertheless, short-term investments allow less risk tolerance than longer-holding horizons, hence the reduction of risk capital for answer a) and an increase for response c) and d). The holding period has no influence on either skew or kurtosis.

Question 12 is one of the easiest for the investor, but crucial for the confirmation of questions 1 to 3 in Part 1 of the questionnaire. For instance if the investor has answered 1(a)/3(a) and checks box "c" in question 12, then there's a need for clarification! On average, the investor filling out the questionnaire should check three to five boxes here, if he is reasonably diversified. Specific preferences will be easy to spot for the investment advisor, who can then adjust the portfolio construction accordingly.

The sum of the volatility shifts equals to zero if one leaves out answer (c). In theory at least, historically low volatility assets like investment grade bonds, cash and money market instruments have the tendency to reduce the volatility of a portfolio, while single stock and commodities rather increase it. It is shaky at best to assess the skew on whole asset classes, so no shift in this category. On the kurtosis side, however, some assets have naturally concentrated or widely spread returns. If the investor frequently uses other assets not listed (answer k), the investment advisor has either to judge the value of the shifts by himself or leave those assets out of the analysis. This should seldom be the case, though.

**Table 11.15**   Attributed points for question 13

| Answer question 13 | Risk | Skew | Kurt. |
|---|---|---|---|
| a | +2% | – | −0.2 |
| b | 0% | +0.2 | – |
| c | −2% | +0.4 | +0.1 |
| d | −3% | +0.6 | +0.2 |

While questions 1–3 give an indication about the investor's *willingness* to take risk, question 13 addresses the investor's *capability* of taking risk. If he needs a regular income from his investments to maintain his living standard, it is prudent to reduce the volatility, to skew the distribution to the right and to concentrate the returns around a target in order to increase the probability of meeting that target. Hence, the relatively large shifts in volatility and skew. If not, the volatility and the kurtosis can be slightly increased. The distribution doesn't need to be skewed to the left, though.

**Table 11.16**   Attributed points for question 14

| Answer question 14 | Risk | Skew | Kurt. |
|---|---|---|---|
| a | +2% | – | −0.3 |
| b | +1% | – | −0.1 |
| c | −1% | +0.1 | – |
| d | −2% | +0.2 | +0.2 |

It is a common practice to invest in higher volatility assets for the young than for more elderly persons, where safety is usually the first priority.

*Summarizing the results*

After the investor has answered the questions, the values of the answers are summed up. The sum of all the volatility shifts from questions 4 to 14 amounts to zero, while the sum of the skew and kurtosis shifts both amount to 2.00. The zero-sum of the volatility shifts represents neutrality in respect of the volatility starting capital assumed in questions 1–3. An investor who has truthfully answered questions 1–3 should remain on average within his initial range as defined in Table 11.4. A very conservative investor starting with a volatility capital of 5% may even reach a negative volatility total. This should be of no concern, as the investments will simply be of the most conservative kind. Respondents whose initial volatility capital shifts by a large amount that changes their category by two (or even more) should be cross-examined further about their investment objectives. Answers to questions 4–14 can result in a single category shift if the investor was on the border of answering differently to one of the questions 1–3.

The large positive skew total results from intentionally framing the questionnaire so as to push the investor towards safety rather than risk. While some specialists may question this practice, it is the author's conviction that right-skewed distributions have, over the long run, better average return rates and lower return volatilities. What's more, a right-skewed distribution of returns is far less likely to anger or disappoint a private banking investor. Conversely, left-skewed distributions are prone to large losses, which is the principal cause for clients' dissatisfaction and their leaving their bank. The high positive kurtosis sum should not come as a surprise. The fact is that making a choice to eliminate one part or the other of a return distribution automatically concentrates the whole distribution over less than the entire range, thus increasing the kurtosis.

Table 11.17 suggests a classification by categories that simplify the interpretation of the numerical results of the Questionnaire. The categories will subsequently be used in examples.

**Table 11.17**   Questionnaire results summary

| Risk (volatility) | <11% | 11%–17% | >17% |
|---|---|---|---|
| Select category: | Low | Medium | High |
| Skew | <−0.4 | −0.4–0.4 | >0.4 |
| Select category: | Left | None | Right |
| Kurtosis | <2.5 | 2.5–3.5 | >3.5 |
| Select category: | Flat | Normal | High |

## 11.4.5  Examples

In order to illustrate practical cases, three examples have been devised. Fictional characters play a role in giving answers as investors and investment advice as advisors. Bob, John and Maria are three different investors, while Marc is their investment advisor. The examples described here will also be used at a later stage to fill the portfolios of the respective characters using products selected according to their answers.

Investor A, Bob Sample, age 62, recently retired, married, bankable assets of EUR 3 million, transfers his funds to investment advisor Marc Council. Bob has no other revenue than what he can earn on his assets, which he has gathered over his life. He fills in the questionnaire with the answers shown in Table 11.18.

**Table 11.18**   Answers to questionnaire from Bob Sample

| Question | 1 | 2 | 3 | 4 | 5 | 6 | 7 | 8 | 9 | 10 | 11 | 12 | 13 | 14 |
|---|---|---|---|---|---|---|---|---|---|---|---|---|---|---|
| **Answer** | a | – | a | – | – | – | – | – | – | – | b | a/f/j | b | d |
| **Scores** | Risk: 4% Skew: +0.4 Kurtosis: +0.2 | | | | | | | | | | | | | |
| **Classification** | Risk category: 1 (low), right skew, normal kurtosis | | | | | | | | | | | | | |

He further comments that his single stock and mutual funds holdings represent less than 10% of his assets. He plans to retire to southern France where he would like to buy a house near the coast in exchange for the house he would sell in the Netherlands. He adds that, with any luck, his house in the North will have a greater value than the house on the coast he plans to buy.

Investor B, John Model, age 49, manager and owner of a small privately-held industrial company, married, father with two children, bankable assets of EUR 2.5 million, transfers most of his funds to his long-time friend Marc Council. His answers to the questionnaire are shown in Table 11.19.

**Table 11.19**   Answers to questionnaire from John Model

| Question | 1 | 2 | 3 | 4 | 5 | 6 | 7 | 8 | 9 | 10 | 11 | 12 | 13 | 14 |
|---|---|---|---|---|---|---|---|---|---|---|---|---|---|---|
| **Answer** | b | a | a | b | c | a | a | b | a | a | c | a/b/d/f | a | c |
| **Scores** | Risk: 13% Skew: +0.7 Kurtosis: +0.7 | | | | | | | | | | | | | |
| **Classification** | Risk category: 3 (medium), right skew, high kurtosis | | | | | | | | | | | | | |

Marc knows from their relationship that John has a good knowledge of FX instruments (his firm operates in foreign countries) and that he invests in stocks of industrial companies with which he does business. Due to the nature of his business, John knows the relationship between risk and reward pretty well, and he is ready to take controlled risk.

Investor C, Maria Case, age 37, no business activity, single, has inherited a large sum from her grandfather who sold a banana plantation just before he passed away. Maria has little experience with investments and no desire to delve into the world of finance, preferring to spend her time with friends. Her last advisor at a competitor bank did such a lousy job that Maria has decided to change her bank and she discusses her fortune – approximately EUR 11 Mio – with Marc Council. Marc asks Maria to fill out the questionnaire, but Maria has trouble with the questions, not making sense of some. After some help through examples, Maria's responses are as shown in Table 11.20.

Marc senses that Maria leads a careless life, traveling around the world to see friends on a whim or buying fashion designer clothes and luxury items for pleasure. She seems to live for the day and likes to see results quickly. The answer to question 11 was difficult to estimate; Maria finally found she didn't like to wait for years for an investment to produce positive results and opted for response (a). Marc agreed as a result of the first impression he got of her. Question 12 could not be answered at all. Her answer to question 13 about her

**Table 11.20** Answers to questionnaire from Maria Case

| Question | 1 | 2 | 3 | 4 | 5 | 6 | 7 | 8 | 9 | 10 | 11 | 12 | 13 | 14 |
|---|---|---|---|---|---|---|---|---|---|---|---|---|---|---|
| **Answer** | b | a | b | b | c | a | a | b | a | b | ?(a) | ? | d | b |
| **Scores** | Risk: 18% Skew: +1.2 Kurtosis: −0.1 | | | | | | | | | | | | | |
| **Classification** | Risk category: 4 (high), right skew, normal kurtosis | | | | | | | | | | | | | |

income requirement makes Marc uneasy; Maria stated that she spends well over a million per year, more than the maximum of 8% stated in the questionnaire (8% of 11 million would make around 880 k).

### 11.4.6 Conclusion

The questionnaire is a handy tool for evaluating the investment preferences of an investor. The discovery of the preferred shape of the distribution of returns of an investor allows a far better investment guideline than was previously available with the mean/return method. The additional information about the preferred skew and kurtosis will enable the advisor to pinpoint the correct investment form for his clients to a much better degree. The reader will have noted that all the examples are right-skewed. Despite that being the case, the assets and products that will fill the portfolios of Bob, John and Maria will be quite different. The portfolio construction process will be described in Chapter 13, after a method for classifying the assets has been presented in the next section.

Although the questionnaire has been thoroughly tested, it is by no means a foolproof investment plan. At the end of the day, no piece of paper can replace human contact and judgment.

# 12
# Return Distributions of Structured Products

## 12.1 PROCEDURE AND DATA

The Questionnaire introduced in Chapter 11 assesses the preferences of an investor in terms of a return distribution shape. There follows the third step of the portfolio construction concept, which consists of finding out assets whose return distribution matches that of an investor's preferences. This study measures the return distributions of classical structures such as capital guaranteed, yield enhancement and participation products, and subsequently to classify them in the risk cube. Four main measures will be calculated:

- the mean return over a holding period;
- the volatility of the returns (as a first measure for risk);
- the skew of the returns (as a second measure for risk);
- the kurtosis of the returns (as a third measure for risk).

The results will enable an investor to select products matching his investment preferences that were determined by means of the Questionnaire. This will be demonstrated in later sections with the hypothetical advisor, who will construct portfolios that match the preferences of his three investors. In order to make the exercise as practical as possible, multiple matching assets will be selected to form a portfolio. This seems obvious from a portfolio management perspective, but the great majority of studies do not consider multiple assets.

This study only determines the *historical* values of the above-mentioned parameters, which will form the basis for considering investments in later sections. In practice, the *forecast* values of the parameters should be the determining factor for investments. The scope of the study will be limited to products based on stock indices and single stocks in EUR and CHF, but it is easy to broaden the scope of the procedure to include other assets and currencies.

### 12.1.1 Back-test time window

For the purpose of the study, 10-year weekly historical data from Bloomberg over the period July 1998 to July 2008 are used. Daily data would have been preferable, especially for products with continuously monitored barriers, where even intraday lows or highs can have a crucial impact on the product.[1] This approximation will be considered in the commentaries where barrier products are tested. This particular 10-year period was selected because 1998 was the year when the structured products were first offered to private investors on a broad scale. It would be useless to start the back-test any earlier, because the majority of products didn't even exist then and those few which were available were only accessible to institutional investors.

---

[1] Unfortunately, the computing power required to handle the large amount of data was not available. The author uses an Intel quadcore 2.4 GHz processor-based computer

As mentioned, the products tested will be based on stocks and stock indices. It has to be kept in mind that there were distinct periods within the back-test period: the LTCM meltdown in 1998 with the ensuing bull run until the dot-com bubble in 2000; the long bear market that followed, including 9/11 and the long bull market from 2003 to mid-2007; finally, the subprime crisis from 2007 onwards. From an FX perspective, we consider a weak EUR against the USD up until 2000 and 8 years of strong bull market afterwards. Yields, especially short-term yields, had strong swings. The Swiss Franc 3-month swap rose from 1.5% to 3.5% in 1999, fell steadily to 0.25% until 2003, and rose back to 3% until the beginning of 2008 only to fall close to zero at the end of that year. In essence, there have been long bull and sharp bear markets for the majority of asset classes, but few enough sideways markets. Since statistical analysis bases its results only on history, history has to repeat itself for the results of this study to be extrapolated into the future as well. In other words, the author wishes once more to express caution about reliance on these results for future decision-making.

## 12.1.2 Product and asset return calculations

A key characteristic of structured products is their predetermined expiry. In order to compare an investment in a product to one in its underlying asset, the procedure must assume the same holding period for the product and the underlying asset. For instance, a one-year holding period will be assumed for a product with a maturity of one year, a two-year holding period for a product with a two-year maturity, and so on. The procedure reflects the stance of a "naïve" investor who buys and holds the product until its maturity, even if it would have been possible to sell it within that timeframe.

The historical returns of the products and those of their underlying assets are calculated over an average of *single holding periods*, in order to be able to compare the relative performance of the product to that of its underlying asset(s). The assumption is that for each holding period, an identical sum is invested in the product and its underlying asset, regardless of the performance of the previous period. Subsequently, the performances of the single periods can be aggregated and averaged, something that would not be strictly mathematically correct for investments over several periods.[2] A return of the products and their underlying assets over the whole back-test period will not be calculated, as it is not the goal to assess whether investments in a string of products over the back-test period as a whole out- or underperformed their underlying asset(s).[3] In turn, this means that the average return shown in the tables starting with Table 12.4 on page 265 will not be the average return the products or their underlying assets would have generated had an investor invested a given capital, say 100, on day one and reinvested the returns over every holding period in new products. For example, Table 12.18 on page 282 shows that the average return of the stock Nokia for a one-year holding period would have been 22.6% over the back-test

---

[2] This is because a retracement followed by a similar recovery in points corresponds to a lower loss and larger gain expressed in percentage. For instance, a 50% drop followed by a 100% rise would only pull the asset back to its initial level. In monetary terms, an investor would be flat, but an average of the percentage returns would yield a wrong positive result. To compute averages over several periods, lognormal calculations must be performed, but that is not the goal here.

[3] The author does not recommend investing in identical structured product strategies on a continuous basis. The belief is rather that structured investments are triggered by certain conditions like current market characteristics, expected market scenarios and investor's risk appetite on an opportunistic basis.

period. That number cannot be multiplied by the amount of holding periods in the sample. Instead, it represents the average performance for a single holding period, which can be compared to the average single-period return of a product with corresponding maturity, in this case a reverse convertible returning on average only 1.6%.

### 12.1.3  Product and back-test construction

A back-tested product's parameters are initially calculated with average conditions of volatility and yield, based on historical data over the back-test period. Each product thus calculated is then hypothetically launched every week over a 10-year period. In that way, for a one-year product, an identical product is launched and expires over 520 times (10 years times 52 weeks per year). If the maturity of the product is five years, the product can only be launched about 250 times. The final performance of each iteration of the product and its underlying asset is calculated and kept on record. Finally, the four statistical measures are calculated from the historical performance: mean return, volatility of the returns, the skew of returns and kurtosis of returns. Figure 12.1 shows the procedure graphically for a one-year product.

Each of the $\sim 250^4$ to 520+ performances for the back-tested product is plotted on a graph. Visual representation makes it easier to identify crucial points and to compare products. A histogram with probabilities of returns provides means of analyzing and comparing the performance of the product to both that of its underlying asset and to that of other products. In addition, each back-tested product has a comparative data table showing statistical numbers like mean return, skew or kurtosis for itself and the underlying asset.

### 12.1.4  Product risk category classification

At the end of a product analysis, the product is classified into a "risk category", being a means to classify it in relation to other products and assets. The risk category is defined by five levels, 1 being the lowest and 5 the highest. This particular ranking has been selected to assess the appropriateness of a product in portfolios used in classical asset and portfolio management.[5] The number attributed to a product in this classification represents the *minimum* risk category below which this particular product should not be implemented. However, it could still be used for higher risk categories when the situation warrants it. The reasoning leading to the value of the risk category is the author's own, and the reader might differ if he assumes other hypotheses. In distinct situations, even the author might reclassify some products into other risk categories. The beauty of structured products is that their uses are not cast in stone but change depending on the current situation.

### 12.1.5  Product construction hypotheses

It is almost impossible to parameterize each product based on the weekly data because one would need the exact level of implied volatility, dividend yield (for stocks and stock indices) and interest rate level at each weekly product launch. Even if the data were available, the question about which product parameter to adjust remains. Suppose, for example, that the

---

[4] For a five-year product.

[5] A risk category of "1" represents a fit of the product in a fixed-income only portfolio, while a risk category "5" would mean that the product should not be implemented in portfolios below the riskiest one.

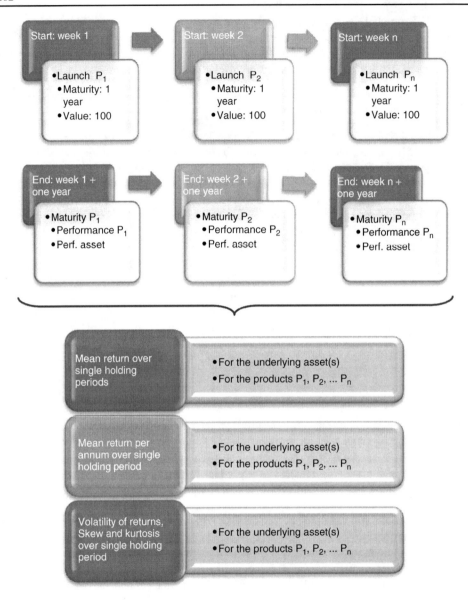

**Figure 12.1** Product statistical data calculation process

product constructed in week 1 featured a capital guarantee of 100%, participation of 100% and a maturity of 5 years. Now imagine that in week 2, the volatility has risen by 5 points; what should the new product look like? Should it feature a lower capital guarantee of 98%, a lower participation rate of 90, or a longer maturity of 6 years? Each node would call for a discretionary decision influencing the result. Since such an undertaking is not practical, identical average construction parameters for all products are assumed. Table 12.1 shows the interest rate levels used for constructing the products:

**Table 12.1** Average interest rate levels assumption

| Interest rate level | 1y | 2y | 3y | 4y | 5y |
|---|---|---|---|---|---|
| EUR | 3.5% | 3.7% | 3.8% | 4% | 4.1% |
| CHF | 1.8% | 2.1% | 2.3% | 2.5% | 2.7% |

Source: Bloomberg, own calculations

For instance a two-year product in EUR will be constructed with an interest rate level of 3.7%, while a four-year CHF-based product will be constructed with a 2.5% interest rate. Once the product's payoff is set, it is maintained over the whole 10 years of the back-test period.

An average volatility level of the underlying assets is used in the construction of the products. An upside or downside shift of a few volatility points (between 1% and 3%) will be applied depending on the product being long or short volatility to reflect the volatility bid-ask spread in the market. Sometimes a slight shift will be made to consider also high or low average volatility skew.

An adjusted dividend yield for stocks and stock indices will be taken according to the long-term average of the underlying asset. For instance, the assumed average dividend yield for the Eurostoxx50 index is 4% and that for the SMI index is 2.5%.

It is clear that, by using average conditions, the products' parameters will end up with conditions either too good or too bad for a given market condition. However, these imperfections should cancel each other out to such an extent that the synthetic products produce a result approaching that which would have been achieved by using the "true" conditions, especially over a 10-year period.

## 12.1.6 Product universe

As mentioned, products of the three main SVSP categories will be considered. Warrants are excluded from this study, as they represent leverage products and are seldom used in portfolio management. The considered products are:

**Table 12.2** Tested types of capital guaranteed products

| Capital guaranteed | Yield enhancement | Participation |
|---|---|---|
| 100% capital guaranteed, no cap | Reverse convertible | Bonus certificate |
| 100% capital guaranteed, capped | Barrier reverse convertible | Capped bonus certificate |
| < 100% capital guaranteed, no cap | Worst-of barrier reverse convertible | |
| < 100% capital guaranteed, capped | | |

For each of the above products and where applicable, several variations of maturity, barrier level, bonus level or cap will be calculated. The emphasis will be put on stocks and stock indices, as these products represent the majority of the total volume outstanding among private banking clients. Once more, the main goal is to assess the historical behavior of the products thereby providing a basis for selecting the appropriate ones when constructing the portfolio according to an investor's preferences.

## 12.2   CAPITAL GUARANTEED PRODUCTS

A 100% participation ratio will always be assumed for capital guaranteed products. The other construction parameters used for the products to be tested are described in Table 12.3.

**Table 12.3**   Details of tested capital guaranteed products

| Product name | Underlying asset | CG* level | Maturity | Currency | Cap |
|---|---|---|---|---|---|
| CG1 | Eurostoxx50 index | 100% | 5 years | EUR | No |
| CG2 | Eurostoxx50 index | 100% | 2 years | EUR | 125% |
| CG3 | Eurostoxx50 index | 94% | 2 years | EUR | No |
| CG4 | Eurostoxx50 index | 94.5% | 1 year | EUR | No |
| CG5 | SMI index | 93% | 5 years | CHF | No |
| CG6 | SMI index | 95% | 2 years | CHF | 135% |
| CG7 | SMI index | 94% | 1 year | CHF | No |

Source: Bloomberg, own calculations *CG: Capital Guarantee

The products have been calculated with the average volatility, interest rate and dividend yield as mentioned in the previous section. They would have been possible to implement *on average* over the ten-year back-test period. Their parameters correspond to real products as often seen in private banking.

### 12.2.1   Capital guaranteed product #1 (CG1)

| Product name | Underlying asset | CG level | Maturity | Currency | Cap |
|---|---|---|---|---|---|
| CG1 | Eurostoxx50 index | 100% | 5 years | EUR | No |

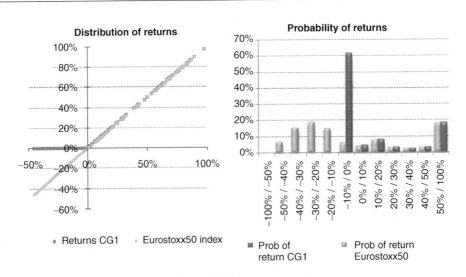

**Figure 12.2**   Distribution and probability of returns for CG1

**Table 12.4** Statistics for CG1

|  | SX5E index | CG1 |
|---|---|---|
| Mean return over h.p.[6] | 1.1% (TR : 12.6%)[7] | 16.9% |
| Mean return p.a.[8] | 0.22% (TR: 2.52%) | 3.38% |
| Volatility of returns | 39.0% | 27.6% |
| Skew | 0.88 | 1.40 |
| Kurtosis | 2.45 | 3.41 |

Source: Bloomberg, own calculations

Let's get familiar with the graphs and tables. The left-hand graph of Figure 12.2 entitled "Distribution of returns" is a scatterplot of all the returns the product CG1 would have generated over the last 10 years. The horizontal axis is the market performance of the underlying asset, here the Eurostoxx50 index, and the vertical axis gives the P&L of the product. The lighter line[9] representing the index returns has the usual 45° straight line. CG1 has the same upside since it has 100% upside market participation rate, but distinguishes itself from the index when the latter falls below its initial price.

The right hand side bar graph entitled "Probability of returns" gives the probability that CG1 or the index achieve a return that falls within a specific range. The horizontal axis is divided into return "buckets"[10] and the vertical axis shows the chance expressed in percent that the return falls in the corresponding bucket. Not surprisingly, CG1 outperforms the index because the distribution is truncated to the left below the capital guarantee level, but there is still an astonishingly high proportion of cases (62%!) where CG1 ends at par, on the capital guarantee level. This means two things: first, in over 60% of the cases, the investor choosing CG1 over the index avoids losses. Second, in over 60% of the cases the investor has no revenue, which for a five-year holding period will represent a problem for most investors!

Table 12.4 shows the essential statistics needed for determining if a product matches the preferences of an investor. Foremost is the mean return, which is expressed over the life of the product in the first row, and per annum in the second. Holding the index for five years any time within the last 10 years would have yielded an average return of 1.1%, which equals to roughly 0.2% per annum. The same strategy with CG1 would have yielded an average of 16.9%, which represents a more decent but still disappointing 3.38% per annum. A short analysis of the time series that led to these results shows that the holding period of the product is too long: the gains a number of products generated in the first years of their life were erased by bear markets that followed. Remember that this study assumes that an investor will buy and hold the product for the whole lifetime.

It is worthwhile knowing if the additional return generated by CG1 was worth its cost: a mean return of 16.9% for CG1 against 1.1% for the Eurostoxx50 index seems like a no-brainer in favor of the product. However, CG1 uses the index's dividends to buy the

---

[6] For the holding period ("h.p.") of the product. In this case, 5 years.
[7] The total return was calculated using the SX5T index.
[8] Per annum.
[9] Actually the line is a series of dots where each dot represents the performance of one back-tested product. For a product on a single asset, the alignment of the dots should closely resemble the payoff at maturity.
[10] Named "classes" in statistics.

downside protection, but the index's performance is shown ex-dividends. In order to compare apples with apples, CG1 should be compared to the total return (TR) index, *including* the dividends. The underlying asset's TR is displayed in parenthesis. In this case, the Eurostoxx50 TR index buy-and-hold strategy for five years any time within the last 10 years would have yielded an average return of 12.6% (2.52% p.a.), which is much more than the 1.1% of the Eurostoxx50 price return index. This example clearly demonstrates the effect of foregone dividends with long-dated products. Nonetheless, the TR index return is still lower than the 16.9% of CG1. The volatility of returns is also somewhat lower in CG1 than in the index. One should not confuse the volatility of returns with the volatility of the index or the product. The volatility of the returns in the table gives an indication about how widely the returns are spread around their mean, *not* how large the variations in the index or the product were. While 27.6% for CG1 is still a large number, it is clearly lower than the 39% of the index. Finally, the skew and kurtosis give an idea of the shape of the returns. In our case, both distributions are right-skewed, but much more strongly in CG1. Since it is capital guaranteed, the positive skew indicates that only positive surprises are possible. Indeed, 18% of the returns are higher than 50% over the five-year period. The kurtosis is also higher in CG1, which is no surprise since the capital guarantee biases the shape to a large extent. The zero-bond floor is initially low, at about 82% due to the long maturity. A change in the interest rate will have a large effect on the product. The more the index rises above its initial value, the higher its delta will rise and the more the product will behave like the index itself, making the product riskier.

Concluding the analysis, it is evident that CG1 adds value compared to the index. However, the long maturity of this product will discourage many investors, and the average return will barely excite many investors. Let's test if other, shorter dated, products yield similar or better results.

**Conclusion:** risk category 3.

### 12.2.2   Capital guaranteed product #2 (CG2)

| Product name | Underlying asset | CG level | Maturity | Currency | Cap |
|---|---|---|---|---|---|
| CG2 | Eurostoxx50 index | 100% | 2 years | EUR | 125% |

In this two-year capped version, the mean return is lower both for the index and for the product when compared to CG1 with a five-year holding period, but much higher than when taken on an annual basis. CG2's return of 6.5% per annum will already appeal to more investors. Actually, the product with a two-year period sacrifices gains to a following bear market much less often than CG1 did with a five-year holding period. CG2 has extremely concentrated returns, mainly due to the relatively low cap. The volatility of returns is very low with 11.9%, which makes it an ideal product for investors with a specific target return. The percentage of times the product ended on the capital guarantee has also decreased to around 40%, but it remains at a relatively high level. Interestingly, a relatively high percentage of the returns for the index is concentrated in the 30% to 40% area, just above the cap of the product. It might be worthwhile constructing a payoff that caps the product at 35% rather than at 25%. It wasn't possible with the average condition assumptions used

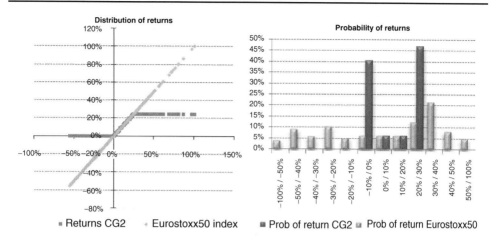

**Figure 12.3**   Distribution and probability of returns for CG2

**Table 12.5**   Statistics for CG2

|                      | SX5E index          | CG2    |
|----------------------|---------------------|--------|
| Mean return over h.p. | 7.2% (TR: 11.6%)   | 13.0%  |
| Mean return p.a.     | 3.6% (TR: 5.8%)     | 6.5%   |
| Volatility of returns | 34.3%              | 11.9%  |
| Skew                 | −0.17               | −0.09  |
| Kurtosis             | 2.09                | 1.08   |

Source: Bloomberg, own calculations

here, but it has been, and should continue to be, common enough to make this set of parameters reasonable.

The skew for the two-year period is negligible both for the index and for the product. In fact, the product has a rather bimodal distribution shape: either no return at all or the maximum, while the same can be observed with the index: chances are that the performance after two years ends either with a strong minus (30% of the returns are below −20%) or with a strong plus (45% of the returns are above +20%). The kurtosis is less meaningful here because of the bizarre shape of the distribution.

Conclusion: the returns are more attractive for CG2 than they were for CG1. CG2 has compelling conditions for specific risk-averse target oriented clients, especially because of the low return volatility. The client advisor who must report to his client on a yearly basis will not have to worry as much about the price variations of the product either. CG2 still outperforms the TR index by a small margin. Despite the high probability of ending a holding period with no return, the even higher chances of ending at the cap level make this product attractive to very conservative investors who might compare CG2 to a short-term bond. Hence, CG2 could be used prudently for investors relying on regular cash flows for income.

**Conclusion**: risk category 1.

### 12.2.3 Capital guaranteed product #3 (CG3)

| Product name | Underlying asset | CG level | Maturity | Currency | Cap |
|---|---|---|---|---|---|
| CG3 | Eurostoxx50 index | 94% | 2 years | EUR | No |

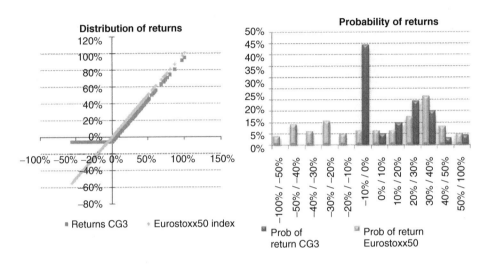

**Figure 12.4**   Distribution and probability of returns for CG3

**Table 12.6**   Statistics for CG3

|  | SX5E index | CG3 |
|---|---|---|
| Mean return over h.p. | 7.2% (TR: 11.6%) | 13.0% |
| Mean return p.a. | 3.6% (TR: 5.8%) | 6.5% |
| Volatility of returns | 34.3% | 20.3% |
| Skew | −0.17 | 0.87 |
| Kurtosis | 2.09 | 3.58 |

Source: Bloomberg, own calculations

Coincidentally, the mean return for this 94% capital guaranteed product without a cap is identical to CG2! The absence of a cap allows for upside surprises, but the first 6% positive performance is lost. The high percentage of occurrences where the product finishes on the capital guarantee level at −6% offsets the times where the product finishes its life high in positive territory, above the cap level that limited CG2. The volatility of returns is accordingly higher, and the distribution is strongly right skewed.

Conclusion: totally risk-averse clients should favor CG2 over CG3. With a nearly 50% chance of finishing with a zero or slightly negative return, CG3 should not be used for clients relying solely on regular cash flows. CG3 fits investors who can take a small loss but would like to leave the door open to large gains. As a matter of fact, risk-seeking investors ought to like this product because of its return characteristics. The strong skewness to the right, a high initial bond-floor (93%) and a short maturity make CG3 a good choice for investors who set high minimum return targets. The upside surprise potential of CG3 is the key characteristic for risk-seeking investors.

**Conclusion:** risk category 2.

### 12.2.4   Capital guaranteed product #4 (CG4)

| Product name | Underlying asset | CG level | Maturity | Currency | Cap |
|---|---|---|---|---|---|
| CG4 | Eurostoxx50 index | 94.5% | 1 year | EUR | No |

Is it possible to construct a viable capital guaranteed product on a yearly basis? CG4 (Figure 12.5 and Table 12.7) attempts to answer this question, and succeeds partially. There is still over a 40% chance of ending a year with a small loss of at most 5.5% (due to the capital guarantee level of 94.5%), but on average the yearly return of 7.3% should satisfy most investors. Again, the shorter time to maturity enables the structure not to lose early

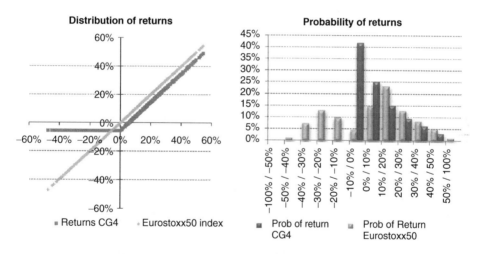

**Figure 12.5**   Distribution and probability of returns for CG4

**Table 12.7**   Statistics for CG4

|  | SX5E index | CG4 |
|---|---|---|
| Mean return over h.p./p.a. | 4.8% (TR: 6.9%) | 7.3% |
| Volatility of returns | 23.5% | 14% |
| Skew | −0.19 | 0.99 |
| Kurtosis | 2.15 | 3.08 |

Source: Bloomberg, own calculations

gains to later bear markets. It also allows the investor to re-enter the market at a lower level and to profit from rebounds or burgeoning bull markets early on. The volatility of the returns is relatively low, which should please investors. Note that CG4 outperforms both the price return index and the total return index. The relatively low kurtosis of the underlying asset is a boon for CG4, as higher returns become more probable. It is worth mentioning that a rule of thumb is that a low kurtosis of the underlying asset is beneficial for nearly all capital guaranteed products.

Conclusion: the chance of a capital guaranteed product ending on the capital guarantee level doesn't seem to fall below 40% regardless of the selected time horizon. This is due to the bumpy road the stock market has experienced in the back-test period. Nevertheless, since in the last 10 years the stock market has not been kind to the investor, much of the stress caused by the sharp negative returns is avoided with CG4 (and other capital guaranteed products, for that matter!). The one-year holding period corresponds to the reporting period of most investment advisors. The low volatility of returns and the generally right-skewed distribution should find favor among conservative investors. The risk of taking a small loss in return for the possibility of a large gain should appeal to them.

**Conclusion:** risk category 1.

### 12.2.5    Capital guaranteed product #5 (CG5)

The next three products address CHF-based investors. The CHF has had low interest rates compared to other currencies and capital guaranteed products have been accordingly difficult to structure. In general, the conditions looked notoriously terrible, and few products with high participation were issued, investors preferring to concentrate on yield enhancement products instead. Let's see if, with CG5 to CG7, it would have been possible to structure acceptable capital guaranteed products.

| Product name | Underlying asset | CG level | Maturity | Currency | Cap |
|---|---|---|---|---|---|
| CG5 | SMI index | 93% | 5 years | CHF | No |

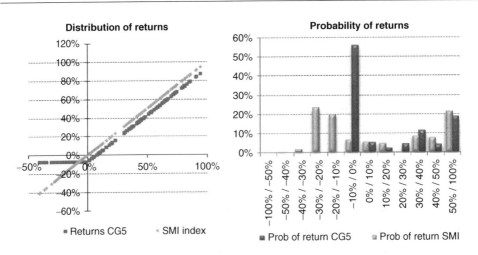

**Figure 12.6**  Distribution and probability of returns for CG5

**Table 12.8**  Statistics for CG5

|                       | SMI index                    | CG5   |
| --------------------- | ---------------------------- | ----- |
| Mean return over h.p. | 12.7% (TR: 23.6%)[11]        | 15.5% |
| Mean return p.a.      | 2.54% (TR: 4.72%)            | 3.1%  |
| Volatility of returns | 37.7%                        | 14%   |
| Skew                  | 0.58                         | 0.99  |
| Kurtosis              | 1.86                         | 3.08  |

Source: Bloomberg, own calculations

The first striking point is the much higher mean return of the SMI as compared to the Eurostoxx50. The reason is that the index seldom dropped by more than 30% over a five-year period. This is inherent to the constituents of the index, with conservative stocks like Nestlé, Novartis and Roche acting as lifeboats in times of crisis. The second surprising element is the very high return average of the total return index, which is double the ex-dividend one. By comparison, CG5's decent average return of 3.1% per annum is beaten by the 4.72% of the TR index. However, the 3.1% return beats the 2.7% average estimated interest rate level for a five-year period assumed in Table 12.1. As with all capital guaranteed products, its volatility of returns is much lower and the distribution of returns more right-skewed when compared to the underlying index. It is interesting to observe that the kurtosis of the returns of the index over a five-year period is very flat! At least CG5's kurtosis is relatively neutral.[12] With the assumed construction parameters of volatility and yield, CG5 could not be constructed with a full 100% capital guarantee and 100% participation, even with a five-year maturity. Hence, it "only" has a guarantee level of 93%. However, large losses would have been prevented, as the index fell between −10 and −30% in over 40% of the cases. These occurrences would have been limited to −7% in the investor's portfolio.

Conclusion: except for the long time to maturity, for which the same conclusions can be drawn as for CG1, CG5 is not as bad a product as one might think. Let's see if lowering the maturity for the subsequent products yields worse, similar or better return results.

**Conclusion:** risk category 3.

## 12.2.6  Capital guaranteed product #6 (CG6)

| Product name | Underlying asset | CG level | Maturity | Currency | Cap  |
| ------------ | ---------------- | -------- | -------- | -------- | ---- |
| CG6          | SMI index        | 95%      | 2 years  | CHF      | 135% |

CG6 is superior to CG5 in several respects: the mean return is much higher for a shorter maturity and, despite the cap, it is more right skewed. Similar to CG2 on the Eurostoxx50, CG6 has a bimodal distribution because of the cap, therefore the skew and especially kurtosis data are biased and of less relevance. Notwithstanding the cap, a low kurtosis, be it of the

---

[11] The total return was calculated using the SMIC index.

[12] Remember that a kurtosis of 3 denotes normality.

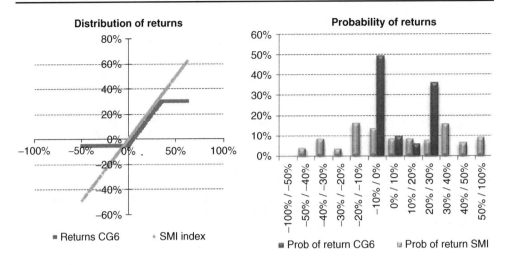

**Figure 12.7**  Distribution and probability of returns for CG6

**Table 12.9**  Statistics for CG6

|                       | SMI index          | CG6    |
|-----------------------|--------------------|--------|
| Mean return over h.p. | 8.3% (TR: 12.2%)   | 9.1%   |
| Mean return p.a.      | 4.15% (TR: 6.1%)   | 4.55%  |
| Volatility of returns | 29.1%              | 15.3%  |
| Skew                  | −0.01              | 0.38   |
| Kurtosis              | 1.94               | 1.32   |

Source: Bloomberg, own calculations

underlying asset or the product, is beneficial for CG6, the reason being the increased chances of the return ending either on the capital guarantee level or on the cap, all else held equal. On average, a flat kurtosis will increase the mean return of the product.

The results of CG6 make it an interesting product for conservative clients: the maximum loss over a two-year holding period is 5%, which amounts to 2.5% p.a. and the volatility of returns is relatively low. The product's returns are again situated mid-way between the price return and the total return index. The product may end on the capital guarantee level every second time, but that "negative" statistic is more than compensated for by the approximately 36% chance it will yield the maximum return of 30%, not counting the in-between returns.

Conclusion: for CHF-based investors, CG6 could be combined with a pure bond portfolio despite its being only 95% capital guaranteed. The historical mean return was at 4.55% more than double the assumed interest rate level for that period and the product would be expected to enhance the returns of the portfolio despite the fact that a small loss of 2.5% p.a. is possible.

**Conclusion:** risk category 1.

### 12.2.7 Capital guaranteed product #7 (CG7)

| Product name | Underlying asset | CG level | Maturity | Currency | Cap |
|---|---|---|---|---|---|
| CG7 | SMI index | 94% | 1 year | CHF | No |

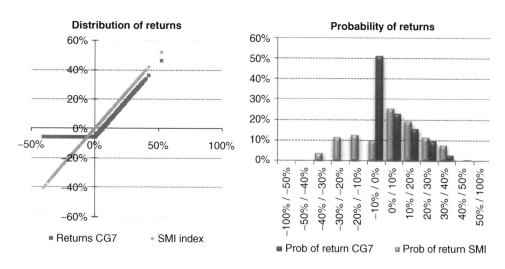

**Figure 12.8** Distribution and probability of returns for CG7

**Table 12.10** Statistics for CG7

|  | SMI index | CG7 |
|---|---|---|
| Mean return over h.p./p.a. | 3.2% (TR: 5.1%) | 3.6% |
| Volatility of returns | 18.6% | 11.2% |
| Skew | −0.15 | 1.07 |
| Kurtosis | 2.24 | 3.19 |

Source: Bloomberg, own calculations

CG7 can be compared to CG4, which has similar conditions, only the former is labeled in CHF. It also has a low capital guarantee level, which allows a short time to maturity. Although CG7 has a lower mean return as compared to CG6, it still has astonishing statistics when compared to bonds or money market: double the mean return compared to the historical interest rate for that period (1.8%) and a low volatility of returns. However, since the maximum loss per annum is 6%, CG7 is less well suited to be implemented as a component of a bond portfolio. Comparing CG7 to stocks mitigates the picture: the TR index performance is much higher on average.

Conclusion: CG7 fits risk-seeking short-term oriented investors who are looking for strongly right skewed distributions. The potential for high gains is realistic (over 40% probability of gains larger than 10% p.a.), but half the time, the investor will be disappointed with a small loss.

**Conclusion:** risk category 3.

### 12.2.8  Conclusion for capital guaranteed products

Many criticisms can be directed at capital guaranteed products. They reduce the expected return, they can be replicated individually at less cost, their valuation is disappointing in the secondary market, etc. Whatever their drawbacks may be, the results of the products tested in this study show that they stand a good chance of having a beneficial effect on a portfolio. For one, capital guaranteed products reduce the effect of small structuring mistakes. Unlike products with *conditional* capital protection, constructed with barrier options, it is not crucial that the capital guarantee be placed at a precise level. The mean return of the product will not vary much whether the guarantee is 95% and the participation 100% or if the guarantee is 97% and the participation 85%. In that sense, capital guaranteed products are easy products. They also reduce the impact of missing the forecast on the underlying asset. There have been many market crashes over the last 10 years, and an investor could have avoided them all by using capital guaranteed products instead of direct investments in the underlying assets. Above all, they do not reduce the expected return, as the results show. If that were the case, capital guaranteed products could be arbitraged.

# 12.3  YIELD ENHANCEMENT PRODUCTS

In this section, we test yield enhancement products, which tend to have left skewed distributions. The vast majority of these products were issued with single or multiple stocks as underlying assets. It would not be thorough to examine only index-based structures; however, it is not practical to depict all the possible stock combinations. The choice has been made to include products on indices and selected stocks that were popular underlying assets in the past few years. In any case, it is not necessary to have the results for every possible product on each stock. The goal is to get a picture of an average return distribution for this product type. That shape, as long as it is representative, can then be applied by default to all the products of the genre. Yield enhancement product returns are more dependent on volatility than many other products. Hence, because the variations of short-term volatility are higher than for long-term volatility, taking an average volatility for the whole back-test period of 10 years will yield less reliable results than for capital guaranteed products.

The products tested are listed in Table 12.11. Some products' results will be compiled in separate tables for space reasons. The same yield and volatility assumptions as for capital guaranteed products are made. The maturity is assumed to be one year for all products.[13] All the results for reverse convertibles, barrier reverse convertibles and worst-of barrier reverse convertibles presented in the following pages can be applied to discount certificates, barrier

---

[13] The one-year maturity has been selected for convenience purposes of this study only. In practice, one should carefully study the volatility surface (the term structure in particular) in order to determine which maturity would best suit the current environment.

**Table 12.11**   Details of tested yield enhancement products

| P. name | Type | Underlying asset | Coupon | Barrier | FX |
|---------|------|------------------|--------|---------|-----|
| YE1 | Reverse Conv. | Eurostoxx50 index | 12% | NA | EUR |
| YE2 | Reverse Conv. | SMI index | 8.75% | NA | CHF |
| YE3 | Reverse conv. | Various stocks* | Various* | NA | Var.* |
| YE4 | Barrier RC | Eurostoxx50 index | 8.75% | 75% | EUR |
| YE5 | Barrier RC | SMI index | 5.75% | 80% | EUR |
| YE6 | Barrier RC | Various stocks* | Various* | Var.* | Var.* |
| YE7 | W-o. Barrier RC | SX5E/SMI/SPX | 8% | 70% | EUR |
| YE8 | W-o. Barrier RC | SX5E/SMI/SPX | 6% | 65% | EUR |
| YE9 | W.-o. Barrier RC | Various stocks* | Various* | Var.* | Var* |

*The results will be regrouped in a table

discount certificates and worst-of barrier discount certificates as well, since these products are identical from a payoff point of view.

## 12.3.1   Yield enhancement product #1 (YE1)

| P. name | Type | Underlying asset | Coupon | Barrier | FX |
|---------|------|------------------|--------|---------|-----|
| YE1 | Reverse Conv. | Eurostoxx50 index | 12% | NA | EUR |

The product's mean return matches the return of the price return index, but not that of the TR index. As suspected, the distribution is strongly left skewed because of the cap at 12%. Despite this, there is an astonishing 75% probability of ending a holding period with

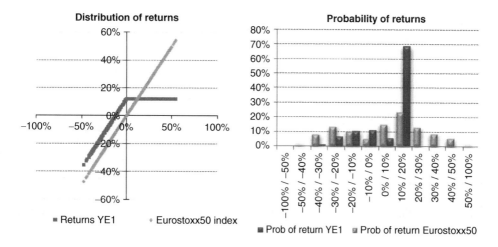

**Figure 12.9**   Distribution and probability of returns for YE1

**Table 12.12** Statistics for YE1

|                          | SX5E index      | YE1   |
|--------------------------|-----------------|-------|
| Mean return over h.p./p.a. | 4.8% (TR: 6.9%) | 4.8%  |
| Volatility of returns    | 23.5%           | 12%   |
| Skew                     | −0.19           | −1.41 |
| Kurtosis                 | 2.15            | 3.64  |

Source: Bloomberg, own calculations

a gain. This contrasts starkly with the probability of returns of CG4 (Figure 12.5, page 269) where for the same holding period over 40% of the return probabilities were negative. Comparing YE1 to CG4 [14] clearly shows the effect on the return distributions caused by the selling (in the case of YE1) and buying (in the case of CG4) insurance premiums. The two distribution shapes show the preferences of investors investing in a product with positive (CG4) versus negative (YE1) skew. While some investors are attracted by the expectation of frequent small to medium gains and do willingly take the risk of the occasional large loss, other investors will accept frequent small losses or flat returns in order to be able to capture occasional high gains. The former sell skewness in the form of yield enhancement and the latter buy it in the form of capital guarantee. The next tests will show if the sellers of protection had better results than those buying it.

**Conclusion:** risk category 3.

### 12.3.2   Yield enhancement product #2 (YE2)

| P. name | Type         | Underlying asset | Coupon | Barrier | FX  |
|---------|--------------|------------------|--------|---------|-----|
| YE2     | Reverse Conv. | SMI index        | 8.75%  | NA      | CHF |

The picture of YE2 is similar to YE1. The mean return of the product is a little disappointing, but the volatility of the returns is very low. Yield enhancement products function best in sideways trending markets. The low mean return of YE2 as well as that of YE1 comes from the fact that in the last 10 years few sideways tending market periods occurred. An analysis of the time series shows that a few crashes destroyed many of the gains. The 8.75% coupon is not high enough to recover the losses due to the crashes. It takes 3 periods of maximum return to recover from one −20% to −30% return event.

The conclusion for YE1 and YE2 is that, while timing is less of an issue with capital guaranteed products, both YE1 and YE2 are sensitive to a few extreme negative market events. It is not advisable to invest in YE1 or YE2 on a continuous basis but to determine investments on an opportunistic basis. Both products are too risky to implement in a bond portfolio. The coupons, about four times as high as the risk-free rate, imply a significant downside risk that cannot be borne by portfolios relying mainly or solely on regular income.

**Conclusion:** risk category 3.

---

[14] And indeed all yield enhancement to capital guaranteed products.

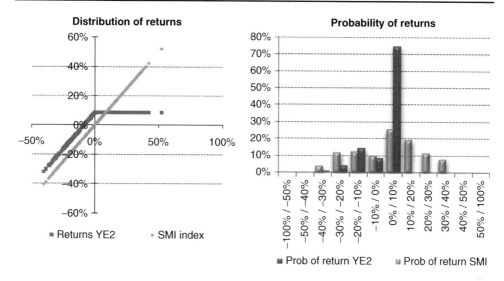

**Figure 12.10** Distribution and probability of returns for YE2

**Table 12.13** Statistics for YE2

|  | SMI index | YE2 |
| --- | --- | --- |
| Mean return over h.p./p.a. | 3.2% (TR: 5.1%) | 3% |
| Volatility of returns | 18.6% | 9.8% |
| Skew | −0.15 | −1.49 |
| Kurtosis | 2.24 | 3.93 |

Source: Bloomberg, own calculations

### 12.3.3 Yield enhancement product #3 (YE3)

| P. name | Type | Underlying asset | Coupon | Barrier | FX |
| --- | --- | --- | --- | --- | --- |
| YE3 | Reverse conv. | Various stocks | Various* | NA | Var. |

A number of stocks that were popular for yield enhancement products have been selected from various industry sectors. While some have chronically low volatilities, others are constantly volatility high-flyers. The products' features and statistics are listed in Table 12.14.

The results are disillusioning. To a large extent, the products underperform their respective underlying stocks, and these are represented ex-dividends. With total returns, the underperformance would be even larger. Only the Novartis reverse convertible keeps up, but after adding approximately 2.5% of dividend yield for the stock, this product underperforms as well. On occasion, the idiosyncratic (or specific) risks of the stocks are so much larger than the premium the investor gets in the form of the coupon, that some of the large drops can never be recovered. For instance, Nokia's probability of return between +100% and +300%

**Table 12.14**  Statistics for YE3 (various stocks)

| Stock. name | Coupon | FX | Stock mean return[15] | Product mean return | Product vol. of returns | Product skew | Product kurtosis |
|---|---|---|---|---|---|---|---|
| Allianz | 12% | EUR | 0.8% | −0.5% | 20.8% | −1.73 | 5 |
| Nokia | 14% | EUR | 22.6% | −1.6% | 18.6% | −1.27 | 3.33 |
| Siemens | 12.5% | EUR | 17.7% | 4.4% | 14.7% | −1.75 | 4.97 |
| TotalFina | 9% | EUR | 9.8% | 6.2% | 6.3% | −2.74 | 10.29 |
| ABB | 11.75% | CHF | 20.5% | −3.2% | 26.2% | −1.38 | 3.18 |
| Nestlé | 7.75% | CHF | 7.7% | 5% | 6.4% | −2.84 | 10.86 |
| Novartis | 6.75% | CHF | 0.8% | 1.7% | 7.7% | −1.43 | 3.92 |
| Roche | 8.5% | CHF | 4.6% | 2.1% | 9.8% | −1.39 | 3.75 |
| UBS | 10.25% | CHF | 5.4% | 3.4% | 14.1% | −2.65 | 9.89 |

Source: Bloomberg, own calculations

over a one-year period was a stunning 12%! Siemens and ABB's probabilities of +100% to +200% were 8% and 10% respectively. However, in these cases, the investors only received the predefined coupon and did not participate in the stock's stellar performance. But in the 15% of the cases where Nokia fell by more than 40%, the investor participated to a large extent (stock loss minus coupon) in the drop. The same is true of Siemens and ABB, the latter falling by more than 50% in 26% of the cases.[16] On low-volatility stocks like Nestlé, Novartis or TotalFina, the distributions are more concentrated around their means. On Total-Fina and Nestlé, the products have finished in positive territory in 90% of the occurrences. On the other stocks, positive occurrences were limited to 70%.

The conclusion seems counterintuitive; investors should invest in single stock reverse convertibles, if at all, only on low volatility stocks with predicable businesses, preferably in the food, pharma or oil industry. Highly volatile stocks should be avoided, as the frequent large losses are unlikely to be recovered because the products' upside performance is capped beyond the level of the coupon. Of course, the nine stocks tested in Table 12.14 are not representative of the total stock universe. However, the author has tested dozens of products on other stocks, and of those, very few have significantly outperformed their underlying stocks.

**Conclusion:** risk category depends on stock, but not less than 3.

### 12.3.4  Yield enhancement product #4 (YE4)

| P. name | Type | Underlying asset | Coupon | Barrier | FX |
|---|---|---|---|---|---|
| YE4 | Barrier RC | Eurostoxx50 index | 8.75% | 75% (A) | EUR |

YE4 compares to YE1 in Section 12.3.1, but the coupon has been lowered by 3.25% to 8.75%. The 3.25% was used to place a protection buffer, protecting the investor's capital

---

[15] Ex-dividends.

[16] The company nearly went bankrupt because of the asbestos claims in the USA but has recovered strongly since.

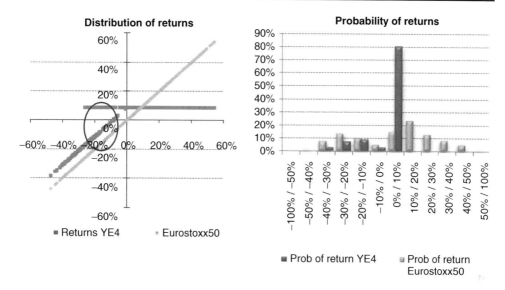

**Figure 12.11**  Distribution and probability of returns for YE4

**Table 12.15**  Statistics for YE4

|                         | SX5E index      | YE4   |
|-------------------------|-----------------|-------|
| Mean return over h.p./p.a. | 4.8% (TR: 6.9%) | 3.2%  |
| Volatility of returns   | 23.5%           | 11.7% |
| Skew                    | −0.19           | −1.85 |
| Kurtosis                | 2.15            | 4.9   |

Source: Bloomberg, own calculations

*conditionally* to the index never trading below 75% of its spot price at the launch date. The knock-in barrier is continuous, American style, meaning it can be breached any time during the life of the product. The lower mean return of YE4 (3.2% as compared to 4.8% for YE1) shows that the barrier was not worth its cost. It was breached all too often: all the payoff points in the circle in the left-hand graph of Figure 12.11 that appear to the vertical below the protection level are instances where a knock-in occurred during the product's lifetime and the index rebounded subsequently.[17] The points to the left of the barrier level are instances where it was breached and the index did not recover to a level above the barrier. Let's see if the returns pick up with YE4′, which features a lower coupon of 7% but a European style barrier, all else remaining equal to YE4.

**Conclusion:** risk category 3.

---

[17] Points included in the circle. As the barrier is American style, one trade below the predefined barrier level is enough to cause a knock-in event. Once this happens, the barrier disappears and the product is transformed into a reverse convertible without barrier.

### 12.3.5 Yield enhancement product #4′ (YE4′)

| P. name | Type | Underlying asset | Coupon | Barrier | FX |
|---------|------|------------------|--------|---------|-----|
| YE4′ | Barrier RC | Eurostoxx50 index | 7% | 75% (E) | EUR |

The European barrier helped shift the mean return upwards by almost 1% and the probability of ending with a positive return by about 10% despite the lower coupon. This leads to an extremely concentrated return distribution with over 90% of all occurrences in the same range. As has been stated earlier, it might be worthwhile decreasing the coupon for the benefit of having a barrier breach only possible at maturity. As can be observed on the left-hand graph of Figure 12.13 as compared to Figure 12.12 (circle), a number of cases where the American barrier was touched and the market rebounded afterwards have been avoided. In the case of YE4′, the barrier was worth the cost. This will probably be the case for single or multiple stock barrier reverse convertibles as well, as we will see shortly.

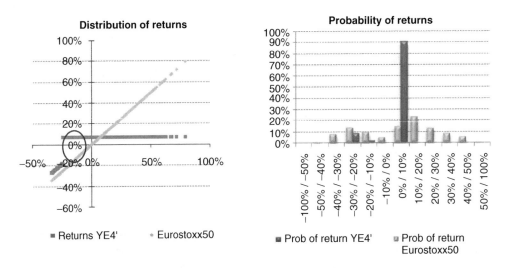

**Figure 12.12**   Distribution and probability of returns for YE4′

**Table 12.16**   Statistics for YE4′

|  | SX5E index | YE4′ |
|---|-----------|------|
| Mean return over h.p./p.a. | 4.8% (TR: 6.9%) | 4.1% |
| Volatility of returns | 23.5% | 8.9% |
| Skew | −0.19 | −2.8 |
| Kurtosis | 2.15 | 8.93 |

Source: Bloomberg, own calculations

Despite its 90% chance of being redeemed with the coupon plus full capital, YE4′ does not fit in a pure bond portfolio. It may, however, be added to portfolios with a small equity allocation if it meets the target return of the investor.

**Conclusion:** risk category 2.

## 12.3.6 Yield Enhancement product #5 (YE5)

| P. name | Type | Underlying asset | Coupon | Barrier | FX |
|---------|------|------------------|--------|---------|-----|
| YE5 | Barrier RC | SMI index | 5.75% | 80% | CHF |

The results for this structure are very poor, as the barrier (American style) destroyed value because of its high cost (3% lower coupon than YE2 in Section 12.3.2). It failed too many times as the index plunged during the stressful times of the bear market of 2000–2003 and the subprime crisis of 2007–2008. It must be emphasized at this point that during these times,

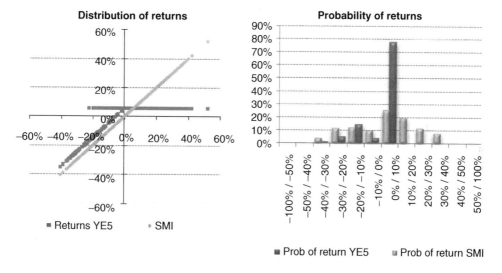

**Figure 12.13**   Distribution and probability of returns for YE5

**Table 12.17**   Statistics for YE5

|  | SMI index | YE5 |
|---|-----------|-----|
| Mean return over h.p./p.a. | 3.2% (TR: 5.1%) | 0.8% |
| Volatility of returns | 18.6% | 9.6% |
| Skew | −0.15 | −1.71 |
| Kurtosis | 2.24 | 4.56 |

Source: Bloomberg, own calculations

mainly because of the high volatility, the market would have allowed much better-looking products with higher barriers or higher coupons. But at other times, such as between 2003 and 2007, the volatility of the market was so low that the present conditions could not have been achieved and investors probably wouldn't have invested in a worse-looking product than an average like YE5 presented here. As mentioned previously, the naïve assumption is made that the structure as calculated for YE5 would have been possible over the last 10 years (1998–2008) on average and held over its lifetime.

A product YE5′, identical in all points to YE5 except for a coupon of 4.5% and a European barrier style, would have yielded an average return of 1%, raising the mean return by 0.2%. Here, the European style barrier didn't add as much value as in the EUR version of YE4′ because its level was too low to begin with: 20% market retracements have been common occurrences over the last 10 years.

**Conclusion:** risk category 3.

Conclusion for YE4, YE4′, YE5 and YE5′: none of the products achieved very convincing results. None was able to beat the average return of their respective price return indices, not to mention TR indices. Overall, investors should prefer European to American style barriers, even if the coupons appear to be quite a bit lower.

### 12.3.7   Yield enhancement product #6 (YE6)

| P. name | Type | Underlying asset | Coupon | Barrier | FX |
|---------|------|------------------|--------|---------|-----|
| YE6 | Barrier RC | Various stocks* | Various* | Var.* | Var.* |

The same stocks as in Table 12.14 are used below with various barriers. The currency of the product is always the same as that of the underlying stock and the maturity remains at one year. The barriers are American style and have been adjusted to the average volatility level of the respective underlying stock.

**Table 12.18**  Statistics for YE6 (various stocks)

| Stock name | Coupon | Barrier | Stock mean return | Product mean return | Product vol. of returns | Product skew | Product kurtosis |
|------------|--------|---------|-------------------|---------------------|-------------------------|--------------|------------------|
| Allianz | 8% | 70% | 0.8% | −2.5% | 20.9% | −1.94 | 5.54 |
| Nokia | 10.75% | 70% | 22.6% | 1.6% | 18.6% | −1.27 | 3.33 |
| Siemens | 8.5% | 70% | 17.7% | 1.4% | 14.6% | −1.94 | 5.58 |
| TotalFina | 6.5% | 80% | 9.8% | 4.9% | 5.7% | −3.83 | 16.98 |
| ABB | 7.75% | 70% | 20.5% | −6.6% | 26.4% | −1.42 | 3.25 |
| Nestlé | 5% | 80% | 7.7% | 3.3% | 6.0% | −3.74 | 16.08 |
| Novartis | 4.5% | 80% | 0.8% | 1.5% | 7.1% | −2.27 | 6.81 |
| Roche | 6.25% | 80% | 4.6% | 1.6% | 9.7% | −1.87 | 5.01 |
| UBS | 7.5% | 75% | 5.4% | 2% | 13.9% | −2.97 | 11.4 |

Source: Bloomberg, own calculations

Again, the barrier reverse convertibles show miserable results, especially for highly volatile stocks. In the sample tested, Allianz and ABB stand out with their average negative returns. The barriers do not hold when they are really needed, and the coupons are too small to recover even from a few significant drops in the shares. On Allianz, for instance, a barrier set at 70% of spot (i.e. a protection buffer of 30%) would have been broken in nearly 40% of cases over the last 10 years, as the stock was shaken by crisis after crisis. This example shows how a barrier can give investors a false sense of safety. Single-stock crashes, representative of the idiosyncratic risk of an individual asset, happen more frequently than with indices. In theory, the higher coupons of single stock reverse convertibles[18] (due to the higher volatility) should compensate the investor for those occurrences overall, but in reality they do not, far from it. The author has tested other stocks (not represented here), with several barrier levels ranging from 80% to 50%, but the products virtually always underperform the stocks on a holding period basis.

Conclusion for YE6: all the single-stock products tested are strongly leptokurtic. The probability of receiving the full coupon plus one's capital back at maturity lies between 60% and 90%, which seems quite attractive at first glance. Here lies the catch with products like the reverse convertible that combines strong leptokurtic with left-skewed distributions: four times out of five, the investor will be pleased by a redemption including the guaranteed coupon plus his full capital. After the two or three first successful investments, he will get used to receiving his high coupon and invest in similar payoffs repeatedly, developing a habit. The longer this lasts, the stronger the habit becomes and the less the investor will look for signs that the structure is not appropriate any more, because of changes in the micro- or macroeconomic environments. He will also be less open to new ideas, concepts, payoffs or underlying assets, because the high coupon of the reverse or barrier reverse convertible often satisfies his return target. An endowment effect takes place, to the point that the investor is often loath to let go of the investment, even if the signs are plain and visible that he should do so. The situation goes so far that the investor ends up implementing a mono-product strategy in his portfolio that concentrates the risk on a single payoff structure.

**Conclusion:** risk category 3.

### 12.3.8  Yield enhancement product #7 (YE7)

| P. name | Type | Underlying asset | Coupon | Barrier | FX |
|---------|------|------------------|--------|---------|-----|
| YE7 | W-o. Barrier RC | SX5E/SMI/SPX | 8% | 70% | EUR |

YE7 is a barrier *worst-of* three indices reverse convertible. YE7 compares to YE4 and YE4'. Adding two indices allowed the barrier to be reduced by 5% to 70%, but the coupon had to be lowered as well by 0.75%. The worst-of feature is noticeable in that the distribution of returns does not resemble a straight line anymore (left-hand graphic of Figure 12.14). The payoff is dependent on the worst-performing index in case the barrier is breached, and it can deviate from the returns of the basket if such a breach occurs. On these occasions, and despite the coupon of 8%, occurrences exist when the structure return is actually worse than

---

[18] Or the higher discounts for discount certificates, or the lower accumulation levels for accumulators, etc.

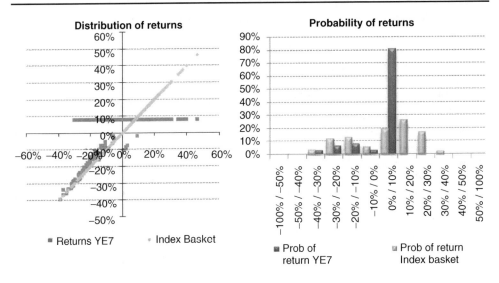

**Figure 12.14**   Distribution and probability of returns for YE7

**Table 12.19**   Statistics for YE7

|                          | SX5E/SMI/SPX | YE7    |
| ------------------------ | ------------ | ------ |
| Mean return over h.p./p.a. | 3.6%       | 2.6%   |
| Volatility of returns    | 17.9%        | 11.7%  |
| Skew                     | −0.47        | −1.91  |
| Kurtosis                 | 2.11         | 5.16   |

the basket return. This means that the worst-performing index lost more than 8% compared to the performance of the basket. In relation to YE4 and YE4′, YE7 fares poorly: its return is lower than that of the basket, and the volatility of returns is equal or higher. The worst-of feature's benefit (a lower barrier), wasn't worth its cost (more frequent barrier breaches combined with worst-of return). In other words, the benefit of shorting the correlation at the issue date by adding two indices in order to lower the barrier was not worth the risk.

**Conclusion:** risk category 4.

### 12.3.9   Yield enhancement product #8 (YE8)

| P. name | Type            | Underlying asset | Coupon | Barrier | FX  |
| ------- | --------------- | ---------------- | ------ | ------- | --- |
| YE8     | W-o. Barrier RC | SX5E/SMI/SPX     | 6%     | 65%     | EUR |

With YE8, a check was done to determine if, by lowering the barrier by 5 percentage points at the expense of the coupon, the mean return of the structure could be improved. With a

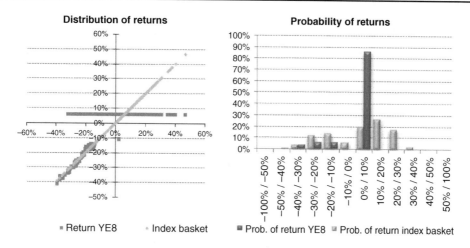

**Figure 12.15**   Distribution and probability of returns for YE8

**Table 12.20**   Statistics for YE8

|                          | SX5E/SMI/SPX | YE8    |
|--------------------------|--------------|--------|
| Mean return over h.p./p.a. | 3.6%         | 1.7%   |
| Volatility of returns    | 17.9%        | 10.9%  |
| Skew                     | −0.47        | −2.33  |
| Kurtosis                 | 2.11         | 6.92   |

mean return of 1.7%, that is clearly not the case. Note that in order to achieve the barrier of 65%, the coupon had to be lowered by two full percentage points!

In a last effort, an attempt was made to lower the barrier by adding the Topix index to the structure and lengthening the time to maturity to three years. This index, representative of the Japanese stock market, is rather poorly correlated with the other three indices, and is often used in private banking. The product became a worst-of structure on the Eurostoxx50, SMI, S&P500 and Topix. The barrier could be lowered to 50%, as low as most issuers will quote barriers. Even so, the average return worsened even more and turned negative. As a case in point, adding risky assets beyond 2 does not pay off. In fact, the maturities of products featuring barriers should be kept between two points in time:

- Long enough to allow the mathematical model used in valuing the structure to think that there's actually a chance for a barrier breach and thus paying something for the embedded short option.
- Short enough in the view of the investor for that worst-case scenario *not* to occur.

In the author's view, it is very difficult to forecast anything meaningful beyond 18 to 24 months for the market as a whole. Hence, it is best to keep maturities below that time span. Unfortunately, empirical observation leads to the conclusion that, for many investors, a 50% barrier over three years on indices seems almost impossible to breach and that such a structure can only be profitable. The framing of such products in this way has been essential to their success amongst private banking investors. The author has seen numerous issues of this kind over recent years. Unfortunately, events like a 50% drop in a stock index happen more often than one might think. Yet when the market falls and the investor starts to think that a breach might actually be possible, it is already too late to sell the product from an emotional point of view for most people. Suppose, for instance, that the initial 50% protection of a product has shrunk to a mere 15% and two years remain until maturity. That product will be quoted far below par, say at 70%, a level at which an investor will be loath to sell. At this point, the endowment effect of the product on the investor will make him keep it until it either knocks in or expires. The long remaining time to maturity then only worsens the chances of the investor to realizing a profit. To summarize, keep away from long-term left-skewed products, especially those featuring a worst-of option.

**Conclusion:** risk category 4.

### 12.3.10   Yield enhancement product #9 (YE9)

| P. name | Type | Underlying asset | Coupon | Barrier | FX |
|---------|------|------------------|--------|---------|-----|
| YE9 | W.-o. Barrier RC | Various stocks | Var. | Var. | CHF |

**Table 12.21**   Statistics for various worst-of barrier reverse convertibles

| Stock name | Coup. | Bar. | Basket mean return | Prod. mean return | Prod. vol. of returns | Prod. skew | Prod. kurtosis |
|------------|-------|------|--------------------|-------------------|------------------------|------------|----------------|
| ALV/SIE | 9% | 65% | 9.3% | −3.5% | 22.8% | −1.6 | 4.13 |
| ALV/SIE/FP | 9.25% | 65% | 9.4% | −3.3% | 22.8% | −1.6 | 4.13 |
| SIE/FP | 7.25% | 65% | 13.8% | 0.2% | 14.8% | −1.97 | 5.65 |
| NES/NOV | 4.75% | 75% | 4.3% | 2.1% | 7.8% | −2.7 | 8.61 |
| NES/ROG/UBS | 10.25% | 70% | 5.9% | 2.2% | 16% | −2.04 | 6.41 |
| NES/NOV/UBS | 9.25% | 75% | 4.6% | 2.3% | 15% | −2.47 | 8.60 |
| ROG/UBS | 7% | 70% | 5% | −0.8% | 15.9% | −2.09 | 6.65 |
| UBS/ABB | 7.75% | 65% | 11.8% | −11.7% | 28.6% | −0.93 | 2.08 |

Source: Bloomberg, own calculations

As expected, the worst-of barrier reverse convertibles based on stocks didn't perform well. The value of the correlation used to lower the barriers or increase the coupon seldom compensated the investor for the additional risk of an additional asset. In CHF, the attempt to construct a product which could be considered as "safe" with Nestlé and Novartis yielded on average slightly more than the assumed average interest rate (1.8% p.a.), and the frequency of positive returns was 90%. Yet on the few occasions the barrier was breached, the negative performance of the worst performer of the two stocks dragged the whole returns down. Figure 12.16 shows that even such a seemingly conservative structure cannot be used as a bond replacement.

The worst product tested was ABB/UBS. Despite a low barrier and an adequate coupon for a CHF structure, the mean return over a single period was strongly negative, while the basket of the two stocks performed well. With this stock pair, the barrier was practically always

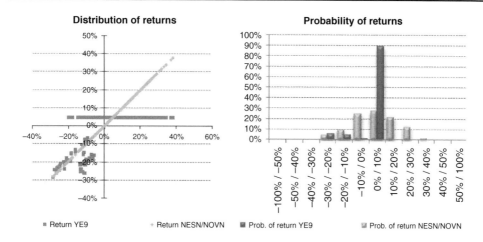

**Figure 12.16**  Distribution and probability of returns for YE9 (Nestlé/Novartis)

hit. On these occasions, the worst-performing stock performed so badly that the product's return was almost always below that of the basket, despite the addition of the coupon. It can be observed on the right-hand side of Figure 12.17 overleaf below that nearly 20% of the returns were below 50%. Note the extremely platykurtic return distribution of the basket, as well as the pronounced "fat tails". While the other multiple stock structures of Table 12.21 have been selected rather randomly based on the popularity among investors, this structure was chosen on purpose to reveal the risk of using multiple uncorrelated single stocks. Both ABB and UBS were once considered "safe" stocks, but at different times. ABB was a successful industrial company before it ran into the asbestos trouble and nearly went broke. UBS was an exemplary global bank, until the subprime debacle had it scrambling for capital. Both stocks declined strongly over significant periods because of severe risks specific to their businesses. The investor is never compensated for such risks over the long run and they absolutely cannot be predicted. The investor is compensated for the average chance of those risks happening, and that average is clearly too low, not even nearly approaching the actual loss experienced on one such occurrence. With the worst-of barrier reverse convertible on uncorrelated stocks, the effect of such occurrences is compounded to the ultimate detriment of the investor. ABB and UBS are not unique examples. Looking at other Swiss large cap stocks over the last 10 years shows a similar picture. Consider Swiss Life that dropped from a level of CHF 500 a share to 50 (−90%!) in two years, Swiss Re which traded at 180 in 2000 and at 60 in 2008; also Adecco, Credit Suisse, Clariant, Ciba, Zürich, which had all major pullbacks at one time or another to which no barrier, however deep, was immune. The same can be said for the majority of the stocks included in other indices, like the Eurostoxx50, S&P500, etc. Consequently, a worst-of yield enhancement structure including any of these stocks would have performed poorly over the last ten years on average.

In addition, it must be remembered that the structures were tested based on weekly data. The results, if anything, would look worse if the data had been based on intraday prices, because the American style barriers can be hit any time. Moreover, the stock average returns over single periods are without dividends. Including the dividends would make the underlying stocks look even better compared to the products.

**Conclusion:** risk category 5.

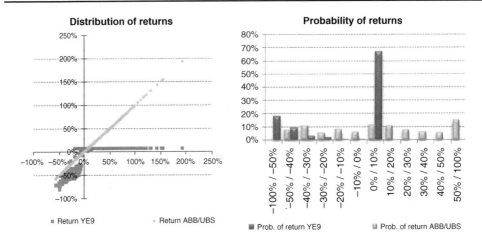

**Figure 12.17**   Distribution and probability of returns for YE9 (ABB/UBS)

### 12.3.11   Conclusion for yield enhancement products

The analysis of the single stock products tends especially to discredit rolling yield enhancement products such as rolling discount certificates or rolling reverse convertible structures.
These structures are invested on a continuous basis in capped, strongly left-skewed and
leptokurtic distributions. At least on single stocks, it has been empirically shown that this
strategy does not work over the long run. It is certainly possible to generate above-average
results with yield enhancement products when they are timed correctly and the market
conditions are optimal. However, a continuous strategy with permanent investments is likely
to perform poorly.

In this section, a small sample of (worst-of barrier) reverse convertibles has been analyzed,
but neither best-of nor relative payoffs have been considered. Products with lookback,
autocallable, or lock-in features were also left out. Of course, all these variations have
their own average return, skew and kurtosis. While some have performed much better and
others worse than the structures presented, they were seldom used in private banking. Was
it chance that made the worst-of barrier reverse convertible the most popular structure in
Switzerland in recent years? Or was it a deliberate move by some market participants to
push a structure that looked good superficially and allowed the issuers to increase their
product volume? The past performance of the products, if anyone had looked, certainly
wouldn't have helped. But then, past performance is no guarantee of future returns.

### 12.3.12   Dos and don'ts

- Products should preferably be based on indices that diversify the unsystematic risk of
  single stocks. The investor should avoid worst-of multiple stock barrier reverse convertibles most of the time, unless he is very convinced of his forecast and market conditions
  are optimal.
- If an investment in a structure with a worst-of feature is made anyway, the investor should
  be aware that on a portfolio management level, it is difficult to assess the risk exposure
  in the portfolio because the worst-of feature can switch one asset for another at any time.

- Yield enhancement products should never be used as bond replacements. The value of even a conservative structure based on low-risk single stocks or indices can fall considerably. Of every structure the author has ever back-tested, not a single one has never had its barrier breached.
- As a final point, investors should bear in mind that, despite the likelihood that four times out of five the product will be redeemed with full coupon and capital, the fifth time is likely to destroy all the revenue generated by the previous coupons and much more. Caveat emptor.

# 12.4   PARTICIPATION PRODUCTS

The product types tested are straight bonus, and capped bonus certificates.[19] After concluding that single stock or multiple stocks with worst-of feature investments seldom outperform their underlying assets, we abstain from testing them here, because it is likely that the results will be largely of similar nature. The structures tested are summarized in Table 12.22. The participation above the bonus level is assumed to be 100% in every structure. The currency is assumed equal to the base currency of the underlying asset. The bonus is expressed in percent above 100% of the spot price. Unless otherwise stated, the barriers are American style, European barriers being represented by an asterisk (*).

**Table 12.22**   Details of analyzed participation products

| P. name | Type | Underlying asset | Bonus | Barrier | Mat. |
|---------|------|------------------|-------|---------|------|
| P1  | Bonus | Eurostoxx50 index | 20% | 75% | 2Y |
| P2  | Bonus | SMI index | 5% | 75% | 2Y |
| P3  | Bonus | Eurostoxx50 index | 10% | 67% | 2Y |
| P3' | Bonus | Eurostoxx50 index | 0% | 65%* | 2Y |
| P4  | Capped bonus | Eurostoxx50 index | 20%/20% | 74% | 2Y |
| P5  | Bonus | Eurostoxx50 index | 7% | 55% | 3Y |
| P5' | Bonus | Eurostoxx50 index | 2% | 55%* | 3Y |

Since advice was given in Part I to keep maturities short, the subsequent analysis will be limited to two and three year products. The bonus certificate, as long as it is uncapped, is usually compared to its underlying asset. As the structure can be considered as a barter trade such as "giving up dividends to purchase protection", it must be compared against the *total return* of the underlying asset.

## 12.4.1   Participation product #1 (P)

| P. name | Type | Underlying asset | Bonus | Barrier | Mat. |
|---------|------|------------------|-------|---------|------|
| P1 | Bonus | Eurostoxx50 index | 20% | 75% | 2Y |

---

[19] For a detailed description of bonus certificates and their behavior during their lifetime, see Sections 3.3.2 and and 4.4.1.

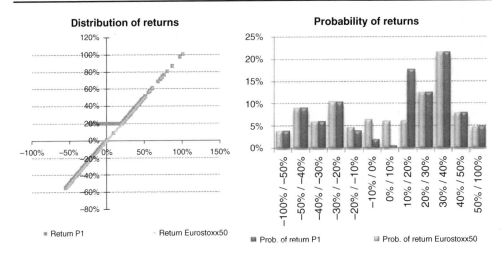

**Figure 12.18**   Distribution and probability of returns for P1

**Table 12.23**   Statistics for P1

|                        | SX5E index        | P1     |
| ---------------------- | ----------------- | ------ |
| Mean return over h.p.  | 7.2% (TR: 11.6%)  | 9.7%   |
| Mean return p.a.       | 3.6% (TR: 5.8%)   | 4.85%  |
| Volatility of returns  | 34.3%             | 34.3%  |
| Skew                   | −0.17             | −0.39  |
| Kurtosis               | 2.09              | 2.17   |

Source: Bloomberg, own calculations

P1, in spite of a high bonus and a decent level of protection, does not succeed in beating the TR index. The volatility of returns is very high, in fact equal to that of the index. In 80% of cases, the return is identical to that of the index. The skew is relatively flat and the kurtosis low. This stands in contrast with yield enhancement and capital guaranteed products, which have strongly leptokurtic distributions, concentrated around the coupon level or around the capital guarantee level respectively. Intuitively, one could assume that the relative wide gap between the bonus and the barrier level (45% in this case) would concentrate the returns around the bonus level. Some concentration happens (around 17% of the returns are concentrated between +10% and +20% level), but far less than in the capital guaranteed products which had concentrations of around 50% at the capital guaranteed level or the yield enhancement products, which had between 70% and 90% of their returns at the coupon level. As a first impression, this structure looks attractive for investors who seek large gains, but who can also bear large losses. Indeed, as mentioned in Part I, the bonus certificate has the highest delta at inception of all the three major product categories. It can be considered as a structure with identical risk as its underlying asset, in the case of P1, a stock index. The 25% protection of the barrier may seem large for a single index structure, but since the lifetime lasts for over two years, it amounts to "only" 12.5% per year. Due to the up and down swings of the stock market in the past 10 years, P1's barrier was broken in approximately

35% of the cases. Later, P3 and P4 will show if that number can be lowered and the return improved.

**Conclusion:** risk category 4.

## 12.4.2  Participation product #2 (P2)

| P. name | Type | Underlying asset | Bonus | Barrier | Mat. |
|---------|------|------------------|-------|---------|------|
| P2 | Bonus | SMI index | 5% | 75% | 2Y |

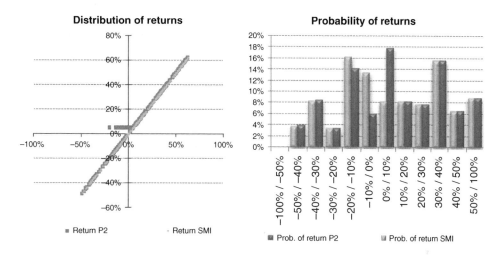

**Figure 12.19**  Distribution and probability of returns for P2

**Table 12.24**  Statistics for P2

|  | SMI index | P2 |
|--|-----------|-----|
| Mean return over h.p. | 8.3% (TR: 12.2%) | 9.4% |
| Mean return p.a. | 4.15% (TR: 6.1%) | 4.85% |
| Volatility of returns | 29.1% | 28.6% |
| Skew | −0.01 | −0.11 |
| Kurtosis | 1.94 | 2.06 |

Source: Bloomberg, own calculations

Similar to P1, the bonus certificate P2 on the SMI fails to beat its corresponding TR index. The same reasoning applies as for P1. The structure is less attractive from a bonus point of view mainly because the SMI has historically lower dividend yields and a lower volatility than the Eurostoxx50. Since these factors are applicable to all versions of CHF based bonus certificates, no other CHF structures on the SMI will be presented, as similar conclusions as for EUR products on the Eurostoxx50 can be drawn.

**Conclusion:** risk category 4.

### 12.4.3 Participation product #3 (P3)

| P. name | Type | Underlying asset | Bonus | Barrier | Mat. |
|---------|------|------------------|-------|---------|------|
| P3 | Bonus | Eurostoxx50 index | 10% | 67% | 2Y |

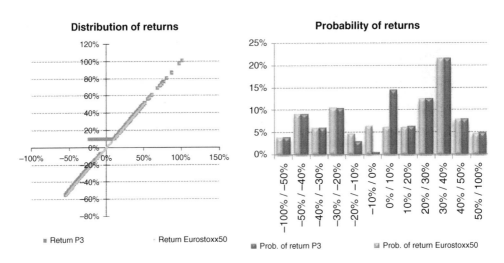

**Figure 12.20**   Distribution and probability of returns for P3

**Table 12.25**   Statistics for P3

|  | SX5E index | P3 |
|--|-----------|-----|
| Mean return over h.p. | 7.2% (TR: 11.6%) | 8.8% |
| Mean return p.a. | 3.6% (TR: 5.8%) | 4.4% |
| Volatility of returns | 34.3% | 33.9% |
| Skew | −0.17 | −0.32 |
| Kurtosis | 2.09 | 2.22 |

Source: Bloomberg, own calculations

With P3 (which compares to P1), a test was made to determine if there is an advantage to lowering the barrier in order to increase the mean return over a period. A "nice to have" effect would have been a significant reduction in the volatility of the returns as well, but neither was the case. The barrier was broken less often (in about 26% of the cases), but the lower bonus level reduced the return when the certificate ended at the bonus level. The kurtosis wasn't raised much either and stayed below the normal level of 3, meaning a platykurtic distribution of returns. Let's see with P3' if a European barrier helps in this respect.

**Conclusion:** risk category 3.

## 12.4.4 Participation product #3′ (P3′)

| P. name | Type | Underlying asset | Bonus | Barrier* | Mat. |
|---------|------|------------------|-------|----------|------|
| P3′ | Bonus | Eurostoxx50 index | 0% | 65% | 2Y |

*European style

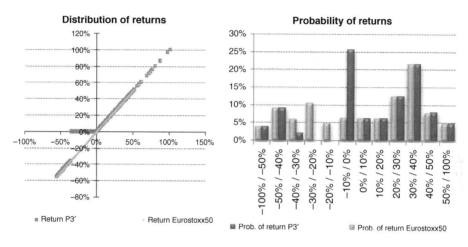

**Figure 12.21** Distribution and probability of returns for P3′

**Table 12.26** Statistics for P3′

|  | SX5E index | P3′ |
|--|-----------|-----|
| Mean return over h.p. | 7.2% (TR: 11.6%) | 11.9% |
| Mean return p.a. | 3.6% (TR: 5.8%) | 5.95% |
| Volatility of returns | 34.3% | 31.1% |
| Skew | −0.17 | −0.49 |
| Kurtosis | 2.09 | 3.03 |

Source: Bloomberg, own calculations

Switching the barrier from American to European style did cost the last 10% that remained of the bonus (the barrier could also be lowered by an additional 2%), but significantly increased the average return over a holding period, even beating the TR index by a small margin. The barrier breach events were reduced dramatically to 12% since they could only be hit at maturity. The volatility of returns stayed quite high, however, making the product still a poor choice for a target-oriented investor. On balance, nearly 15% of all the results were clustered in the −30% to −50% range.[20] P3′ can also be compared to CG3 in Section 12.2.3: for a 6% give-up in the strike, P3′s barrier can be lowered to zero. Otherwise stated, a reduction of the strike by an additional 6% to 94% transforms P3′ into a capital guaranteed product analogous to CG3.

**Conclusion:** risk category 3.

---

[20] The lowest return over a two-year holding period for the Eurostoxx50 was −55%.

### 12.4.5    Participation product #4 (P4)

| P. name | Type | Underlying asset | Bonus/Cap | Barrier* | Mat. |
|---------|------|------------------|-----------|----------|------|
| P4 | Capped Bonus | Eurostoxx50 index | 20%/20% | 74 | 2Y |

*European style

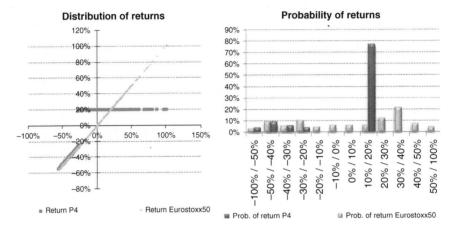

**Figure 12.22**   Distribution and probability of returns for P4

**Table 12.27**    Statistics for P4

|  | SX5E index | P4 |
|--|-----------|-----|
| Mean return over h.p. | 7.2% (TR: 11.6%) | 6% |
| Mean return p.a. | 3.6% (TR: 5.8%) | 3% |
| Volatility of returns | 34.3% | 26.1% |
| Skew | −0.17 | −1.38 |
| Kurtosis | 2.09 | 3.05 |

Source: Bloomberg, own calculations

P4 is a capped bonus certificate with the strike of the bonus at the level of the cap. In addition to the usual construction elements, a call is sold with a strike price at the same level as the down-and-out put, effectively capping the upside potential beyond that point. The premium from the cap is used either to increase the bonus or to lower the barrier. With P4, the strike has been raised to 120% of spot. The premium value of the call was not enough to leave the European barrier at 65% as in P3′, though; it had to be raised to 74%. This had the effect of raising the barrier hit at maturity percentage to over 18%. Overall, the effect of placing a cap on the product can be considered negative. It now resembles a barrier reverse convertible with a non-guaranteed coupon of 10% p.a. Similar to yield enhancement probability of returns, a high concentration (nearly 80%) of outcomes have the product ending at the bonus/cap.

   **Conclusion:** risk category 3.

### 12.4.6 Participation product #5 (P5)

| P. name | Type | Underlying asset | Bonus | Barrier | Mat. |
|---------|------|------------------|-------|---------|------|
| P5 | Bonus | Eurostoxx50 index | 7% | 55% | 3Y |

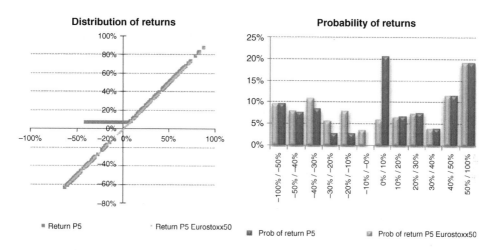

**Figure 12.23** Distribution and probability of returns for P5

**Table 12.28** Statistics for P5

|  | SX5E index | P5 |
|--|-----------|-----|
| Mean return over h.p. | 5.9% (TR: 12.9%) | 9.7% |
| Mean return p.a. | 2.95% (TR: 4.3%) | 3.23% |
| Volatility of returns | 40.9% | 39.4% |
| Skew | 0 | −0.24 |
| Kurtosis | 1.63 | 1.87 |

Source: Bloomberg, own calculations

P5's purpose is to check whether lengthening the maturity to three years and lowering the barrier is beneficial for the mean return or not. It turns out that this is not the case. Moreover, the volatility of returns increased sharply, as even a barrier as low as 55% was breached 21 times out of 100. After all, 45% protection over three years amounts only to 15% per annum, which is less than the 17.5% p.a. of P3 and P3′. The volatility of returns has also increased dramatically, making P5 a longer and riskier product than the preceding bonus certificates. The very flat kurtosis also makes this structure unattractive for target-oriented investors. As shown in Part I, a longer maturity also means a longer time until the protection mechanism has a substantial effect on the secondary market price of the product, making it less attractive to more trading-oriented investors.

**Conclusion:** risk category 3.

## 12.4.7 Participation product #5′ (P5′)

| P. name | Type | Underlying asset | Bonus | Barrier* | Mat. |
|---------|------|------------------|-------|----------|------|
| P5′ | Bonus | Eurostoxx50 index | 2% | 55% | 3Y |

*European style

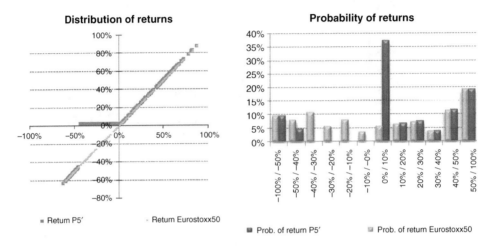

**Figure 12.24** Distribution and probability of returns for P5′

**Table 12.29** Statistics for P5′

|  | SX5E index | P5′ |
|--|-----------|-----|
| Mean return over h. p. | 5.9% (TR: 12.9%) | 14.5% |
| Mean return over h. p. p.a. | 2.95% (TR: 4.3%) | 4.83% |
| Volatility of returns | 40.9% | 35.5% |
| Skew | 0 | −0.44 |
| Kurtosis | 1.63 | 2.63 |

Source: Bloomberg, own calculations

P5′ is identical to P5 with the only difference being a 5% lower bonus, which allowed switching from an American to a European barrier. This helped raise the mean return per holding period substantially, well above the TR index. P5′ thus becomes the second back-tested participation product (after P3′) in which trading the implied dividends for conditional protection was worth its cost.[21] A barrier breach occurred in close to 15% of all cases. In those instances, the returns were strongly negative. P5′ would be suitable for investors with a longer investment horizon capable of bearing the risk inherent to equities but

---

[21] Always calculated on an average basis.

with the intention to protect their investments in all but the most extreme market situations. This seems strange, since most investors would rather have their investments protected in exactly those cases. However, the products were back-tested with average conditions. More often than not, some products, i.e. those with full capital guarantee and full upside potential (uncapped), are not possible for a reasonable maturity because of adverse construction parameters. In those cases, if the forecast scenario is sound, if advantageous construction parameters for a bonus certificate are present and if the investor is capable of bearing the risk of a large loss in an extreme case, a deep barrier bonus certificate can be a good substitute for an otherwise less well-constructed capital guaranteed product.

**Conclusion:** risk category 3.

### 12.4.8 Conclusion for participation products

Bonus certificates may be the riskiest structured products among the three basic product categories, but one of their main attributes – unlimited upside potential – makes them among the best-performing products on average per holding period. They have high volatilities of returns and investors should be able to cope with large gains as with large losses. American style barriers are breached more often than one is prone to think, while European barriers may be worth more than meets the eye, despite the worse conditions in terms of bonus or barrier at first glance. This argument is even more valid when remembering that weekly data have been used to compute the results. As with yield enhancement products, intraday low data would show an even wider result difference in favor of the European barriers. Consequently, the recommendation is clearly for European style barriers whenever possible.

Also, as with reverse convertibles, investors should stay away from single stock or worst-of multiple stock bonus certificates unless there is a strong opinion about a particular stock's forecast evolution and the structuring factors are favorable. Although not presented in detail, single stock bonus certificates are exposed to the sometimes extreme – unforeseeable – idiosyncratic risk for which the investor is not compensated enough. The same reasoning as with for yield enhancement products applies, because the downside conditional protection is achieved with the same building blocks: barrier options. The consequence of implementing only index products is that portfolios will seem dull and narrow when compared to a host of single stock positions. Yet the goal of an investor managing his portfolio should not be to play Action Man, but to optimize the risk-return characteristics of the portfolio in all its aspects. While many large portfolios can be efficiently diversified with single stock, bond, hedge fund and commodity holdings, the majority of portfolios cannot, due to size constraints. In addition, while single stock structured product risks will be diversified to some extent by holding multiple positions, the sum of the risk on the single products will always be higher than the risk on the combined positions as represented by an index.

The tests for the products were done with average conditions over a 10-year period. During that time, a multitude of situations arose where real products would have had widely different conditions than those that were used in the present study. It is obvious that the results would have been different as well. The results presented above should not be taken as highly precise, but as guidance for risk measures and behavior tendency of the products.

The last 10 years have seen long periods of increased volatility in the stock market. Was it because of the wide use of structured products that the volatility increased? It is difficult to say with any certainty, but derivatives as a whole certainly played a decisive role. Factors like faster and global news broadcast, or higher leverage by large players such as banks and hedge funds also contributed to a certain extent to spikes in volatility. Will the markets stay volatile in the future? There's a good chance that they will become even more volatile with new participants from all around the world entering the markets. Globalization will set the same trends for everyone, and will have every participant trying to rush through the same door at the same time whenever an economic event of relevance happens. With increased volatility, capital guaranteed products will become more difficult to structure, and yield enhancement products will seem more attractive with lower barriers or higher coupons. They will not become safer or more profitable, though. Their risk profile will stay the same, as will the profile of the other products, since they are priced at market conditions at all times.

## 12.5   CONCLUSION: PRODUCT CLASSIFICATION

Structured products attempt to concentrate the return distribution of an underlying asset at one or more specific points, or they change the distribution shape as compared to their underlying asset altogether. With the above study, it is now clear which product produces what shape and where the returns are concentrated:

- Capital guaranteed products cut off the distribution to the left at the guarantee level, effectively lowering the probability of returns below that point to zero. In fact, all the lower return probabilities of the asset are replaced with the level corresponding to the capital guarantee, thus eliminating the probability of negative fat tails. This leads to a concentration of the return probability at the level of the capital guarantee. The distribution becomes strongly right-skewed and leptokurtic, with the mean slightly above the level of the capital guarantee. If capped, the distribution becomes bimodal, with all the returns above the cap concentrated at the cap level. Capital guaranteed products buy positive skewness, in the sense that the cut-off of the negative returns has a cost, in theory diminishing the expected return of the product. However, empirical observation shows that the expected return remains at similar levels as the underlying asset. In spite of this, the volatility of returns is significantly lower.
- Yield enhancement products cut off the distribution to the right, significantly raising the probability of the returns at the cap level. All the return probabilities above the cap level are concentrated at that level. Yield enhancement products sell positive skewness, and the premium thus generated is theoretically supposed to increase the expected return of the structure. This empirical study shows that this is seldom the case, though it does happen with the right structures. The shape of the return distribution is extremely leptokurtic and strongly skewed to the left. Placing barriers, especially European style, raises the leptokurtosis even further and produces better results than American-style barriers.
- The participation products tested were all of the bonus certificate type. These have a return distribution that resembles the one of the underlying asset with a slight concentration around the bonus level. Both (fat) tails are open. European barriers tend to make the distribution more concentrated. In general, the distributions have no or only a small skew and are rather meso- to platykurtic, though less so than the assets themselves. Other participation products, while not represented in the study, will have their own shapes. For

instance, tracker certificates have exactly the same return distribution as the underlying asset. Airbag distributions will resemble those of bonus certificates to a large degree. Turbo certificates, because of their caps, will have a left-skewed and leptokurtic shape, as the positive tail is cut off at the cap level, and all return probabilities above the cap are concentrated there. Actually, turbo certificates are the only participation product[22] that resemble the shape of yield enhancement products, and could in theory also be included in that category. Outperformance certificates have a no-skew platykurtic distribution.

With the numerous examples of all the major product categories encompassed in the study, it is now possible to classify each category according to its specific return distribution, as suggested by the return distribution Cube in Figure 11.3. The great majority of products would fit as shown in Figure 12.25.

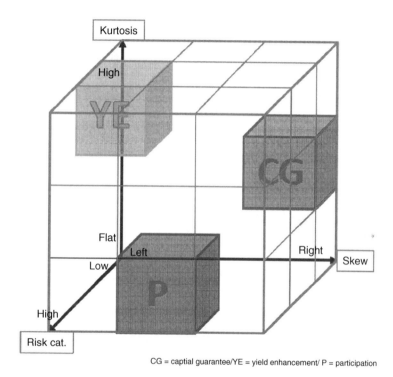

CG = captial guarantee/YE = yield enhancement/ P = participation

**Figure 12.25** Return distribution Cube with product categories

It has been demonstrated that on average, capital guaranteed products generate low-risk, right-skewed medium kurtosis returns. Yield enhancement products have medium-risk, left-skewed and high kurtosis returns. Finally, participation products create rather high-risk, neutral skew and flat kurtosis returns. Of course, this classification represents averages. It is possible to conceive a capital guaranteed product with a medium risk and a high kurtosis, or a participation product with a medium risk and slightly right-skewed, but these would be unusual.

---

[22] Except for the capped bonus certificate P4 presented in Section 12.4.3.

The good news is that each product category effectively covers a different area in the return distribution cube. By combining different product categories, it is possible to structure portfolios that fit any investor preferences, unless they are not achievable. It is also possible to reach any of the 10 distribution classes defined in Table 11.2 by a combination of the product categories. To represent a complete universe, all types of underlying assets should also be included: bonds, equities, hedge funds and commodities as well as FX and any other asset class have their average return distribution. All can be positioned within the risk Cube. For instance, investment grade bonds would be classified as low-risk, right-skewed, high kurtosis assets, while equities have a high-risk, no skew, flat kurtosis profile. Equities actually spread over several risk categories as stocks like Nestlé do not have the same risk parameters as Google, just to take two extremes. Bonds can also be differentiated in the same way; government bonds of the G7 countries will have different parameters than Emerging Market bonds. Once more, the Cube of Figure 12.25 is a simplified representation. A database with the specific return distributions of the investment universe comprising all assets and a greater number of products than analyzed here would be necessary to implement a real-life, complete, portfolio. For professional asset managers, this might actually be a necessary feature in the future. For private investors, such an exercise will be beyond most people's resources. Nevertheless, the above classification provides a good guidance to start with.

# 13

## Structured Portfolio Construction

### 13.1 PORTFOLIO CONSTRUCTION PROCESS

With the three product categories analyzed and parameterized in the return distribution Cube, a *portfolio construction process* can now be established. The goal is to select the individual products that match an investor's preferences to construct a portfolio. The situations in which such a process can be used are manifold. A few of them will be illustrated by means of examples (Table 13.1).

**Table 13.1**  Portfolio construction application examples

|  | Title | Page |
|---|---|---|
| **Example 1** | 13.2 Constructing a structured product portfolio in theory | 302 |
| **Example 2** | 13.3 Preferred return distribution process versus classic portfolio management | 305 |
| **Example 3** | 13.4 Investor portfolios | 311 |

In Example 1, we build a theoretical product portfolio that includes asset and maturity diversification. Example 2 compares a classical portfolio management model to a model including structured products. In Example 3, we revisit our fictional characters Bob Sample, John Model, Maria Case as well as their advisor, Marc Council. But first, let's describe the process both graphically (Figure 13.1) and verbally.

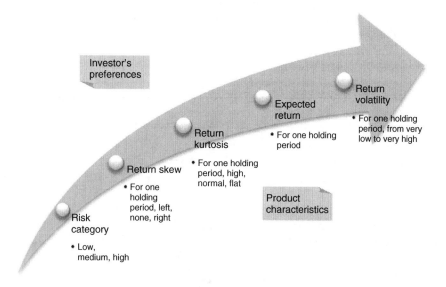

**Figure 13.1**  Portfolio construction process

The investor's preferences are the source of the information used to select the products with matching return distribution characteristics. The preferences act as a filter that eliminates products which would not fit in the portfolio. The construction process begins with the specification of the three risk parameters as defined in the Cube. First, the *risk category* of the investor removes all products and assets considered above the investor's limit. As previously mentioned, the risk category is a reference to the risk classes of traditional portfolio management[1] without being limited to that definition. Only products judged to be at or below the investor's risk category may be considered further. For example, products of the yield enhancement and participation class would be eliminated for an investor with a risk category of one. Classical asset classes like stocks or commodities would also fall out of the investment universe for that investor. Note that *capital guaranteed products* on stocks or commodities can still be taken into account at this stage. In a second and third step, the *skew* and the *kurtosis* of the investor's preferred return distribution both act as further filter, reducing the number of fitting products and classical assets.

In fact, after those three main parameters are known, the preferred product types and the classical asset class(es) have been well identified. The *expected return* over a holding period and the *return volatility* are used to choose between two assets (products) of the same risk, skew and kurtosis category. The investor's investment horizon will in part determine the maturity and thus the holding period of the products. Let's now see how a portfolio consisting only of structured products may be built.

## 13.2   CONSTRUCTING A STRUCTURED PRODUCT PORTFOLIO IN THEORY

Structured products are able to replicate a preferred return distribution with any asset class as underlying. As with a classical portfolio where holdings include stocks, bonds, commodities, etc., a structured product portfolio needs to be diversified in terms of asset classes. In addition, a diversification of the maturities is needed to reduce the reinvestment risk. A structured product portfolio can therefore be depicted with the help of a matrix: the different underlying asset categories combined with the maturities of the products.

The example in Table 13.2, which is in part similar to the case of the fictional character Dominique (page 8), illustrates this well. The assumption is that a global portfolio should be right-skewed, with little or no downside risk, and have a medium-high kurtosis. This return distribution form can be effectively achieved by investing mainly in capital guaranteed products, as mentioned earlier. The strategy is of the type "cut losses and let winners run". The four asset classes considered are equity, fixed income, commodities and FX. The maturities of the products are split between short, medium and long term. Not all the positions need to be filled, and some deviation from the original definition is allowed if the situation warrants it.

In the asset allocation matrix, some slots like short-term equity, short-term fixed income and others are empty. The reason could be either that the structuring parameters were not favorable, or that the investor[2] did not have a view on the market. The shapes of the return

---

[1] For example "Conservative, Balanced and Growth", corresponding to bonds only, 50% bonds and 50% stocks, and stocks only, respectively.

[2] In this case, it could also be the investment advisor or a portfolio manager.

**Table 13.2**   Asset allocation matrix

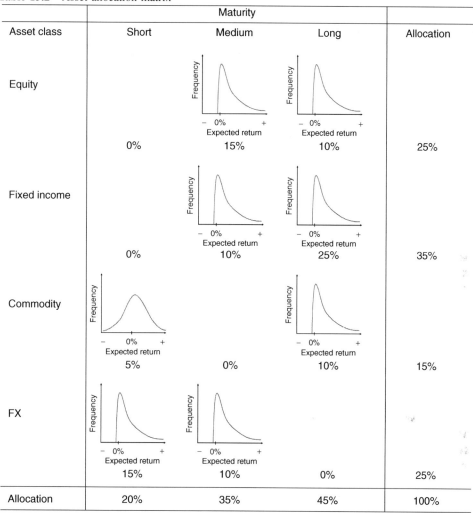

| Asset class | Maturity | | | Allocation |
| --- | --- | --- | --- | --- |
| | Short | Medium | Long | |
| Equity | 0% | 15% | 10% | 25% |
| Fixed income | 0% | 10% | 25% | 35% |
| Commodity | 5% | 0% | 10% | 15% |
| FX | 15% | 10% | 0% | 25% |
| Allocation | 20% | 35% | 45% | 100% |

distributions in the slots are mainly right-skewed, as shown by the graphs. Note that the right-skewed distribution does not necessarily need to be structured to fit rising markets only. It is perfectly conceivable to structure a capital guaranteed product betting on a falling market. The construction of the product differs (in addition to the bond part a put is bought instead of a call), but the return distribution remains the same; only the market view has changed. Depending on the size of the portfolio, a single slot can be filled with several products. For instance, the long-term fixed-income slot with a weighting of 25% could be achieved with four products. In that case, the return distribution shape of the graph would represent the weighted average.

The return distribution shape has been plotted for all invested slots. It is right-skewed, but in this illustrative case, it doesn't promise full capital guarantee: the leftmost part of the distributions starts below 0%. In other words, small losses are possible, while the chance for large gains remains open. In addition, looking at the short-term commodity slot, it is noticeable that the shape of the return distribution form differs from the prerequisite: it has a rather normal bell-shaped curve. However, the low allocation of 5% only influences the overall shape of the distribution to a small degree. The portfolio remains right-skewed overall. Maybe the investment advisor saw a short-term opportunity in the market, or maybe the inclusion of this position helped diversify the portfolio. The little distribution "outsider" has been purposely introduced to underscore the fact that investing, even with structured products, remains an activity based on human decisions and cannot be boiled down to pure mathematical formulas.

The short-, medium- and long-term maturities can be parameterized to the overall holding period of the investor. The allocation weights are hypothetical; in a real portfolio, they should reflect the investor's view of and expectations for the market.

Other asset classes such as hedge funds, real estate, or private equity can be added to the matrix. For these less accessible investments, the investor has to pay increased attention to the cost of implementing a given return distribution. Sometimes the costs are quite high and the expected return would suffer accordingly. In these cases, the investor must make a choice between:

1. implementing a position that does not fit his preferred return distribution;
2. implementing a position fitting his preferred return distribution but at a high cost; or
3. not investing in this asset (class) at all.

The decision has to take into account the benefits or drawbacks of factors like additional diversification, risk impact on the portfolio, change in expected return, etc.

The asset allocation matrix of Table 13.2 is roughly in line with the four steps of Figure 11.1, which described the portfolio construction concept. The investment preferences have been determined according to the framework (risk category, skew and kurtosis preferences, as shown in the return distribution Cube). Consequently, the majority of the positions were selected according to these criteria.

Mention is made of a preferred return distribution that can be structured for rising as well as for falling markets; this would refer to points 5 and 6 of Figure 11.2, describing the forecast for markets and the structuring parameters. If the forecast is for rising markets, a right skew can be achieved through a capital guaranteed product structured by means of a zero-coupon bond and call (Figure 13.2). However, if the forecast is for falling markets, a similar return distribution shape can be achieved by means of a capital guaranteed product constructed with a zero-coupon bond and a put.

All the selected underlying assets had a medium-to-high volatility. They could not have been considered as direct investments in the theoretical portfolio, which was stated to have a low risk appetite. The structured products risk profile took over that of the underlying assets, allowing equity, FX and commodity investments. The upside potential was left open, something that would not have been possible with a bond-only portfolio. The downside was guaranteed, as in a bond investment, and the portfolio was diversified over more asset classes.

This concludes the theoretical approach to constructing a structured product portfolio; let's now see in a second example how structured products can be implemented in a portfolio management context.

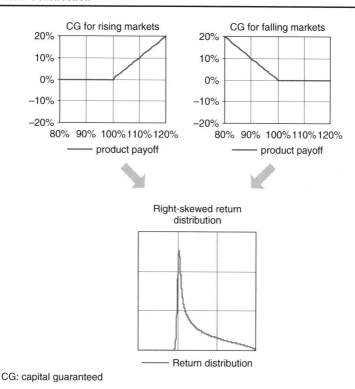

**Figure 13.2** Right-skewed return distributions for bullish or bearish CG products

## 13.3 PREFERRED RETURN DISTRIBUTION PROCESS VERSUS CLASSIC PORTFOLIO MANAGEMENT

Most, if not all, private banks use a risk class system in which their clients are categorized when they decide to give the bank a discretionary mandate. The large majority of banks use the *relative return* concept,[3] in which a portfolio manager will try to outperform a specific benchmark. Benchmarks are generally global stock indices like the MSCI World, bond indices like the Lehman (now Barclays) Bond Aggregate, etc. The risk categories are usually labeled from 1, being the most conservative type of portfolio, to 5, being the most aggressive. Simplifying the five categories to three by using the industry standard terms "Income", "Balanced" and "Growth", the portfolios can be labeled "low risk", "medium risk" and "high risk", as in Table 13.3.

The volatility of the portfolio components is usually taken as a proxy for "Risk". Low-volatility asset classes like money-market instruments and investment grade bonds are usually the only two found in "Income" portfolios. Portfolios with higher risk are constructed with a mix of money-market, bond, stock and alternative investment vehicles. Options, warrants and futures comprise the ultra-high volatility investments due to their leverage

---

[3] As opposed to the absolute return concept, which seeks to generate positive returns for the investors, no matter the direction of the market.

**Table 13.3**  Categories of classical portfolios

| Category | Risk | Bonds | Stocks | Expected return |
|---|---|---|---|---|
| **Income** | Low | 100% | 0% | Low |
| **Balanced** | Medium | 50% | 50% | Medium |
| **Growth** | High | 0% | 100% | High |

effect on a portfolio. Simplifying for illustration purposes, only bonds and stocks as the two basic asset classes will be considered further.

In theory, a portfolio with a higher stock allocation will have the higher expected return. Investors running a low risk have no chances of reaping a higher return than the yield of their bonds, while high-risk investors have both upside and downside potential. While tools exist to measure an investor's willingness and ability to accept risk as represented by volatility, they fall short of encompassing his whole risk spectrum. If risk is divided in two categories, *downside* risk and *upside* risk, then it is reasonable to assume that some investors wish they could get rid of the former while staying exposed to the latter. Volatility, however, always works both ways. Hence, volatility as a unique measure for risk is incomplete, as already mentioned in previous chapters. Yet it is possible to form a portfolio that has a payoff structure where only upside risk is present; it obviously has a cost as will be seen later.

### 13.3.1 Risk sources in a balanced mandate

An illustration using the Balanced mandate with its so-called "medium risk" will demonstrate the concept. A central question for every investor is the source of the majority of the risk. An empirical answer can be found through the following example: in Euro currency, investment grade bonds have an average one-year return between 0% and 10% with a 95% probability. Plotting a historical distribution of returns of an index like the Eurostoxx50 index to represent the stock market over recent years shows a picture where the return distribution approaches a normal shape. Figure 13.3 depicts the yearly return probabilities of the index using monthly data.

It can be observed that the probability of a yearly gain between 0% and 10% similar to bonds amounts to approximately 18%. The returns are lower (i.e. negative) 29% of the time, and higher 53% of the time. Therefore, in total, about 82% of the time, the portfolio's return is principally influenced by the performance of the stocks that either rise far above or fall far below the average yields of the bonds. Hence, the overwhelming majority of the risk comes from the stocks. The downside average below 0% is −18% and the upside average above 10% is +26%. One can reasonably assume that at least some stock investors would like to avoid the 29% chance of getting a −18% return over a one-year period, or that bond investors (precisely because they fear that possible −18% loss) would indeed like to have the 53% chance of reaping +26% on average.

The effect is amplified on a three-year horizon (Figure 13.4). The shape of the return distribution flattens (the kurtosis flattens and becomes platykurtic) and the fat tails are more pronounced. The percentage of cases where the stock returns are in the range of the bond returns decreases to about 8% assuming that the total return on bonds over a 3-year holding period lies between 0% and 20% (not annualized). On this investment horizon, the return of the portfolio is almost entirely attributed to the performance of the stocks. Even taking into

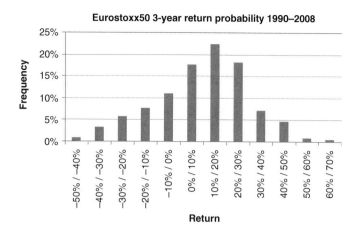

**Figure 13.3**  Eurostoxx50 return distribution over a 1-year holding period[4]
*Source*: Bloomberg, own representation

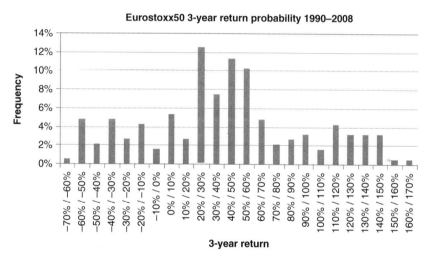

**Figure 13.4**  Eurostoxx50 return distribution over a 3-year holding period
*Source*: Bloomberg, own representation

account rebalancing, a technique used to maintain the ratio of bonds/stocks constant, doesn't change the big picture: stocks make or break the return distribution of the whole portfolio.

### 13.3.2  Keeping only upside risk with a capital guaranteed product

Getting rid of the downside risk while staying exposed to the upside can indeed be achieved by means of a *capital guaranteed product*. As described in Part I, capital guaranteed products

---

[4] Note the difference between Figure 13.3 and Figure 10.1 (page 224). The return distribution changed due to the different time windows taken for the samples. However, even though the changes are noticeable, they are not substantial enough to warrant a dismissal of the back-tests.

combine the least risky asset class (bonds) with the most risky one (options). In the classical portfolios, the upside-but-not-downside risk approach is difficult to achieve because options (representing leverage) are seldom used or outright forbidden. If they are used, it is at best a short-term tactical optimization attempt that hangs on a decision of a portfolio manager or a CIO. In theory, a delta-hedge[5] replicating a guaranteed product could be implemented, but the cost structures of private banks and the size of the mandates (discretionary mandates have on average investable amounts between EUR/CHF/USD 1 and 5 million) prevent such an undertaking. The fact that classical portfolios exclude options, and by corollary structured products, from their core investment process has some drawbacks as will be illustrated in the next section.

### 13.3.3 Comparing a Balanced mandate to a capital guaranteed product

A Balanced mandate and a capital guaranteed product can be compared by listing and evaluating the possible different scenarios over an investment (or holding) period. There are nine in total if the assumption is that interest rates and equity markets may rise, fall or stay stable. It is also useful to make a comparison within a holding period by evaluating the mark-to-market (MtM) performance of the mandate and the product according to the same criteria. Table 13.4 depicts the results using a $+/0/-$ ranking system. The "$+ + + + +$" symbols represents a large positive result, while "$-----$" represents a strongly negative result, the other rankings standing for results in-between.

**Table 13.4**   Comparing a Balanced mandate to a capital guaranteed product

| | | | MtM during lifetime | | For one holding period | |
| --- | --- | --- | --- | --- | --- | --- |
| Scenario | Equities | Interest rates | Mandate | Product | Mandate | Product |
| 1 | Stable | Stable | + | 0 | + | 0 |
| 2 | Stable | Rise | − | − | − | 0 |
| 3 | Stable | Fall | + | + | + | 0 |
| 4 | Rise | Stable | + + | + + | + + + | + + + + + |
| 5 | Rise | Rise | + | + | + + | + + + + + |
| 6 | Rise | Fall | + + + | + + + | + + + + | + + + + + |
| 7 | Fall | Stable | − | − | − − | 0 |
| 8 | Fall | Rise | − | − | − − | 0 |
| 9 | Fall | Fall | − | − | − | 0 |

The results can be divided into three categories:

1. *Equities are stable (scenarios 1, 2 and 3):* No matter what the interest rate does, the product ends flat on its capital guarantee level. The mandate experiences a small variation that depends on the direction of the interest rate variation. Overall, neither the value of the mandate nor that of the product changes much, ending most probably with a low single digit return. In these scenarios, the Balanced mandate holder will be happier than the

---

[5] Delta-hedge is a technique that consists of keeping the exposure of a portfolio neutral or stable in relation to an underlying asset.

product holder, because his bonds and stocks yielded interest and dividends respectively, while the product yielded nothing.

2. *Equities rise (scenarios 4, 5 and 6):* the positive stock performance is reflected on 100% of the assets in the product, but only 50% reflected in the Balanced mandate. It is very likely that the product will strongly outperform the mandate in these scenarios. The product holder will likely be happier than the mandate holder, although the latter will probably be satisfied, having most likely reached his target return.

3. *Equities fall (scenarios 7, 8 and 9):* The product ends again on its capital guarantee level, as in the three first scenarios. The mandate will almost certainly be in negative territory, no matter what the interest rates did. Here as well, it is highly likely that the product will outperform the mandate. While the product holder will hardly jump for joy at not having lost money, the mandate holder will most likely be dissatisfied. Even during its lifetime, it is likely that the product will outperform the mandate.

Several conclusions can be drawn from the above analysis. At maturity, the product is influenced only by the equities and the resulting return distribution is likely to be more concentrated than a Balanced mandate. Six times out of nine, it ends on its capital guaranteed level and yields no profit for the investor. The mandate earns money on a more regular basis (it is in positive territory five times out of nine), but the magnitude of the gains is lower because 50% of the returns are capped by the bond yields. In addition, one large negative stock performance (scenario 7, 8 or 9) can nullify several small positive performances from scenarios 1, 3, or even 5. The product does not behave very differently from the mandate during its lifetime, assuming that the lifetime of the product corresponds to the investment horizon of the investor.

### 13.3.4   The cost of the capital guarantee

It has already been demonstrated that the cost of a capital guaranteed product amounts to the yield of a zero-bond and/or the stock dividends, which are used to buy the protection. It is then a matter of comparing the value of the protection with its costs. Simplifying again for the illustration, let's assume that for a one-year period, the dividend yield on the stock index amounts to 4% and the interest rate of bonds is 4.5%. Compared to a 100% stock portfolio, the cost of the capital guarantee is thus the 4% dividend yield, since the portfolio would not generate any income from the interest rate, having a zero allocation to bonds. Compared to a 100% bond portfolio, the cost of the capital guarantee would be the interest of 4.5% per annum that is forsaken. The dividend yield of the stocks cannot be taken as a cost, as a 100% bond portfolio would not have generated any dividend yield. In the case of a Balanced mandate, the cost is a mix between the 50% bonds and 50% stocks: the weighted 4.5% interest of the bonds adds to the weighted 4% dividends of the stocks, totaling 4.25%. In addition to these costs, one has to consider practical factors like lesser trading flexibility during the lifetime of the product,[6] and product construction costs.

---

[6] Mainly because of the delta and of larger bid–ask spreads.

### 13.3.5   The key: changing the asset allocation split

The drawbacks of the classical Balanced mandate for investors wishing to rid themselves of the potential losses while staying exposed to the potential gains have been elaborated, the returns of the stocks over two periods (one and three years) have been analyzed, and the costs of a capital guaranteed product versus the three classic mandate types have been considered. Now let's combine the concepts. The key is the allocation split of the assets. A Balanced mandate has a 50/50 exposure to bonds and stocks respectively. It is rebalanced periodically to maintain that ratio. Now let's consider a simple capital guaranteed product with 100% capital guarantee and 100% participation on the equity market. Its delta at issue date is around 50%. It has thus the *same equity exposure* as the Balanced mandate when issued. The 'rebalancing' of the product takes place automatically with the equity market movements in the form of higher or lower delta at an *inverse rate* to the rebalancing of the Balanced mandate. If the stock market rises, the delta of the product rises as well, and if it falls, so does its delta. Simply put, a capital guaranteed product effectively sells the risky asset when it falls and buys it when it rises, purely from a delta point of view. It follows a "cut losses and let winners run" type of strategy. A Balanced mandate would sell stocks when they rise and buy them when they fall, following a "buy low/sell high" strategy.

At maturity, the product's delta will be either one or zero: one if the equity markets have risen and zero if the equity markets have fallen. Consequently, if the equity markets have risen, the investor receives the stock performance on 100% of the capital. If the equity markets have fallen, there is no return on 100% of the capital, but losses are avoided as well. This upside potential with downside protection is what many investors would like. A single capital guaranteed product on an equity index might seem much less eye-catching then 25 single stocks handpicked by a portfolio manager or an equity analyst. Then again, even the best 25 stocks may not escape the drag of a substantial bear market.

In conclusion, the inverse rebalancing effect and the capital guarantee are the two main reasons why the capital guaranteed product should be considered at the beginning of the core investment process in private banking Balanced mandates and not only as an option to use opportunistically. The unique return distribution of the product, which differs greatly from that of the mandate, should be made available to investors. If the cost seems bearable and optimal conditions present themselves, there should be no hesitation about switching the entire portfolio into one or several capital guaranteed products. Of course, if the costs seem too high or the conditions are disadvantageous, then a direct investment in stocks will be preferable. In the end, it is a matter of defining the process and setting the criteria. This is why the author proposes the process of Figures 11.1 and 11.2.

The analysis presented above through the example of the Balanced mandate and the capital guaranteed product can be extended to other types of mandates and products. It can also be extended to asset classes other than stocks – commodities, for instance.

This concludes the second example of the use of structured products in a portfolio context. Let's now see a third and last one, in which products with real characteristics are selected to fit the preferred return distributions of the three fictional characters Bob, John and Maria.

## 13.4 INVESTOR PORTFOLIOS

### 13.4.1 Classification of the product universe

For purposes of illustration, only the index-based products that have been tested in the study will be considered. The currency will be limited to the EUR and the asset class "equity" will be limited to the Eurostoxx50 index. In order to round out the picture, additional assets classes such as bonds and cash will be included in the product classification. It is easy to broaden the presented concept to other currencies and indices as well as for single stock/commodity/FX/etc. investments. Table 13.5 summarizes and classifies the products considered. The risk category of the products is described by a number from 1 to 5, denoting the lowest risk class for which each product should be used.

**Table 13.5**  Product classification

| Name | Risk cat. | Return skew | Return kurtosis | Exp. return p.h.p.p.a.[7] | Return volatility |
|---|---|---|---|---|---|
| **Cash** | – | – | High | 3.4% | – |
| **ST IG bonds** | Low (1) | Right | High | 3.7% | Very low |
| **LT IG bonds** | Low (1) | Right | High | 4.1% | Low |
| **ST EM bonds** | Low (2) | Right | High | 6% | Low |
| **LT EM bonds** | Medium (3) | Right | High | 8% | High |
| **Stocks (TR)** | High (4) | None | Flat | 6.5% | Very high |
| **CG1** | Medium (3) | Right | Normal | 3.38% | High |
| **CG2** | Low (1) | None | Flat (dual) | 3.6% | Very low |
| **CG3** | Low (2) | Right | High | 6.5% | High |
| **CG4** | Low (1) | Right | Flat | 7.3% | Low |
| **YE1** | Medium (3) | Left | High | 4.8% | Low |
| **YE4** | Medium (3) | Left | High | 3.2% | Low |
| **YE4'** | Low (2) | Left | High | 4.1% | Very low |
| **YE7** | High (4) | Left | High | 2.6% | Low |
| **YE8** | High (4) | Left | High | 1.7% | Low |
| **P1** | High (4) | None | Flat | 4.85% | Very high |
| **P3** | High (4) | None | Flat | 4.4% | Very high |
| **P3'** | Medium (3) | None | Normal | 5.95% | Very high |
| **P4** | Medium (3) | Left | Normal | 3% | High |
| **P5** | Medium (3) | None | Flat | 3.23% | Very high |
| **P5'** | Medium (3) | None | Normal | 4.83% | Very high |

ST: short term; IG: investment grade; LT: long term; EM: emerging market; TR: total return

With this classification, the elements necessary to construct a portfolio that satisfies the three investors' preferences are now in place:

• A framework of return distributions for different product categories symbolized by the return distribution Cube of Figures 11.3 and 12.25.

---

[7] Per holding period per annum

- The investor's preferences in terms of target return, risk, skew and kurtosis as well as a holding period, which were obtained thanks to the questionnaire starting on page 246 (The answers of Bob, John and Maria are on page 255).
- The distribution of returns and other risk characteristics of assets and products summarized in Table 13.5.

Some of the questions found on page 235 still cannot be answered. For instance, the price for skewness and kurtosis will be difficult to assess for an investor. Nevertheless, progress has been made in answering the most important questions: the overall investment preferences can be matched with appropriate products. In any case, it is the author's view that it is useless to try to determine the exact mathematical value an investor would attribute to skewness or kurtosis. Such an exercise would end with data of little relevance, as the human mind cannot be mathematically quantified. Part of the answer rests effectively with the product specialists, the structurers. They should be able to judge if it is timely to buy or sell skewness, if given the appropriate investment preferences of the investors.

### 13.4.2  Summary and scenario

Portfolios that combine investors' preferences with the appropriate products will now be built. For the purposes of illustration, only two asset classes are used: bonds and equities, the former being split into cash and various types of bonds, while the latter consists of pure equities plus the different product types tested on the Eurostoxx50 index. In real life, other assets (e.g. other equities, FX, commodities, hedge funds, etc.) and products would also have to be considered.

As a reminder, Table 13.6 recaps the investment profiles for Bob Sample, the elderly gentleman who wishes to retire to southern France; John Model, the managing director of an industrial company; and Maria Case, the jet-set lady who inherited a large sum of money.

**Table 13.6**  Summary of example distribution preferences

|            | Risk category | Skew  | Kurtosis |
|------------|---------------|-------|----------|
| **John Model** | Low       | Right | Normal   |
| **Bob Sample** | Medium    | Right | High     |
| **Maria Case** | High      | Right | High     |

Marc Council now reflects on how to implement their respective preferences as concerns distribution of returns and expected return. He has the following additional information at his disposal at the time he receives the funds from his clients:

- His macro research department tells him that their scenario for the Euro area is a slow pickup in the economy, but risks of a recession persist. Interest rates should decrease over the long run as the ECB[8] tries to stimulate the economy, but inflationary pressures remain present and these have to disappear before the ECB moves. At this moment, for the short term, there's even a 30% chance that rates increase.

---

[8] European Central Bank

- On the FX side, the Euro may weaken against the USD if the ECB lowers rates to stimulate the economy, but continuous commodity price increases indicate that investors still see the greenback heading south as they hedge their positions through commodities.
- From the equity market specialists comes the message that equity markets have already suffered substantially and are fairly valued at this point in time. If the economy strengthens as forecast, sudden rebounds and positive trend changes will occur. In any case, the market will remain highly volatile.

This input from the various research departments leaves Marc highly uncertain about the future evolution of the markets in general, and he decides to invest more prudently than he would do otherwise. He has no discretionary power over the assets, and must consult with his clients before taking any decision.

### 13.4.3 Bob Sample's portfolio

According to the results of the questionnaire, Marc knows he cannot risk much for Bob, since the three million EUR is all he has. The portfolio will mostly consist of investment grade bonds. Bob did not want to let go entirely of his stock investments, though. Marc finally convinces him to switch the ~10% stocks Bob mentioned he holds into a capital guaranteed product, mainly because of risk considerations: 50% of the total risk of the portfolio was due to the 10% stock allocation. Since Marc is highly uncertain about the economy, he prefers not to risk destroying the whole portfolio's performance because of a few stocks. Marc and Bob opt for CG2, the two-year capped product on the Eurostoxx50. The high volatility is partly offset by the cap, and since the interest rates are relatively high, the product, while not exceptionally advantageous, has acceptable conditions. Marc and Bob decide to allocate 15% of the portfolio to CG2, while the rest is invested in cash and investment grade bonds. In terms of risk, 15% of CG2 is still massively lower than 10% of single stocks or mutual funds. Even if the stock markets do not perform well over the next two years, the 80% bond allocation should yield enough interest for Bob to live on. On the other hand, if the bullish or rebound scenario from the research department materializes, the up to 25% gain over two years is likely to more than offset any mark-to-market losses that the bond part of the portfolio suffers because of possible interest rate hikes. Most importantly, an issuer with a safe rating has to be found, even if it is somewhat to the detriment of the product's conditions.

**Table 13.7**  Bob Sample's portfolio

|            | %  | Risk cat. | Skew  | Kurtosis |
|------------|----|-----------|-------|----------|
| **Cash**       | 5  | –         | –     | High     |
| **ST IG bonds**| 50 | Low       | Right | High     |
| **LT IG bonds**| 30 | Low       | Right | High     |
| **CG2**        | 15 | Low       | Right | Dual     |

### 13.4.4 John Model's portfolio

The approach to John's profile is quite different. Because of the medium-risk profile and John's understanding of investments, the scope of possible portfolios is much larger. John's target return is clearly above the risk-free rate, and so risky investments are inevitable. During the investment discussion, John mentions that any FX investments would be taken care of through another account, but that the stock and bond allocation would be done at Marc's bank. John is more confident about the economy than Marc's research department is. Marc mentions that the high volatility and implied dividend yield create an interesting opportunity for participation products. John asks Marc to show him an example. Marc, well prepared, shows a first possible portfolio allocation (Table 13.8).

**Table 13.8**   John Model's portfolio #1

|             | %  | Risk cat.  | Skew  | Kurtosis |
|-------------|----|------------|-------|----------|
| **Cash**        | 5  | –          | –     | High     |
| **ST IG bonds** | 20 | Low(1)     | Right | High     |
| **LT IG bonds** | 10 | Low(1)     | Right | High     |
| **ST EM bonds** | 5  | Low(2)     | Right | High     |
| **LT EM bonds** | 10 | Medium(3)  | Right | High     |
| **Stocks**      | 10 | High(4)    | None  | Flat     |
| **P3′**         | 20 | Medium(3)  | None  | Normal   |
| **P5′**         | 20 | Medium(3)  | None  | Normal   |

Marc's thoughts about the allocation were as follows: John is long-term oriented (response (c) to question 11), and does not want to cap his returns (responses (a) and (a) to questions 6 and 7 respectively). The results show that he nevertheless would like a high kurtosis (+0.7 above the normal level of 3), a difficult distribution to create. Since the volatility can be considered high in a historical context, participation products probably have attractive conditions. As Marc is rather uncertain about the future path of the stock market, he very much prefers conditionally protected instruments to direct investments. That, and the fact that John likes to invest in the stocks of companies with which he does business, are the reasons he leaves 10% of direct stock allocation. In fact, had the volatility not been so high, he would have invested a part of the portfolio in capital guaranteed products, but the only one looking even halfway attractive is capped. As an alternative, he opts for the bonus certificates P3′ and P5′. He liked the European-style barriers of these instruments primarily because of the short-term market uncertainty. A crash, even though unlikely but nevertheless possible, followed by a recovery would likely leave the barriers intact. The barriers seem low enough to withstand even a small recession. Sadly, these products do not have the desired return distribution shape. Their skew is so very lightly tilted to the right that it can be considered not skewed, and the kurtosis is normal as well. However, that is still better than the outright stocks, which have more of a flat kurtosis on average. The maturity of the products of two and three years fits more or less into John's horizon of up to five years.

As Marc presents this initial portfolio, John has a few remarks. First, he doesn't need any cash allocation (response (a) to question 13). Second, he is rather bullish on interest rates, so the long-term investment grade bonds don't appeal to him. He would prefer a higher stock allocation. He agrees that the timing is right to try to profit from the high volatility. Marc considers these arguments, and replies that the portfolio already profits from the high volatility with the two participation products.[9] With a potential 50% equity allocation, the portfolio is already quite loaded with this asset class and to increase it further would go beyond the risk category defined by the questionnaire. Marc reminds John that the bonus certificates have a delta of approximately one for most of their lifetimes. One solution might be to switch some long-term bonds into capital guaranteed products with stock exposure, but the high volatility makes most of this product category unattractive. Moreover, if John is bullish on interest rates, any long-term capital guaranteed product would suffer mark-to-market losses if he's proven right. There are only two products Marc can think of, the first being CG2 (as for Bob) or a second one a Shark note as described in Section 3.1.2: 100% capital guaranteed, 100% participation, upper knock-out barrier at about 135% of spot, 18 months' maturity.[10] Marc explains the two capped variants and mentions the advantage of the current high volatility for the Shark note. John thinks that CG2 is not attractive as it is capped at 25%, which amounts to just 12.5% per annum. On reflection, the Shark note appeals to him. The barrier set at 135% of spot for a maturity of 18 months seems like a long way to go, amounting to over 23% per annum. Marc is happy that John likes this idea, as the product probably has a right (bimodal) skew and a high kurtosis, a distribution shape which corresponds to John's profile. Finally, both partners agree on the allocation shown in Table 13.9.

**Table 13.9**   John Model's portfolio #2

|              | %  | Risk cat.  | Skew  | Kurtosis    |
|--------------|----|-----------|-------|-------------|
| **ST IG bonds** | 20 | Low(1)    | Right | High        |
| **LT IG bonds** | 5  | Low(1)    | Right | High        |
| **ST EM bonds** | 10 | Low(2)    | Right | High        |
| **LT EM bonds** | 5  | Medium(3) | Right | High        |
| **Shark note**  | 10 | Low(1)    | Right | High (dual) |
| **Stocks**      | 15 | High(4)   | None  | Flat        |
| **P3′**         | 20 | Medium(3) | None  | Normal      |
| **P5′**         | 15 | Medium(3) | None  | Normal      |

### 13.4.5   Maria Case's portfolio

The construction of Maria's portfolio was a headache for the advisor. How can he meet the high expectations of his client? A failure to reach them will likely result in a withdrawal of funds. The lady was quick enough to transfer her assets to Marc when his competitor showed up with a medium-sized loss. He would have liked to have given the mandate to portfolio management, but Maria expressly wished Marc to make the investment decisions himself and to report to her on the progress of the portfolio's performance in about six months. Marc decides to go for safety, but leaves himself the opportunity open for positive surprises. He invests Maria's funds as shown in Table 13.10.

---

[9] In such an environment, bonus certificates would certainly have better conditions than the average conditions of P3′ and P5′.

[10] This product is not listed in Table 13.5, but a good advisor has more solutions in his head than on a prepared piece of paper.

**Table 13.10**   Maria Case's portfolio

|            | %   | Risk cat.  | Skew  | Kurtosis    |
|------------|-----|------------|-------|-------------|
| **Cash**       | 15  | –          | –     | High        |
| **ST IG bonds**  | 10  | Low(1)     | Right | High        |
| **ST EM bonds**  | 15  | Low(2)     | Right | High        |
| **Shark note**   | 10  | Low(1)     | Right | High (dual) |
| **CG4**        | 35  | Low(2)     | Right | Normal      |
| **P3′**        | 15  | Medium(3)  | None  | Normal      |

Due to the high volatility, some of the funds that he would have otherwise invested in uncapped capital guaranteed products, Marc leaves in cash as a reserve for later use. He plans to wait for a while to see if the markets show a clearer trend. He keeps bonds to a minimum, as the expected return of those instruments does not reach his client's target return. He uses the same Shark note as for John and, despite the high volatility, selects CG4, the one-year 94.5% capital guaranteed product as largest single investment. If the capital guarantee must be lowered to 93%, so be it! Marc doesn't want to take the risk of losing the funds he has only just acquired on the toss of a coin on the direction of stock markets. Their high volatility suggests that they will either have risen or fallen by a large amount by the time the product expires. Marc reasons that if they rise, fine; he'll reach Maria's return requirements. If they fall, well, he hopes that she will give him a second chance, as any loss will be limited to the capital guarantee level. The one-year maturity fits Maria's supposed investment horizon (tentative response a. to question 11) and has the right distribution shape. Her answers to questions 4 and 5 about purchasing protection indicate that, while she doesn't want to spend too much on it, she also doesn't want to be exposed to the possibility of left fat tails. CG4 fulfills Ms Case's requirements in this respect. After a long hesitation, Marc decides to include P3′ in the portfolio as well mainly because of structural diversification considerations. Should the markets indeed decline by a small or medium amount, then CG4 will seem like an unwise investment because it still loses some 5.5 to 7% (depending on the exact level of the capital guarantee), while the performance of the bonus certificate will be higher. Should the markets rise, P3′ will always outperform CG4 by the difference between 100% and the capital guarantee level. Only in a completely bearish scenario will CG4 outshine P3′, but since that is exactly the scenario where Marc risks losing the freshly established relationship, he prefers to keep P3′ at a relatively low weighting. After thinking it over, Marc decides not to give the results of the questionnaire too much weight in his decision process, as he feels that Maria didn't answer with too much thought. As he presents his investment proposal to her, the lady barely acknowledges the positions, saying instead: "Fine, fine. I know you'll do well. Talk to you in about six months. Goodbye, Mr Council".

# 14
## Final Words

I started this book as a compendium, intending to encompass all the major aspects of structured products that I have had to deal with in my career. From unpleasant surprises with volatility products to delightful ones with FX capital guaranteed best-of products, each time I think I have seen it all, I keep being surprised almost daily. That is the fantastic world of structured products: constant innovation. Yet as I kept elaborating on how the products function and what features should be included or avoided when considering an investment, I realized these were simply isolated single-product considerations. After a while, I started to delve into a subject that has been dear to me for some years: how to integrate a product with an asymmetric payoff into a portfolio. This was the hardest part, as I am neither a mathematician nor a seasoned portfolio manager. I hope that the approach I developed, using the return distribution Cube, categorizing investments by risk category, skew and kurtosis, will appeal to investors. The Cube should help assess whether one's portfolio has the correct expected return distribution. Even as I back-tested the many products, I felt that this original approach could actually be quite useful. At least the colleagues and friends to whom I mentioned the approach were quite interested and encouraged me to continue. I would like to thank all of them for supporting this part of the project.

My feeling is that investments by means of structured products will continue in the future because of the simple fact that they cover precise investment needs of investors. What's less certain is how the nature of the business will evolve in the future. I have seen the strong industrialization of the business that led to a kind of monoculture of the discount certificate in Germany, the reverse convertible in Switzerland, and similar structures in other regions of the world. This trend has probably come to an end with the financial crisis of 2008, in which a substantial number of private banking investors experienced large losses on their yield enhancement structures. À propos monoculture, the yield enhancement products episode can be compared to a certain degree with the great Irish Famine of 1845–51, where a large part of the population's diet was dependent on potatoes. As the crops failed, the people hungered and suffered. Likewise, investors who relied purely on yield enhancement structures in their portfolios suffered from the extreme negative stock performances of the financial sector. However, in Ireland, the monoculture was rather forced on the people, while investors subscribed to the financial products of their own free will.

Paradoxically, as investors lost a lot of money on their products, so did most investment banks. The reason, although unknown to most investors, is simple: the banks could not hedge some of their risks and precisely those that they could not hedge went sour. The investors did not hedge their delta (they invested in the products and held them), while the investment banks hedged everything they could, delta, gamma, vega, etc., but couldn't efficiently hedge the correlation and lost massively on that. This occurred because the whole industry focused on the same kind of products and there was simply no two-way market. Every bank in the world had the same correlation positions on their trading ("prop") books and couldn't find a counterparty to offload the risk. When the markets crashed from June 2007 onwards, the losses on the correlation books grew astronomically, erasing any profits made at the time the products were issued. During the booming markets, this was a little-considered consequence of the monoculture in financial markets. When the people suffer and leave for the hope of a better life on new shores, the landlord is seldom spared for long.

So what's next? Will there again be a global preference for one or the other kind of payoff? I certainly hope not. First, a lot of trust in the products has been lost. Second, as any seasoned investor has probably noted several times already, the "too good to be true" investments seldom are. It was thus with the Japanese warrants in the 1990s, with the high-tech stocks at the turn of the millennium, and with the supposedly "safe" worst-of barrier products today. Maybe, and this is my short-term forecast, there will be no global product fashion, trend or preference, as investors who were badly hit by the financial crisis in one way or another reassess their situations and finally make some sensible decisions. That is actually what I hope for in the structured product universe: a rational, diversified payoff market, without habits and laziness; an opportunistic structuring approach, exploiting the timely or local market inefficiencies. In addition, the inclusion of all possible investment vehicles (in the sense of an underlying asset, an option on it or a structured product) in the investment process while considering the investment preferences of each investor.

Over time, I suppose the thought of a modified Modern Portfolio Theory approach including the payoff diversity of new investment vehicles will take root among investors. Of course, this will probably not happen overnight. Many short-term oriented players would dearly like to try to set a new global trend, so they can run their machinery again and profit from economies of scale, large volumes and little effort. The less watchful investors are prone to falling into such a trap again, which is unfortunately human nature. After all, aren't most of us sheep? Let us beware of this mindless herding as we all read the same news, hear about the same subjects inducing the same desires. Complacency is the enemy of efficiency in investments.

Today, the variety of products has become immense. One cannot imagine the legions of quantitative analysts sitting behind their computer models trying to devise new payoffs. If they were working for a space agency, humanity would already be settling on Mars. In structuring, these people are the base of the innovation. Yet most of that innovation is lost on the way and never makes it to the final investor. The bottleneck at this moment lies at the level of the investment advisors and asset and portfolio managers who have difficulties in coping with the diversity and constant innovation. Like the man who tries to catch the rain in a glass misses most of the drops because he only moves fast enough to catch a few of them, so the majority of financial participants are baffled by the constant flow of new products and consider only those they have the resources to analyze. One thing the structured products industry lacks is a coordinated effort to bring all its players up to an adequate level of knowledge. It would make the size of the pie much, much bigger, and the trust in the products would rise exponentially. Most investors will not buy something they do not know, and most structures remain unknown! As I mentioned in the introduction, I believe that only a small minority of the investors in private banking understands the basics of structured products and, of those, a majority does not have a deep enough knowledge about their functioning to make the decision to invest on their own. Many are influenced by the payoff sometimes framed in one way, sometimes another. I personally invest in the products I structure when I find the opportunity compelling. Up to now, if I have been disappointed by an investment I made, it was because of my poor market forecast, but never because of the structure I had chosen.

I also surmise that a deeper knowledge of the products would have led to a greater diversification of the underlying assets. Fixed-income and commodity products have been far too neglected, and I hope to have convinced at least some readers in this respect. Raising the knowledge of market participants would largely prevent the problems of herding and monostrategy investments. It is my guess that investors would have been much more reticent about investing in yield enhancement products had they known the shape of the return distribution and the true risks behind such structures, the more so when the conditions for this product type worsened. Other return distribution opportunities would have received more attention.

I hope the contents of the book have lived up to the expectations of the reader and have brought him useful insight into the world of structured products and I wish everyone who has read this book much success with their future structured product investments. There's much more to know and learn about this fascinating world. There are many more structures, where small variations can make big differences. But who will read a vast tome on structured products? Certainly not busy investors, I'll warrant. Besides, too much unfocused information leads to confusion. As an investor, never hesitate to ask your investment advisor the precise thing you wish to know. As an investment advisor, keep gathering knowledge from your structured product specialists and harass them until they deliver the answer to your request. Their purpose is to come up with a solution to your needs.

# Appendix A
## Glossary of Terms

| | |
|---|---|
| **American style** | 1. Options that can be exercised at any time by the buyer.<br>2. In barrier options, barriers that can be broken through any time during their life.<br>See also European and Bermudan style. |
| **Asianing** | Exotic option, where the final payout depends on the average of a number of observation points taken during the lifetime of the option. Often used in capital guaranteed products to reduce the cost of the call option and increase the participation. |
| **Asset** | Something of value, tangible or intangible. Financial asset examples are stocks, funds or bonds. Unlike nonfinancial assets like real estate or cars, financial assets do not necessarily have a physical form. Structured products use financial assets as underlying. |
| **Asset allocation** | Structure of a portfolio in terms of the weights of underlying assets. For example, the asset allocation of a portfolio could be composed of 60% bonds and 40% stocks. The exposure expressed in percentage of each asset class (bonds, equities, commodities . . . ) should correspond to an investor's preferences. |
| **At-the-money** | In options, the instance where the strike price of the option is at the same level as the spot price of its underlying asset. See also In- and Out-of-the-Money. |
| **Backwardation** | Shape of a forward curve where the front (nearby) futures are more expensive than the futures expiring later. Investments in backwardated commodities through front-month rolling indices produce positive roll-returns. See also Contango. |
| **Barrier** | Feature of an exotic option, designating a point at which the option's payoff has a gap, and where the payoff of the initial option is changed to a new one. Often used in yield enhancement and participation products to realize conditional capital protection (*not* guarantee) linked to the holding of a barrier. See also Knock-in, Knock-out. |
| **Behavioral finance** | Study field, which analyzes the non-rational behavior of persons (subjects) when facing choices involving uncertainty or risk. Empirical behavioral finance studies demonstrate that the purely rational theory like the Modern Portfolio Theory is not applicable to most market participants. |

| | |
|---|---|
| **Benchmark** | A standard by which a portfolio is measured. For instance, a global stock index may act as benchmark for an equity fund or equity portfolio. Benchmarks are often used to measure the relative performance of a portfolio compared to the market. |
| **Bermudan style** | Exotic option feature where a barrier can only be knocked-in or knocked-out within a certain time window, for example only during the last three months of its life. |
| **Bid-ask spread** | The width existing between the prices at which an asset can be bought or sold. |
| **Bond yield** | A rate of return that the holder of a bond earns as direct income. Usually expressed in percent per annum and assuming that the bond is held until maturity. |
| **Break-even** | The value (price) of an asset at which an investor is flat in terms of profits and losses. |
| **Bullet** | In structured products, designates a single lump sum payable upon the maturity of the product. It is not expressed on an annualized basis, but understood over the whole lifetime of the product. |
| **c/bu** | Abbreviation for cent per bushel, the standard measure for major agricultural commodities traded on the Chicago Board of Trade. |
| **Call** | Option giving its buyer the right, but not the obligation, to purchase an underlying asset at a predefined strike price either at maturity (European style), or any time until maturity (American style). |
| **Cap** | The price level of an asset over which a product stops participating to the positive performance of that asset. |
| **Capital guarantee** | One of the three basic groups of structured products. Includes any type of product with an unconditional capital guarantee attached. Quotes usually in percent of nominal value. |
| **Capital guarantee level** | The level in relation to the issue price (often 100%) of the capital guarantee. When the strike of the option is set at-the-money and the capital guarantee is lower than 100%, the difference between 100% and the capital guarantee level is subtracted from any positive performance at maturity. |
| **CDO** | Abbreviation for Collaterized Debt Obligation, which is a type of asset-backed security product in the field of structured credit. Popular belief is that CDOs are supposed to be at the root of the financial crisis of 2008. |

| | |
|---|---|
| **Certificate** | Investment form where no funding from the issuer is necessary. Used mostly for participation products like stock basket certificates, outperformance certificates, etc. |
| **CISA** | Abbreviation for Collective Investment Schemes Act, a law regulating the Swiss fund industry. |
| **Contango** | Shape of a forward curve where the front (nearby) futures are less expensive than the futures expiring later. Investments in contangoed commodities through front-month rolling indices produce negative roll-returns. See also Backwardation. |
| **Correlation** | A statistical measure quantifying how much two assets move in relation to each other. A correlation of 1 indicates that the two move in exact symmetry. At −1, the two move in perfect opposition. At 0, the two assets are said to be uncorrelated. In structured products, correlation is often used in worst-of and best-of products. |
| **Counterparty risk** | Common appellation for credit risk: the issuer's bankruptcy risk borne by the holder of a structured product. |
| **Coupon** | The nominal interest rate paid on an interest-bearing financial instrument, like a bond or a reverse convertible. The coupon, unless otherwise stated, is paid out with certainty. |
| **CPI** | Abbreviation for Consumer Price Index, a measure of inflation for the end consumer. Tracks the price evolution of a standard basket of goods typically representing a consumer's average spending. |
| **Currency risk** | The foreign exchange risk an investor takes when he invests into assets labeled in another currency, or directly into a foreign currency. |
| **Delta** | In options, one of the "Greeks", a risk measure calculating the price variation of a derivative instrument for a price variation in the underlying asset. Also gives an approximation about the chance of an option ending in-the-money. |
| **Delta-hedging** | Trading activity that consists of offsetting the risk of an option or a product by buying or selling an amount of underlying assets that corresponds to the delta of the option or the product. |
| **Derivatives** | General term designating financial instruments whose value changes with the price evolution of an underlying asset. The main types of derivatives are futures, options and swaps. Derivatives are often leveraged in relation to their underlying asset. While structured products have often been designated as derivative products, they should not be confused with pure derivatives. |

| | |
|---|---|
| **Distribution of returns** | The statistical (if calculated from past data) or expected (if calculated with forecast data) returns that an investment form yields on average. The returns can be measured in terms of risk, average return, skew and kurtosis. They are usually represented graphically by a histogram. |
| **Dividend (yield)** | Amount a company pays out to its stockholders. In Europe, dividends are paid out on a yearly basis, while in the US the payouts are quarterly. The dividend yield is the yearly dividend amount expressed in percent of the current stock price. |
| **Duration** | Measure of sensitivity of a bond to a variation in interest rates. In general, the longer the maturity of the bond, the higher its sensitivity to a shift in interest rates, although the bond's coupon also plays a role. Zero-coupon bonds have the highest duration of all bonds, which is equal to their maturity. |
| **Efficient Market Hypothesis (EMH)** | A theory developed by E. Fama which states that markets assume different levels of efficiency (weak, semi-strong and strong), and that it is impossible to generate an outperformance given the fact that all information is reflected in the price of the asset. |
| **European style** | 1. Options which can be exercised only at maturity by the buyer. 2. Barriers which can be broken through only at maturity. See also European and Bermudan style. |
| **Excess return index** | An index including spot plus roll returns, but where the yield component is not included. The GSCI ER and the CMCI ER are excess return indices. See also Total Return Index. |
| **Exotic option** | An option which differs from a standard call or put. Exotic options have special features that influence their behavior, payoff and price. Barrier options, lookback options or quanto options are exotic options, to name just a few. |
| **Fat tails** | An empirical (observed) measure of a return distribution, in which unlikely returns happen far more often than in a normal distribution. |
| **FCOJ** | Abbreviation for frozen concentrated orange juice. |
| **Financial participant** | Any person, company or institution active in the financial market. |
| **Floor** | The price level of an asset below which a product stops to participate in the negative performance of that asset. |

| | |
|---|---|
| **Forward price** | The price of an asset delivered at a future point in time. The forward price of an asset is calculated as the spot price of the asset multiplied by the compounded interest rate minus the dividends paid compounded by the interest rate. |
| **Future** | A standardized contract on a listed exchange for the future delivery of an asset. Some are cash settled, while others are physically settled. The most common financial futures include equity index futures (i.e. on the S&P500, the Eurostoxx50, the SMI ... ) or bond futures (i.e. the 30-year US Treasury Note, the 10-year Bund ... ). |
| **FX** | Abbreviation for Foreign eXchange. The rate at which one currency is exchanged against another. |
| **G7** | Abbreviation designating a group of seven large economies of the world: Canada, France, Germany, Italy, Japan, UK, USA. |
| **Gamma** | In options, one of the "Greeks", a risk measure calculating the rate of change of the delta. See also Delta. |
| **Hedge ratio** | The amount of underlying assets a trader must buy or sell in order to neutralize his exposure to an option or a product. See also Delta-hedging. |
| **Hedging** | Trading activity used to offset risk of an asset or in a portfolio by taking protective measures. Hedging is commonly achieved through long put options or futures. Hedging through put options typically leaves the profit potential open. When futures are used, the upside is capped as well, and the asset or portfolio is said to be neutralized, or immunized. |
| **Interest rate** | The general amount, expressed in percent per annum, that a moneylender asks the money borrower to pay for the use of his capital. |
| **In-the-money** | The instance where the strike price of the option is lower (for calls) or higher (for puts) than the spot price of its underlying asset. See also Out- and At-the-Money. |
| **Intrinsic value** | The value of an option if it were to expire now. In other words, the value of an option minus its time value. The intrinsic value of an option can be calculated by subtracting the spot price from the strike (for calls) or the strike from the spot price (for puts). Negative values indicate that the option is out-of-the-money. |
| **Investment vehicle** | General term designating any type of investment, i.e. a stock, a bond, a product, a future ... Not to be confused with Special Purpose Vehicles, which are financial constructs (mostly asset backed) used, among others, for CDOs or likewise products. |

| | |
|---|---|
| **ISIN** | Abbreviation for the international identification number of a security (International Security Identifying Number). |
| **Issue price** | The price at which a structured product is issued. |
| **Issuer risk** | The risk a structured product holder faces when its issuer fails. The structured product may become worthless when its issuer declares bankruptcy, although a recovery rate might be possible. |
| **Knock-in** | An event causing an exotic option with a barrier to "become alive". A barrier option with a knock-in feature is nonexistent ("dead") until a knock-in takes place. Once this happened, the option becomes a plain vanilla option. See also Barrier, Exotic option and Knock-out. |
| **Knock-out** | An event causing an exotic option with a barrier to "die". A barrier option with a knock-out feature exists ("lives") until a knock-out takes place. "Knock-out", "barrier breach", "barrier event" are all synonyms. See also Barrier, Exotic option and Knock-in. |
| **Kurtosis** | A measure of the concentration of a statistical distribution around its mean. A high kurtosis (leptokurtosis, statistical value greater than 3) designates a distribution that is concentrated around its mean. A low kurtosis (platykurtic, statistical value lower than 3) designates a distribution which is widely spread around its mean, often resulting in "fat tails". A normal distribution is said to be mesokurtic and has a value of 3. |
| **Leverage** | Also called gearing in warrants; uses the available financial resources in such a way that the investment potential outcome is magnified compared to the price variation of the underlying asset. Options, futures and, to a lesser extent, outperformance certificates, have a leverage. |
| **LIBOR** | London Inter-Bank Offered Rate, a short-term (1 to 12 month) interest rate that is a reference to banks lending each other money. The LIBOR exists in all major currencies. The funding rate of a structured product issuer is expressed in LIBOR + x or LIBOR − x, depending mainly on its rating, and influences the parameters of its products at the issue and their price in the secondary market. |
| **Liquidity** | Refers to both the width of the bid-ask spread and the possibility of trading large quantities of an asset without influencing its price. |
| **Lookback** | An exotic option, where the strike can be set by the buyer some time after the option has been issued. More expensive than plain vanilla options. |

| | |
|---|---|
| **Mark-to-market** | Designates the value of an asset at the moment of its evaluation. The asset's price is "marked" at the price where the market values it and thus assumes that value. The mark-to-market *bid* value is often used to determine how much the asset would be worth if it was sold now. |
| **Maturity** | The date at which an asset (option, bond, structured product, etc.) expires. |
| **Modern Portfolio Theory (MPT)** | A financial market theory developed by H. Markowitz assuming that rational investors would invest in efficient portfolios on what is known as the efficient frontier. |
| **Money market** | Short-term financing market. Money market investments are of the safest investment types. The money market rate is used to designate "riskless" investments. See also LIBOR. |
| **Note** | In structured products, investment form which includes treasury funding from the issuer. Necessary for products using bonds as underlying assets, like capital guaranteed products. |
| **Option** | A right but not an obligation to buy (call) or sell (put) an underlying asset at a predefined strike price within a determined period of time. The main influencing factors for an option are the strike price in relation to the spot price of the underlying asset, the implied volatility, the time to maturity, the interest rate and the dividend yield. |
| **OTC** | Abbreviation for "over the counter", as opposed to the listed regulated market. An OTC trade is a direct bilateral agreement between two financial participants without the intervention of a clearing house. Each participant bears the risk of its counterparty. |
| **Out-of-the-money** | The instance where the strike price of the option is higher (for calls) or lower (for puts) than the spot price of its underlying asset. See also In- and At-the-Money. |
| **Par** | In fixed-income trading, denotes a price of 100%. |
| **Participation** | One of the four basic categories of structured products. Most popular participation products include tracker, bonus and outperformance certificates. |
| **Participation rate** | Designates the rate at which a product participates to the price evolution of its underlying asset. |
| **Plain vanilla option** | A call or a put without any special feature. See also Option. |

| | |
|---|---|
| **PPI** | Abbreviation for Producer Price Index, a measure of the average change in the price of goods sold by producers. Usually a good forecast for measuring inflation. Closely linked to the CPI (see CPI). |
| **Premium** | The amount the buyer of an option pays to the seller of that option for the rights (to buy or to sell) attached to it. |
| **Present value** | Today's value of the payment of an asset in the future. Reflects principally the time value of money. |
| **Price index** | An index where the dividend component is not included. Sometimes called ex-dividend index. The Eurostoxx50 or the S&P 500 are price indices. See also Total return index. |
| **Pricing supplement** | The legal document ruling a structured product from A to Z. |
| **Primary market** | Short period of time before the issue date of a product giving investors the opportunity to subscribe to the product, which is still described with indicative conditions. |
| **Prospect** | A chance or a probability. |
| **Prospect theory** | A theory in the field of behavioral finance. See also Behavioral finance. |
| **Prospectus** | See Pricing supplement. |
| **Put** | Option giving its buyer the right, but not the obligation, to sell an underlying asset at a predefined strike price either at maturity (European style), or any time until maturity (American style). |
| **Quanto** | Abbreviation for Quantitative Adjusted Option. An exotic option where the option is expressed in one currency and the underlying asset in another, but where the currency risk has been neutralized. See also Currency risk. |
| **Ratchet** | To increase or decrease in small increments. Technique used in fixed-income based products to place caps on coupon payments. |
| **Rating** | The reliability of an issuer in terms of financial strength, determined by rating agencies like Moody's, S&P and Fitch. AAA denotes the best rating, AA+ the second best, BBB is the lowest investment grade rating, CCC has a high chance of default, and D denotes a company that defaulted on its debt. The rating of issuers of structured products is usually above A−. |

| | |
|---|---|
| **Rebate** | A lump sum paid by the seller to the buyer of a knock-out option when the latter knocks out. Used sometimes in capital guaranteed products like the Shark notes. |
| **Return distribution** | The statistical (if calculated from past data) or expected (if calculated with forecast data) returns that an investment form yields on average. The returns can be measured in terms of risk, average return, skew and kurtosis. They are usually represented graphically by a histogram. |
| **Rhô** | In options, one of the "Greeks", a risk measure calculating the price variation of a derivative instrument for a variation in the interest rate. |
| **Risk aversion** | A behavior of persons tending to seek safety over risk: a risk-averse investor will prefer a bargain with a certain return over an uncertain, but possibly higher, expected return. |
| **Risk (gap-)** | The risk a trader bears when delta-hedging options with barriers (or digital options). The gap risk becomes large especially if little time to maturity remains and the underlying asset trades near the barrier. |
| **Risk seeking** | The inverse behavior of a risk-averse person. See Risk aversion. |
| **Secondary market** | The time from after the issue date until the maturity date for a structured product. |
| **Seed money** | Amount of money pledged by one or more investors to finance the launch of a product. |
| **Swiss Security number** | The Swiss unique identification number for a security. |
| **Sharpe ratio** | A measure of the excess return per unit of risk in an investment. Sometimes referred to as the risk premium. |
| **Skew, skewness** | 1. In statistics, a measure of lopsidedness of a distribution. A negative skew denotes a longer left tail, and is said to be left-skewed. A positive skew denotes a longer right tail, and the distribution is said to be right-skewed. |
| | 2. Denotes the empirical observation that options of different strikes but same maturity on a single asset have different implied volatilities. Also referred to as volatility smile. |
| **Spot price** | The market price of an asset at the moment it is observed. |
| **Strike price** | The price of an underlying asset at which an option can be exercised. |
| **SVSP** | The Swiss Structured Product Association, an association and interest group of the major issuers of structured products in Switzerland. Consult www.svsp-verband.ch for more information. |

| | |
|---|---|
| **Systematic risk** | The risk inherent to the whole market, which cannot be eliminated by diversification. Also called Market risk. |
| **Term-sheet** | A document summarily describing the conditions of a structured product. All the details of the product should be clearly listed on the term-sheet. Although the term-sheet is the most used document for structured products, its legal form is the pricing supplement. |
| **Theta** | In options, one of the "Greeks", a measure calculating the sensitivity of the price of an option to the passage of time (time decay). |
| **Time to maturity** | The amount of days, months or years until a product or an option expires. |
| **Time value** | The value of an option minus its intrinsic value. |
| **Total return index** | An index where the yield and/or the dividend component(s) is/are included. The German stock index DAX or the GSCI TR are total return indices. See also Excess return index or Price index. |
| **Underlying asset** | In structured products, the stock, bond, index, or commodity, etc. upon which the product is structured. The price evolution of the underlying asset(s) is linked to the performance of the product. |
| **Unsystematic risk** | The risk attributed to a single company, which can be eliminated by diversification. Also known as specific or idiosyncratic risk. |
| **Variance** | In statistics, a measure of dispersion of a variable around its mean. The variance is defined as the second central moment of a distribution, the first being the mean. The square root of the variance gives the standard deviation, also known as the volatility. |
| **Vega** | In options, one of the "Greeks", a risk measure calculating the change in the price of an option due to a change in the volatility. |
| **Volatility** | Also referred to as the standard deviation. In finance, volatility is often used as a proxy for risk. It refers to the degree of unpredictable change over time of an asset. A higher volatility denotes a higher degree of risk. Volatility is usually expressed in annualized terms. |
| **Volatility (historical)** | The ex-post (past) volatility that can be mathematically measured over a definite period. |
| **Volatility (implied)** | The ex-ante (expected) volatility that is observable in option markets. |

| | |
|---|---|
| **Warrant** | A securitized option issued by a financial institution. The fourth category of structured products according to the Swiss Structured Product Association, akin to leveraged investments like options. |
| **Yield curve** | In finance, refers to the level of forward interest rates as a function of the time. |
| **Yield enhancement** | One of the three basic groups of structured products. Includes products that have a limited upside but unlimited downside potential. Quotes usually in % of nominal value. |
| **WTI** | Abbreviation for West Texas Intermediate, one of the major crude oil types used as a price benchmark. |
| **Zero-coupon bond** | A bond that doesn't pay a coupon during its whole lifetime. It trades at a discount to its nominal (par) value. A zero-coupon bond, often abbreviated zero-bond, is one of the two elements building a capital guaranteed product (the other being a call option). |

# Appendix B
## Distribution of Returns: An Intuitive Explanation

Words like skew, kurtosis, and return distributions (or distribution of returns) have been mentioned several times throughout this book. This annex gives a simple and intuitive explanation to these terms for those readers who have little experience with them.

Imagine a person: let's revert to the imaginary character at the beginning of the book, Dominic. He is now facing the following problem: he has two six-sided dice in his hand, and would like to know what would be the most likely number on a single roll of both dice. He begins to cast the dice a few times and scribbles the results on a piece of paper, but soon realizes that there must be another, more efficient way to achieve his goal, without using math. After a short period of reflection, he has an idea. He rummages in his cellar and comes back with an old box containing dozens of dice he used years ago. Back at his table, he begins to build stacks of paired dice. He builds eleven stacks, arranging the dice so that on each stack, each pair amounts to one number, from 2 to 12. Each stack also shows all the roll variations that can be reached to end up with one particular number. He starts with the lowest number: 2. There is only one possibility of getting a 2 on a roll with two six-sided dice: a double 1. As a result, the leftmost stack has only one pair of dice, showing two ones. The next number is 3. There are two possibilities to obtain a three: 1 + 2 and 2 + 1. He stacks two pairs of dice showing those numbers. A four can be obtained with 1 + 3, 2 + 2 and 3 + 1 and the stack rises to three pairs of dice. He continues, and notes that after the number 7, the stacks decrease again. After searching for a few more dice to complete his construction, he finishes with the number 12, which can only be reached by a double six.

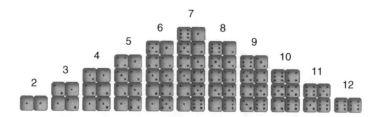

**Figure B.1**

With the eleven stacks of dice, Dominic has produced a return distribution (Figure B.1). It's now clear to Dominic that the most probable number obtained with a roll of two six-sided dice, is 7. There are six possible combinations that end with 7 as a result, with only five combinations for the next best (6 and 8), which are tied in terms of probability. Therefore, the expected value, the expected return, or the mean return amounts to 7. He would now like to know how often, on average, he would roll a 7 with his two dice. For that, Dominic counts the number of total possible rolls, and finds that there are 36 possibilities. He then divides 6 by 36 and finds 16.67%. Great, he now knows that once in every six throws, he will roll a 7. He also notes that he will get a 2 or a 12 only once every 36 rolls.

Dominic observes that the stacks dwindle symmetrically both to the left and to the right of the stack of 7. The dice stacks as arranged in Figure B.1 can be interpreted as a symmetrical return distribution, with an expected return of 7. The stack of 7 has a frequency of 16.67%. Although it is mathematically incorrect, Dominic's dice stacks somewhat resemble a normal distribution, with no skew (or a skew of zero), since it is symmetrical on both sides.

The mean return is also called the first central moment of a distribution. The standard deviation is called the second central moment, skew is the third and kurtosis the fourth. The standard deviation, which is usually taken as a proxy for risk, will not be developed further here, but skew and kurtosis will be.

Dominic now decides to create the following rule: all results on a cast that are lower than 7 will be piled on the stack of 7s. The new expected mean of that stack will be recalculated according to the actual numbers in the stack. The picture changes considerably (Figure B.2).

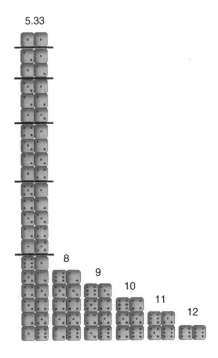

**Figure B.2**

The stacks that were previously to the left of the one with 7s are now piled upon it. This lowers the mean return of the stack: it drops from 7 to 5.33.[1] In addition, the chances of reaching that number have risen to over 58%. Summarizing, the frequency of the highest

---

[1] $(6 \times 7 + 5 \times 6 + 4 \times 3 + \cdots + 1 \times 1)/21 = 5.33$

probable number has risen from 16.67% to 58%, and the left tail of the distribution has disappeared.

The higher frequency of the stack cumulating the numbers from 2 to 7 denotes a higher kurtosis. The distribution of returns shape of Figure B.2 becomes more "pointy", or simply said, taller. A tall distribution occurs when a large amount of returns is concentrated around a certain point, as when Dominic decided to stack all roll results below 7 on the stack of 7. The disappearance of the left tail puts an end to the symmetry of the initial distribution, and skews the distribution to the right. A skewed distribution occurs when its mean is no longer at the center that divides the number of stacks in two equal parts (called the median). The mean of the Figure B.2 remains 7, but it is situated between the leftmost and the second stack to the left. The median is located between the stack of 9s and 10s, dividing the distribution in two even sets of three stacks. Since the mean is to the left of the median, the distribution is right-skewed.

What would have been the shape of the return distribution, if Dominic had instead decided that all results on a cast that are higher than 7 would be piled on the stack of 7s?

This new distribution of returns is left-skewed (the left tail of the distribution is longer than the right one, which has altogether disappeared) and is quite tall, denoting a high kurtosis (Figure B.3).

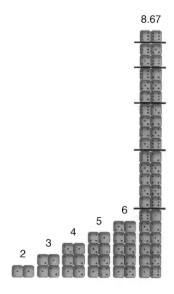

**Figure B.3**

To summarize, four parameters characterize a distribution of return:

- its mean, which in finance is called the expected return of an asset;
- its standard deviation, which in finance is often a proxy for risk;
- its skew; and
- its kurtosis.

The two first parameters are usually known to investors, but the latter two are usually less popular. However, they give unique information about the probability, or chance, that a particular return in a given distribution of returns might actually be achieved. The last two parameters are represented in Figure B.4.

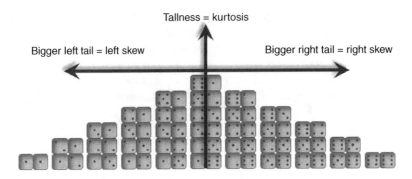

**Figure B.4**

# Appendix C
## Questionnaire

# Investor questionnaire

| Question | Answer |
|---|---|

## Part 1:
In the following situations, when facing a choice between two assets, would you choose the riskless, or the risky one?

1. The riskless asset has an expected return of +4% with no dispersion range, while the risky asset has an expected return of +7% with a dispersion ranging from 0% to +14%
   - ☐ a. I choose the riskless asset (go to question 3)
   - ☐ b. I choose the risky asset (go to question 2)

2. The riskless asset has an expected return of 4% with no dispersion range, while the risky asset has an expected return of 7% with a dispersion ranging from -4% to +19%
   - ☐ a. I choose the riskless asset (go to question 3)
   - ☐ b. I choose the risky asset (go to Part 2, question 4)

3. The riskless asset has an expected return of 4% with no dispersion range, while the risky asset has an expected return of 11% with a dispersion ranging from -4% to +19%
   - ☐ a. I choose the riskless asset
   - ☐ b. I choose the risky asset

## Part 2:
Investment preferences on risky assets. Please give only a single answer for each question

4. Would you be willing to pay for protection (thus reducing your expected return) against market corrections or crashes?
   - ☐ a. No (go to question 6)
   - ☐ b. I would be willing to pay less than 1% annually
   - ☐ c. I would be willing to pay up to 3% annually
   - ☐ d. I would be willing to pay up to 5% annually
   - ☐ e. I would be willing to pay more than 5% annually

5. If you had to choose, which correction would you like to be protected against?
   - ☐ a. The first -10%
   - ☐ b. A correction between -10% and -30%
   - ☐ c. A correction starting from -20%

6. Would you be willing to cap the maximum return on your investment and receive a premium in compensation?
   - ☐ a. No
   - ☐ b. Yes

7. Would you be willing to cap your maximum return in order to buy protection against medium market corrections (-20% to -50%)? The protection vanishes with larger corrections.
   - ☐ a. No
   - ☐ b. Yes

8. Would you be willing to forsake dividends or yield in order to buy protection against medium market corrections (-20% to -50%)? The protection vanishes with larger corrections.
   - ☐ a. No
   - ☐ b. Yes

9. Would you be willing to forsake dividends or yield in order to buy upside leverage?
   - ☐ a. No
   - ☐ b. Yes

If you had the choice between two assets, both with an
expected return closely matching your target but one with
a small dispersion (chances are you can't gain much          ☐ a. I would choose the one with the smaller dispersion.
10  more, but you won't lose much either), and another with   ☐ b. I would choose the one with the larger dispersion.
a greater dispersion (chances are that you will either
gain more or lose more), which one would you choose?

| **Question** | **Answer** |
|---|---|

### Part 3:
**Personal information**

11 On average, for how long do you usually invest?
- ☐ a. Less than a year
- ☐ b. Between one and three years
- ☐ c. Up to five years
- ☐ d. Over 5 years: ...........................

In which asset categories do you invest the largest part
12 of your capital?
(Multiple answers possible)
- ☐ a. Investment grade bonds (funds)
- ☐ b. FX
- ☐ c. Derivatives (warrants, options or futures)
- ☐ d. Structured products (excluding warrants)
- ☐ e. Fund of hedge funds
- ☐ f. Single stocks
- ☐ g. Cash or money-market
- ☐ h. Emerging market bonds (funds)
- ☐ i. Commodities
- ☐ j. Mutual funds
- ☐ k. Others (pls state) ...............................

13 What are the annual cash flows you require or need from
your investments?
- ☐ a. none
- ☐ b. between 1% and 4% of the invested money
- ☐ c. between 4% and 8% of the invested money
- ☐ d. Over 8% of the invested money

14 Please state your age
- ☐ a. Below 30
- ☐ b. Between 30 and 45
- ☐ c. Between 46 and 60
- ☐ d. Over 60

Name:................................................              Date ...................................

Evaluation Questionnaire

|  |  | Volatility | Skew | Kurtosis |
|---|---|---|---|---|
| Questions 1 -3 | (Starting points) |  |  |  |
|  | 1a/3a | 5% | 0 | 0 |
|  | 1a/3b | 9% | 0 | 0 |
|  | 1b/2a/3a | 14% | 0 | 0 |
|  | 1b/2a/3b | 21% | 0 | 0 |
|  | 1b/2b | 27% | 0 | 0 |
| Question 4 | a | 0% | -0.3 | -0.20 |
|  | b | 0% | 0.1 | - |
|  | c | -1% | 0.3 | 0.10 |
|  | d | -2% | 0.6 | 0.20 |
|  | e | -3% | 1 | 0.40 |
| Question 5 | a | 0 | -0.1 | 0 |
|  | b | 0 | 0 | 0 |
|  | c | -1% | 0.3 | 0.1 |
| Question 6 | a | 0 | 0 | 0 |
|  | b | 0 | -1 | 0.7 |
| Question 7 | a | 0 | 0 | 0 |
|  | b | -1% | -0.7 | 0.7 |
| Question 8 | a | 0 | 0 | 0 |
|  | b | 0 | 0.2 | 0.2 |
| Question 9 | a | 0 | 0 | 0 |
|  | b | 2% | 0.1 | -0.2 |
| Question 10 | a | -2% | 0 | 0.5 |
|  | b | 2% | 0 | -0.5 |
| Question 11 | a | -2% | 0 | 0 |
|  | b | 0% | 0 | 0 |
|  | c | 1% | 0 | 0 |
|  | d | 2% | 0 | 0 |
| Question 12 | a | -1% | 0 | 0.2 |
|  | b | -1% | 0 | 0 |
|  | c | 8% | 0 | 0 |
|  | d | -1% | 0 | 0.1 |
|  | e | -2% | 0 | 0 |
|  | f | 3% | 0 | -0.2 |
|  | g | -3% | 0 | 0.3 |
|  | h | 2% | 0 | 0 |
|  | i | 4% | 0 | -0.3 |
|  | j | -1% | 0 | 0 |
|  | k |  |  |  |

|             |   | Volatility | Skew | Kurtosis |
|-------------|---|-----------|------|----------|
| Question 13 | a | 2%        | 0    | -0.2     |
|             | b | 0%        | 0.2  | 0        |
|             | c | -2%       | 0.4  | 0.1      |
|             | d | -3%       | 0.6  | 0.2      |
| Question 14 | a | 2%        | 0    | -0.3     |
|             | b | 1%        | 0    | -0.1     |
|             | c | -1%       | 0.1  | 0        |
|             | d | -2%       | 0.2  | 0.2      |
| **Totals**          | | **0%**  | **2.00** | **2.00** |
| **Totals positive** | | 29%     | 4.1      | 4        |
| **Totals negative** | | -29%    | -2.1     | -2       |

# Appendix D
## List of Figures

# Appendix E
## List of Tables

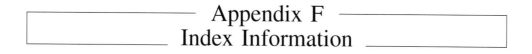

# Appendix F
# Index Information

**Eurostoxx50 index**

Euro STOXX 50® is a trademark of Stoxx Ltd, a joint venture of Deutsche Börse Group, Dow Jones & Company and SIX Swiss Exchange.

**Nikkei 225**

The Nikkei Stock Average Index is an intellectual property of Nikkei Inc.

**S&P 500**

The S&P 500® is a registered trademark of the McGraw-Hill Companies, Inc.

**SMI**

The SMI® is a registered trademark of the SIX Swiss Exchange AG.

**HSI**

The HSI® is compiled and maintained by Hang Seng Indexes Company Ltd.

# Appendix G
## Issuer and Product-Related Websites

| Issuer | Bank's websites |
|---|---|
| ABN AMRO (now RBS) | www.abnamromarkets.com/ |
| Barclays | www.barclaysinvestors.com |
| Barclays | www.barclaysoffshoresolutions.com/ |
| Barclays (English customers only) | www.barclaysstructuredproducts.com/ |
| Bayern Landesbank | www.bayernlb.de/ |
| BHF Bank | www.bhf-bank.com/ |
| BNP Paribas | www.derivate.bnpparibas.com/ |
| Calyon (Crédit Agricole-Lyonnais) | structuredproducts.calyon.com/ |
| Citigroup | equityfirst.citigroup.ch/ |
| Clariden-Leu | www.claridenleu.com/ |
| Commerzbank | portal.commerzbank.de/ |
| Credit Suisse | structuredproducts.credit-suisse.com/ |
| Credit Suisse | structuredinvestments.credit-suisse.com/ |
| Deutsche Bank | www.dbxtrackers.ch/ |
| Deutsche Bank | www.it.x-markets.db.com |
| Dresdner | www.warrants.dresdner.com/ |
| DWS | www.dwsgo.de |
| EFG | www.efgfp.com/ |
| Erste Bank | datacenter.treasury.erstebank.com/ |
| Goldman Sachs | www.goldman-sachs.ch/.de/.it/ |
| HSBC Trinkaus | www2.hsbc-tip.de/ |
| ING | www.structuredproducts.ing.com |
| JP Morgan | www.jpmorganinvestor.com/ |
| JP Morgan | www.jpmorgansp.com/ |
| Julius Baer | www.derivatives.juliusbaer.com/ |
| Merrill Lynch (Bank of America) | www.mlinvest.ch/ |
| Merrill Lynch (Bank of America) | www.merrillinvest.ml.com/ |
| Nomura | www.nomuranow.com/ |
| Nordbank | www.hsh-nordbank.com/ |
| Rabobank | www.rabospecialproducts.nl/ |
| Raiffeisen Centrobank | www.rcb.at/ |
| Royal Bank of Canada RBC | www.rbccm.com/ |
| Royal Bank of Scotland | www.markets.rbs.com |
| Sal Oppenheim | www.oppenheim-derivate.de/ |
| Sarasin | www.saraderivate.ch/ |
| Société Générale (complex products) | www.adequity.ch/ |
| Société Générale | www.warrants.com/home/ |

| Issuer | Bank's websites |
|---|---|
| UBS | keyinvest.ibb.ubs.com/ |
| Unicredito | www.zertifikate.hypovereinsbank.de/ |
| Volksbank | www.strukturierteinvestments.at/ |
| Vontobel | www.derinet.ch/ |
| West LB | www.westlb-zertifikate.de/ |

| Associations | Country |
|---|---|
| www.svsp-verband.ch/ | Switzerland |
| www.derivate-forum.de/ | Germany |
| www.deutscher-derivate-verband.de/ | Germany (same as above) |
| www.zertifikateforum.at/ | Austria |
| www.structuredproducts.org/ | USA |

| Search product sites |
|---|
| www.derilab.com (login requested) |
| www.onvista.de/ |
| www.scoach.de |
| www.warrants.ch |

| Commodity index sites | Provider |
|---|---|
| www.ubs.com/4/investch/cmci/ | UBS |
| index.db.com/dbiqweb2/ | Deutsche Bank |

| Specialized press sites | Language |
|---|---|
| www.structuredproductsonline.com/ | English |
| www.risk.net/ | English |
| www.payoff.ch/ | German |
| www.zertifikate-port.de/ | German |
| www.zertifikatewoche.de/ | German |
| www.derivate-mag.de/online/ | German |
| www.zertifikatejournal.ch/ | German |

# Bibliography

ABN-AMRO (2008). *FX Products Manual*. Retrieved 2008 from ABN-AMRO Corporation website (now RBS): http://www.abnamromarkets.com

ABN-AMRO (2008). *Structured Rates Manual*. Retrieved 2008 from ABN-AMRO Corporation website (now RBS): http://www.abnamromarkets.com

BNP Paribas (2008). *Foreign Exchange Derivatives Handbook*. London.

BNP Paribas (2008). *Interest Rate Derivatives Handbook*. London.

Bodie, Z., A. Kane and A. Marcus (1996). *Investments, Third Edition*. Irwin.

Brennan, M. J. (1979). The Pricing of Contingent Claims in Discrete Time Models. *Journal of Finance*, 34: 53–68.

Coaker, W. J. (2007). Emphasizing Low-Correlated Assets: The Volatility of Correlation. *Journal of Financial Planning*, September: 57–70.

Deutsche Bank (2008). *Deutsche Bank Index Page*. Retrieved 2007–2008, from DB IQ Product Page List: https://index.db.com/

Dubil, R. (2008). Benefits of Protecting Investment Portfolios with Options: A Historical Perspective. *Journal of Financial Planning*, February: 260–270.

EFG Financial Products (2008). Retrieved 2008 from EFG Financial Products: http://www.efgfp.com/

Fama, E. F. (1971). Risk, Return and Equilibrium. *Journal of Political Economy*, Jan–Feb: 30–55.

Goldman Sachs (2006–2008). Know-How. *Anlegermagazin*. Zürich: Goldman Sachs.

He, H. and H. E. Leland (1993). On Equilibrium Asset Price Processes. *Review of Financial Studies*, 6: 593–617.

HSBC Trinkaus (2008). *Zertifikate und Optionsscheine*. Düsseldorf: HSBC Trinkaus.

Julius Baer (2008). Retrieved 2008 from Julius Baer STP: http://www.derivatives.juliusbaer.com/

Kahneman, D. and A. Tversky (2007). *Choices, Values and Frames*. New York: Cambridge University Press.

Leggio, K. B. and D. Lien (2005). Covered Calls: A Lose/Lose Investment? *Journal of Financial Planning*. May: 72–77.

Leggio, K. B. and D. Lien (2008). Leland Model More Accurately Evaluates Efficacy of Portfolio Hedging Strategies. *Journal of Financial Planning*, Article 6: 40–47.

Leland, H. E. (1999). Beyond Mean-Variance: Performance Measurement in a Nonsymmetrical World. *Financial Analysts Journal*, 55(1): 27–36.

Leland, H. E. (1980). Who Should Buy Portfolio Insurance? *The Journal of Finance*, 35(2): 581–594.

Markowitz, H. (1952). Portfolio Selection. *The Journal of Finance*, 12: 77–91.

Montier, J. (2007). *Behavioural Investing*. Chichester: John Wiley & Sons Ltd.

Perold, A. F. (2004). The Capital Asset Pricing Model. *Journal of Economic Perspectives*, Summer: 324.

Sharpe, W. (1964). Capital Asset Prices: A Theory of Market Equilibrium Under Conditions of Risk. *The Journal of Finance*, 19(3): 425–442.

Theil, M. (2002). *Versicherungsentscheidungen und Prospect Theory*. Wien: Springer.

Timmermann, A. and C. W. Granger (2004). Efficient Market Hypothesis and Forecasting. *International Journal of Forecasting*, 20: 15–27.

UBS (2008). *UBS Bloomberg CMCI*. Retrieved 2008 from UBS AG website: http://www.ubs.com/4/investch/cmci/strategy-indices.html

Woo, D., P. Koeva and G. Siourounis (2006). *Should FX be Part of the Porfolios of Non-FX Investors?* London: Barclays Capital.

# Index

*Indexed by Terry Halliday*
*(HallidayTerence@aol.com).*